lonely planet

APR 1 0 2014

Bhutan

Thimphu
p48

Western Bhutan
p73

Central Bhutan
p111

Eastern Bhutan
p136

THIS EDITION WRITTEN AND RESEARCHED BY

Lindsay Brown,

Bradley Mayhew

Contents

PUNAKHA DZONG P96

MONKS AT WANGDUE PHODRANG DZONG P101

PRAYER FLAGS OVER THE WANG CHHU P70

Contents

SPECIAL FEATURES

Welcome to Bhutan

Bhutan is no ordinary place. It is a Himalayan kingdom with a reputation for mystery and magic, where a traditional Buddhist culture carefully embraces global developments.

Surprising Bhutan

Bhutan holds many surprises. It's a country where the rice is red and where chillies aren't just a seasoning but the main ingredient. It's also a deeply Buddhist land, where monasteries are part of the mainstream, and where giant protective penises are painted beside the entrance to many houses. While it visibly maintains its Buddhist traditions, Bhutan is not a museum. You will find the Bhutanese well educated, fun loving and vibrant.

Naturally Bhutan

When you visit Bhutan, you will become one of the few who have experienced the natural charm of the first country where Gross National Happiness is deemed more important than Gross National Product. By law, at least 60% of the country must remain forested for future generations. You will experience Bhutan's natural wonders firsthand when travelling the mountain passes – resplendent with rhododendron blossom in spring. Botanical riches and unique mammals and birds are protected in several national parks, and a mountain trek is one of the best ways to experience the Himalaya.

High-Value Tourism

The Bhutanese pride themselves on a sustainable approach to tourism in line with the philosophy of Gross National Happiness. Firstly, to bust a myth: there is *no* limit to tourist visas. Visitors famously pay a minimum tariff of US$250 per day, making it appear as one of the world's more expensive destinations. However, this fee is all-inclusive – accommodation, food, transport and an official guide are all provided. You don't have to travel in a large group and you can arrange your own itinerary. What you won't find is backpacker-style travel.

Shangri-La?

So why spend your money to come here? Firstly there is the amazing Himalayan landscape, where snowcapped peaks rise above shadowy gorges cloaked in primeval forests. Taking up prime positions in this picture-book landscape are the majestic fortress-like dzongs and monasteries. This unique architecture embodies Buddhist culture and sets the scene for spectacular tsechus (dance festivals). Then there are the textiles and handicrafts, outrageous archery competitions, high-altitude trekking trails, and stunning flora and fauna. If it's not Shangri-La, it's as close as it gets.

Why I Love Bhutan

By Lindsay Brown, Author

As a former conservation biologist, for me there's lots to love about Bhutan. The mountains are carpeted in diverse forests that sing with birds, and it's the opportunity to explore this relatively untouched corner of the Himalaya that keeps me coming back. A highlight of my recent trip was a pair of rufous-necked hornbills feeding right beside the road. Bhutan's Buddhist tradition of respect and reverence for nature plus its amazing festivals and engaging people are the headlines to a rewarding and complex story about a beautiful Himalayan kingdom with a unique outlook on progress.

For more about our authors, see page 304

Above: Buddhist monks performing at the tsechu at Gangte Goemba (p103)

Bhutan

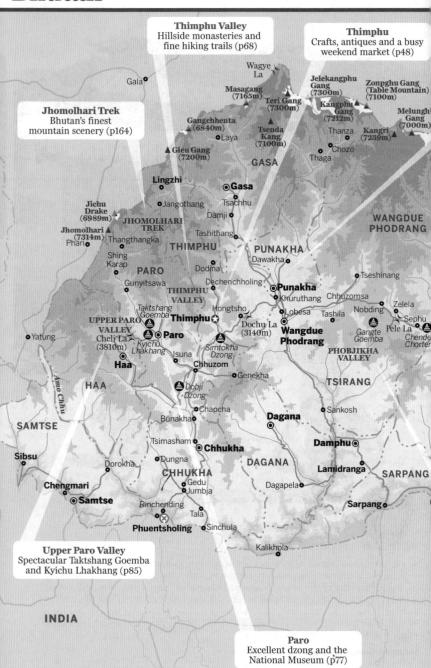

Thimphu Valley
Hillside monasteries and
fine hiking trails (p68)

Thimphu
Crafts, antiques and a busy
weekend market (p48)

Jhomolhari Trek
Bhutan's finest
mountain scenery (p164)

Gala

Wagye La

Masagang
(7165m)

Teri Gang
(7300m)

Jelekangphu
Gang
(7300m)

Zonpghu Gang
(Table Mountain)
(7100m)

Kangphu
Gang
(7212m)

Melungh
Gang
(7000m)

Gangchhenta
(6840m)

Tsenda
Kang
(7100m)

Thanza

Kangri
(7239m)

Laya

Gieu Gang
(7200m)

Chozo

Thaga

GASA

Lingzhi

Gasa

WANGDUE
PHODRANG

Jangothang

Tsachhu

Jichu
Drake
(6989m)

Damji

JHOMOLHARI
TREK

Jhomolhari
(7314m)

Thangthangka

Tashithang

THIMPHU

PUNAKHA

Phari

Dawakha

Shing
Karap

PARO

Dodina

Punakha

Tseshinang

Gunyitsawa

Dechenchholing

Khuruthang

Chhuzomsa

Nobding

Zelela

THIMPHU
VALLEY

Taktshang
Goemba

Thimphu

Hongtsho

Lobesa

Tashila

Sephu

UPPER PARO
VALLEY

Cheli La
(3810m)

Kyichu
Lhakhang

Paro

Dochu La
(3140m)

Wangdue
Phodrang

Gangte
Goemba

Pele La

Chende
Chorter

Yatung

Isuna

Simtokha
Dzong

PHOBJIKHA
VALLEY

Haa

Chhuzom

TSIRANG

HAA

Dobji
Dzong

Genekha

SAMTSE

Chapcha

Dagana

Sankosh

Bunakha

Damphu

Tsimasham

Chhukha

Sibsu

Dungna

DAGANA

Lamidranga

SARPANG

Dorokha

CHHUKHA

Dagapela

Chengmari

Gedu

Jumbja

Samtse

Rinchending

Sarpang

Tala

Phuentsholing

Sinchula

Kalikhola

INDIA

Upper Paro Valley
Spectacular Taktshang Goemba
and Kyichu Lhakhang (p85)

Paro
Excellent dzong and the
National Museum (p77)

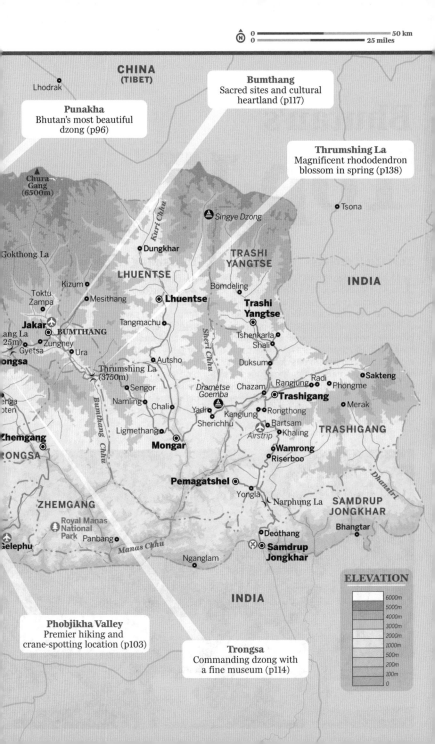

Punakha
Bhutan's most beautiful
dzong (p96)

Bumthang
Sacred sites and cultural
heartland (p117)

Thrumshing La
Magnificent rhododendron
blossom in spring (p138)

CHINA
(TIBET)

Lhodrak

Chura
Gang
(6500m)

Tsona

Singye Dzong

Dungkhar

TRASHI
YANGTSE

Gokthong La

INDIA

Kizum

LHUENTSE

Bomdeling

Toktu
Zampa

Mesithang

◉ **Lhuentse**

Trashi
Yangtse

Jakar
◉ **BUMTHANG**

Tangmachu

Tshenkarla
Shali

ang La
25m)

Zungney

Gyetsa
Ura

Duksum

ongsa

Autsho

Thrumshing La
(3750m)

Rangjung Radi

Sakteng

Sengor

Drametse
Goemba

Chazam

Phongme

enga
ten

Namling
Chali

Yadi

◉ **Trashigang**

Merak

Zhemgang

Ligmethang

Kanglung
Sherichhu

Rongthong

◉
RONGSA

◉ **Mongar**

Bartsam
Airstrip Khaling

TRASHIGANG

Pemagatshel ◉

Wamrong
Riserboo

ZHEMGANG

Yongla

Narphung La

SAMDRUP
JONGKHAR

Royal Manas
National
Park Panbang

Bhangtar

elephu

Manas Chhu

Deothang

⊗◉ **Samdrup**
Jongkhar

Nganglam

INDIA

Phobjikha Valley
Premier hiking and
crane-spotting location (p103)

Trongsa
Commanding dzong with
a fine museum (p114)

ELEVATION

	6000m
	5000m
	4000m
	3000m
	2000m
	1000m
	500m
	200m
	100m
	0

0 ——— 50 km
0 ——— 25 miles

Bhutan's
Top 17

Terrific Tsechus

1 Most of the dzongs and goembas have annual festivals featuring mesmerising dance dramas (p31). The largest of these festivals is the tsechu – with dances in honour of Guru Rinpoche. The dances are performed by monks and laypeople dressed in colourful costumes, and the dancers take on aspects of wrathful and compassionate deities, heroes, demons and animals. During the dances, *atsara* (masked clowns) mimic the dancers and perform comic routines and even harass the audience for money in exchange for a blessing with the wooden phallus they carry! Paro tsechu (p23)

Taktshang Goemba

2 Bhutan's most famous monastery, Taktshang Goemba (Tiger's Nest Monastery; p87) is one of its most venerated religious sites. Legend says that Guru Rinpoche flew to this site on the back of a tigress to subdue a local demon; afterwards he meditated here for three months. This beautiful building clings to the sheer cliffs soaring above a whispering pine forest. The steep walk to the monastery is well worthwhile, providing tantalising glimpses of the monastery, views of the Paro valley and splashes of red-blossom rhododendrons.

Wonderful Wildlife

3 Bhutan has the largest proportion of land designated as protected areas in the world. Its 65% forest and mountain cover comprises a suite of varying habitats and an amazing diversity of plants and creatures. Birdwatchers flock to the monsoon-soaked evergreen forests of southern Bhutan, where hundreds of species can be spotted from the road. Here, you may also spot a troupe of playful golden langurs. The endangered black-necked crane winters in central and eastern Bhutan and the reliably returning cranes of Phobjikha valley (p103) are justifiably renowned.

Golden langur (p252)

Thimphu Weekend Market

4 Thimphu's bustling weekend market (p52) is the biggest and brightest in the country. The food section is an olfactory overload with dried fish competing with soft cheese, betel nut and dried chilli to assault your nostrils. Curly fern fronds (nakey) and red rice are just some of the exotic offerings. Cross the fast-flowing Wang Chhu on the traditional cantilever footbridge to get to the handicraft and textile stalls where you can barter for 'antiques', rolls of prayer flags, reams of material or even a human thigh-bone trumpet.

Trongsa Dzong & the Tower of Trongsa Museum

5 Sprawling down a ridge towards an ominous gorge, Trongsa Dzong (p114) sits in a central position in Bhutan's geography and in its recent history. Both the first and second kings ruled from this strategic position. Inside is a labyrinth of many levels, narrow corridors and courtyards. Overlooking the dzong, the Tower of Trongsa Royal Heritage Museum is housed in the watchtower. This excellent museum is dedicated to the history of the dzong and the royal Wangchuck dynasty and has exhibits ranging from personal effects of the royals to Buddhist statues.

Punakha Dzong

6 Superbly situated where two rivers converge, Punakha Dzong (p96) is postcard perfect and serenely monastic. Built by the Zhabdrung in 1637, it is the winter home of the Je Khenpo and the venue for the coronation of kings of Bhutan. Visit in spring to see the jacaranda trees splash lilac flowers down the whitewashed walls and red-robed monks wandering on a sea of purple petals. The fortress-thick walls are cold and silent one moment, then warmed with the echoes of giggles in another as a horde of young monks head off for a meal.

Souvenir Shopping

7 Bhutan's pride in its handicrafts is on show at the schools of Zorig Chusum (Thirteen Arts) and the numerous handicraft shops. Many items have a utilitarian or religious use, such as bamboo baskets, brass butter lamps or the exquisite wooden bowls hand-turned from intricately patterned burlwood. Silk, cotton, wool and even yak hair is spun, dyed, woven and stitched into cloth and traditional garments. The artistic tradition can be seen in the intricate *thangkas* (religious pictures). Bhutanese stamps will thrill collectors.

Traditional Textiles

8 Hand-woven and embroidered textiles (p237) are generally recognised as Bhutan's premier handicraft. Centuries of tradition have honed the techniques of textile dyeing, weaving and stitching. Most of the weavers are women and it is a rare home in Bhutan that does not 'clunk' to the sound of a loom. In addition to the National Textile Museum in Thimphu, there are small shops throughout the country – particularly in Bumthang and in the far east – selling vibrant fabrics that make a colourful souvenir.

Mountain Treks

9 Bhutan's treks (p156) are physically demanding but hugely rewarding. They generally reach high altitudes and remote regions, and several are justifiably renowned in trekking circles, including the Jhomolhari trek (p164) and Snowman trek (p175). On all treks you will be expertly guided and your pack will be carried by ponies. Trekking takes you beyond the roads and reach of modernisation. Meeting traditionally dressed locals tending their crops and animals according to century-old traditions will be a highlight of your trip.

Jangothang campsite (p167) on the Jhomolhari trek

10

Rinpung Dzong & National Museum

10 Paro's Rinpung Dzong (Paro Dzong; p77) is a hulking example of the fortress-like dzong architecture that glowers protectively over the valley and town. The colourful Paro tsechu is held here in spring; the festival culminates with a *thondrol* (huge religious picture) depicting Guru Rinpoche being unfurled. Above the dzong is an old, round watchtower, the *ta dzong*, home to the excellent National Museum (p79), which has an informative and eclectic collection.

Paro's *ta dzong* (p79)

Buddhist Painting

11 The best place to see Buddhist murals and frescoes is inside the dzongs, goembas and lhakhangs (p236). Stories are told, mandalas mesmerise and major figures are represented, including the Guardians of the Four Directions, Sakyamuni Buddha and Guru Rinpoche. Another common and typically Bhutanese subject depicts the Four Friends (*Thuenpa Puen Shi*), which illustrates the concept and harmony of teamwork and mutual respect between an elephant, monkey, rabbit and bird. Thimphu is the best place to see and purchase traditional and contemporary painting.

Mural at Punakha Dzong (p96)

Forests & Blooms

12 Although the mysterious and ethereal high-altitude blue poppy is the national flower and the cypress is the national tree, no plant is more emblematic of Bhutan than the rhododendron. In spring splashes of red, pink and white rival the multicoloured prayer flags at the high passes from Cheli La (p90) to Thrumshing La (p138). Famous for its forest cover, Bhutan will delight the amateur botanist with its sheer variety of flora and shades of green. Long forest drives are inevitable, so remember to stop the car and smell the flowers.

Rhododendrons (p250)

DIANA MAYFIELD / GETTY IMAGES ©

Kyichu Lhakhang

13 Kyichu Lhakhang (p85) is one of Bhutan's oldest, most venerated and most beautiful temples and it sits just a short distance from the gateway town of Paro. The oldest temple in this twin-temple complex is believed to have been built in AD 659 by King Songtsen Gampo of Tibet. The outside grounds hum with prayers and spinning prayer wheels, while inside a treasured 7th-century statue of Jowo Sakyamuni sits in the sanctuary. Easy day walks can be commenced in the vicinity of this serene lhakhang.

Bumthang

14 The valleys comprising Bumthang (p117) make up the cultural heartland of Bhutan and are ideal for day hikes to monasteries. Bumthang's ancient monasteries and temples figure prominently in Bhutan's early development as well as in the foundation of the unique aspects of Bhutanese Buddhism. Witness the imprint of Guru Rinpoche, hoist Pema Lingpa's 25kg chainmail, and stare into the churning waters of Membartsho, where Pema Lingpa uncovered hidden treasures. Man spinning prayer wheel at Jampey Lhakhang (p124)

Gross National Happiness

15 Gross National Happiness (GNH) has become Bhutan's philosophical banner and a gift to a world grappling with materialistic 'growth economics'. Based on core Buddhist and human values, this measurable index is a counterpoint to the economist's Gross National Product. It is also a revolutionary philosophy that places real value on things such as cultural heritage, health, education, good governance, ecological diversity and individual wellbeing. Importantly, it sees economic growth not as an end but rather as a means of achieving more important ends.

Archery

16 Bhutan's national sport of archery (*datse*) is entertaining to watch, with tournaments held across the country throughout the year (p222). There are two classes of competition: one for the traditional bamboo bows and another for the space-age carbon-fibre bows that propel arrows at astonishing speeds. The targets seem tiny and the distance immense, yet the target is hit quite regularly. Narrow misses, competitive banter, ritual singing and dancing accompany the whoosh of arrows and hoots of delight as the competition heats up.

Thimphu Valley

17 Thimphu valley (p48) delights with its cultural attractions, including the Trashi Chhoe Dzong (p49), which celebrates its tsechu in autumn. The relatively broad valley of Bhutan's capital also provides many out-of-town sights. There are good walks not far from the capital, taking in a handful of perfectly positioned monasteries with excellent views down the valley. And just west of Thimphu's centre at Motithang Takin Preserve (p57) is your best bet for spotting Bhutan's national animal. Trashi Chhoe Dzong (p49)

Need to Know

For more information, see Survival Guide (p259)

Currency
Ngultrum (Nu)

Language
Dzongkha

Visas
Visas are arranged by your tour company and issued on arrival only to those on a prepaid all-inclusive tour.

Money
Tours are prepaid so you'll only need money for drinks, souvenirs and tips; for this, bring cash. ATMs reliable in Thimphu only. Credit cards accepted in some souvenir shops.

Mobile Phones
As long as your phone is unlocked you can buy a B-Mobile or Tashi Cell SIM card for both local and international use and top it up with prepaid cards.

Time
Bhutan Time (GMT/UTC plus six hours; 30 minutes later than India, 15 minutes later than Nepal)

When to Go

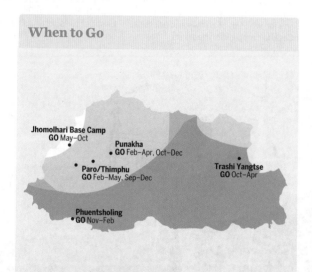

Jhomolhari Base Camp
GO May–Oct

Punakha
GO Feb–Apr, Oct–Dec

Paro/Thimphu
GO Feb–May, Sep–Dec

Trashi Yangtse
GO Oct–Apr

Phuentsholing
GO Nov–Feb

Warm to hot summers, mild winters
Warm to hot summers, cold winters
Mild summers, cold winters
Alpine (cold) climate

High Season
(Mar–May, Sep–Nov)

➡ The weather is ideal in spring and autumn. Book flights well in advance; accommodation options can be limited.

➡ Himalayan views are best in October, while rhododendron blooms peak in March and April.

Shoulder
(Dec–Feb)

➡ Bhutan has seasonal tariffs so, along with fewer tourists, there are good savings to be made by travelling outside the high season.

➡ The weather is still pleasant, though it can be cold in December and January.

Low Season
(Jun–Aug)

➡ Monsoon rains and leeches put an end to most treks, although high-altitude flowers are at their peak.

Useful Websites

Bhutan 360 (www.bhutan-360. com) Introduction to travel in Bhutan.

Tourism Council of Bhutan (www.tourism.gov.bt) Approved tour operators and travel regulations.

Lonely Planet (www.lonely-planet.com/bhutan) Destination information, hotel bookings, traveller forum and more.

Druk Air (www.drukair.com.bt) National airline.

Kuensel (www.kuenselonline. com) National newspaper.

National Portal of Bhutan (www.bhutan.gov.bt) Official government site.

Important Numbers

Bhutan's country code	☏975
International access code	☏00
Ambulance	☏112
Fire	☏110
Police	☏113

Exchange Rates

Australia	A$1	Nu 58
Canada	C$1	Nu 59
Europe	€1	Nu 83
India	Rs100	Nu 100
Japan	¥100	Nu 62
New Zealand	NZ$1	Nu 51
UK	£1	Nu 97
USA	US$1	Nu 61

For current exchange rates see www.xe.com.

Daily Costs

Fixed Daily Rate: US$250

➡ All tourists must pay US$250 per person per day (US$200 a day from December to February and June to August), with a US$40/30 surcharge per person for those in a group of one/two. This covers accommodation, transport in Bhutan, guide, food and entry fees.

➡ Possible extra charges include hot-stone baths, cultural shows, horse riding, rafting and tips.

➡ Children under 12 years are exempt from royalty component (US$65).

Budget: Less than US$150

➡ Only Indian tourists and foreign residents are able to set their own travel budgets.

➡ Budget hotel: US$20–40

➡ Restaurant meal in Thimphu: US$5–15

Top End: US$500–1750

➡ Luxury hotel: US$250–1500 above the daily US$250 tariff

Opening Hours

Opening hours can vary throughout the year. We've provided high-season opening hours; hours may decrease in the shoulder and low seasons.

Government offices 9am to 1pm and 2pm to 5pm in summer, until 4pm in winter Monday to Friday

Banks 9am to 4pm (3pm winter) Monday to Friday, 9am to noon (11am winter) Saturday

Shops 8am to 8pm or 9pm

Nightclubs Open till early next morning on Wednesday, Friday and Saturday

Bars Closed Tuesday, the national 'dry' day

Arriving in Bhutan

As long as you are carrying a copy of your visa approval form, arrival formalities should be smooth and straightforward. Your guide and driver will meet you at Paro airport or a land border, arrange your visa stamp and whisk you away on your tour.

Getting Around

Unless you are on a trek or you're taking advantage of an internal flight, you will be moved around by a late-model minibus, 4WD or car for the bulk of your tour. And the prime concern here is motion sickness on Bhutan's famously winding roads. If you suffer this affliction, bring your favourite preventative remedy and remember to look at the horizon!

For much more on **getting around**, see p275

If You Like...

Fitting in Like a Local

Get a *gho* or a *kira* Locals love it when a *chilip* (foreigner) wears Bhutanese national dress, especially during a holiday or festival. (p66)

Watch an archery tournament There's nothing more Bhutanese than the good-humoured banter of a *datse* (archery) or *khuru* (lawn darts) game. (p222)

Hang some prayer flags Impress your guide and earn some good karma by buying some prayer flags and hanging them at a mountain pass such as Dochu La. (p94)

Overnight in a rural farmhouse The digs are simple but the welcome warm when you spend an evening with a local Bhutanese family – try Ngang Lhakhang (p128) or Khoma (p144).

Sample some local snacks Try the jellied cow skin, dried yak cheese and fresh betel nut at the Paro Sunday Market. (p81)

Himalayan Treks

The best way to experience Bhutan is without doubt on foot, especially if you can combine a trek with a festival and the highlights of Paro and Thimphu. Come in October and November for mountain views and March for rhododendron blooms.

Druk Path trek The walk between Paro and Thimphu takes in high-altitude lakes and remote hermitages. (p160)

Jhomolhari trek Combines some of Bhutan's best high-mountain scenery, with remote villages, high passes and yak pastures. (p164)

Laya–Gasa trek Perhaps the best combination of scenery and culture, with a visit to the unique people of remote Laya. (p171)

Merak–Sakteng trek Excellent cultural trek that leads you to Brokpa communities and remote *migoi* (yeti) habitat in the far east of the country. (p187)

Snowman trek One of the world's toughest, most expensive and ultimate treks across the roof of the Bhutan Himalaya. (p175)

Pampering Yourself

Bhutan's top-end travel is anything but tough. Uber-luxury resorts guarantee six-star treatment, with decadent restaurants and muscle-melting spas.

Hot-stone bath Stone, wood, hot water and artemisia herbs combine to provide the quintessential Bhutanese experience, available at most tourist hotels. (p261)

Termalinca Not quite the Promised Land, but the milk and honey body wrap comes close enough; nonguests are welcome at the spa here. (p63)

Uma Paro Massage, complimentary yoga and Ayurvedic oil treatments, all featuring Comobrand bath products. (p83)

Zhiwa Ling The Menlha (Medicine Buddha) spa here offers a tasty red rice or lemongrass body polish. (p83)

Taj Tashi Choose your mood – invigorating masala spice rub or relaxing coconut skin softener? (p62)

IF YOU LIKE... GIANT STATUES

Crane your neck at the colossal 50m-tall Buddha Dordenma in the Thimphu valley (p57), or the 45m statue of Guru Rinpoche at Tangmachu in remote eastern Bhutan (p143); their little fingers alone are bigger than most statues.

Wildlife & Wildflowers

Bhutan is a paradise for botanists and birders. Mountain goats and langur are easily spotted; red pandas are more commonly seen in bottled form.

Phobjikha valley Winter (end of October to mid-February) offers guaranteed sightings of one of over 300 black-necked cranes. (p103)

Dochu La One of the best places to wander through a magical forest of pink, white and yellow rhododendron blooms (March and April). (p94)

Motithang Takin Preserve Get up close to Bhutan's odd-looking and endearing national animal, said to have inspired the legend of the golden fleece. (p57)

Royal Manas National Park Tourism is in its infancy here but the wildlife and bird-spotting in this subtropical forest ranks as some of Asia's best, if you don't mind roughing it. (p135)

Day Walks

Sometimes it's just nice to get out of the car and hike to a hillside monastery or temple. Lose the crowds and meet monks, villagers and fellow pilgrims on an equal footing.

Tango & Cheri Goembas Excellent excursion from Thimphu to two of Bhutan's most historic monasteries, Tango Goemba and Cheri Goemba, with longer hikes possible. (p70)

Taktshang Goemba If the two-hour hike up to the Tiger's Nest Monastery in the Paro valley isn't enough, you can continue up to a handful of little-visited temples and cliffside viewpoints. (p87)

(Above) Zhiwa Ling hotel (p83)
(Below) A monk cleans and fills the butter lamps at Tango Goemba (p70)

Bumthang valley The best single destination for day hikes to silent meditation retreats and valley viewpoints. Link them together for a hotel-based, multiday hike. (p126)

Ura & Shingkhar Hike between charming villages, Ura (p133) and Shingkhar (p132), up to a retreat with stunning views or into nearby Thrumshing La National Park (p138).

Phobjikha valley Spot black-necked cranes as you follow easy walks in this charming hidden valley. (p103)

Sacred Sites

Protector deities, spirits and saints lurk behind every pass, river junction and lake in Bhutan. These pilgrim spots are imbued with sacred significance and hold a key to understanding how Bhutanese see their world.

Taktshang Goemba Bhutan's most revered site, tied on to the cliff face by little more than the hairs of angels. (p87)

Gom Kora Pilgrims flock to this remote chorten for its collection of rock footprints, relics and bizarre sin tests. (p150)

Changangkha Lhakhang Always bustling with mothers and their babies seeking a blessing from the red-faced protector Tamdrin. (p57)

Membartsho The serene and sacred 'burning lake', where Pema Lingpa found underwater treasures and performed miracles. (p130)

Hidden Gems

Bhutan's big shows are its dzongs and festivals but don't overlook the charm of the country's smaller, less-visited monasteries and temples.

Juneydrak Hermitage The Haa valley is a great place to get off the beaten track and this timeless hermitage is its highlight. (p93)

Kila Nunnery Perched just below the Cheli La, Kila is an hour's walk and about two centuries off the main highway. (p92)

Dumtse Lhakhang Pilgrim paths wind upwards at this snail-shell-shaped chapel past some of the country's best medieval murals. (p80)

Tago Lhakhang A charming and easily missed 15th-century chapel inside a chorten, just south of Paro. (p90)

Dechen Phodrang Sacred stones and towering cypress trees mark this pilgrimage site, seemingly lost in time in the furthest corner of the kingdom. (p152)

Festivals

Many people time their entire trip around one of Bhutan's colourful tsechus (dance festivals). Expect swirling mask dances, playful clowns, spectacular costumes and superb photo opportunities.

Paro tsechu Popular with groups and with good reason; perhaps too popular for many people's taste. (p23)

Ura yakchoe A quiet rural festival, though the dates are notoriously changeable. Camping is a good idea here. (p24)

Punakha Domchoe One of Bhutan's most unusual festivals re-enacts an ancient battle; held in February or March. (p23)

Kurjey tsechu Brave the monsoon rain and avoid the tourists, plus you can hit the nearby Nimalung tsechu at the same time. (p24)

Arts & Crafts

Bhutan's arts and crafts vary from sacred murals to bamboo bows. For high religious art visit the dzongs and monasteries but for handicrafts try these fascinating workshops.

National Institute for Zorig Chusum Watch students perfect the 13 traditional arts and crafts. (p52)

Jungshi Handmade Paper Factory View the whole paper-making process. (p60)

National Textile Museum Thimphu's impressive new complex showcases Bhutan's most impressive art form. (p56)

Tshenden Incense Factory Breathe in the fragrance of juniper, sandalwood and high-altitude herbs at this family-run workshop near Bondey. (p90)

Khoma village, Lhuentse Every household has a loom in this remote centre of 'brocade-style' weaving excellence. (p144)

Yathra workshops, Zungney Shop for hand-woven woollen blankets at these roadside looms on the drive to Bumthang. (p117)

Month by Month

February

The mercury stays low in Paro and Bumthang but things are warmer in the lower elevations of Punakha and the east, and there are loads of festivals, with few crowds.

Losar

Bhutanese mark their New Year by painting their houses, visiting the local monastery, and throwing epic archery and darts tournaments. The event follows the lunar Bhutanese calendar and there are lots of regional variations, so it can happen anytime between mid-January and mid-March.

Punakha Domchoe & Tsechu

The balmy Punakha valley hosts this unique event, whose highlight is a dramatic recreation of a 17th-century battle featuring hundreds of costumed *pazaps* (warriors). A three-day tsechu then ensues. The festival follows the lunar calendar, so it can fall in March.

Chorten Kora

Thousands of pilgrims from eastern Bhutan and Arunachal Pradesh circum-ambulate this stupa during two festivals set two weeks apart. Unlike monastic festivals, this celebration feels more like a local fair. The main festival is from the 13th to 15th of the first lunar month, so can fall in March.

Nomad's Festival

Highlanders from as far away as Laya and Sakteng attend this tourism fair in the upper Bumthang valley, selling such local products as conical hats from Laya and fermented cheese from Sakteng. Traditional games and masked dances make it an interesting (if slightly contrived) addition to the festival scene.

March

Spring, from March to May, is an excellent time to visit Bhutan, for both touring and trekking. Mountain views can be cloudy, but the magnificent rhododendrons are in bloom and bird life is abundant.

Gom Kora

Hundreds of people travel to this pilgrimage site in the east of the country for a night of celebrations and ritual circumambulations of the sacred black rock. It takes place between the 8th and 10th of the second lunar month, so can fall in April.

April

April is the second most popular month to visit Bhutan, partly because temperatures are comfortably warm. The Paro tsechu is a big draw and trekking is good.

Paro Tsechu

This very popular festival features four days of *cham* (religious ritual dance) followed by the predawn unfurling of a giant *thangka* (religious picture) depicting

TOURISM FESTIVALS

Several new tourism-oriented festivals have been inaugurated in Bhutan in recent years. While they may lack the authenticity of Bhutan's main religious tsechus, they can be fun and are worth a visit if you are in the region. All offer traditional sports like archery, wrestling and darts, plus mask dances, cultural dances and plenty of local foods and products. Apart from the Nomad's Festival in upper Bumthang, try the Alpine Festival in Haa in the first or second weekend in July, the Mushroom Festival in Ura in August and the Takin festival at Gasa in the third weekend in February.

the eight manifestations of Guru Rinpoche. The first day's ceremonies are in Paro Dzong, before the action moves outside. It can also fall in March.

Trekking

Warm weather and continued rhododendron blooms at higher elevations make this a fine time to trek, but there's less chance of blue skies at the top of the mountain. Bring some rain gear just in case.

May

The end of spring brings warm and dusty weather, with rain and cloud increasing towards the end of the month. The lighter crowds and good weather still make it a fine month to visit, though it's already hot at lower elevations.

Ura Yakchoe

A small-town vibe marks this three-day festival featuring religious processions, dances and local moonshine. The only problem is that dates are notoriously unreliable. The

festival can fall in April but is only fixed a few weeks in advance.

Monk Processions

On the first day of the fourth lunar month, the entire monk body moves from Punakha to their summer residence in Thimphu. The procession includes the Je Khenpo (Chief Abbot) and several sacred relics, and local people line up along the route for a blessing.

June

Monsoon clouds can obscure views and cancel flights at Paro airport. As the rains intensify, roads can wash away. The spectacular wildflowers at this time of year in the high valleys are a botanist's dream.

Nimalung Tsechu

Bumthang is the place to visit in the fifth lunar month. Nimalung Goemba has a three-day festival starting on the eighth day, with the final day coinciding with the nearby Kurjey tsechu. Dates can fall in July.

Kurjey Tsechu

Monks from Trongsa Dzong perform religious dances for this one-day festival in Bumthang. The date also marks the birthday of Guru Rinpoche, which is celebrated by prayer ceremonies across Bhutan. A three-day tsechu at Nimalung Goemba starts two days before Kurjey tsechu.

Monsoon Madness

The summer monsoon (June to September) dominates Bhutan, which receives more rainfall than any other Himalayan region. The rains peak during July, making road travel to the east precarious, but the lush foliage and fresh mushrooms, mangoes and avocados go some way to compensate.

September

The first half of the month is still rainy but by the end of the month the monsoon has washed the Himalayan skies clear and several big festivals coincide with the beginning of the main tourist season.

Thimphu Tsechu

Crowds can be thick during the four days of spectacular monk dancing in Trashi Chhoe Dzong (over 3000 tourists attend each year). The event can also fall in October. The preceding three-day *dromchoe* festivities (celebrating the defeat of the Tibetans in the 17th century) are generally open to Bhutanese only.

✈️ Haa Tsechu

Sleepy Haa only truly wakes up during this festival. Monk dances are held on the eighth and ninth days of the eighth lunar month in the courtyard of the Lhakhang Kharpo, before the final day's action moves to nearby Wangchulo Dzong.

✈️ Tamshing Phala Choepa

The Bumthang valley offers a double shot of festivals in the eighth lunar month. From the ninth to 11th you can enjoy dances at Tamshing Goemba, before relocating three days later to nearby Thangbi Goemba for three days of festivities. Both festivals can fall in October.

✈️ Gasa Tsechu

You may have to camp to catch this remote three-day festival, but you'll get to see masked dances and the performance of a 300-year-old folk song called *goenzhey*, believed to have been composed by Zhabdrung Ngawang Namgyal when he first came to Bhutan via Laya in 1616.

October

October is the single most popular month to visit Bhutan. Temperatures are warm, mountain views are clear and tour groups are everywhere. Make your hotel and flight bookings well in advance.

✈️ Jampey Lhakhang Drup

Cham dances and bonfires commemorate the estab-lishment of this 7th-century temple. The first evening features a famous midnight 'naked fire dance'. The fun lasts from the 15th to 18th of the ninth lunar month, so it can fall in November. The four-day Jakar tsechu occurs a week before.

✈️ Prakhar Duchoed

This three-day festival at Prakhar Goemba in the Chumey valley shares the same dates as the Jampey Lhakhang Drup so you can easily double up.

🏃 Trekking Heaven

Trekking is superb everywhere in Bhutan in October and this is when most tour companies operate their treks. Nights can be cold at high elevations but the views of snowy peaks such as 7314m Jhomolhari are superb.

November

A good month weather-wise, though pack a jumper for the evenings. Several smaller festivals offer an alternative to the over-visited Paro and Thimphu tsechus.

👁️ Black-Necked Crane Festival

This modern festival in Phobjikha is held on 11 November. Local children perform dances in crane costumes in the courtyard of Gangte Goemba to celebrate the winter return of more than 300 black-necked cranes.

✈️ Mongar Tsechu

Mongar offers a smaller, more intimate festival experience than most others in Bhutan, with more opportunities for photography and cultural interaction. The little-visited Trashigang tsechu occurs on the same three days, which can fall in December.

✈️ Ngang Bi Rabney

Three-day festival at the Ngang Lhakhang (Swan Temple) in upper Bumthang that features some unusual dances by noblemen from two local clans, as well as masked dances. The festival can fall in December.

December

December marks the beginning of winter, with possible snow at higher elevations, though it's not a bad time for touring western Bhutan. The high passes to Haa and the east may be temporarily snowbound.

✈️ Lhuentse Tsechu

Very few tourists make it to this remote monastic festival, way out in the extreme northeast of the country. Festivities also take place simultaneously in nearby Dungkhar. The festival can fall in January.

✈️ Trongsa Tsechu

One of the oldest and least-visited festivals in the country. Three days of dancing run from the ninth to the 11th of the 11th lunar month, so it can fall in January. The final day features the hanging of a giant *thondrol* (a special-occasion *thangka*).

Itineraries

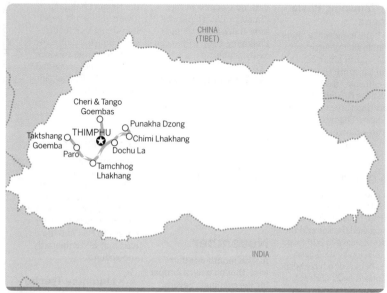

CHINA
(TIBET)

Cheri & Tango
Goembas

Punakha Dzong

THIMPHU

Taktshang
Goemba
Paro

Chimi Lhakhang

Dochu La

Tamchhog
Lhakhang

INDIA

A Long Weekend in Paro & Thimphu

If you have limited time or money, you can get a good impression of Bhutan in just four days by concentrating on Thimphu and Paro. Count on two full days in picturesque **Paro**, visiting Paro Dzong and the National Museum. On the second day, hike up to the dramatic Tiger's Nest at **Taktshang Goemba** and visit lovely Kyichu Lhakhang. After lunch make the three-hour drive to **Thimphu**, stopping at the charming **Tamchhog Lhakhang** en route.

On day three you could squeeze in a long day trip over the **Dochu La** to **Punakha Dzong**, the most beautiful dzong in the country. In March, budget an hour to walk through the colourful rhododendron forests above the Dochu La pass. On the way back to Thimphu, pop into the nearby **Chimi Lhakhang**, the temple of the 'Divine Madman'.

Day four is in **Thimphu**. Go to the weekend market and visit **Cheri Goemba** or **Tango Goemba** in the upper Thimphu valley. If handicrafts are your thing, hit the National Textile Museum and National Institute for Zorig Chusum. Late in the afternoon drive back to Paro; most flights depart early in the morning.

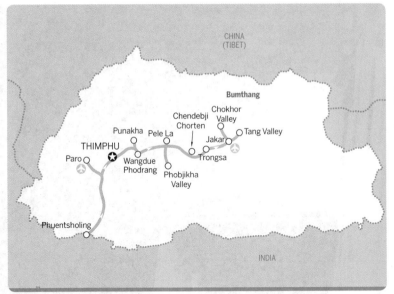

To Bumthang

A 10-day itinerary should just about allow you two or three days in Bumthang, with overnight stops in Paro, Thimphu and Wangdue Phodrang and quick stops in **Punakha** and **Trongsa**, but a full two weeks will let you see the same places in more depth and at a much more relaxed pace, with time for a couple of great day hikes.

Follow the four-day itinerary for your first days. From **Thimphu**, a night in the **Phobjikha valley** will give you a chance to see Gangte Goemba and also view the rare and endangered black-necked cranes (November to February). If you like to explore places on foot, set aside an extra half-day's hiking in Phobjikha.

From Phobjikha it's a day's drive over the **Pele La** to the superb dzong and museum at **Trongsa** and on to **Jakar** in Bumthang. Leave early, as there's lots to see en route, including the Nepali-style **Chendebji Chorten**, which is a perfect place for a picnic.

If you have two full days in Bumthang, spend one day doing a loop in the **Chokhor valley**, taking in the Jampey Lhakhang, Kurjey Lhakhang and walking to Tamshing Goemba. Your second day here should be spent exploring the **Tang valley**, visiting Membartsho (Burning Lake) and the interesting Ogyen Chholing Museum near Mesithang. If you have an extra day, overnight in the Ogyen Chholing Guest House and hike down to the road via the remote rural chapels of Choejam Lhakhang and Narut (Pelphug) Lhakhang.

The Bumthang valley is another good place for some hiking, so budget half a day to stretch your legs after a week's driving. From Jakar it's a two-day drive back to **Paro**, so spend a night at **Wangdue Phodrang**. Alternatively, fly back on the new Druk Air flight from Bumthang to Paro, if it's running.

If you intend to visit India in conjunction with Bhutan, consider driving from Thimphu or Paro to **Phuentsholing** instead of flying, which will add a day to the itinerary. From here you are only a few hours from Darjeeling, Kalimpong and Sikkim, as well as the airport at Bagdogra, which has frequent flights to Delhi and Kolkata (Calcutta).

LEE FROST / GETTY IMAGES ©

Above: Punakha Dzong (p96)

Left: Chortens at the summit of Dochu La (p94)

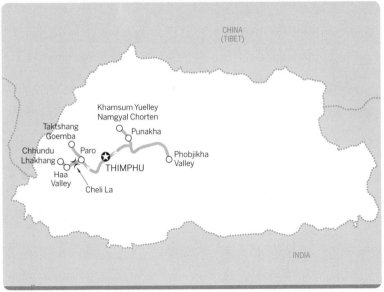

Haa to Punakha

If you're thinking about a four-day trip, consider a seven-day trip. It's not that much more money and, really, when are you next going to be in Bhutan? A week gives you more time to get a feel for Bhutanese culture and enables you to get off the beaten track in either the Haa or Phobjikha valleys, while still seeing the major dzongs and monasteries of western Bhutan.

With the extra days you can definitely add an overnight trip over the mountains to **Punakha**. This way you'll have time to make the 1½-hour return hike to the nearby **Khamsum Yuelley Namgyal Chorten**, as well as visit Chimi Lhakhang, and maybe even a short rafting or mountain-biking trip if that's your thing.

To get off the beaten track, add on an overnight trip to the **Haa valley**, on the road that links Paro to Thimphu. The road goes over the highest motorable pass in Bhutan, the **Cheli La**, and it's worth the couple of hours hiking to visit Kila Nunnery. Arrive in Haa at lunchtime, and spend an afternoon and maybe the next morning exploring the Juneydrak Hermitage and **Chhundu Lhakhang**, before continuing on to **Thimphu**.

Figure on two full days in **Paro**, including visits to **Taktshang Goemba**, Kyichu Lhakhang and Drukyel Dzong in the Paro valley, and a full day (or two) in Thimphu. A few tips: try to be in Thimphu on a Saturday or Sunday to see the weekend market and avoid Paro on Monday, when the National Museum is closed. If you're lucky, you may be able to catch a weekend archery tournament, most likely in Thimphu.

If you don't visit Haa, you might be able to add on a day trip to the **Phobjikha valley**, especially worthwhile in winter (November to February) when the valley's black-necked cranes are roosting. Bring some warm clothes and a torch (flashlight).

At some point during your trip ask your guide to arrange a Bhutanese hot-stone bath, available in most tourist hotels (for a charge). Throw in a festival and you have the perfect introductory visit to Bhutan.

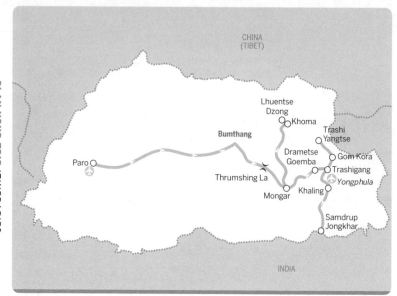

 Eastern Explorations
16 DAYS

It takes at least two weeks to make a trip out to the little-visited far east and we'd suggest throwing in a couple of extra days to allow for some rest and recuperation. There's a lot of driving involved (up to five hours a day in eastern Bhutan) but it is now possible to fly back to Paro from **Yongphula** (near Trashigang). With this itinerary you can also avoid the long drive back to Paro by exiting Bhutan at Samdrup Jongkhar, as long as you have arranged an Indian visa in advance. This is a particularly good trip if you're interested in traditional weaving.

Follow the earlier itineraries from **Paro** as far as Bumthang, from where you can see the highlights of the east in five or six days. From Bumthang, day one takes you on a dramatic drive over the **Thrumshing La** (3750m) and Bhutan's wildest road to **Mongar**. Stay here for two nights and make a scenic day trip up to remote **Lhuentse Dzong** and the nearby traditional weaving village of **Khoma**. To cut down on the driving, consider instead a day's hiking off the beaten track around Mongar.

Day three takes you on to funky **Trashigang**, with an optional two- or three-hour detour along the way to **Drametse Goemba**, Bhutan's most important Nyingma monastery. Accommodation standards in the east are not as good as western Bhutan, so bring a sense of humour as well as bug spray.

Figure on two nights at Trashigang, with another great day excursion to **Trashi Yangtse**, with stops en route at the pilgrimage site of **Gom Kora**, the old Trashi Yangtse dzong and the Nepali-style Chorten Kora. March and April bring two important pilgrimage festivals to this region. Spend a second day here to go crane-spotting in Bomdeling Wildlife Sanctuary or to hike here via Dechen Phodrang pilgrimage site.

From Trashigang it's a full day's winding drive down to the plains at steamy **Samdrup Jongkhar**; stop to check out the traditional weaving at the National Handloom Development Project in **Khaling**. From Samdrup Jongkhar, take a three-hour taxi ride to Guwahati (check in advance for planned strikes) then fly to Kolkata, Delhi or Bangkok, or take the overnight train to West Bengal for Darjeeling and the Nepal border.

Plan Your Trip
Festivals

The exotic visuals and otherworldly mysteries of Bhutanese culture are showcased during its deeply religious, vibrant and colourful dance festivals. Most dzongs and many goembas host an annual festival, the largest of which is the tsechu, where strikingly costumed dancers mesmerise and delight dedicated audiences of locals and travellers alike.

The Tsechu

Tsechus feature a series of dances *(cham)* performed by spectacularly masked and elaborately robed dancers in honour of Guru Rinpoche. See p239 for a description of the *cham* dances. The dates and duration of the tsechus vary from one district to another but usually take place on or around the 10th day of the Bhutanese calendar, which is dedicated to Guru Rinpoche.

Usually the tsechus are performed in the dzong courtyards, which can become crowded as onlookers vie for a view. The tsechu is a grand event, drawing people from the surrounding districts. They are not solemn occasions, but are marked by a holiday atmosphere as people put on their finest clothing and jewellery, share their food and exchange news. A small fair is often set up just outside the dzong or goemba. The festival is an opportunity to catch up with far-flung friends and relatives, and to be immersed in Buddhist teachings. The Bhutanese believe that they will create merit by attending the tsechus and watching the performances of the ritualised dances.

The highlight of many tsechus is the unfurling of a giant *thangka* (religious picture) from a building overlooking the dance arena before sunrise. Such *thangkas* are called *thondrols*. The word means 'liberation on sight', and it is believed that one's sins are washed away upon viewing one of these impressive relics.

Top Tips

Book Early

Hotel rooms and flights into Bhutan fill up quickly around the time of the most popular festivals, such as the Thimphu and Paro tsechus.

Go Further

The smaller festivals and tsechus held in regional dzongs far from Thimphu and Paro are less frequented by tourists and provide a more intimate and traditional experience.

What to Pack

Snacks, a collapsible stool or a cushion – the dances are long and you won't want to lose your hard-fought-for position. Zoom lenses get you closer to the action – don't let your desire for a close-up get in the way of the dancers or block the view of other spectators.

EITAN SIMANOR / GETTY IMAGES ©

Above: Dancer preparing for Tamshing Phala Choepa (p25)

Left: Masked dancers perform at Ura Yakchoe (p133)

You & the Tsechu

Consider getting a *gho* or *kira* to wear to the tsechu (see the boxed text, p66). During the tsechu dances *atsara* (clowns) mimic the dances and perform comic routines wearing masks with long red noses. While entertaining the onlookers, they also help to keep order and have developed the habit of harassing tourists for money. Take it as a good-natured game. If you contribute, you may even receive a blessing from the wooden phallus they carry.

Wherever there is dancing you should be willing to take part. Traditionally, everybody, including visitors, enthusiastically takes part in the final dance (Tashi Lebey), which concludes all festivities or dance performances. Don't feel shy, just follow the person in front of you and smile for the cameras!

PHOTOGRAPHY ETIQUETTE

During festivals you can photograph from the dzong courtyard where the dances take place. Remember, however, that this is a religious observance and that you should behave accordingly – use a telephoto lens without a flash. Don't intrude on the dance ground or on the space occupied by local people seated at the edge of the dance area, and if you do end up in the front row, please remain seated. Don't photograph a member of the royal family, even if you happen to be at a festival or gathering where they are present.

Punakha Domchoe & Tsechu

The Thimphu and Paro tsechus are by far the most popular festivals with tourists, though more and more visitors are discovering the theatrical *domchoe* in beautiful Punakha. The Punakha Domchoe (or *dromchoe*) festival in February/March is a dramatic celebration of a 17th-century battle scene. In 1639 a Tibetan army invaded Bhutan to seize its most precious relic, the Rangjung Kharsapani, a self-created image of Chenresig. The Zhabdrung concocted an elaborate ceremony in which he pretended to throw the relic into the Mo Chhu, after which the disappointed Tibetans withdrew.

On the final day of the five-day *domchoe* a group of 136 people dressed as *pazaps* (warriors) perform a dance in the main courtyard, then shout and whistle as they descend the front stairs of the dzong. Next, a procession of monks led by the Je Khenpo proceeds to the river to the accompaniment of cymbals, drums and trumpets. At the river the Je Khenpo throws a handful of oranges symbolising the Rangjung Kharsapani into the river. This is both a recreation of the Zhabdrung's trick and also an offering to the *naga* (*lu* in Dzongkha), the spirits in the river. The singing and cheering warriors then carry their general als back into the dzong as firecrackers explode around them. Mask dances then celebrate the Zhabdrung's construction of the dzong. The three-day Punakha tsechu, with *cham* dances in honour of Guru Rinpoche, immediately follows the *domchoe*, and on its final day a *thondrol,* which features an image of the Zhabdrung, is displayed.

Other Festivals

In addition to the well-known tsechus there are other religious festivals and cultural celebrations throughout the Bhutanese year (see p23). Notable non-religious festivals include Bumthang's Nomad's Festival and Phobjikha's Black-Necked Crane Festival.

Festival Dates

Festival dates are determined by the Bhutanese calendar, which in turn is based on the Tibetan calendar, but differs from the latter by one day. So be careful if you are using an online Tibetan calendar calculator. There are Bhutanese versions available, even a Bhutanese calendar app! By far the easiest way to determine festival dates is to find the dates on the **Tourism Council of Bhutan** (www.tourism.gov.bt) website, where over 30 festivals are listed with their dates.

Booking Your Trip

Despite its image as an exclusive, remote destination, Bhutan is not a difficult place to visit. You can easily organise a journey as a group of friends, couple or even as a solo traveller, and there is no limit to the number of tourists who can enter the country.

Fixed Rate Pricing

Fixed Daily Rates

The daily tariff for tourists is US$250 per person per day in the high and shoulder seasons. The rate drops to US$200 per person per day in the low seasons (December to February, June to August).

Groups of one/two people pay an additional surcharge of US$40/30 per person.

Tariff Discounts

Children up to five years old travel free while those aged six to 12 years are exempt from the US$65 government royalty, which is a component of the US$250 daily tariff, and pay only 50% of the rest of the daily tariff.

Full-time students aged under 25, with valid identity cards, get a 25% discount if booking directly with a Bhutanese tour operator.

Discounts are offered on the royalty (not the daily tariff) for longer-stay visitors – 50% (ie US$32.50) from the ninth night and 100% after the 15th night.

Tourists are allowed a royalty-free night (ie US$65 discount) if overnighting in the border towns of Phuentsholing, Samdrup Jongkhar or Gelephu.

When to Book

Bhutanese tour operators generally need a minimum of one month to arrange the logistics, including bank transfers, visa and booking Druk Air tickets. Pinning down your itinerary and tour price may take several weeks of emailing beforehand. If you're timing your trip to coincide with a popular festival, you will need to start several months prior to book Druk Air flights and secure accommodation.

Booking a Tour

Unlike most countries, government regulations require foreign visitors to travel with a prepaid and preplanned itinerary organised through a Bhutanese tour company. You can join a prepackaged group tour or arrange a custom-made program with a Bhutanese operator. Generally there is a great deal of freedom as to where you can go and what you can do. The one thing you can't do is travel without a guide.

Your visit to Bhutan must be arranged through an officially approved tour operator, either directly or through an overseas agent. By dealing with an overseas agent you will avoid complicated payment procedures and also have a home-based contact in case of queries or special needs, but you'll generally pay more for your trip. If you deal directly with a Bhutanese tour operator you will have lots of scope to individualise your itinerary, but you'll have to spend time exchanging emails and organising an international bank transfer.

Just because you are paying a high tariff, don't imagine you'll have Bhutan to yourself. During the high season, tourist hotels, the major dzongs and festivals hum with tour groups, especially in Paro. For a more exclusive experience you'll have to head to the lesser-visited monasteries in Haa and central Bhutan, choose the shoulder season, or venture out to eastern Bhutan.

If you're not used to travelling on an organised tour, we suggest you break up your itinerary with the occasional hike, bike ride or visit to a remote monastery to give you that independent travel vibe.

INDIAN TRAVELLERS

Indian nationals are categorised differently from other international tourists. Indians do not require a visa and may pay local rates for food, transport and accommodation. They may travel independently throughout most of Bhutan, though a special permit is required. For more details, see p269.

are held by the Bhutanese government and only released to the operator at the end of the tour, so you have safeguards no matter which company you choose. In the event of a problem with your Bhutanese tour company, the **Tourism Council of Bhutan** (TCB; ☎02-323251; www.tourism.gov.bt) can provide advice and assistance.

Which Tour Company?

There are more than 200 licensed tour companies in Bhutan, ranging from one-person operations to large organisations with fleets of vehicles and their own hotels.

Large companies, such as Norbu Bhutan Travel, Etho Metho Tours and Treks, Bhutan Tourism Corporation Limited (BTCL), Yangphel Adventure Travel, International Treks and Tours, Rainbow Tours and Treks, and Gangri Tours and Trekking, have more clout to obtain reservations in hotels (some of which they own) and on Druk Air, but they are focused on groups and so may have less time to answer individual enquiries.

One Bhutanese hotelier suggested that the following companies would be large enough to handle overseas queries, but still small enough that the owner would pay personal attention to your program: Bhutan Travel Bureau, Bhutan Mountain Holiday, Bhutan Mandala Tours and Treks, Sakten Tours and Treks, Thunder Dragon Treks, Windhorse Tours and Yu Druk Tours and Treks.

If you wish to go trekking, consider one of the companies that specialises in this activity, such as Bhutan Trekking & Hiking Services.

All operators in Bhutan are subject to government regulations that specify services, standards and rates, and tour funds

Daily Tariff

Bhutan's tourism mantra is 'high value, low impact'. Although there is no restriction on visitor numbers, there is a minimum daily tariff fixed by the government, which is the same whether you stay in hotels or camp on a trek. From this daily tariff US$65 goes to the government as a 'royalty'.

The costs seem steep at first, but when you factor in what that gets you – accommodation, food, private transport, guides, entry fees, permits, a fully organised trek etc – it's not a bad deal. The personal service can be remarkable. For a solo trek we had a staff of six, plus six horses! On the other side of the coin, the standards of accommodation and food in the remote east don't reach 'value for money' status.

Solo travellers and couples can easily travel in Bhutan, though you will pay a surcharge. In fact, the most common group size visiting Bhutan is two people.

Because of the daily tariff there's little difference in price between agencies. A few travel agencies will offer some discount to people who book with them directly, effectively passing on to you the commission they pay to international companies. Another advantage to booking directly with a local agent is that with no commission to pay, the agent has more funds to allocate to better accommodation. If you book through an Indian or Nepalese agent, you may find the Bhutanese agent has less funds to book you in a better hotel, since a commission is going to the agent abroad.

The daily tariff doesn't include luxury accommodation, for which you will have to pay a surcharge, which amounts to paying the bulk of the normal hotel rate. Some agents include visa fees, drinks and perhaps a cultural show in the daily tariff, while most charge separately for this. Activities such as rafting and mountain biking entail additional fees.

Special Categories

➡ **Group leaders** A discount of 50% is given to one person in a group of 11 to 15 people. A free trip is allowed for one member per group exceeding 16 people.

➡ **Travel agents** Established tour companies intending to put Bhutan into their programs may apply for a discounted familiarisation tour. This requires both a pretrip and a post-trip briefing.

Payment Procedure

Tours must be fully paid for in advance in order to get visa authorisation. If you have arranged your trip directly with a travel agent in Bhutan, you must make a wire transfer into a Bhutan National Bank (BNB) account which is held in one of the following foreign banks: Standard Chartered (New York, Tokyo, London, Frankfurt branches) or Bank of America (New York). Your agent will advise on all the banking details for transferring the funds and also ask you to send them a copy of the transfer so that it can be matched with BNB's records. The agent will advise BNB to transfer the funds to the TCB (and Druk Air or a luxury hotel if applicable). The ultimate beneficiary is your travel agent in Bhutan, but the funds will be held by the TCB until your travel is completed; therefore you have more protection against default on the part of the tour company.

Delays & Cancellation

There is no daily tariff for days of delay in your arrival or departure due to weather conditions, Druk Air problems or road-blocks. In cases of delayed departure, tour operators will simply charge the actual expenses for accommodation, food, transport and any other services required.

Each agency has its own cancellation policy, so check the fine print with your agency. There is no refund if you have to cut a trip short once in Bhutan. Travel insurance is a very worthwhile investment, given that you must make full payment upfront.

Bhutanese Tour Operators

The following list includes a selection of the largest companies. For a complete list, see the websites of the **Tourism Council of Bhutan** (www.tourism.gov.bt) and the **Association of Bhutanese Tour Operators** (ABTO; www.abto.org.bt):

All Bhutan Connection (☑02-327012; www.abc.com.bt)

Bhutan Journeys (☑02-333890; www.bhutanjourneys.com)

Bhutan Mandala Tours and Treks (☑02-323676; www.bhutanmandala.com)

Bhutan Men-Lha Adventures (☑02-321555; www.trekkingbhutan.com)

Bhutan Mountain Holiday (☑02-320115; www.bhutanmountainholiday.com)

Bhutan Tourism Corporation Limited (BTCL; ☑02-324045; www.kingdomofbhutan.com)

Bhutan Travel Bureau (☑02-332105; www.btb.com.bt)

Bhutan Travel Club (☑02-334523; www.bhutantravelclub.com)

Bhutan Travel Service (☑02-340370; www.bhutantravel.com.bt)

Bhutan Trekking & Hiking Services (☑02-325472; www.trektobhutan.com)

Bhutan Your Way (☑17641224; www.bhutanyourway.com)

Bridge to Bhutan (☑02-331766; www.bridgetobhutan.com)

Dragon Trekkers and Tours (☑02-323599; www.dragontrekkers.com)

Etho Metho Tours and Treks (☑02-323162; www.bhutanethometho.com)

Gangri Tours and Trekking (☑02-323556; www.gangri.com)

Inner Bhutan (☑77110111; www.hotel-bhutan.com)

International Treks and Tours (☎02-326847; www.intrekasia.com/bhutan.htm)

Jojo's Adventure Tours (☎02-333940; www.jojos.com.bt)

Keys to Bhutan (☎02-327232; www.keystobhutan.com)

Lhomen Tours and Trekking (☎02-324148; www.lhomen.com.bt)

Lingkor Tours and Treks (☎02-323417; www.lingkor.com)

Namsay Adventure (☎02-325616; namsay@druknet.bt)

Norbu Bhutan Travel (☎02-340151; www.triptobhutan.com)

Rainbow Tours and Treks (☎02-323270; rainbow@rainbowbhutan.com)

Raven Tours and Treks (☎02-326062; www.raventourstreks.com)

Sakten Tours and Treks (☎02-325567; www.bhutanhimalayas.com)

Snow Leopard Trekking Co (☎02-321822; www.snowleopardtreks.com)

Thoesam Tours and Trekking (☎02-365101; www.bhutanthoesamtoursandtreks.com)

Thunder Dragon Treks (☎02-321999; www.thunderdragontreks.com)

Village Tours and Treks (☎02-334325; www.bhutanvillagetour.com)

White Tara Tours and Treks (☎02-333224; wtara@druknet.bt)

Windhorse Tours (☎02-326026; www.windhorsetours.com)

Yangphel Adventure Travel (☎02-323293; www.yangphel.com) Operates fly-fishing tours and encourages a 'catch and release' approach.

Yu Druk Tours and Treks (☎02-323461; www.yudruk.com)

Tours from Abroad

Many overseas travel agencies and adventure travel companies offer trips to Bhutan, though few are real specialists. In addition to removing the hassle of transferring money, they will also arrange your flights with Druk Air. Most group tours to Bhutan fly to Paro together.

Australia

Intrepid Travel (☎1300 364 512; www.intrepidtravel.com.au)

Peregrine Adventures (☎1300 791 485, 03-8601 4444; www.peregrineadventures.com)

World Expeditions (☎1300 720 000; www.worldexpeditions.com.au)

Continental Europe

Explorator (www.explorator.fr)

Hauser Exkursionen (☎89-235-0060; www.hauser-exkursionen.de; Spiegelstrasse 9, D-81241 Munich, Germany)

Snow Leopard Adventures (☎070-388 3261; www.snowleopard.nl; Netherlands)

UK

Audley Travel (☎01993-838300; www.audleytravel.com)

Blue Poppy Tours & Treks (☎0207-700 3084; www.bluepoppybhutan.com)

Exodus (☎0870-240 5550; www.exodus.co.uk)

Explore Worldwide (www.explore.co.uk)

KE Adventure Travel (☎17687-73966; www.keadventure.com)

Mountain Kingdoms (☎01453-844400; www.mountainkingdoms.com)

USA & Canada

Above the Clouds (☎802-482 4848; www.aboveclouds.com)

Adventure Center (☎800-228 8747; www.adventurecenter.com)

Asian Pacific Adventures (☎800-825 1680; www.asianpacificadventures.com)

Bhutan Travel (☎800-950 9908; www.bhutantravel.com)

Geographic Expeditions (☎800-777 8183; www.geoex.com)

Journeys International (www.journeys-intl.com)

Mountain Travel Sobek (☎888-831 7526; www.mtsobek.com)

Wilderness Travel (☎510-558 2488, 800-368 2794; www.wildernesstravel.com)

Planning Your Trek

Dzongs and tsechus are only the starting point of Bhutan's draws. Where the roads and tour buses peter out begins an untouched wilderness of Himalayan valleys and remote villages linked only by a network of little-travelled footpaths. To explore this pristine side of Bhutan there's no other way around it: you have to trek. This chapter gives an overview of how to plan a trek in Bhutan; for details of the treks themselves see the Treks chapter.

Best Treks

Best Trek for Bragging Rights

Gruelling, expensive (minimum US$5000) and treacherous, the Snowman trek is Bhutan's ultimate adventure and a brutal way to earn your trekking stripes.

Best Trek for Himalayan Peaks

The Jhomolhari trek takes you within an arm's reach of Jhomolhari and Jichu Drakye, two of Bhutan's most beautiful summits.

Best Trek for Mountains & People

Experience the unusual culture of the Layap people in a village at 3700m on the Laya–Gasa trek.

Best General Trek

Atmospheric monasteries and breathtaking alpine scenery converge on the Druk Path trek between Paro and Thimphu.

Best Trek to Spot Yetis

The Merak–Sakteng trek passes through isolated valleys and interesting ethnic groups in eastern Bhutan; hike it before the roads arrive.

When to Go

The first thing to consider while planning your trek is weather. The second half of October provides the best window for trekking in Bhutan; mid-April comes a close second. However, both these periods fall within high tourist seasons, when flights are booked out and hotel rooms at a premium, so book well in advance. The popular trekking routes also see a steep rise in human traffic during these periods. No matter when you trek, you are likely to have sporadic – and sometimes heavy – rain.

Best Times

➡ **October–November** The best overall season, with vivid blue skies common and dazzling views. The bright sun makes for pleasant daytime temperatures upward of 20°C, falling to around 5°C at night. Mornings are crisp and clear. Clouds and wind tend to build up after 1pm, but typically disappear at night to reveal spectacular starry skies.

➡ **March–May** Affords warmer weather and suits those who fancy rhododendrons and other exotic Himalayan flora. However, there is a higher chance of rain, and high passes can be snowed under, especially through March.

→ **December–February** Winter is the time to tackle the new lowland treks such as the Nabji or Salt treks. The weather is warm but not oppressively hot.

Avoid

→ **June–August** This is when the monsoons descend on Bhutan in all their fury, and it can sometimes rain for days on end. Mudslides are common, trails get dangerously wet and slippery, and there's an army of bloodthirsty leeches waiting to jump on you along the way.

→ **September** Alpine wildflowers are in bloom, but the mud remains deep and soggy due to rain. Mountain views are generally blocked out by passing clouds, barring the odd sunny morning.

READ UP

For a comprehensive low-down on Bhutan's mountain trails as well as a sea of information on the flora, fauna, environment and geology of the region, pick up Bart Jordans' *Bhutan: A Trekker's Guide*.

Kevin Grange's travelogue *Beneath Blossom Rain: Discovering Bhutan on the Toughest Trek in the World* isn't our favourite trekking book but it does give a flavour of group trekking in Bhutan.

For more inspiration, look at www.greathimalayatrail.com.

Booking Your Trek

Government rules dictate that all treks in Bhutan must be arranged as full-fledged camping trips booked through a tour operator. This is essential, since most routes pass through uninhabited and un-developed forest areas, and parties must therefore be self-sufficient in terms of provisions, personnel and equipment.

It's also mandatory for trekkers to be escorted by a licensed guide registered with the Tourism Council of Bhutan (TCB). Guides in Bhutan come with varied levels of work experience, and a seasoned trek leader is often hard to find. If you're trekking in the high season, ask your tour operator to arrange for a knowledgeable guide well in advance.

Trekking in Bhutan also involves obtaining a slew of permits for entering national parks, walking through protected areas and engaging in activities such as fishing. Brief your tour operator about your exact plans, so that these permits can be duly obtained.

Although many Bhutanese agents can arrange treks on the most popular routes, you should go with a specialised agent if you're headed off the beaten track. The biggest trek operators are Yangphel Adventure Travel, International Treks and Tours, Yu Druk Tours and Treks, Lhomen Tours and Trekking, and Namsay Adventure; see p36 for details.

What to Pack

Trekking gear is not widely available in Bhutan, so bring all personal equipment with you, preferably in a lockable duffel bag. While packing for the trek, limit your baggage to 15kg. Each pack animal carries 30kg, and it's expected that one animal will carry the luggage of two trekkers.

Your trek operator will provide two-person tents with thin foam mattresses, eating utensils, kitchen equipment, a kitchen tent and a toilet tent. Sleeping bags are not provided, so bring your own. Regulations specify that the operator should provide a first-aid kit and a pressure bag (portable altitude chamber) for high-altitude treks.

Schedule Changes

Despite all the planning and advance arrangements involved, itineraries can often be disrupted by several unforeseen factors. Unexpected showers can make trails slippery, snow can block out tracks, horses can fail to appear on schedule, or horse drivers may consider the trail too dangerous for their animals. These happen more frequently than you might imagine. Be prepared to take any disappointment in your stride.

LAYA–GASA

Difficulty Medium–hard
Duration 12 days
Season April to June, September to November
Good For Remote mountains and communities
Summary This trek is an extension of the Jhomolhari trek. It offers diverse flora and fauna, as well as a good opportunity to spot blue sheep. (p171)

JHOMOLHARI

Difficulty Medium–hard
Duration 8 days
Season April to June, September to November
Good For Mountain views
Summary Bhutan's most popular trek offers spectacular views of the 7314m Jhomolhari from a high camp at Jangothang. (p164)

JHOMOLHARI 2

Difficulty Medium
Duration 6 days
Season April to June, September to November
Good For Mountain views with less time
Summary The shorter and earlier version of the main Jhomolhari trek goes to the Jhomolhari base camp at Jangothang, returning the same or an alternate route. (p169)

Wagye La
Jelekangphu Gang
Teri Gang
Kangphu Gang
Masagang
Zonpghu Gang (Table Mountain)
Gangchhenta
Tsenda Kang
Gieu Gang
Thanza
Gasa
Tserim Kang
Jichu Drake
Kang Bum
Jhomolhari
Dodina
Punakha
Drukgyel Dzong
Motithang
Paro
THIMPHU
Dochu La
Wangdue Phodrang
Cheli La
Haa
Sele La
Talakha Peak
Dagana
Chhukha
Damphu
Samtse

DRUK PATH

Difficulty Medium
Duration 6 days
Season February to May, September to December
Good For An introductory taste of trekking in Bhutan
Summary One of the most scenic and popular treks in Bhutan, following a wilderness trail past several remote lakes. Although it is a short trek, it goes to a high altitude. (p160)

DAGALA THOUSAND LAKES

Difficulty Medium
Duration 5 days
Season April, September to October
Good For Trekking off the beaten track
Summary A short trek, near Thimphu, to a large number of lovely high-altitude lakes; far fewer, however, than the name suggests. (p163)

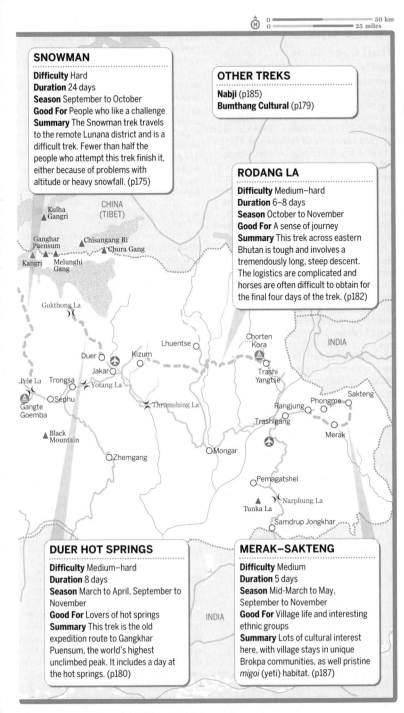

0   50 km
0   25 miles

SNOWMAN

Difficulty Hard
Duration 24 days
Season September to October
Good For People who like a challenge
Summary The Snowman trek travels to the remote Lunana district and is a difficult trek. Fewer than half the people who attempt this trek finish it, either because of problems with altitude or heavy snowfall. (p175)

OTHER TREKS

Nabji (p185)
Bumthang Cultural (p179)

RODANG LA

Difficulty Medium–hard
Duration 6–8 days
Season October to November
Good For A sense of journey
Summary This trek across eastern Bhutan is tough and involves a tremendously long, steep descent. The logistics are complicated and horses are often difficult to obtain for the final four days of the trek. (p182)

Kulha Gangri

CHINA (TIBET)

Ganghar Puensum   Chisangang Ri
Chura Gang
Kangri   Melunghi Gang

Gokthong La

Lhuentse

Chorten Kora

INDIA

Duer   Kizum
Jakar

Pele La   Trongsa
Gangte Goemba   Sephu   Yotang La

Trashi Yangtse

Sakteng
Rangjung   Phongme
Trashigang   Merak

Thrumshing La

Black Mountain

Zhemgang

Mongar

Pemagatshel

Narphung La
Tunka La

Samdrup Jongkhar

DUER HOT SPRINGS

Difficulty Medium–hard
Duration 8 days
Season March to April, September to November
Good For Lovers of hot springs
Summary This trek is the old expedition route to Gangkhar Puensum, the world's highest unclimbed peak. It includes a day at the hot springs. (p180)

INDIA

MERAK–SAKTENG

Difficulty Medium
Duration 5 days
Season Mid-March to May, September to November
Good For Village life and interesting ethnic groups
Summary Lots of cultural interest here, with village stays in unique Brokpa communities, as well pristine *migoi* (yeti) habitat. (p187)

On the Trail

Trail Conditions

Treks in Bhutan are quite physically demanding due to their lengths, altitude and drastic changes in elevation but a lot of this depends on the trek. The average daily gain is about 500m spread over 8km to 12km, with the odd 1000m ascent thrown in when campsites are few and far between. There's a lot of side-hill climbing on steep slopes, which means more up-and-down climbing around vertical cliffs, avalanche tracks and side canyons. Campsites are sometimes spaced out over long distances, requiring you to walk seven to nine hours in a day. Other days, however, may involve just three or four hours of brisk walking.

Many treks follow ancient trade routes that fell into disuse once roads were built. Some of these trails, especially in eastern Bhutan, have seen scant maintenance for several decades, and route conditions are thus often difficult to predict. It's always possible to encounter snow, especially on high passes. The terrain is amazingly rocky, and you might often have to traverse long stretches of round river rocks, which is hard on your feet. Trails are often extremely muddy, especially in spring and early summer, and diversions are quite common.

TOPOGRAPHIC MAPS

Good quality maps of Bhutan are extremely difficult to obtain. The entire country has been mapped by the Survey of India at 1:50,000, but these are restricted documents, as are a related series of topographic maps produced by the Survey of Bhutan. Another series is the 1:200,000 Russian Military Topographic set which takes 10 sheets to cover Bhutan, but its text is in Russian cyrillic.

In cooperation with an Austrian project, the Tourism Council of Bhutan (TCB) produced large-scale contour maps of the Jhomolhari and Dagala Thousand Lakes treks based on the Survey of Bhutan series. These are the best (although not entirely accurate) trekking references available, if you can track one down.

Guides & Camp Staff

For a small group, a trekking party typically contains a guide, a cook, a helper and a horseman with his animals. Porters are generally not used in Bhutan, unlike neighbouring Nepal. The guide makes important decisions, and often teams up with the cook to handle the logistics. Larger groups are accompanied by a 'trek organiser' who oversees sundry campsite activities, packers to manage and streamline porterage, and a couple of 'waiters' who serve food and handle kitchen duties. On our solo trek along the Druk Path we had six staff and seven ponies!

Accommodation

You will sleep in a tent, with foam pads placed on the floor as a mattress. All your gear goes into the tent with you at night. Staff will often bring you a bowl of warm water each morning to wash with. In some places, there is a stone building that the staff can use for cooking and shelter and may be available for trekkers to use as a dining room or emergency shelter.

Along some treks such as the Merak–Sakteng and Nabji treks you have the opportunity to stay in village homestays. At other villages you might stay in community-run campgrounds, where profits go into a community fund.

Food

The food on a Bhutan trek is pampering, to say the least. Most cooks are adept at tossing together a reasonable variety of Western and Asian dishes. You can rely entirely on camp meals, which are quite elaborate, and your cook can look after any special dietary requirements if given advance notice. All rations are carried from the start of the trek, and food is cooked over stoves fueled by bottled gas.

Breakfast at camp generally starts with tea in bed and moves on to cereal or porridge, jam, toast and sometimes eggs, served with instant coffee or tea. You'll sometimes even be served French fries for breakfast, more proof (if you need it) that Bhutan really is Shangri-La. Midday meals are hot, usually prepared at breakfast time and packed beforehand in a thermos-style metal container with a flask of hot tea. For dinner, you're likely to be served red or white rice, chapatis, lentil soup and

PERSONAL EQUIPMENT CHECKLIST

Clothing
➡ fleece
➡ waterproof jacket or poncho, plus umbrella
➡ hiking pants or skirt
➡ wicking or quick-drying T-shirts or blouses
➡ long-sleeved shirt
➡ sun hat that covers your ears

Footwear
➡ water-resistant trekking shoes with hard Vibram soles (properly broken in)
➡ camp shoes, thongs or sandals
➡ socks (polypropylene)

Equipment
➡ daypack
➡ sleeping bag (down-filled for high-altitude treks)
➡ silk sleeping bag liner
➡ water bottle (preferably metal to cool boiling water)
➡ torch (flashlight) and spare batteries

Miscellaneous Items
➡ toiletries
➡ toilet paper and cigarette lighter in a Ziploc bag
➡ pocket knife
➡ sunscreen (SPF 30+) and lip balm
➡ travel towel
➡ biodegradable laundry soap
➡ medical and first-aid kit
➡ hand sanitiser
➡ water filtration or chemical purification
➡ blister gear and tape
➡ sewing kit
➡ goggles or sunglasses, and spare spectacles
➡ books for the long evenings
➡ stuff sacks for organisation and sturdy plastic bag to keep your sleeping bag dry
➡ second duffel bag or suitcase to leave your city clothes in
➡ trekking poles

For Treks above 4000m
➡ down- or fibre-filled jacket
➡ long underwear
➡ woollen hat or balaclava
➡ gloves
➡ gaiters
➡ mountain trekking boots (properly broken in)

vegetables. Fresh meat may be served on the first two nights, and canned fruit cocktails are often thrown in for dessert. Bhutan is one place where you might actually gain weight on a trek! All you need to bring is a few muesli bars and a slab of chocolate for moral support.

Pack Animals

In the absence of porters, pack horses (and at higher elevations, yaks) form the lifeline of treks in Bhutan. They carry all personal and common trekking gear, freeing you up to trek with nothing but a daypack. Contractors arrange for animals at the starting point, and their owners accompany them on the trek to arrange their loads and ensure their overall wellbeing. The ancient *dolam* system in Bhutan allocates specific grazing grounds to each village. For this reason, pack animals don't cross *dzongkhag* (administrative district) boundaries. Messages are sent ahead so that replacement animals are (with any luck) waiting at the boundary.

Responsible Trekking

Fires

➜ Campfires are prohibited and you should decline the offer if your staff suggest one. Bring enough warm clothing and you won't need to stand around one. It's a real dilemma, though, if the packers build a fire, or if one is struck as part of a 'cultural show' in a village.

➜ Since 1996 cooking meals over a fire has been prohibited by law, and staff are required to carry a supply of fuel. However, it's a hard rule to enforce, and animal herders sometimes violate the code and cook their own meals over wood.

➜ Burning garbage is offensive to deities, especially within sight of a sacred mountain such as Jhomolhari.

Rubbish

➜ Encourage your guide and staff to pack out all your group's waste. Don't overlook easily forgotten items such as silver paper, cigarette butts and plastic wrappers, including those left behind by others. They weigh little and can be stored in a dedicated rubbish bag.

➜ Sanitary napkins, tampons and condoms cause serious damage to the environment if they are not carried out of a trek.

Human Waste Disposal

➜ Contamination of water sources by human faeces can lead to the transmission of hepatitis, typhoid and intestinal parasites, and poses severe health risks to trekkers as well as local residents and wildlife. A toilet tent will be set up at each camp.

➜ Where there is no toilet tent, consider burying your waste. Dig a hole 15cm deep and at least 100m from any watercourse. Consider carrying a trowel for this purpose. Cover the waste with soil and a rock. Use toilet paper sparingly, and burn it or bury it with the waste. In snow, dig down to the soil or your waste will be exposed when the snow melts.

Washing

➜ Detergents and toothpaste, even biodegradable ones, pollute watercourses. For personal washing, use biodegradable soap and a basin at least 50m away from any watercourse. Widely dispersing the waste water allows the soil to filter it fully before it makes it back to the watercourse.

Erosion

➜ Hillsides and mountain slopes are prone to erosion. Sticking to existing tracks and avoiding short cuts helps to prevent it. If you blaze a new trail straight down a slope, it will turn into a watercourse with the next rainfall and soil loss and scarring will result.

➜ Sometimes a track passes right through a mud patch. Walking through the mud preserves the trail while walking around the edge will increase the size of the patch.

➜ Avoid removing or disturbing plants that keep the topsoil in place.

Cultural Conservation

➜ Thoughtful travellers respect the culture and traditions of local village, camp staff and horse drivers.

➜ Giving sweets, money, medicines or gifts to local people, particularly children, encourages begging.

➜ Buying local household items or religious artefacts from villagers could deprive them of family heirlooms or precious relics and utensils that are difficult to replace. It could also be considered disrespectful.

Regions at a Glance

Which region of Bhutan you decide to visit will most likely depend on how much time you can afford to spend here. The vast majority of visitors quite naturally focus on the west and Thimphu. With its excellent tourist infrastructure, fantastic sights and spectacular festivals, it allows you to see the most of Bhutan in the shortest amount of time.

Central Bhutan, on the other hand, sees fewer tourists and is a quieter, dreamier collection of alpine valleys and historical monasteries. The winding roads east are for adventurers, weaving researchers and *migoi* (yeti) hunters. It offers warmer, wetter and wilder climes, tougher travel and, some would say, the 'real' Bhutan, untouched by group tourism or even much of the modern age.

Thimphu

Shopping
Museums
Modern Bhutan

Handicrafts

It's not just that Thimphu has the best handicraft shops in the country (it does), it's also the best place to actually see the products being made, from traditional paper and incense factories to local silversmiths and weaving workshops.

Textiles & Traditions

The best general museums are not in Thimphu (try Paro and Trongsa instead), but for specialised interests such as Bhutanese medicine, traditional country life and the country's rich textile tradition, this is the place.

Cafes & Culture

Thimphu is the beachhead for globalisation in Bhutan. It's the place for contemporary Bhutanese art and culture, as well as espresso coffee and pizza. And there's nowhere better to witness cultural collisions that sum up Bhutan's inherent quirkiness – monks with mobiles and lamas with laptops are a daily sight.

p48

Western Bhutan

Architecture
Trekking
Scenic Views

Dzongs & Monasteries

If you only visit two towns in Bhutan, make them Paro and Punakha. The west is blessed with not only the country's loveliest dzong (Punakha), but also its loveliest lhakhang (Kyichu Lhakhang) and the most dramatic monastery (Taktshang Goemba). These are the big sights that you simply have to see.

Ancient Trails

From awesome Jhomolhari to the remote land of Laya, and the well-worn trails of the Druk Path, Bhutan's most popular trek, the west offers you the opportunity to combine the best of the cultural sights with a walk in the mountains.

Himalaya Panorama

In October or November, a trip to the Dochu La, with its view of Himalayan peaks framed by chortens and prayer flags, is a literal highpoint, rivalled only perhaps by views of Jhomolhari from the upper Paro valley.

p73

Central Bhutan

Architecture
Hiking
Buddhism

Venerable Temples

The heartland of central Bhutan is Bumthang, a delightful collection of Swiss-style valleys sprinkled with golden-roofed chapels, remote red-walled goembas and sacred temples, including the fabulous 1500-year-old Jampey Lhakhang.

Village Encounters

Bumthang offers the best day hikes through bamboo forest and yak meadows, past chortens to remote monasteries. The delightful Bumthang Cultural trek goes through moss-covered forests, while the villages of Ura and Shingkhar are great for strolls.

Sacred Sights

The line separating fact and fiction can be fuzzy in Bhutan. Stand where Guru Rinpoche wrestled a snow lion, run your hand over meditation caves etched with the body prints of saints and peer into a lake full of treasure visible only to the virtuous. It's a sacred landscape.

p111

Eastern Bhutan

Off the Beaten Track
Dramatic Drives
Handicrafts

Pure Bhutan

Bhutan's wild east is for the hardy. Long, winding drives on rough roads ending in simple accommodation is the norm here. Life is more rural and led at a slower pace. And you're likely to have it to yourself. Just don't come during the monsoon...

High Mountain Passes

Roads in the east regularly inch along sheer cliff faces on a ledge not wide enough for two vehicles. Throw in dense fog and a monsoon downpour and you can expect a thrilling drive. The variety of landscapes is equally impressive, from the heights of Thrumshing La and the lush Himalayan foothills down to the subtropical.

Traditional Textiles

Eastern Bhutan is the heartland of the country's rich weaving traditions. Enthusiasts can wander the village looms of Khoma and find out which natural dye comes from insect secretions at Khaling.

p136

On the Road

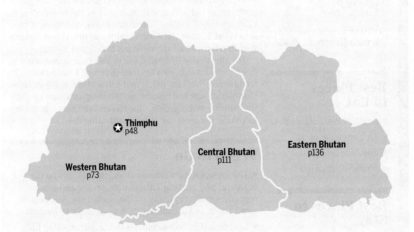

Thimphu
p48

Central Bhutan
p111

Eastern Bhutan
p136

Western Bhutan
p73

Thimphu

🔊 02 / POP 95,100 / ELEV 2320M

Best Places to Eat

➡ Seasons Restaurant (p64)

➡ Ambient Café (p63)

➡ The Zone (p63)

➡ Bhutan Kitchen (p63)

Best Places to Stay

➡ Druk Hotel (p62)

➡ Hotel Jumolhari (p61)

➡ Taj Tashi (p62)

➡ Hotel Pedling (p61)

Why Go?

The capital of one of the world's most intriguing destinations, Thimphu has all but shrugged off the friendly village tag. The city buzzes with a commercial exuberance that constantly challenges the country's natural conservatism and Shangri La image. Vehicle traffic, unheard of a handful of years ago, now courses through the ever-growing road network nourishing a construction boom. However, the juxtapositions of old and new remain part of Thimphu's charm. Crimson-robed monks, Indian labourers, government ministers clad in *ghos* and *kiras* (traditional dress) and camera-wielding tourists all share the pot-holed pavements.

For the visitor Thimphu offers the best opportunity to briefly break away from the tour itinerary. In addition to its traditional Buddhist sights and attractions, it offers cafes, bars, nightclubs and restaurants. Finding a balance between the esoteric and espresso – the old and the new – is the key to getting the most out of this captivating city.

When to Go

➡ The improving autumn weather, clear skies and the colourful and exciting Thimphu *dromchoe* and tsechu festivities make September to November the peak season, when flight and accommodation bookings can be tight.

➡ In spring the rhododendrons in the surrounding hills erupt in blossom and the Je Khenpo leads the annual procession of monks from Punakha to their summer residence in Thimphu.

➡ Saturday is a good day to be in the city throughout the year, with archery tournaments, expanded opening hours at the dzong, the Weekend Market and the liveliest nightlife, though some sights and all government offices are closed.

◉ Sights

★Trashi Chhoe Dzong   BUDDHIST, DZONG
(Map p50; ⊘5-6pm Mon-Fri, 8am-6pm Sat & Sun, to 5pm in winter) This splendid dzong, north of the city on the west bank of the Wang Chhu, seems to fit seamlessly into the valley, lending the city both regal splendour and monastic weight. The dzong was the site of the lavish formal coronation of the fifth king in 2008 and hosts the city's biggest annual bash, the colourful tsechu festivities.

The building you see is actually not the original Thimphu dzong. In 1216 Lama Gyalwa Lhanangpa built Dho-Ngen Dzong (Blue Stone Dzong) on the hill above Thimphu where Dechen Phodrang now stands. A few years later Lama Phajo Drukgom Shigpo, who brought the Drukpa Kagyu lineage

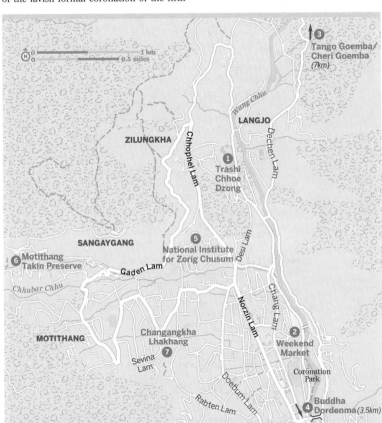

Thimphu Highlights

❶ Roam the peaceful courtyards of the grand and serene **Trashi Chhoe Dzong** (p49)

❷ Plunge into the pungent, bustling **Weekend Market** (p52) for incense and artefacts

❸ Hike through whispering pines and rhododendrons to the serene solitude of **Tango Goemba** (p70) or **Cheri Goemba** (p70)

❹ Look up in awe at the mighty **Buddha Dordenma** (p57) that gazes over the city

❺ Marvel at the skill and artistry of Bhutanese arts and crafts at the **National Institute for Zorig Chusum** (p52)

❻ Inspect and photograph the seriously odd-looking takins at **Motithang Takin Preserve** (p57)

❼ Join the pilgrims at colourful **Changangkha Lhakhang** (p57), Thimphu's liveliest temple

Greater Thimphu

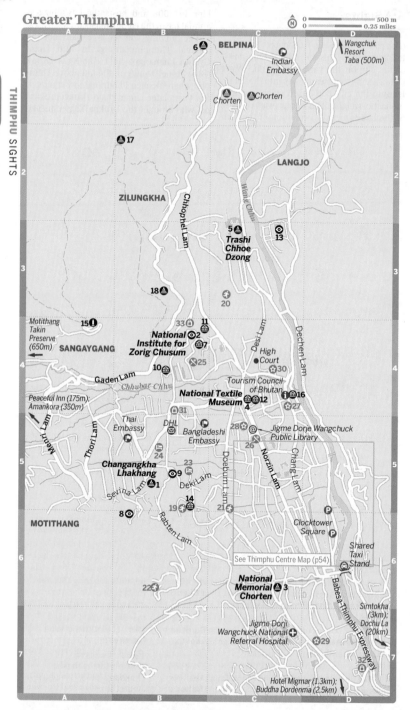

N

0 ————— 500 m
0 ————— 0.25 miles

BELPINA

Wangchuk
Resort
Taba (500m)

Indian
Embassy

Chorten   Chorten

LANGJO

17

ZILUNGKHA

Chhophel Lam

Wang Chhu

5
Trashi
Chhoe
Dzong

13

18

33   11
National   2
Institute for   7
Zorig Chusum

20

Motithang
Takin
Preserve
(650m)

15

SANGAYGANG

25

High
Court

30

Desi Lam

Dechen Lam

10

Gaden Lam

Chhubai Chhu

National Textile
Museum   12
4

Tourism Council
of Bhutan

16
27

Peaceful Inn (175m);
Amankora (350m)

Thai
Embassy

31

DHL

Bangladeshi
Embassy

28

26

Jigme Dorje Wangchuck
Public Library

Menri Lam

Thori Lam

24

23

Changangkha
Lhakhang
9

Deki Lam

Norzin Lam

Chang Lam

Doebum Lam

8

19

14

21

See Thimphu Centre Map (p54)

MOTITHANG

Rabten Lam

Sevina Lam

Clocktower
Square

P

P

Shared
Taxi
Stand

22

National
Memorial
Chorten   3

29

Jigme Dorji
Wangchuck National
Referral Hospital

Babesa–Thimphu Expressway

Simtokha
(3km);
Dochu La
(20km)

32

Hotel Migmar (1.3km);
Buddha Dordenma (2.5km)

Greater Thimphu

to Bhutan, took over the dzong. In 1641 the Zhabdrung acquired the dzong from the descendants of Lama Phajo and renamed it Trashi Chhoe Dzong (Fortress of the Glorious Religion). He arranged to house both monks and civil officials in the dzong, but it was too small so he built another dzong lower down in the valley for the civil officials. The 13th *druk desi*, Chhogyel Sherab Wangchuck (1744–63), later enlarged Trashi Chhoe Dzong so that it could again accommodate both civil officials and monks.

The original upper dzong was destroyed by fire in 1771 and was abandoned in favour of the lower dzong, which was expanded. That dzong itself suffered a fire in 1866, and twice again since then. The five-storey *utse* (central tower) was damaged in the 1897 earthquake and rebuilt in 1902.

When he moved the capital to Thimphu in 1962, King Jigme Dorji Wangchuck began a five-year project to renovate and enlarge the dzong. The royal architect performed the repairs without touching the *utse,* Lhakhang Sarpa (New Temple) or any other of its chapels at the centre. Other than these structures, the entire dzong was rebuilt in traditional fashion, without nails or architectural plans. The dzong once housed the

National Assembly and now houses the secretariat, the throne room, and offices of the king and the ministries of home affairs and finance.

The dzong's whitewashed two-storey outer structure has three-storey towers at the four corners projecting out over the walls and capped by red-and-gold, triple-tiered roofs. There are two main entrances on its eastern side. The southern entrance leads to the administrative section (off limits to visitors), while the northern leads to the monastic quarter, the summer residence of the *dratshang* (central monk body).

Entering the dzong from the northeast entrance you are greeted by the four guardian kings, while the steps are flanked by images of Drukpa Kunley, Thangtong Gyelpo and Togden Pajo with consort. Upon entering the **dochey** (courtyard) it's hard not to be impressed by the splendid proportions of the architecture, the enclosed silence broken only by the flight of pigeons, the shuffle of feet and the whirr of prayer wheels. A large *utse* separates the northern monastic courtyard and its Lhakhang Sarpa from the southern administrative courtyard. The northern **assembly hall** houses a large statue of Sakyamuni (the historical Buddha)

THIMPHU IN...

Most of the major attractions will already be included in your itinerary. Here are a few suggestions if your itinerary allows some free time in Thimphu.

One Day

After your hotel breakfast head down to the **Weekend Market** and explore the traditional produce stalls before crossing the atmospheric cantilever bridge to the souvenir stalls on the east bank of the Wang Chhu. If the market isn't on, check the **Changlimithang Archery Ground** (p57) for any activity or drop into the **National Textile Museum** (p56), **National Institute for Zorig Chusum** (Painting School) or **Voluntary Artists Studio Thimphu** (p57) to watch artisans at work or track down that unique souvenir. Visit the **Mid Point** (p63) or **Musk** (p63) restaurants for a light lunch or the trendy **Ambient Café** (p63) or **Karma's Coffee** (p65) for coffee and cake. Round off the afternoon by checking out the numerous shopping centres for handicrafts, books or Bhutan's extravagant postage stamps. As beer o'clock approaches, head towards **The Zone** (p63). After-dinner entertainment can be found in one of the many clubs or a late-night live-music haunt such as **Mojo Park** (p65).

and the thrones of the current king, past king, past king and Je Khenpo. Look to the ceiling for fine painted mandalas.

It is sometimes possible to enter the utse. If you're allowed in, look for the 3rd-floor funeral chorten of the 69th Je Khenpo, where pilgrims receive the blessing of betel nut from his nut container. If this intrigues you, head next door to visit the toilet of the Zhabdrung in his former living room.

Northeast of the dzong is an excellent example of a traditional cantilever bridge. To the southeast is the unassuming residence of the current king, while across the river you can see the impressive **SAARC building** (Map p50), which houses the National Assembly. The small Neykhang Lhakhang, west of the dzong, houses the local protective deities Gyenyen Jagpa Melen and Dorji Daktshen, and is off limits to visitors. The large open-air courtyard on the north side of the dzong hosts the dances of the annual tsechu festival in September. The dzong's huge Sangay Tsokhorsum *thondrol* (a painted/embroidered religious picture) is unfurled here at the climax of the tsechu.

★ Weekend Market   MARKET

(Map p54; ⊙ Sat & Sun) The Weekend Market occupies stalls on both banks of the Wang Chhu, just north of Changlimithang Stadium. Vendors from throughout the region start arriving on Thursday and Friday, and remain until Sunday night.

Wander around and you'll find a pungent collection of dried fish, strips of fatty pork and balls of *datse* (homemade soft cheese).

During the winter you can even pick up a leg of yak (with the hoof still attached). The incense area is one of the more interesting sections, full of deliciously aromatic raw ingredients, as well as pink cubes of saffron that look like dice but are used to flavour the holy water given to pilgrims in lhakhangs. The bags of mixed grains and grasses are for throwing in the air during religious rituals.

Depending on the season, look out for banana pods, jackfruit and the curly fern fronds known as *nakey*. The cereals section has red rice and tsampa, the ground roasted barley beloved by highland Bhutanese and Tibetans.

Across the cantilever footbridge, known as the Kundeyling Baazam, on the west bank, is a collection of clothing stalls as well as a handicraft market. Products include wooden bowls, mala beads, printing blocks, amulets, yak tails and prayer wheels, some of which are made in Nepal. There are some gems amid the junk. Bargaining is very much in order; your guide can advise you on the quality of your intended purchase.

★ National Institute for Zorig Chusum   ART SCHOOL

(Map p50; ☑ 322302; izc@druknet.bt; Pedzoe Lam; ⊙ 10am-noon & 2-3.30pm Mon-Fri, 10am-noon Sat) This institute, commonly known as 'the painting school', operates four- to six-year courses that provide instruction in Bhutan's 13 traditional arts. Students specialise in painting (furniture, *thangka*s – painted religious pictures, usually on canvas), woodcarving (masks, statues, bowls), embroidery (hangings, boots, clothes) or statue-making (clay).

Most tour operators include a visit to the school in their sightseeing program. Though large groups of visitors can disrupt the classes, the craft demonstrations are a photographer's dream and it's hard not to be impressed with the skill and discipline of the young students.

There are several handicraft shops nearby.

★ **National Memorial Chorten** BUDDHIST, CHORTEN

(Map p50; Chorten Lam) This large Tibetan-style chorten is one of the most visible religious structures in Thimphu, and for many Bhutanese it is the focus of their daily worship. It was built in 1974 as a memorial to the third king, Jigme Dorji Wangchuck (1928–72).

The whitewashed chorten, with its golden finial, is decorated with richly painted annexes facing the cardinal directions, and features elaborate mandalas, statues and a shrine dedicated to the popular king.

Throughout the day people circumambulate the chorten, whirl the large red prayer wheels and pray at a small shrine inside the gate. Particularly charming is the dedicated group of old-timers hauling away at room-size giant prayer wheels beside the main entrance. Early morning is especially tranquil as elderly people shuffle in, and spruced-up kids on their way to school whiz in and out to pay homage.

Folk Heritage Museum MUSEUM

(Phelchey Toenkhym; Map p50; ☑ 327133; Pedzoe Lam; SAARC national/adult Nu 25/150; ⊙ 9am-4.45pm Mon-Fri, 10am-1pm Sat & Sun) This restored three-storey, rammed-earth and timber building replicates a traditional farmhouse and is furnished as it would have been about a century ago. A guided tour of this almost-living museum is included in the admission and provides an interesting glimpse into rural Bhutanese life. Details that jump out include the antique noodle press, the leopard-skin bags and Brokpa yak-hair 'spider' hats. The restaurant here serves Bhutanese lunches (Nu 250).

National Library MUSEUM, LIBRARY

(Map p50; ☑ 333301; www.library.gov.bt; Pedzoe Lam; ⊙ 9am-5pm Mon-Fri summer, to 4pm winter) The National Library was established in 1967 to preserve ancient Dzongkha and Tibetan texts. For tourists it's of interest mainly as a fine example of traditional Bhutanese architecture, but it's also a good resource for books about Bhutan.

Traditional books and historic manuscripts are kept on the top floor and include texts from the famous Tibetan printing presses of Derge and Narthang. Scriptures from all religious schools are represented, including the Bön tradition. Most of the books are Tibetan-style, printed or written on long strips of handmade paper stacked between pieces of wood and wrapped in silken cloth. Other displays include some great historic photos, a copy of a letter sent from the *druk desi* (secular ruler) to British army officer and surveyor Samuel Turner in 1783, and carved wooden blocks used for printing books and prayer flags.

National Institute of Traditional Medicine MUSEUM, CLINIC

(Map p50; ☑ 324647; Serzhong Lam; admission Nu 100; ⊙ 9am-3pm Mon-Fri, to 1pm Sat) Established in 1978, this interesting government facility researches, prepares and dispenses traditional herbal and other medicines. The small museum details ingredients that range from herbs and minerals to animal parts, precious metals and gems. The institute collects medicinal plants from remote corners of the Bhutanese Himalaya such as Lingzhi, Laya and Lunana and then distributes pills, tablets, ointments and medicinal teas to regional health-care units around the country.

Of particular interest is *yartsa goenbub* (cordyceps), the high-altitude cure-all 'Himalayan Viagra' that is actually a caterpillar that has been mummified by a fungus. The curious 'worm-root' sells for up to US$25,000 per kilogram in China.

DON'T MISS

BHUTAN, THE BIG BOOK

At the National Library, be sure to check out the copy of the world's largest published book. Aptly entitled *Bhutan*, and weighing in at 68kg and over 2m tall, this heavyweight tome could crush any coffee table. Its huge illustrated pages are turned one page per month (when it's not awaiting repair). Details on the book and how to buy a copy (US$15,000 for a full-sized edition, US$100 for the smaller version) can be found at www.friendlyplanet.org. You can also see a copy of the book close up in the library of the Uma Paro hotel.

Thimphu Centre

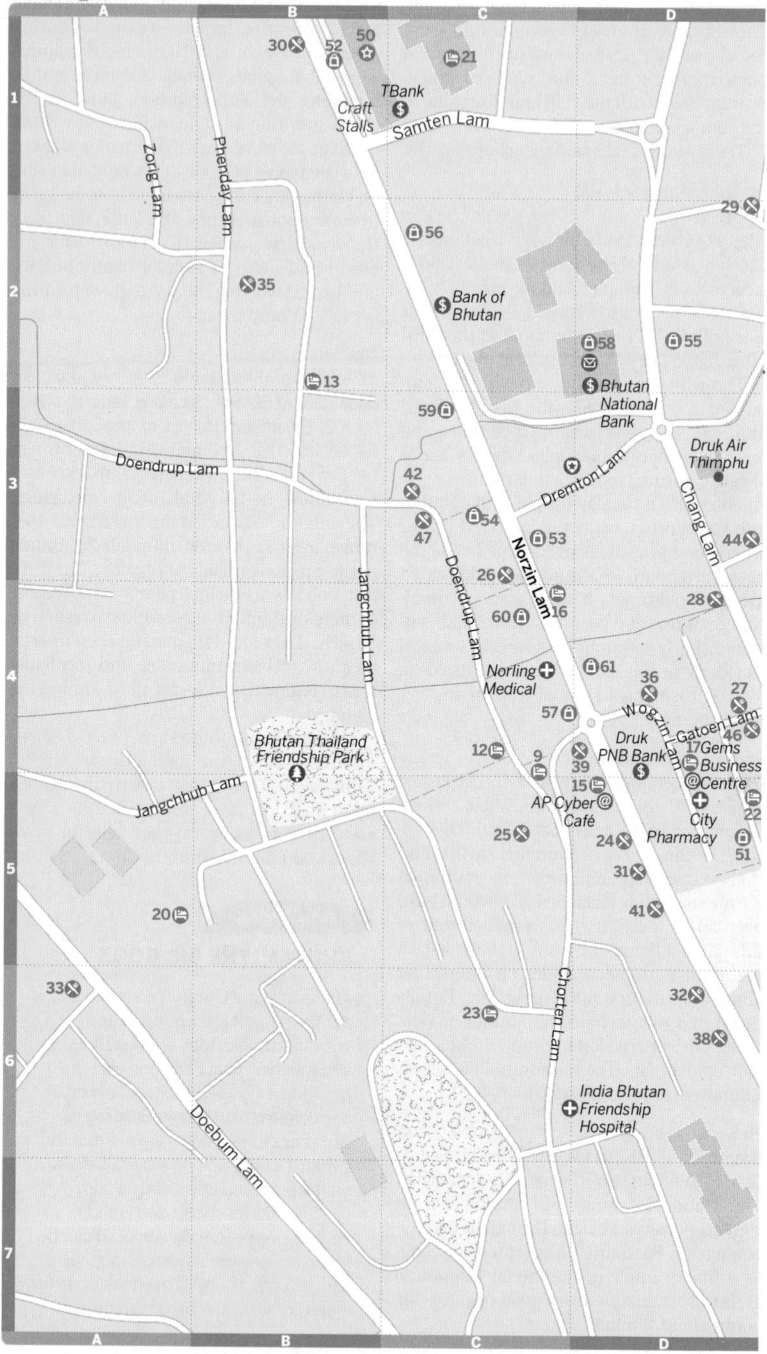
A
B
C
D
1
2
3
4
5
6
7
30
52
50
21
TBank
Craft Stalls
Samten Lam
Zorig Lam
Phenday Lam
29
56
35
Bank of Bhutan
58
55
Bhutan National Bank
13
59
Druk Air Thimphu
Doendrup Lam
Dremton Lam
42
47
54
53
Chang Lam
44
Norzin Lam
26
16
28
60
Jangchhub Lam
Doendrup Lam
Norling Medical
61
36
27
57
Wogzin Lam
Gatoen Lam
46
Bhutan Thailand Friendship Park
12
9
39
Druk PNB Bank
17
Gems Business Centre
Jangchhub Lam
15
AP Cyber Café
City Pharmacy
22
25
24
51
31
20
41
33
32
23
Chorten Lam
38
India Bhutan Friendship Hospital
Doebum Lam

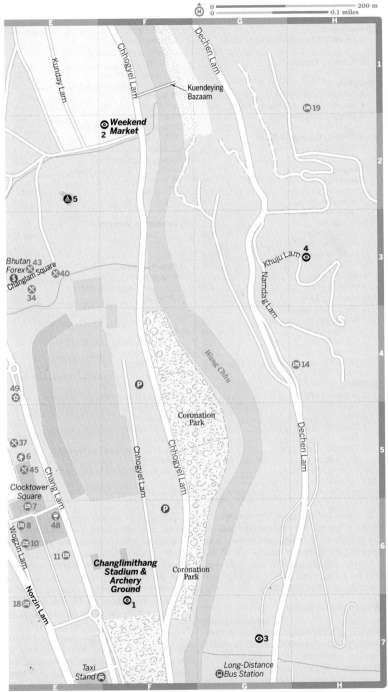

0   0   200 m
0   0.1 miles

Kunday Lam

Chhogyel Lam

Dechen Lam

Kuendeying
Bazaam

19

Weekend
Market
2

5

Bhutan 43
Forex Changlam Square 40

34

Khuju Lam

4

Namdag Lam

Wang Chhu

14

49

Coronation
Park

37

6

45

Chang Lam

Dechen Lam

Clocktower
Square
7

8

48

Chhogyel Lam

Chhogyel Lam

Wogzin Lam

10

11

Changlimithang
Stadium &
Archery
Ground
1

Coronation
Park

18

Norzin Lam

3

Taxi
Stand

Long-Distance
Bus Station

THIMPHU SIGHTS

Thimphu Centre

If you're feeling under the weather, the on-site clinic will tell you if your wind, bile and phlegm are in balance and prescribe appropriate medicines or treatments, all free of charge. *Lasgang* root is said to do wonders for a sore throat; we're not quite sure about the elephant's gallstone.

★**National Textile Museum**　MUSEUM, ARTS CENTRE
(Map p50; ☑321516; Norzin Lam; SAARC national/adult Nu 25/150; ◷9am-4pm Mon-Sat) Thimphu's National Textile Museum is worth a visit to learn about Bhutan's living national art of weaving. The ground floor focuses on *cham*

(religious ritual dance) costumes, while the upper floor introduces the major weaving techniques, styles of local dress and type of textiles made by women and men. There is usually a small group of weavers working their looms inside the shop, which features work from the renowned weaving centre of Lhuentse in northeastern Bhutan. Each item is labelled with the name of the weaver, at prices costing Nu 1500 to Nu 25,000.

When we visited the museum was in the process of moving across the road to its impressive new home in front of the **Royal Textile Academy** (Map p50; www.royaltextileacademy.org). It will house a conservation centre, shop and cafe, while a weaving centre will operate at the adjacent academy.

Buddha Dordenma BUDDHIST, MONUMENT

The huge 50m-tall steel statue of Buddha Dordenma commands the entry to the Thimphu valley. The huge three-storey throne will eventually hold several chapels, while the body itself is filled with 125,000 smaller statues of Buddha. The statue was made in China (of course), cut into pieces and then shipped and trucked in from Phuentsholing (we would love to have seen the faces of the local farmers as the supersized features of the Buddha drove by!). See www.dordenma.org for more details on the impressive construction. The drive or bike up the paved road to the Changri Kuensel Phodrang site is worth it to gauge the immense size of the statue as well as for the great views of Thimphu.

★ Changlimithang Stadium & Archery Ground STADIUM

(Map p54; Chhogyel Lam) The national stadium occupies the site of the 1885 battle that helped establish the political supremacy of Ugyen Wangchuck, Bhutan's first king. You might catch the occasional football match here, but the next-door archery ground is much more fun. It's worth checking to see if there's an archery tournament going on: whether it's traditional bamboo or high-tech carbon-fibre bows, the skill, camaraderie and good-humoured ribbing are always entertaining. Traditional songs and victory dances are all part of the fun. Archers often practise here in the mornings.

Voluntary Artists Studio Thimphu & Alaya Gallery GALLERY

(VAST; Map p50; ☑ 325664; www.vast-bhutan.org; Tarayana Centre, Chang Lam, Chubachu) The impressive Voluntary Artists Studio Thimphu is the capital's main centre for artists. The goal of the studio is to promote both traditional and contemporary works of Bhutanese art, to provide vocational training for young artists and to act as a creative meeting venue for artists. It's a great place to plug into the Thimphu art scene and chat with artists. Art by the students and instructors is sold here at the Alaya Gallery, as well as at the Art Shop Gallery (p66).

Simply Bhutan MUSEUM

(Map p50; www.bhutanyouth.org; SAARC national/adult Nu 50/100; ⊙9am-1pm & 2-5pm Mon-Sat) Simply Bhutan is an interactive 'living'

VALLEY VIEW

One of the best views of the Thimphu valley comes from the prayer-flag-strewn hillside just below the 2685m **telecommunications tower** (Map p50), high above the town in an area known as Sangaygang. The lovely half-hour walk to **Wangditse Goemba** (Map p50) starts from here, as do several hiking, running and mountain-biking trails (see the map at the site). The access road attracts fitness fans after work and becomes a lovers' lane after dark. Photography is best in the afternoon, but be careful not to photograph the telecommunications installation.

---

museum developed for and by the youth of Bhutan through the Bhutan Youth Development Fund. Visit before the lunch break for the 'magic moment' live performance. Visitors learn about Bhutanese traditions, get to dress up in traditional clothes and be photographed in front of painted backdrops. There are also craft displays and a souvenir shop.

Motithang Takin Preserve ZOO

(Sangaygang) A short distance up the road to the telecommunications tower viewpoint is a trail leading to a large fenced enclosure that was originally established as a zoo. Some years ago the fourth king decided that such a facility was not in keeping with Bhutan's environmental and religious convictions, and it was disbanded. The animals were released into the wild, but the takins, Bhutan's national animal, were so tame that they wandered around the streets of Thimphu looking for food, and the only solution was to put them back into captivity. It's worthwhile taking the time to see these oddball mammals, and the new visitor centre and cafe should be open by the time you visit. Also, expect an entrance fee to have been introduced. The best time to see them is early morning when they gather near the fence to feed.

★ Changangkha Lhakhang BUDDHIST, TEMPLE

(Map p50; Sevina Lam) This popular fortress-like temple perched on a ridge above central Thimphu regularly hums with pilgrim activity. It was established in the 12th century on a site chosen by Lama Phajo Drukgom

PRAYER WHEELS

Spinning prayer wheels are a ubiquitous sight in Bhutan. The revolving cylinders are filled with printed prayers that are 'activated' each time the wheel is turned. Prayer wheels can be intricately decorated hand-held affairs (*mani lhakhor*) or building-sized (*mani dungkhor*) and every size in between. Some are effortlessly turned by diverted streams of water (*mani chhukhor*) or even hot air above a flame, whereas monks and devotees turn human-powered wheels to gain merit and to concentrate the mind on the mantras and prayers they are reciting. Remember to always turn a prayer wheel clockwise.

Shigpo, who came from Ralung in Tibet. Parents traditionally come here to get auspicious names for their newborns or blessings for their young children from the protector deity Tamdrin (to the left in the grilled inner sanctum, next to Chenresig). Don't leave without taking in the excellent view from the back *kora* (pilgrim path), with its lovely black and gold prayer wheels.

Zilukha Nunnery   BUDDHIST, NUNNERY
(Map p50; Gadem Lam) After visiting the telecommunications tower, take Gaden Lam for great views of Thimphu and Trashi Chhoe Dzong. Just above the road is this modern nunnery, which is also called Drubthob Goemba. The site has links to Thangtong Gyelpo, and there's an interesting enclosed chorten in the main courtyard.

Dechen Phodrang   BUDDHIST, MONASTERY
(Map p50; Gaden Lam) At the end of Gaden Lam is Dechen Phodrang, the site of Thimphu's original 12th-century dzong. Since 1971 it has housed the state monastic school, providing an eight-year course to more than 450 students. The 12th-century paintings in the goemba's Guru Lhakhang have been restored, and the upper floor features a large figure of Zhabdrung Ngawang Namgyal as well as a *goenkhang* (chapel dedicated to protective deities).

Zangto Pelri Lhakhang   BUDDHIST, TEMPLE
(Map p54) This private chapel, built in the 1990s by Dasho Aku Tongmi, a musician who composed Bhutan's national anthem, is southwest of the Weekend Market. It's

beside the older Mani Dungkhar Lhakhang and is a replica of Guru Rinpoche's celestial abode. Inside is an array of large 4m-high statues, including several Guru Rinpoches. Look for the elephant skull in a box – reputedly unearthed while digging the foundations.

🏃 Activities

You will probably be too busy sightseeing, trekking or shopping to swim, cycle or go rock climbing, but these activities are available if you are interested.

There are tennis courts, squash courts and a basketball court at the north end of Changlimithang Stadium, and a public swimming pool at the **Sports Complex** (Map p50; ☑ 322064; Doebum Lam; ⊙ 4-8pm Mon-Fri, 1-6pm Sat & Sun Feb-Nov).

Royal Thimphu Golf Club   GOLF
(Map p50; ☑ 325429; www.golfbhutan.com; Chhophel Lam; green fees SAARC national/adult Nu 1500/US$40, per day club hire US$20; ⊙ 8am-5pm Tue-Sun) The Royal Thimphu Golf Club has a delightful nine-hole course beautifully situated above Trashi Chhoe Dzong. Resident Indian Brigadier General TV Jaganathan got permission from King Jigme Dorji Wangchuck to construct a few holes in the late 1960s, and the course was formally inaugurated in 1971. How often do you get to tee off in sight of a Bhutanese dzong and have to dodge chorten hazards?

Schoolboy caddies are available for around Nu 300. You don't need to make an appointment to play, but you may have to wait to tee off on weekends. The clubhouse canteen (closed Monday) has decent food and fine views of the greens.

Yu-Druk Tours & Treks   MOUNTAIN BIKING
(Map p54; ☑ 321905; www.yudruk.com) Local company Yu-Druk Tours & Treks organises rides and rents mountain bikes (US$35 per day, including helmet). It can arrange to have you and the bike transported to the start of several rides.

Vertical Bhutan   ROCK CLIMBING
(☑ 322966; www.verticalbhutan.com) Bhutan's only rock-climbing club, Vertical Bhutan, gathers most weekends to climb on **The Nose** (Map p50), a rock face high above the southwest part of Thimphu. There are several fixed routes with names such as 'Wedding Present' and 'Reach and Preach'. Contact the club secretary for the climbing schedule.

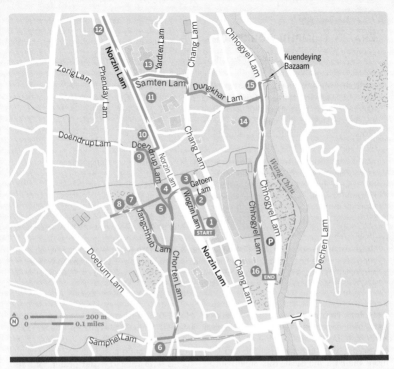

🏃 City Walk
Downtown Thimphu

START CLOCKTOWER SQ
END CHANGLIMITHANG ARCHERY FIELD
LENGTH 4KM; TWO TO THREE HOURS

Start at **①Clocktower Sq** and head north along Wogzin Lam, past shops like **②Dawa Norbu Religious Shop** (for prayer flags and cloth) and **③Gasep Sangay Wangdi Tsongkhhang** (a monks' outfitters), before reaching the famous **④traffic circle** with the arm-snapping police. Go uphill to the **⑤Swiss Bakery**, the time-warp decor of which hasn't changed since 1970, and head southwest along Chorten Lam to the **⑥National Memorial Chorten** (p53) to observe the circumambulating locals.

Backtrack to the Swiss Bakery, turning left at Jangchhub Lam, which takes you north to spin the giant prayer wheel of the timeless **⑦Droma Lhakhang**. The adjacent **⑧Thai Pavilion** marks the Bhutan Thailand Friendship Park.

Head downhill and north along Doendrup Lam. By Seasons Restaurant, take a look at

⑨Samphel Traditional Furniture, selling painted chests and tantric drums, before squeezing down the vegetable market alley of Hong Kong Market. Turn left up Norzin Lam and after 50m you'll pass the **⑩Sephub Gyeltsen Tsongkhang** (p66), with its excellent range of traditional cloth, prayer flags and carpets. The **⑪National Handicrafts Emporium** (p67) and **⑫National Textile Museum** (p56) are both worthwhile detours before popping into the opulent lobby and coffee shop of the **⑬Taj Tashi** hotel.

Head east down Samten Lam to Chang Lam and then down Dungkhar Lam, passing local-style Chhodon Restaurant. Pop into the **⑭Zangto Pelri Lhakhang** (p58) to spin the giant prayer wheel of the Mani Dungkhor Lhakhang and continue to the **⑮Weekend Market** (p52). Finally, head south along Chhogyel Lam to **⑯Changlimithang Archery Field** (p57), checking for signs of an entertaining archery match.

WORTH A TRIP

CRAFTY THIMPHU WORKSHOPS

Thimphu has a small arts and crafts industry. Ask your tour company to arrange a visit to the following workshops and traditional factories in Thimphu.

Jungshi Handmade Paper Factory (Map p54; ☎ 323431; www.gawaling.com; Khuju Lam; ⊗ 8.30am-5pm Mon-Sat) This small factory produces traditional Bhutanese paper handmade from the bark of the daphne bush. You can see the whole process, from soaking and boiling the bark to sorting, crushing, pulping, layering, pressing and drying. Products for sale include lovely decorated paper (Nu 350 per sheet), as well as cards, notebooks, lampshades and calendars. *Jungshi* means 'natural'.

Nado Poizokhang Incense Factory (Map p50; ☎ 323107; www.nadopoizokhang .com; Changangkha; ⊗ 9am-5pm Mon-Fri) Easily Thimphu's sweetest-smelling excursion, this traditional workshop churns out about 10,000 sticks of handmade incense monthly. You can learn about the various ingredients (juniper, cloves, cardamom) and see the production process at the main workshop just above the Changangkha Lhakhang, or simply browse for the final product at the showroom (Map p50; Rabtem Lam).

Goldsmiths Workshop (Map p54; ⊗ 9am-1pm & 2-5pm Mon-Fri) This government workshop behind the bus station is a bit rough and ready, but it's a good place to see copper and silver chasing and the production of everything from fine jewellery to large monastery pieces like *torana*s (arches found over statues) and finials.

Deer Park Thimphu MEDITATION
(Map p50; www.deerparkthimphu.org; Nazhoen Pelri Youth Development Centre) For those whose pursuits tend towards the spiritual more than the physical, this small centre offers Tuesday-evening meditation classes, short weekend retreats and Buddhist discussions for adults and children, as well as a Friday movie night. See its website for the schedule.

★✪ Festivals & Events

Thimphu really comes alive during the annual *dromchoe* and tsechu festivities, held consecutively over eight to 10 days in September/October, corresponding with the eighth lunar month in the Bhutanese calendar. Many businesses are closed during the main dates.

🛏 Sleeping

If you are on a normal tourist visa, you will be booked into one of the comfortable midrange hotels unless you have paid a premium for a top-end hotel (shown here as luxury hotels). If you are an Indian national or you're working in Bhutan on a project, you have the option to choose a more moderately priced hotel. The local budget hotels are not as comfortable as the tourist hotels but they're quite adequate.

Hotel Zey Zang LOCAL $
(Map p54; ☎ 334707; Norzin Lam; r Nu 800-1500) Like all the budget hotels, nothing exceptional here, but it has clean and comfortable rooms with cable TV and heater, and also has a pure vegetarian restaurant.

Hotel Tandin LOCAL $
(Map p54; ☎ 322380; Norzin Lam; r from Nu 1150) The rooms are plain and not immune to noise, but the bathrooms are clean and the bedrooms heated, and it has a pretty good Bhutanese/Indian restaurant.

R Penjor Lodge LOCAL $
(Map p54; ☎ 325578; Norzin Lam; s/d Nu 750/1000) Upstairs from Ambient Café and run by the same friendly folk, the good-value rooms are clean and each come with a bathroom.

Hotel Singye LOCAL $
(Map p54; ☎ 333229; hotelsingyethimphu@yahoo.com; Norzin Lam; r/deluxe Nu 1500/2000) A decent, clean and friendly option with a multicuisine restaurant and bar, and the opportunity to haggle to get a better rate.

Hotel Yoedzer LOCAL $
(Map p54; ☎ 324007; mendrell@druknet.bt; City Centre Complex, Wogzin Lam; r/deluxe Nu 660/1320) Rooms are a bit rundown, with thin mattresses and hot water in the mornings only (deluxe rooms have their own geyser), but they are essentially clean and it's very central.

★ **Hotel Jumolhari**   HOTEL $$
(Map p54; ☎ 322747; www.hoteljumolhari.com;
Wogzin Lam; s/d Nu 3600/4200, deluxe Nu 4440/
5040; ☎) This centrally located hotel bills it-
self as a boutique hotel and boasts a classy
ambience and stylish decor. The rooms are
tasteful, carpeted and comfortable; there
is a health club with free sauna and steam
room, and an excellent restaurant serving
good Indian dishes, among others. All in all
a good choice if you can secure a room with-
out needing to pay a surcharge.

Hotel Pedling   HOTEL $$
(Map p54; ☎ 325714; www.hotelpedling.com; Doen-
drup Lam; s/d Nu 3240/3840, deluxe r Nu 4080;
☎) The rejuvenated Hotel Pedling is stylishly
decorated in muted tones with comfy beds,
though the bathrooms seem to have been
slapped together a bit too quickly and without
much skill. The pleasant staff are a great as-
set, as is the excellent breakfast set-up with an
eggs-to-order chef typical of more expensive
hotels. The hotel is owned by Gangte Monastery and often gets visiting Buddhist groups.

Namgay Heritage Hotel   HOTEL $$
(Map p54; ☎ 337113; www.nhh.bt; Jangchhub Lam;
s/d Nu 3680/4255, deluxe Nu 5750/6325; ☎)
Sitting at the top end of the tourist class is
this stylish place with an impressive atrium.
Rooms are comfortable and sport Buddhist
decor, plus there's a Bhutanese restaurant,
and a free sauna, steam room and gym.
Visiting lamas should splash out on the
suite, which comes with its own meditation
throne. Unlike most Thimphu hotels, wi-
fi isn't free. The swimming pool should be
ready by the time you arrive.

Hotel Kisa   HOTEL $$
(Map p54; ☎ 336495; www.hotelkisa.com; Chang
Lam; r/ste from Nu 4800/7800; ☎) The Kisa
remains one of the best-regarded hotels in
town. It's central and stylish, with 35 very
comfortable rooms and one of the best hotel
restaurants in town. It sits at the top end of
the tourist class and is recommended.

Yeedzin Guest House   GUESTHOUSE $$
(Map p54; ☎ 325702; yeedzin@druknet.bt; Jangch-
hub Lam; s/d/ste Nu 1650/1980/2200; ☎) This
modest but quiet and friendly guesthouse
overlooks central Thimphu and oozes old-
world charm. It's popular with local NGO
staff and consultants, who like the five suites,
each with a kitchen. The cosy ground-floor
restaurant is warmed by an 'open' fire, and
the resident weavers add a homey touch.

Hotel Galingkha   HOTEL $$
(Map p54; ☎ 328126; www.hotelgalingkha.com;
Doendrup Lam; s/d from Nu 3360/3960; ☎) This
central hotel overlooking the southern traffic circle has been extensively remodelled
and externally exhibits some Parisian flair.
Inside you will find teak flooring, autumnal
tones and modern decor. The ground-floor
cafe-restaurant would be great for a coffee if
the espresso machine was working.

Bhutan Suites   HOTEL, APARTMENT $$
(Map p50; ☎ 333377; www.bhutansuites.com;
Changangkha; s/d from Nu 3795/4600; ☎) Busi-
ness travellers and tourists alike are sure to
appreciate the separate sitting room, under-
floor heating and minikitchens here, plus
the sweeping private-balcony views over
Thimphu. The location is more convenient
for visiting government ministries than hav-
ing dinner in town, but you can order room
service from its good vegetarian restaurant.

Wangchuk Hotel   HOTEL $$
(Map p54; ☎ 323532; www.wangchukhotel.com;
Chang Lam; s/d incl breakfast Nu 2875/3335; ☎)
This hotel overlooks the stadium and is a favourite of many expats. The wood-panelled,
carpeted rooms are spacious, light and comfortable, so don't be put off by the rather
gloomy lobby. The restaurant has a good
reputation.

Jambayang Resort   GUESTHOUSE, APARTMENT $$
(Map p54; ☎ 322349; www.jambayangresort.com.
bt; Dechen Lam; s/d from Nu 2750/3300, ste/
apt Nu 5400/2970; ☎) High above the Wang
Chhu on the east bank is this old-fashioned
but charming resort. The sprawling guest-
house has 18 comfortable (but not luxurious)
rooms, many with balcony and excellent

DON'T MISS

TRAFFIC STOPPER

Thimphu is apparently the world's only
capital without traffic lights. A set was
installed a few years back, but residents
complained in classic Bhutanese fash-
ion that it was too impersonal, which
is why the beloved white-gloved police
continue to direct the increasing traf-
fic with the balletic grace of someone
doing a 1980s robot dance. As well
as being a classic Bhutanese anach-
ronism, it may well be the city's most
photographed spectacle.

views, and four private apartments with kitchens. Note there are lots of stairs to negotiate. Locals recommend the restaurant, with its great views over Thimphu, outdoor seating and barbecue.

Hotel Riverview
HOTEL $$
(Map p54; ☑ 325029; hotelriverview@druknet.bt; Dechen Lam; s/d/ste from Nu 3480/4080/5400; ☎) On the east bank of the Wang Chhu is this hefty 47-room hotel. All of the rooms have river and town views, which are slightly better from the upper-floor rooms that boast private balconies. The architecture certainly isn't charming and it's a little inconvenient for exploring the town, but many people like the quiet location, and there's a restaurant, business centre and spa.

Hotel Phuntsho Pelri
HOTEL $$
(Map p54; ☑ 334970; phuetshopelri@druknet.bt; Phenday Lam; s/d/deluxe from Nu 2875/3450/4025; ☎) This contemporary and central hotel has rooms set around a courtyard, with polished floorboards, thicker-than-usual mattresses, and tea and coffee facilities. The businessy vibe is tempered by the bar and Turkish-style spa.

Peaceful Resort
HOTEL $$
(☑ 337012; www.bhutanpeacefulresort.com; Motithang; s/d Nu 2200/2875, deluxe Nu 2875/3450, ste Nu 3450/4025; ☎) Nestled among well-to-do mansions in the forested hills of Motithang, this place is far removed from the distractions of the city, so a little inconvenient for longer stays. The seven standard rooms are in the attic and the deluxe rooms make for a better choice. Expansion plans include a spa, conference hall and double the current number of rooms.

Hotel Dragon Roots
HOTEL $$
(Map p54; ☑ 323256; droots@druknet.bt; Wogzin Lam; s/d Nu 2400/2900; ☎) The old-fashioned and somewhat noisy rooms at the Dragon Roots are cosy enough and centrally located, but definitely at the lower end of the tourist spectrum and overdue for sprucing up. The staff seem to be always preoccupied elsewhere and there were maintenance issues when we visited.

Taj Tashi
LUXURY HOTEL $$$
(Map p54; ☑ 336699; www.tajhotels.com; Samten Lam; r/ste from US$624/960; ☎☒) The striking dzong-like architecture of the five-star Taj Tashi signals the understated yet stylish luxury found inside. The bar and outdoor terrace are both elegant places for a quiet drink. The four deluxe rooms with balcony come with a sun deck and day bed, and are a good choice. Corner rooms are also popular for the excellent views. Guests enjoy a top-end gym and indoor pool; and couples will love the candlelit aromatherapy oil massage, followed by a rose-petal bath and a bottle of champagne.

★ Druk Hotel
HOTEL $$$
(Map p54; ☑ 322966; www.drukhotels.com; Wogzin Lam; s/d Nu 6600/8160, ste Nu 12,000; ☎) This hotel was for a long time the best in Thimphu but it's had a lower profile over recent years despite extensive renovations. It is in the centre of town, overlooking Clocktower Sq and boasts a stylish bar, a multicuisine restaurant noted especially for its Indian food, a 24-hour business centre, and a health club with a gym, sauna and steam bath.

Amankora
LUXURY HOTEL $$$
(☑ 331333; www.amanresorts.com; Thori Lam; s/d incl full board US$1740/1860; ☎) On the 'less is more' theme comes this five-star resort on the forested fringes of town. Amankora looks like a mini dzong, its stone-paved passageways inspiring hushed tones from the reverential guests. Inside the open-plan rooms, plenty of wood and tan-coloured textiles mellow the monastery asceticism. The traditional *bukhari* wood heaters are a nice touch. As with other Amankora hotels, there is a luxurious spa, and airport transfers and meals are included in the tariff.

Khang Residency
HOTEL $$$
(Map p50; ☑ 339111; www.khangresidency.com; Lower Motithang; r from Nu 6600; ☎) This modern block close to the Changangkha Lhakhang eschews the ubiquitous pine cladding found in so many hotels, opting instead for a sleek international vibe in its spacious rooms. There's underfloor heating, balconies, separate showers and bath, and all the amenities you could need, including a tastefully designed bar and restaurant and a free sauna for guests.

Hotel Migmar
HOTEL $$$
(☑ 338901; www.hotelmigmar.bt; Thimphu Expressway, Olakha; s/d Nu 4025/5175, ste Nu 8625; ☎) The Migmar is at the top end of the tourist class, for which you may well be paying a premium. It features a bar and restaurant, and 27 spacious and luxurious rooms with facilities like hairdryer and safe. The

location out of town in the southern suburbs is quiet, as long as you request a room away from the expressway, and is a little inconvenient if you would like to venture out for a stroll.

Termalinca Resort & Spa   LUXURY HOTEL $$$
(☎ 351490; www.termalinca.com; Babesa; r/ste US$420/540; 🖥) This luxury option is 7km from Thimphu, down the valley on the banks of the Wang Chhu. The 30 stone-and-pine rooms are spacious, sleek and stylish, with picture windows, open-plan bathrooms and traditional Chinese furniture. There are no balconies, so spend your time instead at the delightful riverside bar or the impressive yoga room-gym-spa. The resort is owned by the eldest wife of the fourth king.

🍴 Eating

Thimphu is the one place in Bhutan where you can break out of the same-same hotel buffets and track down some authentic local tastes.

🍴 Clocktower Square & Around

Lower Norzin Lam is lined with cheap hotels offering simple and inexpensive vegetarian Indian food at lunch and dinner for Nu 30 to Nu 70; try the **Hotel New Grand** (Map p54; ☎ 324290; mains Nu 60-120) or **Hotel Ghasel** (Map p54; mains Nu 55-180) for their good South Indian vegetarian dishes; and the **NT Hotel** (Map p54; ☎ 323458; mains Nu 50-160) for its inexpensive curries and liquid Tuesday special.

Mid Point Restaurant   BHUTANESE, INDIAN $
(Map p54; ☎ 321269; Wogzin Lam; mains Nu 45-100; ⏱10am-10pm Mon-Sat) This is a favourite of many Bhutanese for its generous servings, particularly *dosas* and other South Indian dishes, at very reasonable prices. The fish curry is excellent, as is the *hogey* (cabbage, carrot and chilli) salad. The outdoor seats are one of the few places in town for alfresco dining.

Musk Restaurant   BHUTANESE $
(Map p54; ☎ 323388; Clocktower Sq; mains Nu 70-120, set meals Nu 140-180; ⏱9am-10pm Tue-Sun) This Clocktower Sq hang-out is a great spot to join the locals who sit outside to shoot the breeze and puff surreptitiously on cigarettes. The menu consists mostly of Bhutanese dishes, but there are

also a few Thai and Indian dishes. Thursday features a Nepali thali (set meal) and Friday is the day for Bhutanese *bangchung* (lunchbox).

★**Ambient Café**   CAFE $$
(Map p54; Norzin Lam; coffee Nu 50-100, mains Nu 110-175; ⏱9am-9pm Tue-Sun; 🖥) A central, bright and well-run place, popular with expats, offering free wi-fi, good espresso coffee, homemade cakes and daily lunch specials, including grilled sandwiches and wraps. It's upstairs overlooking Norzin Lam.

★**The Zone**   WESTERN $$
(Map p54; ☎ 331441; Chang Lam; mains Nu 150-280; ⏱11am-10pm Wed-Mon) This expat favourite models itself on an American diner with a Bhutanese twist. There's burgers and fries, house-made ice cream, ribs (including yak), pizza, *momos* (deep-fried or steamed dumplings), hot dogs, and fish and chips. The outdoor pub-style seats are a great place to read the paper over an Illy coffee and a homemade doughnut, or come for an evening beer.

★**Bhutan Kitchen**   BHUTANESE $$
(Map p54; ☎ 331919; Gatoen Lam; set menu Nu 350; ⏱noon-3pm & 6.30-9.30pm) This elegant restaurant showcases Bhutanese cuisine in a spacious but warm setting that features traditional seating and a standout kitchen. It was designed with tour groups in mind, so you can dive into the *ema datse* and other local dishes without calling for the fire brigade. Get things going with a complimentary shot of *arra* (the local firewater) or *sud-ja* (butter tea) at lunch.

Plums Café   BHUTANESE, CONTINENTAL $$
(Map p54; ☎ 324307; Chorten Lam; mains Nu 110-180; ⏱noon-2.30pm & 6-9pm Mon-Sat) This cosy restaurant above the main junction is an ideal place to try *ema datse* (chillis with cheese), *shamu datse* (mushrooms and cheese) or some fried *nakey* (ferns), followed by scrumptious apple pie. Come early and grab a window seat and you'll get prime views of the police directing traffic below you.

Hotel Jumolhari   INDIAN $$
(Map p54; ☎ 322747; www.hoteljumolhari.com; Wogzin Lam; mains Nu 60-190; ⏱7am-10pm) This delightful restaurant in one of Thimphu's more appealing hotels is notable for its delicious tandoori and curries, delicate naans, cold beer and relaxed atmosphere.

Relish Restaurant & BBQ
MULTICUISINE $$

(Map p54; ☑ 335655; Changlam Sq; Nu 150-380; ☺10am-9pm) Looking a lot like its former incarnation as a Chinese restaurant, this romantic eatery has a menu that includes Bhutanese, Italian and Chinese mains plus juicy barbecued meats. Sit indoors or out in the courtyard warmed by a brazier. From the barbecue choose satays, kebabs, fish, prawns or spicy chicken wings, and wash it down with a cold Red Panda.

Rice Bowl
CHINESE $$

(Map p54; ☑ 333844; Norzin Lam; mains Nu 60-275; ☺9am-10pm Mon-Sat) Decent chilli pork, Sichuan chicken and crispy shredded lamb Hunan-style are made to be shared, though the service is slow and some dishes such as the Singapore noodles occasionally miss the mark.

Cup N Slice
CAFE $$

(Map p54; Norzin Lam; coffee Nu 45-100, mains Nu 150-340; ☺9am-9pm; 🛜) This is the newest of Thimphu's cafes offering decent espresso coffee and free wi-fi. In addition you can also sit down to snacks and substantial meals such as pizza and pasta. It overlooks Norzin Lam and Clocktower Sq but is entered from the rear. If the building is locked, take the lane alongside the south of the building.

✕ Other Locations

Chhodon Restaurant
BHUTANESE $

(Map p54; ☑ 323679; Dungkhar Lam; mains Nu 70-100; ☺9am-7.30pm) If you really fancy going local, this family restaurant in an old traditional house is known for the city's best spicy *tsidro* (ribs). Order these with some *shikam* (dried beef with chillis), rice and *sud-ja* for a totally authentic Bhutanese meal.

Cypress Hotel
NEPALESE $

(Map p54; ☑ 334453; 2nd fl, FCB Bldg, Norzin Lam; mains Nu 40-150, set veg/nonveg meals Nu 150/200; ☺9am-10pm Mon-Sat; 🍴) An unpretentious and charming family-run place serving delicious and spicy Bhutanese and Nepali food (the *shahi paneer* – paneer cheese in mildly spiced gravy – is recommended), with a popular Friday-night thali of eight dishes.

Sonam Tshoey Ice Cream
ICE CREAM $

(Map p54; Changlam Plaza; 100/500ml Nu 65/280) A Swiss-watch shop (look for the Tissot sign) that doubles as a purveyor of delicious homemade ice cream! The all-natural

vanilla and chocolate ice creams are safe and scrumptious, plus seasonal fresh-fruit sorbets should be available by the time you visit.

Zombala
BHUTANESE $

(Map p54; Doendrup Lam; momos per plate Nu 50; ☺9am-9pm Mon-Sat) Any local Thimphupa will tell you the best *momo*s in town are at Zombala's, a cheap and cheerful local dive near Hong Kong Market. Choose between beef or cheese, and expect to fight for a seat.

Art Café
CAFE $

(Map p54; ☑ 327933; Doendrup Lam; cakes & soups Nu 90-130; ☺9am-7pm Tue-Sun; 🛜) Smart and cosy best describe this well-hidden favourite. Although awaiting a new chef when we visited, expect to find decent coffee and delicious cakes, hearty soups, pasta and burgers when fully operational. It's near the Swiss Bakery.

Jichu Drakey Bakery
BAKERY $

(Map p54; ☑ 322980; Doebum Lam; pastries from Nu 40; ☺7.30am-9pm) Stroll up the hill for pretty good takeaway cakes and pastries (there are no tables). The apple pie and strudel are our favourites.

Big Bakery
BAKERY $

(Map p50; cakes from Nu 40; ☺9am-7pm Mon-Fri, 10am-5pm Sat & Sun) This project trains young Bhutanese with a learning disability as bakers. It's worth your support, especially as all that this involves is popping in for a cup of coffee and a croissant.

★ Seasons Restaurant
ITALIAN $$

(Map p54; ☑ 327413; Doendrup Lam; pizzas Nu 190-430; ☺10am-3pm & 4-9pm Wed-Mon) This deservedly popular restaurant specialises in pizzas, but also offers daily specials, such as steaks and spare ribs, and excellent salads, including a smoked beef, blue cheese and pear salad. The alfresco patio overlooking bustling Hong Kong Market is the perfect place to enjoy a Red Panda beer. Desserts include old favourites such as apple pie and ice cream, and there's espresso coffee.

Chula
INDIAN $$

(Map p50; ☑ 336275; Norzin Lam; mains Nu 120-290; ☺noon-2.30pm & 6-9pm Mon-Sat) Chula gets our vote for the best Indian food in town. The chicken *tikka masala, dal Lakhnavi* and *palak paneer* are all great, as are the good-value set lunch thalis (Nu 250). The dishes are tuned to tourist tastes, so if you like it spicy make sure you request it.

★ Karma's Coffee
CAFE $$

(Map p54; Tashi Rabten Bldg, Phenday Lam; coffee Nu 75-120, mains Nu 160-195; ⊙10am-9pm; ☎) A cosy cafe with every conceivable version (hot, iced or frappéd) of what we reckon is the best coffee in Thimphu. There's comfy seating, plenty to read, all-day breakfasts, burgers, fried chicken, delicious brownies, and even a smoking room out the back.

Baan Thai
THAI $$

(Map p54; ☏339966; 4th fl, Karma Kangzang Bldg, Norzin Lam; mains Nu 130-275, set lunch Nu 180; ⊙noon-3pm & 6-9pm Wed-Mon) The Thai food here is authentically spicy, and the curries are big enough for two. The bubbly Thai owner can offer recommendations, or try the delicious *tom kha ghai* (chicken coconut soup) and *som tam* (green papaya salad), perfectly favoured with lime and fish sauce.

Bhutan Orchid
BHUTANESE $$

(Map p54; ☏336660; Chang Lam; set menus from Nu 350; ⊙9am-2pm & 4-10pm) A well-organised buffet restaurant frequented by tour groups where you get to try Bhutanese cuisine without an overdose of chilli. Notable are the regional specialities, such as *hentey* (buckwheat *momos* stuffed with spinach) from Haa, and *puta* (buckwheat noodles) from Bumthang.

Kar Gyal
INDIAN $$

(Map p54; ☏336037; Changlam Sq; mains Nu 100-150; ⊙10am-10.30pm Mon-Sat) This rather dim but friendly restaurant boasts an extensive and inexpensive menu featuring North and South Indian dishes, tandoori and thalis.

Self-Catering

For fresh produce, remember the busy Weekend Market and the street stalls in **Hong Kong Market** (Map p54).

Tashi Supermarket
SUPERMARKET $

(Map p54; ☏322980; Clocktower Sq; ⊙8am-7.30pm) Excellent range of imported and local groceries, with a convenient central location.

Sharyang Enterprise
SUPERMARKET $

(Map p54; Changlam Plaza; ⊙10am-8pm Tue-Sat, noon-8pm Sun) Also known as 'Wangdi's Supermarket' and offering perhaps Thimphu's best selection of foodstuffs, much of it imported from Thailand.

Sharchhogpa Grocery
SUPERMARKET $

(Map p50; Norzin Lam; ⊙7am-9pm) Friendly grocery shop with cereals, bread and plenty of packaged foodstuffs.

🍷 Drinking & Entertainment

Recommended places for coffee include Ambient Café (p63) and Karma's Coffee.

Thimphu has lots of corner-shop bars, but only a handful could be recommended for outsiders looking for more than a game of *carom* (finger snooker) and a swig of cheap whisky. As well as the hotel bars, there are numerous small bars throughout the town. Alcohol won't be served until after 1pm, and bars are closed on Tuesday, the national dry day. Bars close at 11pm on weekdays and midnight on Friday and Saturday.

Entertainment is patchy, but you can ask your guide to take you to a local *drayang* bar: members of the audience request songs at Nu 100 each, which are then sung in traditional style by locals or the resident group.

For a small town there's a fair bit of competition and lots of turnover in the club scene. Depending on the night and the time you rock up, a small admission may be asked of men. Clubs generally close at midnight on weekdays and at 2am Friday and Saturday.

Hi Jinks
BAR

(Map p54; Wogzin Lam; ⊙1-11pm Wed-Mon) The Druk Hotel's sultry leather-and-wood bar is ideal for a relaxing pre- or postdinner drink.

Om Pub
BAR

(Map p54; ☏326344; Jojo's Shopping Complex, Chang Lam; ⊙6pm-late Wed-Mon) A relaxing place for young professionals on the 2nd floor of the rather derelict Jo Jo's building; the entrance is on the north side.

Mojo Park
LIVE MUSIC

(Map p54; Chang Lam; ⊙7pm-late Wed-Mon) Thimphu's premier live-music venue and bar. Musicians start about 9pm.

City Cinema
CINEMA

(Map p50; ☏17608471; City Mall, Chubachhu; tickets from Nu 150) Modern cinema screening Bhutanese movies in a new mall development that also boasts a supermarket, restaurant and coffee shop.

Club Ace
NIGHTCLUB

(Map p50; Phenday Lam; ⊙9pm-midnight Wed, to 2am Fri & Sat) Popular place just outside central Thimphu, with a big dance floor, DJs and thumping electronic beats.

Space 34
NIGHTCLUB

(Map p54; Chang Lam; ⊙9pm-1am Wed, Fri & Sat) Cosy and thumping, and downstairs from Lungta Handicraft.

Khuju Luyang
CULTURAL PERFORMANCE

(Map p50; ☑328649; khujuluyang@druknet.bt; Gongphel Lam; performance per group Nu 5000) This troupe of 12 performs a popular hour-long selection of religious, regional and folk songs and dances, including *cham* masked dances and songs from Laya and Sakteng, accompanied by live music on the zither, flute, fiddle and *drangyen* (lute). It's stagey but enjoyable and worth it, especially if you haven't timed your trip with a major festival.

Royal Academy of Performing Arts
CULTURAL PERFORMANCE

(Map p50; ☑322569; Chhophel Lam; ⊙8.45am-4.30pm Mon-Fri) The home of the Royal Dance Troupe works to preserve Bhutan's folk-dancing heritage and trains professional dancers who perform several of the dances at the Thimphu tsechu. With advance notice they will provide a one-hour performance for visitors, or ask your guide if there's a practise session you could attend.

Nehru-Wangchuck Cultural Centre
PERFORMING ARTS

(Map p54; ☑322664; Tashi Centre, Norzin Lam) This centre in front of the Taj Tashi hotel runs performance programs, documentaries and lectures on South Asian, particularly Indian, culture. There's also a library covering the religion and culture of South Asia and Tibet, plus a yoga room. Check its Facebook page for current programs.

🛍 Shopping

Thimphu has a plethora of 'general' shops selling everything from prayer flags to canned fish. To provide even more variety, some corner shops also sell hard liquor by the glass and their sign may read 'shop-cum-bar' or the all-encompassing 'general-cum-bar-shop'.

Many 'souvenirs' are actually made in India or Nepal, but there are lots of interesting Bhutanese products, especially textiles, baskets, jewellery, incense, books, *atsara* (clown masks) and religious items. Local products also include Tsheringma safflower- and gooseberry-flavoured herbal teas and the organic lemongrass oil and sprays made by **Bio Bhutan** (www.biobhutan.com). There is a long row of **craft stalls** (Map p54; Norzin Lam) opposite the Tashi Centre where you should be able to find that perfect souvenir. And don't neglect the handicraft section at the Weekend Market (p52), where you can put your bargaining prowess to the test.

Art Shop Gallery
ARTS & CRAFTS

(Map p54; ☑325664; Wogzin Lam; ⊙11am-5pm) Located near the Clocktower, the Art Shop Gallery has art supplies, traditional paper and handicrafts, and contemporary paintings from the Voluntary Artists Studio Thimphu (p57).

Gagyel Lhundrup Weaving Centre
CLOTHING

(Map p50; ☑327534; Changzamtog; ⊙9am-5pm Mon-Fri) This private centre at the south end of Thimphu produces handwoven textiles and has a selection of cloth and ready-made garments for sale. This is one of the few places where you can watch weavers at work. A finely embroidered *kira* can take a year to make and cost over US$1000; cheaper ones start at US$50.

LOCAL DRESS: GRAB A KIRA & GHO

Getting your very own *gho* or *kira* (traditional dress for man and woman, respectively) is a novel idea for a souvenir, and you could don it before heading to a festival or event in Bhutan. Many shops in Thimphu, including the souvenir shops, sell off-the-rack *gho*s and *kira*s.

According to Chimmi at **Sephub Gyeltsen Tsongkhang** (Map p54; Norzin Lam; ⊙8am-9pm), one of Thimphu's best cloth stores, ready-made *gho*s cost from Nu 1500 for cotton-wool blends, or Nu 2500 for 'silk-look' varieties, with handwoven cloth costing as much as Nu 6000. A *kira* costs from Nu 750 and the *toego* (short-waisted jacket) costs Nu 400 (traditional) to Nu 700 (modern). For a better fit, Chimmi recommends allowing a couple of days to get a tailor-made item. Don't forget you'll also need to invest in a *kera* (narrow woven belt; Nu 250), while men also need a white *lhagey* (inner liner) and *omso* (socks), and women will need a *wonju* (blouse).

Once you have your *gho* or *kira*, you'll probably need help learning how to wear it. You'll also need some instruction on storing the *gho*, which involves folding the pleats origami-style.

DSB Books
BOOKS

(Map p54; ☑323123; Chang Lam; ☺9am-8pm) Thimphu's best selection of magazines and newspapers, as well as coffee-table and other books on Buddhism, Bhutan and the region. It's located on the ground floor of Jojo's Shopping Complex; enter from the lane behind Chang Lam.

National Handicrafts Emporium
HANDICRAFTS

(Map p54; Norzin Lam; ☺9am-1pm & 2-6pm) This government-run souvenir emporium has fixed prices and is on many itineraries. It closes an hour earlier from November to February.

Lungta Handicraft
HANDICRAFTS

(Map p54; www.lungtahandicraft.com; Chang Lam; ☺8.30am-8.30pm) The best buys here are the larger items like bamboo boxes, carpets, metal ewers, and even horse saddles and monastic trumpets. The antiques all have stamped seals from the National Commission of Cultural Affairs (NCCA), which mean they are safe to take through customs. Like many shops, it can arrange pricey but convenient DHL shipping.

Tsering Dolkar Handicrafts
HANDICRAFTS

(Map p54; Shop 36, Norzin Lam) Unlike many Thimphu craft shops, this one stocks mostly Bhutanese crafts, and is strong on jewellery. Visa cards accepted.

Choki Handicrafts
HANDICRAFTS

(Map p50; ☑324728; www.chokischool.com; Thori Lam) Choki sells masks, *thangkas*, paintings and painted lama tables called *choektse*. Many products come from the affiliated Choki Traditional Art School.

Yarkay Central Building
HANDICRAFTS

(Map p54; Norzin Lam) If you prefer to keep the legwork to a minimum, this shopping complex has several craft stores under one roof, including Druk Handicrafts, Kelzong Handicrafts and Kurtoe Handicrafts.

Sangay Arts & Crafts
HANDICRAFTS

(Map p50; ☑327419; Pedzoe Lam) You can purchase works by students of the National Institute for Zorig Chusum at this nearby shop, run by a former student.

Philatelic Bureau
STAMPS

(Map p54; ☑322296; Dremton Lam) Alongside the main entrance at the post office, this display shop proffers the best selection of souvenir sheets of Bhutanese stamps. Also for collectors, a tiny stall on the ground floor of Hotel Tandin (p60) has a small selection of postcards and many unusual stamps.

Norling Audio
MUSIC

(Map p54; Norling Centre, Norzin Lam) CDs of Bhutanese and Bollywood songs are available here from Nu 200 to Nu 400.

Sachok Enterprise
OUTDOOR EQUIPMENT

(Map p54; ☑333880; Norzin Lam) If you are missing a piece of gear for your trek, this place has both genuine and fake brand-name equipment, and the owner is honest about what's what.

DD Shop
OUTDOOR EQUIPMENT

(Map p54; Etho Metho Plaza, Norzin Lam) The Chinese-made King Camp brand sold here isn't top-notch, but there are useful items like water bottles, socks and gaiters, plus imported hiking shoes. The big-name brands here are fakes from Nepal.

ℹ Information

EMERGENCY
Police station (Map p54; Dremton Lam)

INTERNET ACCESS
There are a dozen or so internet cafes spread around town, all charging around Nu 60 per hour. Most hotels have wi-fi and usually it is provided for free. They also have business centres with internet access available for a fee.

AP Cyber Café (Map p54; Norzin Lam; ☺9am-8pm; ☎) Hidden on the 1st floor.

Gems Business Centre (Map p54; City Centre Complex, Wogzin Lam; ☺10am-8pm) Near Hotel Yoedzer.

Jigme Dorje Wangchuck Public Library (Map p50; ☑322814; Norzin Lam; per hour Nu 50; ☺12.30-6.30pm Mon-Fri, 11am-3pm Sat) This tiny place feels like a British village library and has a dog-eared collection of books on Buddhism and Bhutan, as well as internet access.

MEDICAL SERVICES
Pharmacies can supply medications, including over-the-counter antibiotics. Consider also the clinic at the National Institute of Traditional Medicine (p53).

City Pharmacy (Map p54; ☑321382; City Centre Complex, Wogzin Lam; ☺8.30am-9pm Mon-Sat, 10am-9pm Sun) Near Hotel Yoedzer, this pharmacy also sells veterinarian supplies.

India Bhutan Friendship Hospital (Map p54; ☑322485; Chorten Lam) Local hospital.

Jigme Dorji Wangchuck National Referral Hospital (Map p50; ☑322496; Gongphel Lam) Bhutan's best hospital.

Norling Medical (Map p54; Norling Centre, Norzin Lam) Pharmacy on the ground floor of the plaza.

MONEY

Most hotels can change money at government rates, although they usually have a limited supply of cash. Bank of Bhutan (BOB) and Druk PNB ATMs accept Visa and MasterCard.

Bank of Bhutan (Map p54; ☑ 322266; Norzin Lam; ⊙ 9am-1pm Mon-Fri, to 11am Sat) This main branch (with ATM) tends to be busy. There's a smaller branch on nearby Wogzin Lam, and two ATMs outside Hotel Tandin on Norzin Lam.

Bhutan Forex (Map p54; Room 24, 1st fl, Changlam Plaza; ⊙ 9am-7pm Mon-Sat) Changes cash US dollars at the bank rate, with no commission, and keeps longer hours than the banks.

Bhutan National Bank (Map p54; ☑ 322767; Chang Lam; ⊙ 9am-4pm Mon-Fri, to 11am Sat) In the same building as the post office, this bank changes cash, but not euro travellers cheques.

Druk PNB Bank (Map p54; ⊙ 9am-1.15pm & 2-4pm Mon-Fri, 9am-noon Sat) Has an ATM that accepts Visa and MasterCard.

TBank (Map p54; Norzin Lam; ⊙ 9am-1pm & 2-4pm Mon-Fri, 9am-noon Sat) Opposite the Taj Tashi hotel, changes cash and travellers cheques.

POST

Many hotels and shops sell stamps; it is safe to simply drop cards and letters into post boxes here.

DHL (Map p50; sangay_wangmo@dhl.com; 19-13 Thori Lam)

Post office (Map p54; Chang Lam; ⊙ 9am-5pm Mon-Fri, 10am-1pm Sat) Well-organised, with a postcard and philatelic shop.

❶ Getting There & Away

The long-distance bus station (Map p54) is below the east end of the *zampa* (bridge) at the southern end of town. (Even the bus depot has a prayer wheel in the courtyard and names its bus companies after the eight auspicious symbols!). There are over two dozen daily buses (so-called 'vomit comets') to Phuentsholing (Nu 91 to Nu 121, Coaster Nu 210), plus several daily to Paro (Nu 60), one to Haa (Nu 115), and less frequent departures to longer-distance destinations.

Shared taxis depart just outside the bus station for Phuentsholing (per seat Nu 650), Paro (Nu 200) and Wangdue Phodrang (Nu 200).

❶ Getting Around

If you are on a normal tourist visa, you will have a car/minibus, driver and guide available throughout your stay in Bhutan. Most shops and points of interest are within easy walking distance of Thimphu's major hotels, so it's easy to pop out for a walk, drink or shopping trip.

Although usually well signposted, street names are used by very few locals, including taxi drivers; landmarks and building names will serve you better when asking for or giving directions.

TO/FROM THE AIRPORT

You can book a taxi outside Paro airport at a fixed rate of Nu 800 to Thimphu. A taxi to the airport from Thimphu's long-distance bus station can cost half this rate. It is 53km from the airport to Thimphu; the journey takes less than two hours.

If your tour operator has not arranged transport for your departing flight, the most reliable option is to have your hotel arrange a vehicle. If you have an early-morning flight from Paro (and most are), it's best to spend the night in Paro.

TAXI

Most of Thimphu's taxis are small cars and minivans with meters that the drivers rarely use. Taxi drivers have a habit of charging foreigners, including Indians, as much as they can – one of Bhutan's few rip-offs. A short ride around town costs approximately Nu 60 or you can hire a taxi for the day for about Nu 800. The taxi stand on Chang Lam has shared taxis that shuttle across the valley when full.

AROUND THIMPHU

North of Thimphu

As you travel up the east side of the Wang Chhu, you'll pass the impressive SAARC building (National Assembly) and banquet hall. On the opposite side of the river you may catch a glimpse of Samtenling Palace, the cottage that is the king's residence.

Six kilometres north of Thimphu centre is the suburb of Taba, where you can stay at the atmospheric **Wangchuk Resort Taba** (☑ 365262; www.wangchukhotel.com; off Dechen Lam; s/d from Nu 2875/3680). The resort is associated with the Wangchuk Hotel in town and has a restful, pine-forest location, hotstone baths, an antique museum and a private goemba built on the ruins of a former palace; perfect for meditation. There are great valley views from the balconied rooms.

The large **Dechenchoeling Palace** was built in 1952 and is used by the royal family and government and so is off limits to visitors. North of the palace is the Royal Body Guard (RBG) facility.

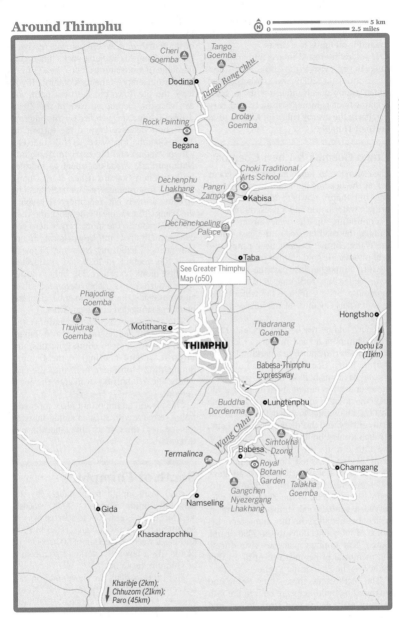

See Greater Thimphu
Map (p50)

Pangri Zampa

North of Dechenchoeling is Pangri Zampa, two imposing buildings beside two huge cypress trees. Founded in the early 16th century, Zhabdrung Ngawang Namgyal lived here after he arrived in 1616 because this temple appeared in the vision that directed him from Tibet to Bhutan. The complex is a centre for traditional astrology, and the head astrologer was entrusted to divine the auspicious date for the king's coronation in 2008.

The nearby **Dechenphu Lhakhang** is home to Gyenyen, the valley's protective deity, and is off limits to tourists.

If you're interested in arts and crafts, arrange to pay a visit to the **Choki Traditional Art School** (☑ 380219; www.chokischool.com), which trains disadvantaged kids in traditional arts of painting, sculpture and carving. It's in the nearby village of Kabisa, 10km north of Thimphu.

Tango Goemba & Cheri Goemba

The excursion to Tango and/or Cheri goembas at the head of the valley is an excellent one, but there's nowhere to eat nearby so bring a water bottle and a packed lunch.

Continuing up the valley from Pangri Zampa, the road crosses to the east side of the Wang Chhu at Begana, near a huge and very photogenic gold-painted **rock painting** of Guru Rinpoche. Just past the bridge are some 'self-arisen' rock images of a fish and mongoose. Soon you'll see the white buildings of Cheri Goemba on the hillside in the distance.

A few kilometres beyond Begana, 12km from Thimphu, a road branches right and climbs a short distance to a parking lot. The trail to Tango Goemba is a climb of 280m and takes about half an hour if you follow the steeper short cut, or about an hour if you take the longer, more gradual trail. Lama Gyalwa Lhanampa founded the site in the 12th century, and the 'divine madman', Lama Drukpa Kunley, built the present building in the 15th century. In 1616 Zhabdrung Ngawang Namgyal visited Tango Goemba and meditated in a nearby cave. The head lama, a descendent of Lama Drukpa Kunley, presented the goemba to the Zhabdrung, who carved a sandalwood statue of Chenresig, which he installed in the monastery. Because of its connections to the Zhabdrung, Tango is a popular place to visit during the memorial of his death in April or May, known as the Zhabdrung Kuchoe.

The picturesque three-storey tower and surrounding buildings were built in the 18th century by the eighth *desi*, Druk Rabgye, and Zhabdrung Jigme Chhogyel added the golden roof in the 19th century. Tango functions as a university of Buddhist studies for monks and is the residence of Gyalse Rinpoche, an important *trulku* (reincarnated lama) who is recognised as the seventh reincarnation of the fourth *desi*, Gyalse Tenzin Rabgye (the founder of Taktshang Goemba).

There are several chapels to visit, including the 3rd-floor *zimchung* (living quarters) of the fourth *desi*, where you can receive a blessing from his walking stick. Tango gets its name (it translates to 'horse head') from the natural shape of the rock outcrop. If you leave the site down the short cut path, you can visit the meditation cave of the Zhabdrung (Tandin Ney) perched on this outcrop.

A short distance beyond the turn-off to Tango Goemba, the road ends at Dodina (elevation 2600m) and the entry to Wangchuk National Park. A walk of about 45 minutes leads to Cheri Goemba (Cheri Dorji Dhen), Bhutan's first monastery. The trail starts by crossing a lovely covered bridge that spans the Wang Chhu (a fine picnic spot), and then climbs steeply to the monastery, where you can normally spot tame brown goral (mountain goats). Zhabdrung Ngawang Namgyal built this goemba in 1620 and established the first monk body here. His father's ashes were interred in a richly decorated silver chorten inside the upper goemba after the body was smuggled here from Tibet.

The next-door *goenkhang* features the two protector deities of Cheri and Tango. From here it's a steep climb (pilgrims aim to do it without pausing) to the Demon-Subjugating Monastery, built into the cliff where the Zhabdrung overcame the local demons.

Cheri is still an important place for meditation retreats, with 30 or so monks here for the standard three years, three months and three days.

South of Thimphu

A road leads uphill from Babesa to the **Royal Botanical Garden** (SAARC national/adult Nu 30/50; ⊘ 9am-4pm, to 5pm summer) at Serbithang, which was inaugurated in 1999 and has a weedy collection of 500 species of plants. It's a favourite weekend picnic spot of Thimphu residents.

From the garden's far viewpoint you can see across the valley to the **Gangchen Nyezergang Lhakhang**, an ancient lhakhang that was rebuilt and reconsecrated in 2001.

Simtokha Dzong

Simtokha is about 5km south of Thimphu on the old road to Paro and Phuentsholing. The junction with the road to eastern Bhutan is just before Simtokha.

DAY WALKS AROUND THIMPHU

In addition to the short walks to Tango Goemba and Cheri Goemba, there are several day walks to monasteries and lookout points around Thimphu. *Mild and Mad Day Hikes Around Thimphu* by Piet van der Poel and Rogier Gruys details 27 hikes, as well as numerous alternatives and side trips. You can download the text and hiking maps from www.bhutan-trails.org/index.html.

Wangditse Goemba

A flat 30-minute walk with great views of Trashi Chhoe Dzong takes you from the San-gaygang telecommunications tower to Wangditse Goemba, which was founded in 1750. The inner chapel houses a two-storey statue of Sakyamuni Buddha. There are views north towards Samtenling Palace, home to the current (fifth) king, and the Dhey and Dorje Drak meditation retreats on the hillside above. From Wangditse you can descend steeply southeast, veering right to Zilukha Nunnery, or you can descend even more steeply northeast to Dechen Phodrang.

Drolay Goemba

It's a two- to three-hour round trip from the parking lot below Tango Goemba to Drolay Goemba at 3400m. The walk offers amazing views of the Thimphu valley and you can combine it with a visit to Tango Goemba.

Thadranang Goemba

A strenuous two-hour uphill hike leads to Thadranang Goemba (3270m). Start at the Yangchenphug High School and climb steeply up the ridge through a blue-pine forest.

Lungchuzekha Goemba

Perhaps the best easy walk in the area is the four-hour round trip from Dochu La to Lungchuzekha Goemba. It affords excellent views of the Himalaya and you can return via the same route or descend to Trashigang Goemba and Hongtsho. From the 108 chortens the trail gradually climbs into rhododendron forest for 1½ hours with some steep sections, before branching left to Lungchuzekha Goemba and right to Trashigang. Combine the hike with dawn views from Dochu La for a great half-day excursion or do it after a morning visit to Punakha.

Phajoding Goemba

It is a 5km walk uphill from upper Motithang to Phajoding Goemba (3950m), a large monastic complex with 10 lhakhangs and 15 monastic residences, many of them used for extended meditation retreats. Togden Pajo, a yogi from Tibet, founded the site in the 13th century, though most of the buildings were constructed in 1748 through the efforts of Shakya Rinchen, the ninth Je Khenpo, whose image is the central figure in the main Khangzang Lhakhang here. The monastic school is housed in the Jampa Lhakhang and offers a more secluded environment than the Dechen Phodrang School in Thimphu.

From Phajoding you can ascend another 300m to Thujidrag Goemba. This is the last day of the Druk Path Trek (p160) in reverse.

Talakha Goemba

This 15th-century goemba (3080m) offers spectacular views of the Bhutan Himalaya and Thimphu valley. You can drive part way and then set out on foot, or visit it on the last day of the Dagala Thousand Lakes Trek (p163). From the small goemba you could make a strenuous six- to nine-hour hike up to 4280m Talakha peak.

Trashigang Goemba

It's two hours from the hillside below Hongtsho to Trashigang Goemba (3200m). This goemba, built in 1786 by the 12th Je Khenpo, is an important meditation centre, and there are numerous pilgrim guesthouses here. In addition to about 15 monks, there are a few *anims* (Buddhist nuns). Inside the lhakhang are statues of the several Je Khenpos who meditated here.

Officially known as Sangak Zabdhon Phodrang (Palace of the Profound Meaning of Secret Mantras), Simtokha Dzong was built in 1629 by Zhabdrung Ngawang Namgyal. It is often said to be the first dzong built in Bhutan. In fact, there were dzongs in Bhutan as early as 1153, but this was the first dzong built by the Zhabdrung, was the first structure to incorporate both monastic and administrative facilities, and is the oldest dzong to have survived as a complete structure. Just above the dzong is the Institute for Language and Culture Studies.

During its construction Simtokha Dzong was attacked by an alliance of Tibetans and five Bhutanese lamas from rival Buddhist schools who were opposed to the Zhabdrung's rule. The attack was repelled and the leader of the coalition, Palden Lama, was killed. In 1630 the Tibetans again attacked and took control of the dzong. The Zhabdrung regained control when the main building caught fire and the roof collapsed, killing the invaders. Descriptions of the original Simtokha Dzong were provided by the two Portuguese Jesuit priests who visited here in 1629 on their way to Tibet.

Expansion and restoration of the dzong was performed by the third *druk desi,* Mingyur Tenpa, in the 1670s. It has been enlarged and restored many times since, most recently by a team of Japanese architects.

The site is said to guard a demon that had vanished into the rock nearby, hence the name Simtokha, from *simmo* (demoness) and *do* (stone). The site is also, of course, a vitally strategic location from which to protect the Thimphu valley and entryway to the Dochu La and eastern Bhutan. The dzong is about 60 sq metres, and the only gate is on the south side (though the original gate was on the west side.)

The **utse** is three storeys high, and behind the usual prayer wheels around the outside there is a line of more than 300 fine slate carvings depicting saints and philosophers. The large central figure in the central lhakhang is of Sakyamuni, flanked by the eight bodhisattvas. The dark murals inside this lhakhang are some of the oldest and most beautiful in Bhutan. In the **western chapel** are statues of Chenresig, green and white Taras, and an early painting of Zhabdrung Ngawang Namgyal, which was cleaned in 1995 but is still cracked. Check out the tigers' tails and guns hanging from the pillars in the eastern *goenkhang*. The **protector chapel** is dedicated to the protectors of Bhutan, Yeshe Goenpo (Mahakala) and Pelden Lhamo.

Western Bhutan

Best Places to Stay

➡ Gangtey Palace (p81)

➡ Lechuna Heritage Lodge (p92)

➡ Dewachen Hotel (p105)

➡ Uma Punakha (p100)

Best Places to Eat

➡ Bukhari Restaurant (p84)

➡ Sonam Trophel Restaurant (p84)

➡ Phuenzhi Diner (p100)

Why Go?

Whether you arrive by air at the dramatic, mountain-bound Paro valley or by road at steamy Phuentsholing, it soon becomes clear that you have arrived at a special destination. Prayer flags flutter from nearly every rooftop, men and women dress in traditional garb, chortens and stupas decorate river and road junctions, and fortresslike monasteries command the mountain tops.

The west is the region of Bhutan that most tourists see and for good reason. It's the heartland of the Drukpa people and is home to the major airport, the capital, the most popular festivals and the most spectacular dzongs (fort-monasteries) in the kingdom. Throw in the trekking, the scope to get off the beaten track and the minimal driving times, and the appeal is obvious. Whether it's the beginning of your trip or the only part of Bhutan that you will explore, the west is a spectacular introduction to this magical country.

When to Go

➡ September to November are the ideal months to visit Bhutan. You'll get great weather, clear mountain views from Dochu La, and dramatic festivals at Thimphu and Wangdue Phodrang.

➡ Black-necked cranes arrive in the Phobjikha valley in late October and early November. March and April are also popular, with the Paro tsechu a major draw, as lovely spring rhododendron blooms decorate the high passes.

Western Bhutan Highlights

1 Explore the picturesque dzong at **Punakha** (p96), the capital of Bhutan from the 17th to the 19th centuries

2 Hike to the dramatic cliff-hanging **Taktshang Goemba** (p87), Bhutan's most famous sight

3 Visit the hulking **Paro Dzong** (p77) and take a crash course in Bhutanese culture and history at Paro's **National Museum** (p79)

4 Spot black-necked cranes or hit the hiking trails in the remote **Phobjikha valley** (p103)

5 Make the pilgrimage to the **Kyichu Lhakhang** (p85), one of Bhutan's oldest and most beautiful temples

6 Hunt for rare Himalayan flowers and visit remote monasteries in the little-visited **Haa valley** (p92)

7 Be blessed with a 10-inch penis, if only for a day, at **Chimi Lhakhang** (p96), the monastery of the Divine Madman!

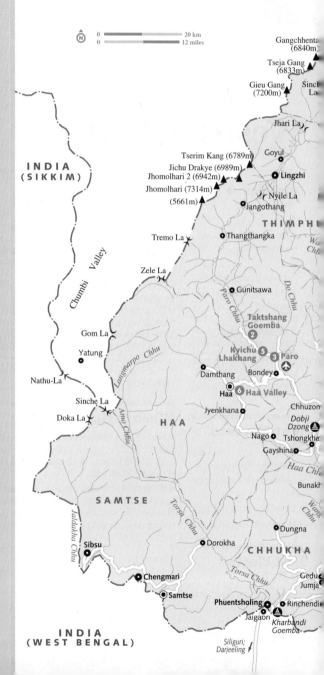

PARO DZONGKHAG

With our passage through the bridge, behold a curious transformation. For just as Alice, when she walked through the looking-glass, found herself in a new and whimsical world, so we, when we crossed the Pa-chhu, found ourselves, as though caught up on some magic time machine fitted fantastically with a reverse, flung back across the centuries into the feudalism of a mediaeval age.

Earl of Ronaldshay, *Lands of the Thunderbolt* (1923)

Paro, Thimphu & Punakha Valleys

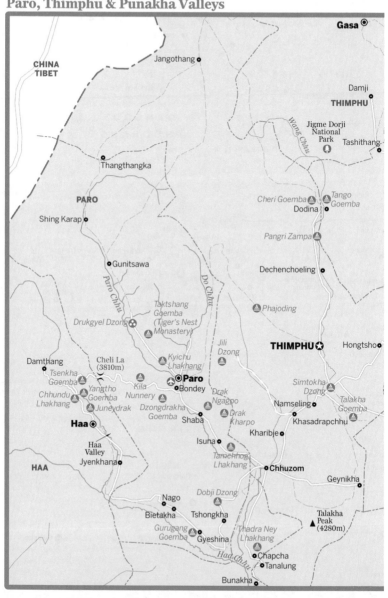

The Paro valley is without doubt one of the loveliest in Bhutan. Willow trees and apple orchards line many of the roads, white-washed farmhouses and temples complement the green terraced fields, and forested hills rise on either side to create a beautiful, organic and peaceful whole.

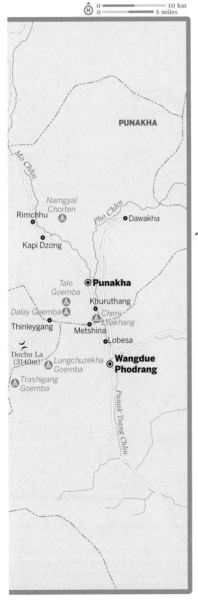

The fertile land, clement climate and network of trade routes from Tibet have provided the people of Paro with a solid economic foundation. For most of the 19th century, Paro held the seat of government and was the commercial, cultural and political centre of the country.

Several treks begin in or near Paro. The Druk Path trek climbs east over a 4200m pass before descending to Thimphu. The Jhomolhari, Laya–Gasa and Snowman treks all lead west from Drukgyel Dzong on to Jhomolhari base camp and the spectacular alpine regions of Gasa and Laya.

Paro

08 / ELEV 2280M

The charming town of Paro lies on the banks of the Paro (or Pa) Chhu, just a short distance northwest of the imposing Paro Dzong. The main street, only built in 1985, is lined with colourfully painted wooden shop fronts and restaurants, though these appear under threat as the town grows and multistorey concrete buildings continue to propagate. For now Paro remains one of the best Bhutanese towns to explore on foot and is worth an hour or two's stroll at the end of a day of sightseeing.

⊙ Sights

★ Paro Dzong   BUDDHIST, DZONG

(Rinpung Dzong; Map p78; ⊙ 9am-5pm) The Paro Dzong is one of Bhutan's most impressive and well-known dzongs, and perhaps the finest example of Bhutanese architecture you'll see. The massive buttressed walls that tower over the town are visible throughout the valley.

The dzong's correct name, Rinchen Pung Dzong (usually shortened to Rinpung Dzong), means 'Fortress on a Heap of Jewels'. In 1644 Zhabdrung Ngawang Namgyal ordered the construction of the dzong on the foundation of a monastery built by Guru Rinpoche. The fort was used on numerous occasions to defend the Paro valley from invasions by Tibet. The British political officer John Claude White reported that in 1905 there were old catapults for throwing great stones stored in the rafters of the dzong's veranda.

The dzong survived the 1897 earthquake but was severely damaged by fire in 1907. It was formerly the meeting hall for the National Assembly and now, like most dzongs, houses both the monastic body and district government offices, including the local courts.

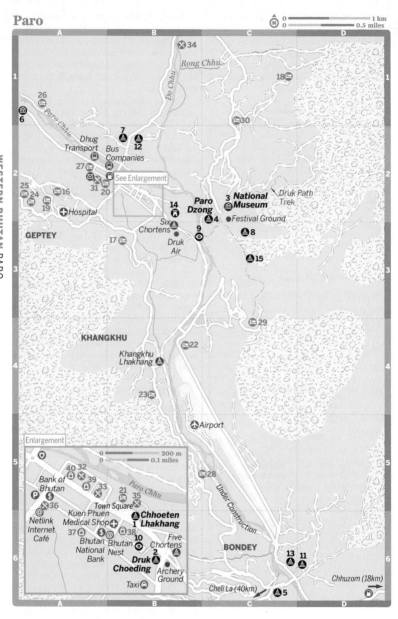

The dzong is built on a steep hillside, and the front courtyard of the administrative section is 6m higher than the courtyard of the monastic portion. The road to the National Museum branches down to the dzong's northeastern entrance, which leads into the **dochey** (courtyard) on the 3rd storey. The **utse** (central tower) inside the *dochey* is five storeys tall and was built in the time of the first *penlop* (governor) of Paro in 1649. To the east of the *utse* is a small **lhakhang** dedicated to Chuchizhey,

Paro

WESTERN BHUTAN PARO

an 11-headed manifestation of Chenresig. The richly carved wood, painted in gold, black and ochres, and the towering white-washed walls reinforce the sense of established power and wealth.

A stairway leads down to the **monastic quarter**, which houses about 200 monks. The **kunre**, which functions as the monks' classroom, is in the southeast corner (to the left). Look under the vestibule for the mural of the 'mystic spiral', a uniquely Bhutanese variation on the mandala. The large **dukhang** (prayer hall) opposite has lovely exterior murals depicting the life of Tibet's poet-saint Milarepa. The first day of the spring **Paro tsechu** is held in this courtyard, which fills to bursting point. The views from the far windows are superb.

Outside the dzong, to the northeast of the entrance, is a stone-paved area where masked dancers perform the main dances of the tsechu. A *thondrol* – huge *thangka* (painted or embroidered religious picture) – of Guru Rinpoche, more than 18m square, is unfurled shortly after dawn on the final day of the tsechu – you can see the huge rail upon which it is hung. It was commissioned in the 18th century by the eighth *desi* (secular ruler of Bhutan), also known as *druk desi,* Chhogyel Sherab Wangchuck.

Below the dzong, a traditional wooden covered bridge called **Nyamai Zam** (Map p78) spans the Paro Chhu. This is a reconstruction of the original bridge, which was washed away in a flood in 1969. Earlier versions of this bridge were removed in time of war to protect the dzong. The most picturesque pictures of Paro Dzong are taken from the west bank of the river, just downstream from the bridge.

The dzong courtyard is open daily, but on weekends the offices are deserted and most chapels are closed.

An interesting side note: scenes from Bernardo Bertolucci's 1995 film *Little Buddha* were filmed here.

★ **National Museum**   MUSEUM
(Gyelyong Damtenkhang; Map p78; ☑271257; SAARC nationals/adult Nu 50/150, monks, nuns & children under 10yr free; ⊙9am-4.30pm, closed national holidays) At the top of the hill above Paro Dzong is an old watchtower that was renovated in 1968 to house the National Museum. The unusual round building is said to be in the shape of a conch shell, with 2.5m-thick walls; it was completed in 1656 and was originally the *ta dzong* (watchtower) of Paro Dzong, which lies undefended below. An underground tunnel is said to lead from the watchtower to the water supply below.

At the time of research, the *ta dzong* was closed owing to the damage suffered in the 2009 and 2011 earthquakes. A sample of the museum's exhibits are currently on display in an adjacent annexe, in what was the portrait gallery. Restoration of the *ta dzong* is expected to be completed in 2015.

Cameras are not allowed inside the museum, but you can photograph the *ta dzong* and surrounding grounds.

Displays in the various galleries include an impressive collection of *thangkas,* both ancient and modern, depicting Bhutan's important saints and teachers, as well as fearsome festival masks. There's a natural-history gallery, while the Heritage Gallery displays a collection of religious statues and early stone carvings, plus a few original iron links from the nearby Tamchhog Bridge (p90).

Driving to the museum involves a 4km loop into the Dop Shari valley. After visiting, you can walk down a path from the museum to the dzong and back to the town, enjoying good views of the valley and of the Ugyen Pelri Palace.

Ugyen Pelri Palace   PALACE
(Map p78) The secluded wooded compound of the Ugyen Pelri Palace was built by the Paro *penlop,* Tshering Penjor, in the early 1900s and is now a residence of the queen mother, thus closed to the public. It is designed after Guru Rinpoche's celestial paradise, Zangto Pelri, and is a beautiful example of Bhutanese architecture. For views of the palace from above, head to the dzong.

On the road beside Ugyen Pelri Palace are five square **chortens** (Map p78) that were built in memory of the first king of Bhutan, Ugyen Wangchuck.

★ **Chhoeten Lhakhang**   BUDDHIST, TEMPLE
(Map p78) The towerlike Chhoeten Lhakhang is southeast of the town square. The caretaker may allow you to visit the upstairs chapel, which features a central Jowo Sakyamuni, with Guru Rinpoche and Chenresig to the side.

★ **Druk Choeding**   BUDDHIST, TEMPLE
(Map p78) Also known as Tshongdoe Naktshang, the quiet and peaceful Druk Choeding is the town temple. It was built in 1525 by Ngawang Chhogyel (1465–1540), one of the prince-abbots of Ralung in Tibet and an ancestor of the Zhabdrung Ngawang Namgyal. The main statue is of a seated Jampa (future Buddha). Also present are the local protectors Gyenyen, Jichu Drakey and Hong Gyelri, surrounded by a fearsome collection of old Bhutanese shields and weapons.

Dumtse Lhakhang   BUDDHIST, TEMPLE
(Map p78) To the west of the road leading to the National Museum is Dumtse Lhakhang, an unusual chorten-like temple that was built in 1433 (some sources say 1421) by the iron-bridge builder Thangtong Gyalpo. The temple was built to subdue a demoness and so is chained firmly to the ground. Its three floors represent hell, earth and heaven, and hold some of the finest murals in Bhutan. It's essential to bring a good torch. Your travel agency may need to have Dumtse listed on your permits, so mention you'd like to stop here in advance.

Beyond Dumtse Lhakhang, to the east of the road, the tiny **Puna Lhakhang** (Map p78) is said to date from the 7th century.

PARO SHORT HIKES

There are several options if you're interested in a day hiking the Paro valley. Southeast of Kyichu Lhakhang in the direction of Paro are the hilltop **Tingchok Goemba** (Map p86) and **Dranjo Goemba** (Map p86), home to Tserim, the goddess of wealth, both of which can provide an excuse for a short hike. From here you could walk back to Paro via the Olathang Hotel. More ambitious is the cardio day hike up from the hospital to **Gorena Lhakhang**, high on the ridge behind the Olathang Hotel.

A great way to end a visit to the National Museum is with a hike along the forested hillside to **Zuri Dzong** (Map p78) and then down to the Uma Paro hotel, where your vehicle can pick you up. En route you'll pass **Gönsaka Lhakhang** (Map p78), a charming place that predates Paro Dzong. Don't miss the meditation cave here. The views down over the valley and dzong are wonderful. Zuri Dzong was built in 1352 and is well protected by double walls. It is home to the valley's local protector gods.

Druk Home Museum   MUSEUM
(Map p78; ☑ 77224488; admission Nu 150; ☺9am-5pm Mar-Oct, to 4pm Nov-Feb) This small private museum has been developed in a traditional house on the road to Taktshang with the aim of providing 'Bhutan at a glance'. On display are festival masks, examples of regional dress and explanations of the *kabney* (scarf) hierarchy. The dried foods and herbs display is comprehensive (including a bowl of Cornflakes!), and you can also taste local snacks and wine.

Paro Sunday Market   MARKET
(Map p78) Paro's weekly vegetable market isn't very large but it has a traditional feel and is a fine introduction to some of Bhutan's unique local products. You'll see strings of *chugo* (dried yak cheese), either white (boiled in milk and dried in the sun) or brown (smoked). The fruit that looks like an orange egg is actually fresh husky betel nut, imported from India. The jars of pink paste contain lime, which is ingested with the betel nut. There are also exotic-looking ferns, powdered juniper incense, squares of dried jellied cow skin known as *khoo* (a local snack) and slabs of *datse,* the cheese used in almost every Bhutanese dish. The market is busiest between 6.30am and 10am.

After visiting the market check out the action in the **archery ground** (Map p78) to the southeast.

🛌 Sleeping

Paro's better accommodation options are in resort-style hotels scattered around the valley, not in the town itself. The closest options to town are on the hillside west of Paro, in a suburb known as Geptey, which offers great views over the valley.

Hotels increase their rates significantly during the spring Paro tsechu, when every hotel and even local farmhouses are full to bursting point. Some hotels stage dance performances around a campfire when there are enough guests to warrant it.

Hotel Jigmeling   LOCAL $
(Map p78; ☑271444; jighotel@hotmail.com; s/d Nu 1430/1650, deluxe Nu 1430/1870; ☎) Of the nearly identical local hotels in Paro town that are popular with Indian tourists, the Jigmeling is probably the best, with stylish, clean rooms, porch and balcony seating, and also a decent restaurant-bar. Wi-fi costs just Nu 200 for your entire stay.

ⓘ A TASTE OF TRADTIONAL BHUTAN

Most tour companies can arrange a hot-stone bath and/or Bhutanese meal at a traditional farmhouse. One popular place in Paro is the **Tshering Farm House** (Map p78) in the Dop Shari valley, which serves great traditional food (set meal Nu 420) and adds artemisia herbs to its traditional-style wooden baths (Nu 550).

Hotel Peljorling   LOCAL $
(Map p78; ☑ 271365; s/d Nu 550/750) Operated by the same group as the Peljorling in Phuentsholing, this basic but central local-style hotel has rather ordinary rooms with private bathrooms, and a good restaurant that serves a mean breakfast of beans on toast!

★ Gangtey Palace   BOUTIQUE HOTEL $$
(Map p78; ☑ 271301; www.gangteypalace.net; s/d Nu 3360/3840, deluxe Nu 4200/4800; ☎) This 19th-century, traditional Bhutanese building was once the residence of the *penlop* of Paro and it oozes historical charm. The spacious deluxe rooms in the main tower come with creaking staircases and a few antique pieces, but the standard rooms are also pleasant and have sublime garden and valley views. Ask staff to show you the murals in the main tower's altar room. The views from the restaurant balcony are also great and there's a very cosy bar. This is one place where you want to arrive early in order to savour the atmosphere.

Olathang Hotel   HOTEL $$
(Map p78; ☑ 271304; www.bhutanhotels.com.bt; s/d Nu 2875/3450, cottage s/d Nu 3450/4025, deluxe cottage s/d Nu 4025/4600, ste from Nu 6325; ☎☒) This hotel was built in 1974 for guests invited to the coronation of the fourth king and, though getting on a bit, it still maintains a whiff of grandeur. The main building's rooms are set around a lovely courtyard; the peaceful standard cottages share a lounge, so are particularly good for families and small groups; and the private deluxe cottages among the whispering pines are better for couples.

Tenzinling Resort   HOTEL $$
(Map p86; ☑ 272503; www.tenzinling.com.bt; Lango; s/d Nu 3600/4200, ste Nu 3500; ☎) Quiet and

rural, this stylish complex above Lango village, 6km from Paro, is an excellent option. The spacious wood-floored rooms come with free wi-fi and balcony views. The atmospheric 'Zomsa' bar has a *bukhari* (wood stove) heater, and downstairs the cosy tearoom serves regional teas, espresso coffee, and pizzas and snacks. There's also a multicuisine restaurant.

Janka Resort
HOTEL $$

(Map p86; ☏ 272352; www.jankaresort.com; Nemjo; s/d Nu 2530/3220, deluxe Nu 4025/4600) There's a rural feel at this resort, yet it's just 2.5km from Paro town. The standard rooms frame the courtyard, with five stylish deluxe rooms in the main building. The resort has a huge prayer wheel and staff can arrange for guests to visit the chapel in the owner's attached farmhouse. Look for the small archery ground just by the turn-off.

Ugyen Phendeyling Resort
HOTEL $$

(Map p86; ☏ 272017; www.upresortparo.com; s/d incl breakfast from Nu 1800/2400, deluxe Nu 2400/3000; ☎) This quiet, comfortable place with simple concrete cottages is particularly popular with Buddhist groups. It's run by local Rinpoche Ugyen Dorji, who offers his next-door chapel for guest meditation. Hiking trails behind the property lead to the hillside Dosu Lhakhang.

Dewachan Resort
HOTEL $$

(Map p86; ☏ 271744; www.dewachanresort.com; Nemjo; s/d from Nu 3000/3600, ste Nu 4800; ☎) The views over the terraced valley from the *bukhari*-warmed dining room are what sold us on this hillside collection of ochre-coloured buildings, as well as the proximity to local hiking trails. The rooms with balconies are worth seeking out, though it can be windy up here.

Tashi Namgay Resort
HOTEL $$

(Map p78; ☏ 272319; www.tnr.bt; Damsebu; s/d Nu 3278/3393, deluxe Nu 4025/4485, lodge d Nu 4600, ste Nu 13,800; ☎) This well-run place on the west bank is directly across Paro Chhu from the airport and features great views of the river and Paro Dzong. Deluxe riverside rooms are spacious and decorated with Tibetan carpets; standard rooms are in a block above the main building. One of the few places to charge for wi-fi.

Tiger Nest Resort
HOTEL $$

(Map p86; ☏ 271310; www.tigernest.bt; s/d Nu 3600/4200, ste Nu 5760; ☎) Just beyond the turn-off to Taktshang in the upper valley, this delightful resort, 9km from Paro, offers rare views of Taktshang Goemba and, on clear days, the snowcapped peak of Jhomolhari. It has well-appointed rooms with modern underfloor heating configured in twin cottages or in the main building, which has a sun-warmed terrace.

Khangkhu Resort
HOTEL $$

(Map p78; ☏ 272393; www.khangkhuresort.com; Khangkhu; s/d Nu 3450/3795, ste from Nu 5750) This newish resort is located across the river from the airport southwest of Paro town. It lacks intimacy but the spacious rooms are well equipped and come with private balcony seating. There's a multicuisine restaurant and bar, and a meditation centre.

Kichu Resort
HOTEL $$

(Map p86; ☏ 271468; www.intrektour.com; Lango; r Nu 3105, deluxe Nu 4255, ste Nu 8050; ☎) A large complex 5km from Paro, past the Kyichu Lhakhang and popular with trekking groups and Indian tourists. The rooms are in octagonal cottages, each with eight rooms, and the deluxe versions are worth the extra expense.

Pelri Cottages
COTTAGE $$

(Map p78; ☏ 272473; www.pelricottages.com; Olathang; s/d Nu 3000/3600, ste Nu 4800; ☎) On a hill above the Olathang Hotel, Pelri Cottages is a low-key collection of cottages in a former apple orchard. More old-school than luxurious, the clean wood-clad rooms are decorated with Tibetan carpets to give a cosy feel and the small wooden balconies are pleasant.

Dechen Hill Resort
HOTEL $$

(Map p78; ☏ 271392; www.dechenhillresort.com; Geptey; s/d from Nu 2070/2875) This hotel, in a secluded area below the road and 2km from central Para, is a favourite with expats and has some of the best Indian food in the valley. It has a pleasant garden, though rather ordinary rooms; the best have a balcony while others are small and dark.

Hotel Galingkha
HOTEL $$

(Map p78; ☏ 272498; www.hotelgalingkha.com; Geptey; s/d from Nu 1800/2160; ☎) This hotel is run by the folks from Hotel Galingkha in Thimphu. The renovations by the new owners have included laying down lots of linoleum, though rooms still vary quite a bit with some boasting balcony seating.

Sonam Trophel Hotel
HOTEL $$

(Map p78; ☎ 274444; www.trophelttraveltour.com; s/d Nu 2160/2400, deluxe r/ste Nu 3360/4200; ☎) If you want to be based in central Paro, this neat and comfortable lodge straddles the local and tourist markets. It doesn't have the peace of the valley resorts but it does allow you to grab a local beer in town, if you can put up with a little extra street noise.

Rema Resort
HOTEL $$

(Map p78; ☎ 271082; www.pororemaresort.com; r Nu 2040, deluxe Nu 2400, ste Nu 3000; ☎) A compact resort of only 10 rooms, 1.5km from Paro, this resort is surrounded by farmhouses on the quieter north side of valley, with panoramic views from the restaurant, bar and cottages. Features include an archery field and hot-stone bath, and the restaurant uses its own organic vegetables.

Hotel Tashi Phuntshok
HOTEL

(Map p78; ☎ 272254; www.hoteltashiphuntshok. com; Changnanka; r Nu 2400, deluxe Nu 3000) Right at the end of the runway, this mid-range hotel is certainly convenient to the airport. Although not exceptional, the pine-scented rooms are spacious, clean and comfortable, and the bar and restaurant can provide multicuisine dishes. Avoid the attic rooms on the top floor if low ceilings are not to your liking.

Valley View
HOTEL $$

(Map p78; ☎ 272541; valleyview@druknet.bt; s/d Nu 1800/2280) None of the pine-clad rooms here actually take advantage of the touted views owing to the building's alignment, but they are comfortable enough and there's a cosy bar and restaurant. The location is useful for Druk Path trekkers.

★ Uma Paro
LUXURY HOTEL $$$

(Map p78; ☎ 271597; www.uma.paro.como.bz; superior/deluxe r incl breakfast US$360/480, ste US$720, villa US$840-1320; ☎ ☒) Kudos goes to the Uma for combining traditional architecture with top-of-the-line facilities to create the best hotel in town. Highlights are the excellent restaurant and spa, with a gym, heated indoor pool and herbal hot-stone bath. All rooms are luxurious, but deluxe rooms offer balconies with a view and are the best choice. Activities include complimentary yoga and archery lessons. During the Paro tsechu the hotel requires a minimum stay of five nights.

Zhiwa Ling
LUXURY HOTEL $$$

(Map p86; ☎ 271277; www.zhiwaling.com; Satsam Chorten; s/d incl breakfast from US$312/342, ste US$446) This impressive luxury hotel, 8km from Paro, boasts a central lodge, with an impressive lobby, surrounded by a collection of stone towers. Antiques, plush sofas and a spa (Thai, Shiatsu and Swedish massage) temper the austerity, and there's even a temple on the 2nd floor, built with 400-year-old pillars from Gangte Goemba. Most rooms have a balcony and the royal suite even comes with its own altar room. Pottery is handmade and painted on the premises.

Nak-Sel Boutique Hotel & Spa
LUXURY HOTEL $$$

(☎ 272992; www.naksel.com; Ngoba; r superior/ deluxe/luxury US$138/201/397, ste US$200-300; ☎) Luxury at tourist prices is what this opulent resort promises and indeed it compares very well to properties charging twice as much. It offers Indian, Western and Bhutanese cuisine in the excellent restaurant, as well as a cafe, and the wellbeing spa has a yoga room. The rooms feature underfloor heating and balconies with views to Jhomolhari and Taktshang Goemba (Tiger's Nest Monastery). It's 3km up a secluded side valley on the edge of a forest that has hiking options. Rate discounts of 20% are possible.

Haven Resort
LUXURY HOTEL $$$

(Map p78; ☎ 270999; www.haven-bhutan.com; Dop Shari; r/ste US$300/660) Haven is a Thai-built luxury resort secluded in the quiet Dop Shari valley. The restaurant features stunning panoramic windows, rough-hewn furniture, and a menu of northern Thai and Bhutanese cuisine. The standouts are the aforementioned Thai cuisine and the luxury spa, including hot-stone bath.

Amankora
LUXURY HOTEL $$$

(Map p86; ☎ 272333; www.amanresorts.com; s/d full board US$1855/1995; ☎) 'Designer dzong' is the theme here, with the half-dozen sleek rammed-earth buildings secreted among the blue pines. The rooms benefit from the woodland setting and muted home-spun fabrics, a romantic open-plan bathroom and traditional *bukhari*. The spa has a wide range of muscle-melting treatments and there's an intimate restaurant and reading room. It's certainly sleek and stylish, but it's hard to justify the price tag. Most guests are on a packaged Amankora multiday journey. The resort is near Balakha village, about 14km from Paro, not far from Drukgyel Dzong.

SHOP LIKE A LOCAL

Paro has several interesting traditional shops that are aimed squarely at locals rather than tourists. They have no fixed hours. Dophu Dolma General Shop and Lama Tshering Dorji General Shop, both marked by a line of prayer wheels, are monks' supply shops that sell prayer flags, incense, statuary, butter lamps, trumpets and nonreligious items like khuru darts and bamboo arrows. On the main street, the **Zhayden Nagtsho Traditional Boot Unit** (Map p78; ☑272345) is the place for traditional handmade Bhutanese boots; prices start at US$150 for an embroidered pair.

Udumwara Resort　LUXURY HOTEL $$$
(Map p86; ☑ 271133; www.udumwara.com; Satsam; s/d Nu 9600/10,800; ☎) This very large resort was also very new when we visited and was lacking some finishing touches. The rooms are certainly spacious, comfortable and well appointed, but the extensive use of plywood somewhat dampens the feeling of luxury. Other facilities include a chapel, multicuisine restaurant, alfresco dining and two bars.

🍴 Eating

Most tourists eat dinner in their hotels but you can request to visit the following places for lunch.

Tshernoyoen's Café　CAFE $
(Map p78; coffee Nu 90, cakes Nu 50-70; ☉10am-9pm Tue-Sun; ☎) Paro's first real cafe serves up reviving espresso and fine carrot cake in a relaxed environment down by the river. It's a good place to take a break, read the papers and recaffeinate.

★Sonam Trophel Restaurant　BHUTANESE $$
(Map p78; ☑271287; mains Nu 35-80, set meal Nu 480) Upstairs, Sonam has excellent home-style Bhutanese cooking adapted to foreign tastes and is popular with small groups as meals are brought to the table (no buffet). Lunch consists of a minimum of seven dishes. The momos (dumplings), boneless chicken, ginger potatoes and hentshey datse (spinach and cheese) are all excellent.

Yue-Ling Restaurant　RESTAURANT $$
(Map p78; ☑272802; set meal Nu 420) Good reliable place frequented by tour groups with fine curries, vegetable dishes, naan and puri breads. If you want to try some fiery local dishes, ask your guide to bring a plate of the food provided to the drivers and guides.

Chharo Restaurant　MULTICUISINE $
(Map p78; ☑272642; mains Nu 60-110) This pleasant tourist restaurant (chharo means friendship) has a good range of Indian, Chinese and Bhutanese dishes, and can prepare Bumthang-style buckwheat pancakes and noodles with advance notice.

Chharo and Dho Restaurant　RESTAURANT $$
(Map p78; ☑272802; set meals Nu 420) Offers some fine set meals for groups.

★Bukhari Restaurant　RESTAURANT $$$
(Map p78; ☑271597; Uma Paro hotel; mains Nu 450-1800, set meal Nu 3000; ☎) The sophisticated restaurant at the Uma is considered the best in the valley. The menu changes every three days; when we visited it included a warming roast beetroot soup and a Bhutanese hogey salad with Sechuan pepper and lime dressing. For lunch, the popular Uma burger features a yak pattie and Bumthang 'Gouda' cheese. There are also set Bhutanese or Indian meals.

🛍 Shopping

There are numerous handicraft shops in town offering everything from stamps to jewellery, and most take credit cards.

Chencho Handicrafts　HANDICRAFTS
(Map p78) Chencho has an interesting selection of local handicrafts, and is particularly strong on weavings and embroidery; it also has weavers working on-site.

Made in Bhutan　HANDICRAFTS
(Map p78) This slick operation has some expensive pieces like silver amulets and lutes, alongside cheaper souvenirs, rare stamps and postcards.

Vajrayana Art Gallery　ARTS & CRAFTS
(Map p78; chhidorj@hotmail.com) Vajrayana Art Gallery features art by self-taught Bhutanese artist Chimmi Dorje, who incorporates Buddhist themes such as prayer flags and mandala motifs into his abstract art. The gallery is often closed outside the high season.

ℹ️ Information

Bank of Bhutan (Map p78; ☏271230; ⊙9am-1pm Mon-Fri, to noon Sat) Has an ATM.

Bhutan National Bank (Map p78; ⊙9am-4pm Mon-Fri, to 11am Sat)

Bhutan Nest (Map p78; ☏272689; per min Nu 3; ⊙9am-9pm) Besides internet service, it also rents mountain bikes for Nu 1500 per day, plus trekking equipment.

Hospital (Map p78; ☏271571) On a hill to the west of town and accepts visitors in an emergency.

Kuen Phuen Medical Shop (Map p78) Basic medical supplies; opposite Made in Bhutan.

Netlink Internet Café (Map p78; per min Nu 1; ⊙9am-8.30pm)

Police station (Map p78) Northwest of the town square, near the bridge over the Paro Chhu.

Post office (Map p78; ⊙9am-5pm Mon-Fri, 8.30am-12.30pm Sat)

ℹ️ Getting There & Away

Paro airport (Map p78) is 7km south of Paro town and 53km from Thimphu. There's a branch of Druk Air (Map p78) in Paro near the six chortens and the bridge leading to the dzong.

A shared taxi to Thimphu costs Nu 200 per seat or Nu 600 per minivan; to Phuentsholing it costs Nu 400 to Nu 500 per seat. Daily Coaster buses to Thimphu (Nu 45) and Phuentsholing (Nu 200) leave from Dhug and Metho Transport at the northwest end of town.

Upper Paro Valley

The Paro valley extends west all the way to the peaks on the Tibetan border, though the road only goes as far as Sharna Zampa, near Drukgyel Dzong, about 20km beyond Paro. En route it passes half a dozen resorts, rural scenery and some of Bhutan's most famous sights. Beyond the dzong, a side valley leads to the Tremo La, the 5000m pass that was once an important trade route to Tibet and also the route of several Tibetan invasions.

Kyichu Lhakhang

A short drive from Paro is Kyichu Lhakhang (Map p86), one of Bhutan's oldest and most beautiful temples. The temple is popularly believed to have been built in 659 by King Songtsen Gampo of Tibet, to pin down the left foot of a giant ogress who was thwarting the establishment of Buddhism into Tibet. Additional buildings and a golden roof were constructed in 1839 by the *penlop* of Paro and the 25th Je Khenpo.

As you enter the intimate inner courtyard you'll see a mural to the right of the doorway of King Gesar of Ling, the popular Tibetan warrior-king, whose epic poem is said to be the world's longest.

The third king's wife, Ashi Kesang Wangchuck, sponsored the construction of the Guru Lhakhang in 1968. It contains a 5m-high statue of Guru Rinpoche and another of Kurukulla (Red Tara), holding a bow and arrow made of flowers. To the right of Guru

WESTERN BHUTAN UPPER PARO VALLEY

SUBDUING THE DEMONESS

When the Tibetan king Songtsen Gampo married the Chinese princess Wencheng in 641, her dowry included the Jowo Sakyamuni, a priceless Indian statue of the Buddha as a small boy. As the statue was transported through Lhasa, it became stuck in the mud and no-one could move it. The princess divined that the obstruction was being caused by a huge supine demoness, lying on her back with her navel over a lake where Lhasa's main temple, the Jokhang, now stands.

In 659 the king decided to build 108 temples in a single day to pin the ogress to the earth forever and, as a by-product, convert the Tibetan people to Buddhism. Temples were constructed at her shoulders and hips, which corresponded to the four districts of central Tibet, and her knees and elbows, which were in the provinces. The hands and feet lay in the borderlands of Tibet, and several temples were built in Bhutan to pin down the troublesome left leg.

The best known of these temples are Kyichu Lhakhang in Paro, which holds the left foot, and Jampey Lhakhang (p124) in Bumthang, which pins the left knee. Other lesser-known temples have been destroyed, but it is believed that, among others, Konchogsum Lhakhang in Bumthang, Khaine Lhakhang south of Lhuentse, and two temples in Haa may have been part of this ambitious project.

Upper Paro Valley

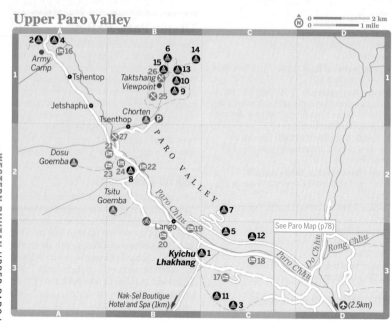

Rinpoche is a chorten containing the ashes of Dilgo Khyentse Rinpoche, the revered Nyingma Buddhist master and spiritual teacher of the queen mother, who passed away in 1992, and was cremated nearby. There is a statue of him here, as well as some old photos of the fourth king's grandmother and the first king of Bhutan. In the corner of the lhakhang is a pile of iron links forged by the famous bridge builder Thangtong Gyalpo. The ornately carved wooden pillars are superb.

The inner hall of the main **Jowo Lhakhang** conceals the valley's greatest treasure, an original 7th-century statue of Jowo Sakyamuni, said to have been cast at the same time as the famous statue in Lhasa. In front of the statue you can feel the grooves that generations of prostrators have worn into the wooden floor. King Songtsen Gampo himself lurks up in the upper left niche. The main door is superbly gilded. The former quarters of Dilgo Khyentse to the left are closed to visitors.

Further north, outside the temple and up a side road by the huge Zhiwa Ling hotel, is the site where Dilgo Khyentse was cremated in 1991. His reincarnation lives in the complex, which is generally closed to visitors. The small and inconspicuous **Satsam Chorten** (Map p86) by the turn-off once marked no man's land between two ri-

val *penlop*s. The dirt road that leads from Satsam Chorten back to Paro is an excellent option for mountain bikers.

Sanga Choekor Shedra

At night you'll see the Sanga Choekor Shedra (Map p86) spotlit up high on the top of a hill on the north side of the valley. The *shedra,* a Buddhist college, is home to about 100 monks and is worth a visit mainly for the fine views from the switchbacking drive up. Look for the stuffed bear in the main entryway. On the way back down pop into the small and charming **Kuenga Choeling Goemba** (Map p86), where monks can show you the walking path down to nearby **Tsendo Girkha Goemba** (Map p86).

Sanga Choekor is 12km up the unpaved north bank road. Mountain bikers could cycle up this road, then cross the footbridge to Kyichu Lhakhang.

Taktshang Goemba

The Taktshang Goemba (which translates as Tiger's Nest Monastery) is the most famous of Bhutan's monasteries, miraculously perched on the side of a sheer cliff 900m above the floor of Paro valley, where the only sounds are the murmurs of wind and water

Upper Paro Valley

and the creaking of the prayer wheels. It is said that Guru Rinpoche flew to the site of the monastery on the back of a tigress (a manifestation of his consort Yeshe Tshogyel) to subdue the local demon, Singey Samdrup. He then meditated in a cave here for three months.

The site has long been recognised as a *ney* (holy place). Milarepa is said to have meditated here, Thangtong Gyalpo revealed a *terma* (treasure text) here and Zhabdrung Ngawang Namgyal visited in 1646. Pilgrims from all over Bhutan come to the site. The *penlop* of Paro, Gyalse Tenzin Rabgye, built the primary lhakhang in 1692 around the Dubkhang (also called the Pelphu), the holy cave in which Guru Rinpoche meditated.

On 19 April 1998 a fire (which some rumour was arson, to disguise a theft) destroyed the main structure of Taktshang and all its contents. It had suffered a previous fire and had been repaired in 1951. Reconstruction started in April 2000 at a cost of

130 million ngultrum and the rebuilt site was reconsecrated in the presence of the king in 2005. Tradition says that the original building was anchored to the cliff-face by the hairs of *khandroma* (*dakinis;* female celestial beings), who transported the building materials up onto the cliff on their backs. The renovation team had only a cable lift for assistance.

The paved road to the Taktshang parking lot branches right, 8km north of Paro, and climbs 3km past a white chorten and a small lhakhang to the trailhead at 2600m.

◎ Sights & Activities

Taktshang Goemba   BUDDHIST, MONASTERY
(Tiger's Nest Monastery; Map p86; ⊘ 8am-1pm & 2-5pm daily Oct-Mar, until 6pm Apr-Sep) Tourists can enter the **monastery**, as long as your guide has arranged the standard permit in advance. Bags, phones and cameras have to be deposited at the entrance, where you must register with the army.

As you enter the complex you pass underneath images of the Rigsum Goempo (Jampelyang, Chenresig and Chana Dorje). Look to the right for the relic stone; Bhutanese stand on the starting line, close their eyes and try to put their thumb into a small hole in the rock as a form of karmic test.

Most groups then visit the **Dubkhang** (Pelphu Lhakhang), the cave where Guru Rinpoche meditated for three months. Outside the cave is a statue of Dorje Drolo, the manifestation the Guru assumed to fly to Taktshang on a tigress. The inner cave is sealed off behind a spectacularly gilded door. Murals of Guru Tshengye, the eight manifestations of Guru Rinpoche, decorate the walls. Behind you, sitting above the inside of the main entrance, is a mural of Thangtong Gyalpo holding his iron chains.

From here ascend to the **Guru Sungjem Lhakhang**, which has a central image of Pema Jungme, another of the eight manifestations of Guru Rinpoche. This statue replaced a famous 'talking' image that was lost in the 1998 fire. Various demonic animal-headed deities and manifestations of the deity Phurba decorate the walls, while outside is an image of the protector Tseringma riding a snow lion.

The next chapel on the left has connections to Dorje Phagmo, with a rock image of the goddess' crown hidden in a hole in the floor. The inner chorten belongs to Langchen Pelgye Tsengay, a 9th-century

WESTERN BHUTAN UPPER PARO VALLEY

disciple of Guru Rinpoche, who meditated in the cave. Behind the chorten is a holy spring.

Further on inside the complex, to the left, is the Drole Lhakhang, where the monks hand out *sungke* (blessed threads), while to the right is the **Guru Tsengye Lhakhang**, which features an image of the monastery's 17th-century founder, Gyelse Tenzin Rabgay. Ask a monk to show you the trap door! Further up is a butter lamp chapel (light one for a donation of Nu 20). You can also peer into the original Tiger's Nest cave just above the chapel but it's too dangerous to climb down into.

After visiting the Tiger's Nest and re-ascending to the previous viewpoint, it is possible to take a signed side trail uphill for 15 minutes to the **Machig-phu Lhakhang** (Map p86), where Bhutanese pilgrims come to pray for children. Head to the cave behind the chapel and select the image of the Tibetan saint Machig Labdron on the right (for a baby girl), or the penis print on the cave wall to the left (for a boy). The main statues inside the chapel are of Machig and her husband Padampa Sangye.

➡ **Hike to Tiger's Nest Monastery**

The only way up to the Tiger's Nest is to walk, ride a horse or fly up there on the back of a magic tiger (the latter generally reserved for tantric magicians). The 1¾-hour hike is a central part of any tourist itinerary and is unmissable for the spectacular views. It's also a good warm-up hike if you are going trekking. If the full hike sounds a bit tough you can walk (or ride horses) for the first hour to the 'cafeteria', a wooden teahouse-restaurant, which offers a good view of the monastery. If you require horses (Nu 500/800 to the cafeteria/monastery), be sure to mention this to your guide in advance. Wear a hat and bring water.

The trail climbs through blue pines to three water-powered prayer wheels, then switchbacks steeply up the ridge, where a sign exhorts you to 'Walk to Guru's glory! For here in this kingdom rules an unparalled benevolent king!' If you have just flown into Paro, walk slowly because you are likely to feel the altitude.

Once you reach the ridge there are excellent views across the valley and southwest towards Drukgyel Dzong. After a climb of about one hour and a gain of 300m you will reach a small chorten and some prayer flags on the ridge. Be watchful here as the trail crosses an archery ground. It's then a short walk to the cafeteria (2940m), where you can savour the impressive view of the monastery over a well-deserved cup of tea. The **cafeteria** (Map p86; ☏17601682; tea & biscuits Nu 84, buffet lunch Nu 420; ⊙noon-3pm; ☏) also serves full vegetarian meals; if you arrange your schedule accordingly, you can have a simple breakfast or full lunch here.

The trail continues up for another 30 minutes to a spring and the basic monastery guesthouse. If you still have hunger pangs, a side trail leads to the **Tashi Tashi Cafe** (Map p86; set meals Nu 410). A **cave** and plaque marks the birthplace of a previous Je Khenpo; his former residence is just up the hill. A short walk further along the main trail brings you to a spectacular **viewpoint** (Map p86) at 3140m that puts you eyeball to eyeball with the monastery, which looks like it is growing out of the rocks.

From this vantage point Taktshang seems almost close enough to touch, but it's on the far side of a deep valley about 150m away. The trail curves past a charming chapel of butter lamps and descends to a waterfall by the **Singye Pelphu Lhakhang** (Snow Lion Cave), a meditation retreat associated with Guru Rinpoche's consort Yeshe Tshogyel and jammed into a rock crevice, before climbing back up to the monastery entrance.

➡ **Taktshang Hiking**

Instead of returning to the parking lot the way you came you can make an adventurous two- to three-hour hike to higher chapels before descending steeply to the parking lot. Just to the side of the Machig-phu Lhakhang a trail climbs a couple of perilous log ladders and then branches right for 15 minutes to the Ugyen Tshemo Lhakhang, or left up to the **Zangto Pelri Lhakhang** (Map p86), named after Guru Rinpoche's heavenly paradise and perched on a crag with great views from the back down to the Tiger's Nest. Roll the dice inside the chapel to double your chances of conceiving more kids. From here the trail descends past a charming holy spring (behind a wooden door) and down to the monastery guesthouse.

The **Ugyen Tshemo Lhakhang** (Map p86) has an unusual set of four exterior protectors. Inside is a 3D mandala and some charred statues rescued from a fire around 60 years ago. If you're keen, you can continue up to the **Yosel Choekhorling** (Yoselgang; Map p86) before returning.

BUMDRA TREK

It's no myth: you can approach Taktshang Goemba from above, though not on the back of a flying tiger. The overnight Bumdra trek takes you high above Taktshang on the first day so that you spend the second day descending through forests to reveal the famous Tiger's Nest. The trek and campground have been developed by **Bhutan Trekking & Hiking Services** (☑02-325472; www.trektobhutan.com), and can be organised through your Bhutanese agent.

This hike starts from Sanga Choekor Shedra (p86), at 2800m, from where it climbs steadily through blue pine, to a forest of mighty oaks with a red-flowering rhododendron understorey. Four hours from the start you reach the Chhoe Chhoe Lhakhang, high on a spur overlooking the Paro and Do rivers, where Himalayan views and a hot lunch miraculously appear.

After lunch it's a short walk to the camping ground in an open yak pasture beside **Bumdra Lhakhang** (3900m). If you have the energy, you can ascend a peak to the north for views of the snowcapped peaks, and visit the cliff-hugging lhakhang with its statue of Guru Rinpoche.

After a hot breakfast on day two, start heading downhill beneath larch and tall silver pines to the Ugyen Tshemo Lhakhang, at 3300m, which is directly above the still-invisible Taktshang Lhakhang. Two hours from the start you cross a stream that powers prayer wheels and later falls off a cliff beside Taktshang, before reaching the main trail to the Tiger's Nest. After visiting Taktshang Goemba (p87) take the trail to the parking area and rest those weary legs.

From the Ugyen Tshemo Lhakhang, descend steeply down the valley for 15 minutes to a right turn-off, past a chorten to the cliff-face **Shama Lhakhang** (Map p86), just next to Taktshang but inaccessible from there. Look out for *jaru* (mountain goats) here.

Back at the junction, trails drop steeply for 45 minutes down to the three water prayer wheels just before the car park. Figure on six hours for the entire hike up to Taktshang and down this alternative route. The descent is best not attempted in wet weather.

✖ Eating

Yak Herders Hut RESTAURANT **$$**
(Map p86; ☑17111142; set breakfast/lunch/dinner Nu 240/420/450) Your guide can reserve breakfast, lunch or dinner at this cosy place with traditional seating and a great atmosphere on the side road to Taktshang.

Drukgyel Dzong

Near the end of the road, 14km from Paro, stand the ruins of **Drukgyel Dzong** (Map p86; ☺8am-5pm). This dzong was built in 1649 by Zhabdrung Ngawang Namgyal in a location chosen for its control of the route to Tibet. The dzong was named *'Druk'* (Bhutan) *'gyel'* (victory) to commemorate the victory of Bhutan over Tibetan invaders in 1644. One of the features of the dzong was a false entrance that lured the returning Tibetan invaders into an enclosed courtyard during a second attack.

The dzong sits at the point where the trail from Tibet via the Tremo La enters the Paro valley. Once the Tibetan invasions ceased, this became a major trade route, with Bhutanese rice being transported to the Tibetan town of Phari Dzong in barter for salt and bricks of tea. Trekking groups have largely replaced the trade caravans and you may see mule men here preparing for the Jhomolhari trek.

The building was used as an administrative centre until 1951, when a fire caused by a butter lamp destroyed it. You can still see the charred beams lodged in the ruined walls. There have been a few attempts at renovation, but all that has been accomplished is the installation of a new roof on the five-storey main structure to stop it from eroding and collapsing.

As you walk up to the dzong you'll pass a small chapel on the left, a chorten on the right, and then the remains of the large towers and the walled tunnel that was used to obtain water from the stream below during a long siege. There's not much left to the dzong except the front courtyard and *ta dzongs* (watchtowers) behind.

Back in the village you can take a nice stroll up to the small **Choedu Goemba** (Map p86), which houses a statue of the local protector, Gyeb Dole.

The road to the dzong passes Jetshaphu village, several army camps and the Amankora resort. On a clear day (most likely in October or November) there are fine views of Jhomolhari's snowy cone from this stretch, which makes for a great bike ride.

Southeast of Paro

Twin roads lead south from Paro to Bondey, with a new road being constructed between the river and the airport at the time of research. From Bondey roads head west to Haa and southeast to the confluence at Chhuzom, 24km from Paro and 18km from Bondey.

Paro to Bondey

6KM

The west-bank road south of Paro passes above the airport and Khangkhu village to Bondey, which straddles the Paro Chhu to the southeast of the airport. A couple of turnouts offer great views of planes taking off or landing at the airport.

Beyond the turn-off to the Cheli La is the 400-year-old **Bondey Lhakhang** (Map p78), on the west bank of the river. On the east side of the Paro Chhu, beside the main road near the Bondey Zam, is the charming and unusually shaped **Tago Lhakhang** (Map p78), founded by Thangtong Gyalpo. A circular chapel occupies the upper floor; ask for the key at the next-door Tharpala General Shop if the caretaker is not around. A 15-minute uphill hike (or short drive) above Tago is the small **Pelri Goemba** (Map p78), a rare Nyingmapa-school chapel that was reduced in size after an unwise dispute with the dominant Kagyu school.

Cheli La

If you don't have time to visit the Haa valley, the 35km drive up to the 3810m Cheli La makes an interesting day excursion from Paro and is an excellent jumping-off point for day walks to Kila Nunnery. On a clear day there are views of Jhomolhari from the pass, as well as down to the Haa valley. For details of the drive over the pass to the Haa valley, see p91.

Paro to Thimphu

53KM

Figure on two hours driving from Paro to Thimphu, longer if you stop en route.

Bondey to Chhuzom

18KM / 30 MINUTES

If you're coming from the airport you'll first reach the settlement of Bondey, where there are some lovely traditional houses and chapels.

Just 1km from Bondey is the family-run **Tshenden Incense Factory** (☎271352; ⊗Mon-Sat), where you can see the boiling,

---

THE IRON-BRIDGE BUILDER

Thangtong Gyalpo (1385–1464) was a wonder-working Tibetan saint and engineer who is believed to be the first to use heavy iron chains in the construction of suspension bridges. He built 108 bridges throughout Tibet and Bhutan, earning himself the nickname Lama Chakzampa (Iron Bridge Lama).

In 1433 he came to Bhutan, originally in search of iron ore, and built eight bridges in places as far removed as Paro and Trashigang. You can see some of the original iron links at Paro's National Museum and at Kyichu Lhakhang in the Paro valley. Sadly, the only surviving Thangtong Gyalpo bridge, at Duksum on the road to Trashi Yangtse in eastern Bhutan, was washed away in 2004.

This medieval Renaissance man didn't rest on his engineering laurels. Among his other achievements was the composition of many folk songs, still sung today by people as they thresh wheat or pound mud for house construction, and the invention of Tibetan *lhamo* opera. He was also an important *terton* – discoverer of *terma* (sacred texts and artefacts hidden by Guru Rinpoche) – of the Nyingma lineage and attained the title Drubthob (Great Magician), and in Paro he built the marvellous chorten-shaped Dumtse Lhakhang. His descendants still maintain the nearby Tamchhog Lhakhang.

Statues of Thangtong Gyalpo depict him as a stocky shirtless figure with a beard, curly hair and top knot, holding a link of chains.

dyeing, extruding and drying processes if your guide rings in advance. Two kilometres further on at Shaba are two cliff-face sites. A short hiking trail near the army camp leads to **Drak Ngagpo** (Black Cliff) hermitage, while a little further on a rough road heads up to **Drak Kharpo** (White Cliff), a cliffside monastery where Guru Rinpoche meditated for several months. At Isuna, 12km from Bondey and 8km from Chhuzom, the road crosses a bridge to the south bank of the Paro Chhu.

About 5km before Chhuzom, the road passes **Tamchhog Lhakhang**, a private temple across the river owned by the descendants of the famous Tibetan bridge-builder Thangtong Gyalpo. The traditional iron bridge here was reconstructed in 2005 using some of Thangtong's original chain links from Duksum in eastern Bhutan. A small cave above the bridge supposedly marks Thangtong's iron mine, as well as the mouth of the snake-shaped hillside that the chapel is built on.

You can almost feel the clocks slowing down as you step into the 600-year-old temple. The lovely murals have been darkened by centuries of yak-butter lamps. A *kora* (circumambulation) path in the main chapel leads around central murals of Thangtong Gyalpo and his son Dewa Tsangpo. The doorway of the upper-floor *goenkhang* (protector chapel) is framed by rows of skulls and a hornbill beak and is dedicated to the local protector Maza Damsum. It's a magical place to visit.

Chhuzom, better known as 'the Confluence' is at the juncture of the Paro Chhu and the Wang Chhu (*chhu* means 'river', *zom* means 'to join'). Because Bhutanese tradition regards such a joining of rivers as inauspicious, there are three **chortens** here to ward away the evil spells of the area. Each chorten is in a different style – Bhutanese, Tibetan and Nepali.

Chhuzom is also a major road junction, with roads leading southwest to Haa (79km), south to the border town of Phuentsholing (141km) and northeast to Thimphu (31km). Local farmers sit by the side of the road selling vegetables, apples and dried cheese.

Chhuzom to Thimphu

31KM / 1 HOUR

As the road ascends the Wang Chhu valley, the hillsides become surprisingly barren. Three kilometres past Chhuzom a rough side road leads to Geynikha (Geynizampa) and the start of the Dagala Thousand Lakes trek.

After turn-offs to Kharibje and the former hydro plant at Khasadrapchhu, the valley widens at the small village of **Namseling**. Above the road are numerous apple orchards. Much of the fruit is exported, particularly to Bangladesh. In the autumn people sell apples and mushrooms from makeshift stalls at the side of the road.

The Thimphu 'expressway' drops towards the valley floor and enters Thimphu from the south. A second, older road travels via Babesa and Simtokha, enabling you to visit the Simtokha Dzong or bypass Thimphu completely on the way to Punakha.

HAA DZONGKHAG

The isolated Haa valley lies southwest of the Paro valley, hidden behind the high ridge of the Cheli La. Despite easy access to Tibet, the remote valley has always been off the major trade routes and continues to be on the fringes of tourism. The valley is the ancestral home of the Dorji family, to which the queen grandmother, Ashi Kesang Wangchuck, belongs.

Less than 10% of visitors to Bhutan make it to Haa, but it's a picturesque valley that is ideal for mountain biking and hiking, and there is real scope here for getting off the beaten track. There are at least a dozen monasteries in the valley. Perhaps the best way to visit is to spend a day cycling to the nearby sights.

There are two roads into Haa. One climbs from Paro, crossing the 3810m Cheli La. The other diverges from the Thimphu–Phuentsholing road at Chhuzom and travels south, high above the Wang Chhu, before swinging into the Haa valley.

Paro to Haa via Cheli La

68KM / 2½ HOURS

From the turn-off at Bondey, south of Paro, it's 2½ hours to Haa over the high Cheli La on the highest motorable road in Bhutan. As you start to climb, a side road branches left for 2km to **Dzongdrakha Goemba**, where four chapels and a large white Nepali-style chorten perch dramatically on a cliff ledge. The site is one of several where Guru Rinpoche suppressed local demons and is worth the detour.

As you drive up to the pass, look for the roadside *drub chuu* (spring) with rock paintings of Guru Rinpoche and his two wives. About 20km from the turn-off to Dzongdrakha is an easily missed turnout (and possible picnic spot) where a road leads to Kila Nunnery.

When you finally crest the Cheli La, join the Bhutanese in a hearty cry of '*lha-gey lu!*' (May the gods be victorious!). A sign says the elevation of the pass is 3988m, but it's really more like 3810m. If it's raining in Paro, it's likely to be snowing here, even as late as the end of April. During the clear skies of October and November you can take hiking trails up the mountain ridge for 1½ hours to spectacular mountain views towards Jhomolhari. If you like getting off the beaten track and want to stretch your legs, consider a visit to **Kila Nunnery**, established as a meditation site in the 9th century and reputedly the oldest nunnery in Bhutan. A trail leaves Cheli La and heads down to the nunnery from where you can continue downhill to meet the main road and your waiting car.

As you make the steep switchbacking 26km descent from the pass to Haa, you'll soon see the golden roof of the Haa Dzong.

Haa

📞 08 / ELEV 2670M

The town of Haa sprawls along the Haa Chhu and forms two distinct areas. Much of the southern town is occupied by the Indian Military Training Team (IMTRAT) camp (complete with a golf course that has sand 'greens') and a Bhutanese army training camp. Near here is the dzong and monastery. The central bazaar to the north has the main shops and local restaurants.

The three hills to the south of town are named after the Rigsum Goempo, the trinity of Chenresig, Chana Dorje and Jampelyang; they also represent the valley's three protector deities.

The scenic road to the north continues past the Talung valley and Chhundu Lhakhang, and ends at Damthang, 15km from Haa town. It would be prudent to turn around before you reach the gates of the large Bhutanese army installation.

◉ Sights

Wangchulo Dzong　　　　　DZONG

Haa's Wangchulo Dzong is one of Bhutan's newest, built in 1915 to replace a smaller structure. It is inside the Indian army compound (an impressive chorten marks the entrance) and so houses several army offices and a rations shop.

Haa Dratshang　　　　　MONASTERY

The 70-strong monk body is housed not in the dzong but in the Haa Dratshang, also known as the Lhakhang Kharpo (White Chapel), at the southern entrance to town. An annual **tsechu** is held here on the eighth and ninth day of the eighth lunar month, before a large *thangka* is displayed on the 10th day at Wangchulo Dzong. A 10-minute walk behind the *dratshang* (central monk body) is the Lhakhang Nagpo (Black Chapel), from where trails lead to Shek Drak.

Shek Drak　　　　　CHAPEL

A short excursion up the valley behind the Haa Dratshang is Shek Drak, a tiny retreat centre perched on the hillside. Take the side road just south of the Haa Dratshang, by Domcho village, and continue halfway (3.5km) up the hillside towards Takchu Goemba. From here, a 10-minute walk climbs to the small and charming chapel attended by one lama and one monk.

🛏 Sleeping & Eating

★ **Lechuna Heritage Lodge**　　HERITAGE $$

(📞347984; www.bhutanlhl.com; Lechu; s/d Nu 3300/3810; 🅟) This beautiful lodge comprises a wonderfully restored farmhouse of just seven rooms sharing three bathrooms and four separate toilets. It's much more comfortable than it sounds because the renovation has been so careful to blend modern comforts within the traditional architecture. There's a cosy bar downstairs, filter coffee and tea in the common room, and a communal dining table is attached to the separate kitchen. The lodge is 10km north of Haa town in the picturesque village of Lechu and is a great base for short and long walks on the valley rim.

Risum Lodge　　　　　HOTEL $$

(📞375350; risum_77@yahoo.com; Wantsa; s/d Nu 2400/2640) Standard accommodation is available here in clean and cosy pine-clad rooms, with hot-water bathrooms, heaters and, on the upper floors, balconies. An excellent photo album in the restaurant has information on outlying monasteries, including Wantsa Goemba, a short walk behind the resort. The hotel is east of the road linking the two sections of town.

Hotel Lhayul   RESTAURANT **$**

(☎375251; mains Nu 70-85) This is an OK place for lunch, with comfy sofas and a bar, but your guide will need to have made a booking. Though this hotel is primarily used as a restaurant, there are also basic, overpriced rooms available (singles/doubles Nu 1800/2280). It's in the central bazaar area of town.

Around the Haa Valley

Juneydrak

About 1km north of Haa, by the Two Sisters Hotel and the hospital and just before the main bridge, a 4WD track branches east 1km to Katsho village, from where you can take a lovely hike to **Juneydrak hermitage** (also known as Juneydrag). The cliffside retreat contains a footprint of Machig Labdrom (1055–1132), the female Tibetan tantric practitioner who perfected the *chöd* ritual, whereby one visualises one's own dismemberment in an act of 'ego annihilation'.

From the village a trail follows the stream past a *mani* wall to a two-legged archway chorten (known as a *khonying*). Cross the bridge and ascend the trail through a charming rhododendron forest. At a red sign in Dzongkha (the national language of Bhutan), take the trail to the left and climb up to a chorten that marks the entry to the hermitage. A sign here asks visitors not to disturb the hermits, so don't try to enter the lhakhang. In case you needed persuading, a green-faced demon guards the entryway.

From here, a set of exposed log ladders ascend the cliff and the trail curves round the exposed bluff. Don't attempt this if you are afraid of heights or if it's raining. The trail curves around to **Katsho Goemba**, which has fine views down to Katsho village. Your vehicle can meet you here.

A less strenuous alternative is to drive up to Katsho Goemba and then walk down to Juneydrak from there.

Yangtho Goemba & Around

North of the turning to Katsho, the main road crosses to the river's south bank and passes several villages as it heads up the valley. About 5km from Haa, a side road branches right over the river past Yangthang village to several remote monasteries which offer some good exploring.

Follow the road as it swings into the side valley and you'll pass the Yangthang ceremonial ground that is still used for annual sacrifices to the local deity Chhundu. At the Makha Zampa bridge take the right branch 1.5km to **Yangtho Goemba**, up on the ridge. The monastery's charming upper chapels feature murals depicting Zangto Pelri (the paradise of Guru Rinpoche) and also the *tshomen* (water deities) that are said to inhabit the pool just outside the monastery. Ask the monk to show you the excellent medieval rat trap!

Back at the bridge, the left branch takes you further up the valley for 2km to Talung village and **Tsenkha Goemba** (signposted Changkha). Hard-core explorers can take the branch road here for 2km to curve around to Jangtey Goemba. An enticing two-day trek continues up the Talung valley and over the Saga La to Drukyel Dzong.

Chhundu Lhakhang

Three kilometres further along the main road (11km from Haa) is the Chhundu Lhakhang (Getsu Lhakhang), one of several shrines dedicated to the valley's protective deity. The timeless chapel is a five-minute walk down a concrete path below Chenpa Haatey (Lechu) village, just past the Yakchu Zam bridge. Call the **caretaker** (☎77210520) if the temple is closed. Blue-faced Chhundu and his red-faced cousin Jowya glower in glass cabinets on either side of the main altar.

POPPY PURSUITS

If you wish to photograph the famous Himalayan blue poppy (*Meconopsis grandis*, Bhutan's national flower), you should take a hike from Haa. From mid-June to late July, several varieties of *Meconopsis* open their showy blooms on the high passes surrounding Haa. Cheli La and Tsungsikha are popular destinations. There are five species of Himalayan blue poppy found in Bhutan, as well as red, yellow and white poppies. Aficionados seek the large cream-white *M. superba*, which is endemic to Haa. Summer is also the time numerous other alpine flowers strut their stuff, though flower-spotters must be prepared for lots of rain and the odd leech!

Troublesome Chhundu was banished to Haa by the Zhabdrung after an altercation with Gyenyen, Thimphu's protector. He also had a quarrel with Jichu Drakye of Paro, resulting in Paro's guardian stealing all of Haa's water – and that's why there is no rice grown in Haa. Annual sacrifices to Chhundu are still carried out in nearby Yangthang, highlighting how deeply Bhutan's roots run to its pre-Buddhist animist past.

Haa to Chhuzom

79KM

From Haa town it's 6km to Karnag (also called Karna), 2km further to Jyenkana and then 19km to Nago, with its picturesque water prayer wheels. A few kilometres further is **Bietakha**, its small dzong in precarious ruin after the 2009 and 2011 earthquakes. At Km 40, shortly before the village of Gyeshina, look for the photogenic **Gurugang Goemba** just below the road.

Now high above the river, the road swings into a huge side valley, passing below the village of Susana en route to Mendegang. Near the houses and basic restaurants of **Tshongkha** is a road leading 15 minutes uphill to Phundup Pedma Yoeling Shedra. The road traverses in and out of side valleys, passing above **Dobji Dzong**, which served as Bhutan's central prison from 1976 and is now a small religious school for 22 monks (the old prison cells are now classrooms!). Milarepa is said to have spent the night here. At the time of research a new road was being built to the dzong replacing the current hairy road that goes via a stone quarry.

The road continues its descent into the Wang Chuu valley to join the main road at Chhuzom. From Chhuzom it's 24km (45 minutes) to Paro or 31km (one hour) to Thimphu.

PUNAKHA DZONGKHAG

Thimphu to Punakha

76KM / 2¾ HOURS

The drive from Thimphu to Punakha, along the National Hwy and over the Dochu La, leads from the cool heights of Thimphu to the balmy, lush landscapes of the Punakha valley.

Thimphu to the Dochu La

23KM / 45 MINUTES

From Thimphu, the route to the east leaves the road to Paro and Phuentsholing and loops back over itself to become the east–west National Hwy. About a kilometre past the turn-off there is a good view of Simtokha Dzong. The route climbs through apple orchards and forests of blue pine to the village of **Hongtsho** (2890m), where an immigration checkpoint controls all access to eastern Bhutan. Your guide will present your restricted-area travel permit, giving you the chance to haggle for walnuts, apples and dried cheese from the roadside vendors.

High on a ridge across the valley to the south is **Trashigang Goemba**, which you can visit by taking a trail from just below Hongtsho (see p71).

The road climbs to the **Dochu La** (3140m), marked by a large array of prayer flags and an impressive collection of 108 chortens. On a clear day (only really likely between October and February), the pass offers a panoramic view of the Bhutan Himalaya – some groups make special predawn trips up here to catch the views. The collection of chortens was built in 2005 as atonement for the loss of life caused by the flushing out of Assamese militants in southern Bhutan. Bring your own prayer flags to add to the collection.

The adjacent **Druk Wangyal Lhakhang** is well worth a visit to view its cartoon-style modern murals. Images include the fourth king battling Indian rebels in the jungle, monks using a laptop, and a Druk Air plane, alongside a modern history of the kingdom. It's a quintessentially Bhutanese fusion of the 21st and 15th centuries. The nearby Druk Wangyel Cafe Dochu La, with a gift shop, hot drinks and snacks, should be open by the time you read this. On 13 December the **Dochu La Wangyal Festival** is held beside the lhakhang.

The hill above the chortens is covered in a lovely rhododendron forest, part of the 47-sq-km **Royal Botanical Park**. If you are here between mid-March and the end of April it's well worth taking some time to wander in the forest and take in the wonderful blooms. It is also a good area for birdwatching. The **Dochu La Nature Trail** (1.2km, one hour) starts near the Dochu La cafe and ends on the road at Lamperi. The **Lumitsawa Ancient Trail** (4.7km, two hours) continues downhill from here to again meet the road at Lumitsawa. Both trails are sections of the original route between Thimphu and Punakha. If you have more time, you can take an excellent half-day hike back to Hongtsho via Lungchuzekha and Trashigang goembas (see p71). There is also a full-day ridge trail from Tharana (above Hongtsho) to Dochu La.

On the hill just below the pass is the **Dochu La Resort** (✆02-380404; www.dochularesort.com; s/d Nu 1920/3000), where many people break for tea (breakfast/lunch Nu 360/480). The proprietor also has a business making embroidered *thangkas* including some large *thondrols* for tsechus, and there's a small gift shop here. It's a popular overnight stop in October and November, when views are clearest.

There is a powerful binocular telescope here, a gift from the Kyoto University Alpine Club after members made the first ascent of Masang Gang (7165m) in 1985. A photograph nearby labels the peaks on the horizon (with different spellings and elevations from those used in this book). Gangkhar Puensum (7541m) is the highest peak that is completely inside Bhutan; Kulha Gangri (7554m) is higher, but it is on the border with Tibet. Using the telescope, it's also possible to see Gasa Dzong, a small white speck almost 50km to the north.

The area near the pass is believed to be inhabited by numerous spirits, including a cannibal demoness. Lama Drukpa Kunley, the 'Divine Madman', built Chimi Lhakhang in the Punakha valley to subdue these spirits and demons.

Dochu La to Metshina

42KM / 1½ HOURS

The vegetation changes dramatically at the pass from oak, maple and blue pine to a moist mountain forest of rhododendron, alder, cypress, hemlock and fir. There is also a large growth of daphne, a bush with bark that is harvested for making traditional paper. The large white chorten a few kilometres below the pass was built because of the high incidence of accidents on this stretch of road.

About 11km below the pass at Lamperi is the entrance to the **Royal Botanical Park** (admission Nu 50; ☺9am-5pm), where you can hire a bicycle (Nu 200 per hour) or take a downhill hike on the ancient trail to Lunitsawa (two hours).

It's a long, winding descent past Lumitsawa to **Thinleygang**, during which the air gets warmer and the vegetation becomes increasingly tropical with the appearance of cactus, oranges and bamboo. Every November (on the first day of the 10th month), the Je Khenpo and *dratshang* overnight here on their two-day journey from their summer residence in Thimphu to their winter residence in Punakha.

Monasteries soon start to appear on the surrounding hills; first the striking hilltop Jakar Goemba and then Dalay and Talo goembas. The road passes a chorten that flows with *drub chhu* (holy water), said to have its source in a lake far above.

The road continues its descent, looping in and out of a side valley, to the road junction and petrol station at Metshina, where the road to Punakha branches left off the National Hwy. If you are continuing the 8km to Wangdue Phodrang, stay on the main road. If you fancy a spicy lunch, stop at the **Kumar Restaurant & Bar** (✆02-376052; Metshina; mains Nu 50-140; ☺7am-10pm), opposite the Metshina vegetable market on the main road. It's an authentic Nepalese *dhaba* (basic roadside restaurant) with curries, samosas, dahl and noodles.

Metshina to Punakha

11KM / 30 MINUTES

The road to Punakha makes a switchback down past a collection of restaurants and houses at **Sopsokha**, from where you can visit the Chimi Lhakhang. Beyond here, the road crosses the small Teop Rong Chhu and swings round a ridge into the valley of the Punak Tsang Chhu. The quiet tarmac road on the far side of the valley offers several mountain-biking options.

After another 2km or so, by the village of Wolakha, a road peels off to the left and climbs to the Meri Phuensom and Zangto Pelri hotels. Just above the hotels is an *anim goemba* (nunnery) and huge Nepalistyle chorten, financed by the fourth king's father-in-law, and visible from the main road as you descend into the valley.

High up on the hillside, this side road continues relentlessly uphill for 15km to **Talo Goemba**. You need a permit specifying Talo in order to visit the monastery. Up on the nearby ridge, the village of Norbugang reportedly has several fine lhakhangs but is closed to visitors since it is home to the family of the fourth king's four wives. A 1km side road branches off 5km before Talo to **Dalay Goemba**, a *lobdra* (monastic school) which is home to a young *trulku* (reincarnated lama). The monastery was founded by the seventh Je Khenpo and is also known as Nalanda, after the famous Indian Buddhist university.

Back on the main road, just under 2km from the junction and 6.5km from Metshina, is the new town of Khuruthang. All of Punakha's shops were relocated to this charmless concrete grid in 1999. There are several restaurants, local hotels and a Saturday vegetable market.

To the side of the road is the new **Khuruthang Goemba**, built by the Royal Grandmother and consecrated in 2005. The main Zangto Pelri Lhakhang here has excellent ceiling mandalas. The murals on the far wall depict the Zhabdrung and the various dzongs he established. The large Nepali-style chorten here was built by the Indian guru Nagi Rinchen and is said to enshrine a speaking image of Guru Rinpoche known as Guru Sungzheme.

It's a further 3km to a middle school and small park with an excellent viewpoint over the Punakha Dzong. A kilometre further on is a parking area and the footbridge leading across the Mo Chhu to gorgeous Punakha Dzong.

Chimi Lhakhang

On a hillock in the centre of the valley below Metshina is the yellow-roofed Chimi Lhakhang, built in 1499 by the cousin of Lama Drukpa Kunley in his honour after the lama subdued the demoness of the nearby Dochu La with his 'magic thunderbolt of wisdom'. A wooden effigy of the lama's thunderbolt is preserved in the lhakhang, and childless women go to the temple to receive a *wang* (blessing or empowerment) from the saint. Newborns are also brought here to be named, and all leave with the same name: Chimi (or Chimmi).

Most visitors take the 20-minute trail across fields from the road at Sopsokha to the temple (take a hat and be prepared for wind, dust or mud). The trail leads downhill across rice fields to Yoaka (which means 'in the drain') and on to the tiny settlement of Pana, which means 'field'. It then crosses an archery ground (keep your eyes peeled!) before making a short climb to Chimi Lhakhang. More and more guides are taking their vehicles down the narrow rough road to Pana village.

There are a few monks at the temple, which is surrounded by a row of prayer wheels and some beautiful slate carvings. The bodhi tree here is believed to have been brought from Bodhgaya. You'll see the central statue of the lama and his dog

Sachi, as well as statues of the Zhabdrung, Sakyamuni and Chenresig. Make a small offering and you'll be rewarded with a blessing from the lama's wooden phallus, tusk and his iron archery set. Mothers-to-be pray to a fertility goddess and then select their future baby's name from a collection of bamboo slips. The small chorten on the altar is said to have been crafted by Drukpa Kunley himself. Murals to the right of the chapel depict events from Kunley's colourful life.

The well-run **Chimi Lhakhang Cafeteria** (🖉 17612672; set meals Nu 420) in Sopsokha is a great place for lunch or tea, with tables lined up against the window overlooking Yoaka and Pana villages. The nearby **Village Restaurant** (Sopsokha; set meals Nu 420) is a similar, though much less professional, operation with some very rickety stairs to negotiate.

Punakha & Khuruthang

🖉 02 / ELEV 1250M

Punakha sits in a sultry, fertile and beautiful valley at the junction of the Mo Chhu (Mother River) and Pho Chhu (Father River). Commanding the river junction is the gorgeous Punakha Dzong, perhaps Bhutan's most impressive building.

Punakha served as Bhutan's capital for over 300 years. The first king was crowned here in 1907 and the third king convened the Bhutan National Assembly here for the first time in 1952. In 2008 the fifth and current king underwent a secret ceremony in the dzong, receiving the royal raven crown, before proceeding to a formal coronation in Thimphu.

The low altitude of the Punakha valley allows two rice crops a year, and oranges and bananas are in abundance. Punakha also has one of the most famous festivals in the country, the springtime *domchoe* (see p33), dedicated to the protector deity Yeshe Goenpo (Mahakala).

All of Punakha's shops and facilities are in the unappealing new town of Khuruthang, 4km to the south.

◎ Sights

★ **Punakha Dzong**   DZONG
(🕗 8am-5pm) This dzong was the second dzong to be built in Bhutan and it served as the capital and seat of government until Thimphu was promoted to the top job

THE DIVINE MADMAN

Lama Drukpa Kunley (1455–1529) is one of Bhutan's favourite saints and a fine example of the Tibetan tradition of 'crazy wisdom'. He was born in Tibet, trained at Ralung Monastery and was a contemporary and disciple of Pema Lingpa. He travelled throughout Bhutan and Tibet as a *neljorpa* (yogi) using songs, humour and outrageous behaviour to dramatise his teachings to the common man. He felt that the stiffness of the clergy and social conventions were keeping people from learning the true teachings of Buddha.

His outrageous, often obscene, actions and sexual antics were a deliberate method of provoking people to discard their preconceptions. Tango Goemba is apparently the proud owner of a *thangka* (religious picture) that Kunley urinated on! He is also credited with having created Bhutan's strange animal, the takin, by sticking the head of a goat onto the body of a cow.

His sexual exploits are legendary, and the flying phalluses that you see painted on houses and hanging from rooftops symbolise the lama, also known as the Divine Madman. Kunley's numerous sexual conquests often included even the wives of his hosts and sponsors. On one occasion when he received a blessing thread to hang around his neck, he wound it around his penis instead, saying he hoped it would bring him luck with the ladies.

He spoke the following verse on one occasion when he met Pema Lingpa:

I, the madman from Kyishodruk,

Wander around from place to place;

I believe in lamas when it suits me,

I practise the Dharma in my own way.

I choose any qualities, they are all illusions,

Any gods, they are all the Emptiness of the Mind.

I use fair and foul words for Mantras; it's all the same,

My meditation practice is girls and wine;

I do whatever I feel like, strolling around in the Void,

Last time, I saw you with the Bumthang trulku;

With my great karmic background, I could approach.

Indeed it was auspicious, to meet you on my pilgrim's round!

For a biography and collection of songs, poems and bar-room anecdotes concerning Drukpa Kunley, try Keith Dowman's *The Divine Madman*.

in the mid-1950s. It's arguably the most beautiful dzong in the country, especially in spring when the lilac-coloured jacaranda trees bring a lush sensuality to the dzong's characteristically towering whitewashed walls. Elaborately painted gold, red and black carved woods add to the artistic lightness of touch.

Guru Rinpoche foretold the construction of Punakha Dzong, predicting that '...a person named Namgyal will arrive at a hill that looks like an elephant'. When the Zhabdrung visited Punakha he chose the tip of the trunk of the sleeping elephant at the confluence of the Mo Chhu and Pho Chhu as the place to build a dzong.

A smaller building called Dzong Chug (Small Dzong) housed a statue of the Buddha here as early as 1326. Construction on the current dzong began in 1637 and was completed the following year, when the building was christened Pungthang Dechen Phodrang (Palace of Great Happiness). Later embellishments included the construction of a chapel to commemorate the victory over the Tibetans in 1639. The arms captured during the battle are preserved in the dzong.

The Zhabdrung established a monk body here with 600 monks from Cheri Goemba in the upper Thimphu valley and the dzong is still the winter residence of the *dratshang*.

Punakha Dzong is 180m long and 72m wide and the **utse** is six storeys high. The gold dome on the *utse* was built in 1676 by local ruler Gyaltsen Tenzin Rabgye. Many of the dzong's features were added between 1744 and 1763 during the reign of the 13th *desi,* Sherab Wangchuk. One item he donated was the *chenmo* (great) *thondrol,* a large *thangka* depicting the Zhabdrung that is exhibited to the public once a year during the tsechu festival. A brass roof for the dzong was a gift of the seventh Dalai Lama, Kelzang Gyatso.

Frequent fires (the latest in 1986) have damaged the dzong, as did the severe 1897 earthquake. In 1994 a glacial lake burst on the Pho Chhu, causing damage to the dzong that has since been repaired.

In addition to its strategic position at the river confluence, the dzong has several features to protect it against invasion. The steep wooden entry stairs are designed to be pulled up, and there is a heavy wooden door that is still closed at night.

The dzong is unusual in that it has three **docheys** instead of the usual two. The first (northern) courtyard is for administrative functions and houses a huge white chorten and bodhi tree. In the far left corner is a collection of stones and a shrine to the Tsochen, queen of the *nagas* (snake spirits), whose image is to the side. The second courtyard houses the monastic quarters and is separated from the first by the *utse.* In this courtyard there are two halls, one of which was used when Ugyen Wangchuck, later the first king, was presented with the Order of Knight Commander of the Indian Empire by John Claude White in 1905.

In the southernmost courtyard is the temple where the remains of the *terton,* Pema Lingpa, and Zhabdrung Ngawang Namgyal are preserved. The Zhabdrung died in Punakha Dzong, and his body is still preserved in the **Machey Lhakhang** (*machey* means 'sacred embalmed body'), which was rebuilt in 1995. The casket is sealed and may not be opened. Other than two guardian lamas, only the king and the Je Khenpo may enter this room. Both come to take blessings before they take up their offices. The unprecedented abdication of the fourth king meant a fifth person, the king's father, could also enter the lhakhang.

At the south end is the **'hundred-pillar' assembly hall** (which actually has 54 pillars). The exceptional murals, which were commissioned by the second *druk desi,* depict the life of Buddha. The massive gold statues of the Buddha, Guru Rinpoche and the Zhabdrung date back to the mid-18th century, and there are some fine gold panels on the pillars.

Bhutan's most treasured possession is the **Rangjung ('Self-Created') Kharsapani**, an image of Chenresig that is kept in the Tse Lhakhang in the *utse* of the Punakha Dzong. It was brought to Bhutan from Tibet by the Zhabdrung and features in Punakha's famous *domchoe* festival. It is closed to the public.

After you exit the dzong from the north you can visit the *dzong chung* and get a blessing from a wish-fulfilling statue of Sakyamuni. The building marks the site of the original dzong. North of the dzong is a cremation ground, marked by a large chorten, and to the east is a royal palace.

Upper Punakha Valley   VALLEY
The road up the west side of Mo Chhu valley passes several country houses owned by Bhutan's nobility, including the Phuntsho Pelri palace, a royal summer residence. The fourth king's father-in-law built many of the lhakhangs in the valley and owns several hotels, including the Damchen Resort.

Just 1km north of the dzong is the **Nazhoen Pelri Training Centre** (☑584664; www.bhutanyouth.org; ☯9am-4pm), a program that offers a one-year course to train girls to produce handicrafts. Products include handwoven bags, slippers, embroidered purses and table mats, prayer-flag bookmarks and Christmas decorations. Products are well designed, prices are reasonable and it's a worthy cause.

On the left side of the road, 4.5km from Punakha, look out for the **Dho Jhaga Lama Lhakhang**, the pretty gardens of which surround a huge boulder split miraculously in two. It is said that the Indian guru-magician Nagi Rinchen sent lightning and hail to split the rock to liberate his mother who was trapped inside. The chapel houses a statue of the guru (to the far right), who is recognisable by the scriptures in his top knot. Rinchen meditated in a cave across the river (behind Sona Gasa, the former palace of the third king), and so is depicted here as a long-haired *drubthob* (hermit-magician). To the far left is a statue of the local female protector, Chobdra, riding a snow lion.

In Yambesa, 7km north of Punakha, is the huge **Khamsum Yuelley Namgyal Chorten**, perched high on a hill on the opposite bank of the river. The 30m-tall chorten (also known as the Nyzergang Lhakhang) took eight years to build and was consecrated in 1999. The chorten is dedicated to the fifth king and serves to protect the country, so it is stuffed with a veritable 'who's who' of Bhutanese demonography; some with raven or elephant heads, others riding snow lions or *garudas,* and most covered in flames. Look in the ground-floor stairwell for one protector riding a brown, hairy *migoi* (yeti). Go to the roof for fine views of the valley.

A bridge provides access to a sweaty 45-minute hike uphill to the chorten. Head off in the morning to avoid the subtropical heat. Ask your guide to point out the wonderfully fragrant *tingye* (flower pepper) plants that grow along the trail beside fields of chillis and beans.

The bridge is also a put-in spot for relaxing rafting and kayaking float trips down the Mo Chhu to Punakha Dzong (see p261). Beyond the chorten, the road leads up past Kabesa village and the Uma Punakha resort to Tashithang and then continues all the way to the Gasa hot springs and the ending point of the Laya–Gasa trek.

 Activities

Punakha's mountain-bike trails offer one of the best chances to break out the fat tyres, though you'll have to bring your own bike as there's nowhere to rent locally.

A 27km-loop route from Khuruthang crosses the bridge there and heads up the east side of the valley along a feeder road to Samdingkha (14km), then returns along a trail to Punakha Dzong (7.5km), finally coasting back to Khuruthang along the paved road.

A longer 40km loop starts from the new town of Bajo, just north of Wangdue Phodrang, and heads up the east side of the valley to Jangsabu (14km), before climbing a technical trail (some carrying required) to Olodama and Tschochagsa (9.5km). From here you can detour to Lingmukha or coast down 10km to the Aumthekha junction, across the river from Chimi Lhakhang, and then pedal back to Bajo and Wangdi.

WESTERN BHUTAN PUNAKHA & KHURUTHANG

GASA DZONG & HOT SPRINGS

The road along the Mo Chhu valley leads north out of Punakha and enters **Gasa Dzongkhag** and **Jigme Dorji National Park**. Until recent times you had to trek much of this route, and though the road is steadily being improved, it remains a rough, slow drive. The drive from Punakha to Gasa (about 133km return from Khamsum Yuelley Namgyal Chorten) takes a full day. The rewards are the magical views, wonderful bird-watching and the dzong. The hot springs, on the other hand, are primarily a destination for the sick and elderly seeking relief in the thermal waters.

Just 19km from Khamsum Chorten is the village of **Tashitang**. Here the road hugs the Mo Chhu and is wrapped in verdant forests that sing with bird life. Just stop the car and wander quietly along the roadside to spot shimmering sunbirds, pure blue flycatchers and crested laughing thrushes. Even non-twitchers will be amazed at the bird show.

It's another rough 47km drive through forests, terraces and villages to Gasa's **Trashi Thongmoen Dzong**, a venerable and remote fortress nestled in a rugged mountain setting. Though damaged several times by fires, the dzong's eclectic treasures remain on display in the Chanzho Lhakhang: the skeleton of the sheep that followed the Zhabdrung on his journey from Ralung Monastery in Tibet, and the Zhabdrung's remarkably preserved saddles in a metal chest.

The steep trail down to the **Gasa tsachhu** (hot spring) is punishing on the knees, so it's just as well that the hottest of the four communal baths is beneficial for joint pain. The other baths are beneficial for a plethora of other ailments. The 'vapour spa' above the baths is a stinky grotto where sulphurous fumes whoosh out of soft-drink bottles that have been fashioned into funnels and jammed into crevices. Good for the sinuses apparently!

🛏 Sleeping

Many people visit Punakha as a day trip from Thimphu or visit en route to Wangdue Phodrang, where there are several more hotels.

★ Meri Puensum Resort   HOTEL $$

(📞584195; www.meripuensum.com.bt; s/d Nu 2300/2500, deluxe Nu 2500/2760; 🛜) This welcoming hotel is 6km south of Punakha, 1.2km up a side road, on a hill above the Punakha valley. Comfortable, warm rooms are in a central building and cottages that hug the steep hillside overlooking the rice terraces of the Punakha valley. The garden gazebo (with wi-fi) is a great place to breakfast or sip on a relaxing beer after a long day's touring.

Hotel Y.T.   HOTEL $$

(📞376014; hotelyt@druknet.bt; s/d from Nu 2160/3000; 🛜) Above the road department complex in Lobesa, 1.5km from Metshina en route to Wangdue Phodrang, this friendly, family-run hotel was established in 1991 and is still a popular choice. Slightly old-fashioned, its charm comes from the enthusiasm of the owners, who were adding new rooms when we visited. The owner is an ex-forester, which is why the gardens are stuffed with mango, avocado and papaya trees.

Hotel Zangto Pelri   HOTEL $$

(📞584125; hotzang@druknet.bt; s/d Nu 2000/2400, deluxe Nu 2300/2760, ste Nu 6000; 🛜) Named after the paradise of Guru Rinpoche, this hotel has 45 rooms in the central building and quieter surrounding cottages (upper-floor rooms are best). Most rooms have a balcony. If you stay here (or nearby), consider getting up at dawn and driving 8km up the paved road to Laptshaka (1900m) for a beautiful view of the mountains.

Damchen Resort   HOTEL $$

(📞584354; www.damchenresort.com; s/d Nu 2300/2530, deluxe from Nu 2990/3220) On the banks of the Punak Chhu, below Khuruthang, this riverside resort boasts a great setting, but it feels a bit glum and institutional, with uninspiring decoration and a soulless dining room reminiscent of a school camp. The proximity to Khuruthang means you can visit the town or goemba by yourself. Some deluxe rooms have balcony vews of the river.

★ Uma Punakha   LUXURY HOTEL $$$

(📞584688; www.comohotels.com; r US$480-960; 🛜) Upstream along the Mo Chhu valley, 14km from Punakha, in a lush rural location just north of the Khamsum Yuelley Namgyal Chorten, the Uma is a delightful boutique retreat of just 11 luxury rooms. The views from the main patio over fields towards the river and chorten are sublime. Booking enquiries should be made through the sister hotel in Paro (p83).

Kunzang Zhing Resort   LUXURY HOTEL $$$

(📞584705; www.kunzangzhingresortbhutan.com; r/ste Nu 13,200/19,800; 🛜) This new hotel with striking 'stone-and-wood' architecture is close to the established Meri Puenum Resort. Fully appointed rooms boast modern bathrooms and views. The lobby has a business centre, a library and gift shop, while the multicuisine dining room is accompanied by two bars, the outdoor one with a bonfire.

Amankora   LUXURY HOTEL $$$

(📞584222; www.amanresorts.com; s/d full board US$1740/1860; ❄🛜) This is the most intimate of Aman's uberluxury resorts, with only eight rooms in three buildings. The main farmhouse (now the restaurant and reading room) was the former residence of the Queen Mother and features a traditional altar room. The spa reception is in the old farmhouse kitchen, and the outdoor dining area is surrounded by rice fields and orchards. Park at the suspension bridge over the Mo Chhu, 6km north of Paro, and take a golf cart up to the resort.

🍴 Eating

★ Phuenzhi Diner   BHUTANESE $

(📞584145; Dungkhar Lam; set breakfast/lunch Nu 300/350) The 'Four Friends' is easily the best place in Khuruthang and is well known to travel guides. The food is delicious and reliable (as is the welcoming air-con) and if you're lucky there will be pancakes on the menu. If you don't eat here, your guide will probably book lunch at one of the tourist hotels.

ℹ Information

Bank of Bhutan (Khuruthang; 🕑9am-1pm Mon-Fri, to 11am Sat) Changes cash and travellers cheques and has an ATM.

WANGDUE PHODRANG DZONGKHAG

The scenic *dzongkhag* (administrative district) of Wangdue Phodrang is centred on the once-magnificent dzong of that name and stretches all the way to the Pele La and Phobjikha valley. South of Wangdi, as it is known locally, towards the southern region of Tsirang, is the giant Indian-financed Punatsangchuu hydroelectric project.

Punakha to Wangdue Phodrang

21KM / 30 MINUTES

It's a half-hour drive from Punakha to Wangdue Phodrang. Follow the road back to Metshina and drive 1.5km to Lobesa, following the Punak Tsang Chhu. Soon the dramatic ruins of Wangdue Phodrang Dzong come into view, along the end of a ridge above the river. There is a police checkpoint before the bridge across the Punak Tsang Chhu.

The modern bridge over the Punak Tsang Chhu replaced the original 17th-century wooden cantilever structure that was washed away by floods in 1968.

Wangdue Phodrang & Bajo

🎵 02 / ELEV 1240M

Legend says that the Zhabdrung Ngawang Namgyal met a small boy named Wangdi playing in the sand on the banks of the Punak Tsang Chhu and was moved to name his new dzong Wangdi – later Wangdue – Phodrang (Wangdi's Palace).

The ramshackle old town that once lined the road to the dzong has been relocated 4km north to the rather soulless grid of Bajo new town.

◉ Sights

Wangdue Phodrang Dzong   BUDDHIST, DZONG
(⊙8.30am-5pm) The Wangdue Phodrang Dzong was founded by the Zhabdrung in 1638 atop a high ridge between the Punak Tsang Chhu and the Dang Chhu, clearly chosen for its commanding view of the valleys below. Legend relates another reason for choosing this spot: as people searched for a site for the dzong, four ravens were seen flying away in four directions. This was considered an auspicious sign, representing the spreading of religion to the four points of the compass.

Wangdi is important in the history of Bhutan because in the early days it was the country's second capital. After Trongsa Dzong was established in 1644, the *penlop* of Wangdue Phodrang became the third most powerful ruler, after the *penlops* of Paro and Trongsa. The dzong's strategic position gave the *penlop* control of the routes to Trongsa, Punakha, Dagana and Thimphu.

The dzong caught fire (believed to be due to an electrical fault) on 24 June 2012 and was virtually destroyed save for the lower walls. Almost immediately funds were raised for its restoration and the first steps of this huge task were underway at the time of writing.

Wangdue Phodrang

The Guru Tshengye *thondrol*, depicting Guru Rinpoche, is unfurled here each year in the early hours of the final day of the autumn tsechu festival. While the dzong is being rebuilt the tsechu will be held on a field at the nearby Army Training Centre.

★ Radak Neykhang   BUDDHIST, TEMPLE

By the tall cypress trees of the district court, before the dzong, is this timeless 17th-century temple dedicated to an ancient warrior king. There's a collection of helmets, knives and shields in the anteroom. Inside are five versions of the local protector deity, as well as a statue to the far right of a *tshomen* (water spirit) who lived in the river and was an obstacle to the construction of this building.

Make an offering and roll the chapel dice and the resident monk will read your future.

🛏 Sleeping

There's not a great deal of demand for hotel rooms in Wangdi. Many travellers just make a day trip to see the dzong or stay in Punakha (30 minutes' drive away) and continue straight through to Gangte, Trongsa or Bumthang. At tsechu time in autumn, however, the town is packed and rooms are at a premium.

Hotel Tashiling   LOCAL $

(📞481403; tashilinghotel@gmail.com; Dzong Lam; s/d Nu 1800/2160; 🛜) This local hotel near the dzong has 16 pine-walled rooms and fragrant chillis drying on the roof. It's only worth considering for Indian tourists, who pay 50% less than the rate for foreigners. The giant fridge full of cold beers will raise spirits.

Punatsangchhu Cottages   HOTEL $$

(📞481942; www.punacottages.bt; s/d Nu 2645/3220, deluxe Nu 3795/4370, ste Nu 5175; 🛜) Also known as Puna Cottages, this is good choice, below the road and next to the river, 5km from Wangdi. Modern rooms vary in size and some have lovely sunny balconies overlooking the river. The restaurant is good and the lawn is perfect for a cold a beer on a warm afternoon.

Dragon's Nest Resort   HOTEL $$

(📞480521; www.dragonsnesthotel.com; s/d from Nu 2400/3120, deluxe Nu 2760/3360; 🛜) This trusty place is on the west side of the river, 4km below Wangdi and diagonally across from Bajo. The spacious rooms and lush grounds overlook the river and the new town. The hotel was undergoing renovation, so expect freshly furnished rooms.

Kichu Resort   HOTEL $$

(📞481359; www.intrektour.com; r/ste Nu 3105/5175) In Chhuzomsa (9km east of Wangdi), this tranquil resort has 24 well-appointed rooms in a lovely landscaped garden overlooking the rushing Dang Chhu. The son of the owners is a *rinpoche* (title given to a revered lama), so the restaurant serves only vegetarian food. But there is a bar and a lovely garden for relaxing drinks. Ask for a riverside balcony room and pack insect repellent against the sand flies.

ⓘ Information

Bank of Bhutan (Bajo; ⊘ 9am-1pm Mon-Fri, to noon Sat) Changes cash and travellers cheques. It's in Bajo, 2.5km north of Wangdue Phodrang.

National Bank of Bhutan (Bajo; ⊘ 9am-4pm Mon-Fri, to 11am Sat) Changes cash and travellers cheques.

Wangdue Phodrang to Pele La

61KM / 1¾ HOURS

The beautiful drive east towards the Pele La offers access to central Bhutan and the Phobjikha valley, known for its winter population of black-necked cranes. The pass itself takes you over the Black Mountains, the physical boundary between western and central Bhutan.

Leaving Wangdue Phodrang, the road traverses bare hillsides high above the Dang Chhu. The large riverside building below the road is a jail for prisoners serving life imprisonment.

By the time the road reaches Chhuzomsa at the confluence of the Pe Chhu and the Dang Chhu, 9km from Wangdi, it is level with the river (Chhuzomsa means 'meeting of two rivers'). Below the small village is the idyllic riverside Kichu Resort.

Just beyond Chhuzomsa is a ropeway that climbs 1340m in 6km to Tashila. The ropeway is primarily used to carry goods up to the village and to bring logs back down the hill, but it makes two special trips daily (8am and 5pm) to carry people. Passengers sit in an open wooden box and dangle high above the trees for 45 minutes to the top.

At Tikke Zampa, 4km past Chhuzomsa, the road crosses to the south bank of the Dang Chhu and begins a gradual climb to the Pele La. A further 10km and you'll see a superbly located lhakhang atop a hillock to the left. The road gets steeper as it climbs the valley. In many places the road has been blasted out of the cliff and hangs high above the deep forests of the valley below.

The road detours frequently into side valleys, passing the village of **Kalekha** (or Khelaykha), the end of the Shasi La hike (see the boxed text, p105) from the Phobjikha valley. From here it's 12km to the village of Nobding (2640m), where the tourist-friendly **Kuenphen Restaurant** (442000; set lunch Nu 420) offers a useful lunch stop. A further 7km on is Dungdung Nyelsa, where the old (disused) road to the Pele La branches off. In spring the upper hillsides here are covered with red, white and pink rhododendron blossoms. The road climbs steeply up the hillside for 5km, to the turn-off to Gangte in the Phobjikha valley.

From the turn-off, it's a final 3km through forests to the top of the Pele La (3420m), which is marked by a chorten and an array of prayer flags. On a clear day (which is rare in these parts) there is a view of Jhomolhari (7314m), Jichu Drakye (6989m) and Kang Bum (6526m) from a viewpoint 500m down the old road between Nobding and the Pele La. There are no mountain views from the pass itself. The Pele La marks the western border of the Jigme Singye Wangchuck (formerly the Black Mountains) National Park and is the gateway to central Bhutan.

Phobjikha Valley

02 / ELEV 2900M

Phobjikha is a bowl-shaped glacial valley on the western slopes of the Black Mountains, bordering the Jigme Singye Wangchuck National Park. Because of the large flock of black-necked cranes that winters here, it is one of the most important wildlife preserves in the country. In addition to the cranes there are also muntjacs (barking deer), wild boars, sambars, serows, Himalayan black bears, leopards and red foxes in the surrounding hills. The Nakey Chhu drains the marshy valley, eventually flowing into the lower reaches of the Punak Tsang Chhu. Some people refer to this entire region as Gangte (or Gangtey), after the goemba that sits on a ridge above the valley.

The road to Phobjikha diverges from the main road 3km before the Pele La. It's then a 1.5km drive through forests to the Lowa La (3360m), where you may encounter a few stray yaks. After the pass the trees disappear and the scenery switches dramatically to low-lying dwarf bamboo as the road descends to Gangte village and goemba. From the goemba junction, the road switchbacks down past the turn-off to the Amankora resort to the valley floor, past extensive russet-coloured fields of potatoes. Gangte potatoes are the region's primary cash crop and one of Bhutan's important exports to India.

The valley is snowbound during the height of winter and many of the valley's 4700 residents, including the monks, shift to winter residences in Wangdue Phodrang during December and January, just as the cranes move in to take their place. The local residents are known as Gangteps and speak a dialect called Henke.

⊙ Sights

★**Gangte Goemba**   BUDDHIST, MONASTERY

Gangte Goemba enjoys the valley's prime chunk of real estate, on a forested hill overlooking the green expanse of the entire Phobjikha valley. The extensive complex consists of the central goemba, monks' quarters, a small guesthouse and outlying meditation centres.

During a visit to the Phobjikha valley, the 15th-century treasure-finder Pema Lingpa prophesied that a goemba named *gang-teng* (hilltop) would be built on this site and that his teachings would spread from here. Pema Thinley, the grandson and reincarnation of Pema Lingpa, built a Nyingma temple here in 1613, and the larger goemba was built by the second reincarnation, Tenzing Legpey Dhendup. The current Gangtey *trulku*, Kunzang Pema Namgyal, is the ninth reincarnation of the 'body' of Pema Lingpa.

The **tshokhang** (prayer hall) is built in the Tibetan style with eight great pillars, and is one of the largest in Bhutan. The inner sanctum houses the funeral chorten of founder Tenzing Legpey Dhendup. Much of the interior and exterior woodwork of the 450-year-old goemba was replaced between 2001 and 2008 due to a beetle-larvae infestation. A three-day **tsechu** is held here from the eighth to 10th day of the eighth lunar month (September/October), with *cham* (religious dances) and the hanging of a large *thondrol* on the final day.

The long white building on the hill to the north of the goemba is **Kuenzang Chholing**,

Phobjikha Valley

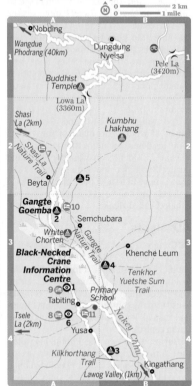

a *drubdey* (retreat and meditation centre for monks). The normal period of meditation is three years, three months and three (sometimes seven) days, during which time the monks remain inside and eat food passed in to them by another monk.

The Valley VALLEY

The beautiful glacial valley below the goemba is peppered with villages, hiking trails, potato fields, lhakhangs and, if you time your visit right (November to mid-February), black-necked cranes. It's a great place to hike and explore surrounding valleys, so make sure you budget an extra half-day here to do this.

Your first stop should be the Royal Society for Protection of Nature's (RSPN) **Black-Necked Crane Information Centre** (☑442536; ⏰5am-1pm & 2-5pm Mon-Fri, 9am-noon Sat & Sun Nov-Mar, from 9am Apr-Oct), which has informative displays about the cranes

and the valley environment; you can use the centre's powerful spotting scopes. If the weather's iffy you can browse the library and handicraft shop, and watch videos at 10am and 3pm (Nu 200 per group). This is also the centre of the valley's fledgling ecotourism initiative and it can arrange local hiking guides, an overnight stay in a local homestay or lectures.

A further 1.5km on is the village and hotels at Tabiting. Behind the Phuntsho Chholing Guest House is the small **Wangmo Hand-Woven Carpet Factory** (☑442553). Established in 1992 by a local woman, Dorji Wangmo, it produces about 30 carpets a year.

Further on, the road becomes a rough 4WD track as it continues past Yusa village to the small **Domchoe Lhakhang**, said to be the oldest in the valley, dating to the 7th century. It's a 45-minute walk from Tabiting.

Across the valley from Tabiting is the 15th-century **Khewang Lhakhang**, which has a **tsechu** on the third day of the ninth month, when local men (not monks) do the dancing, celebrating an ancient victory over local demons.

⌂ Sleeping

Electricity has arrived, with much of the infrastructure underground, maintaining the valley's picturesque, crane-friendly scenery, though the supply is not all that reliable. The high-altitude valley can be very chilly so bring warm clothes.

Phuntshocholing Farm House GUESTHOUSE $
(☑442554; s/d Nu 1320/1870) This traditional farmhouse belonging to the sister of the Gangte *trulku* was converted to a hotel in 1994. It has creaking wooden floors, wall paintings, a cosy dining room and a chapel on the 2nd floor, though the rooms themselves are pretty simple for the money, with clean shared bathrooms. If you value experience over mod-cons, this is a good opportunity to get a close-up look at the traditional architecture of rural Bhutan.

★**Dewachen Hotel** HOTEL $$
(☑442550; www.dewachenhotel.com; s/d Nu 3840/4440) This impressive stone-and-wood building in Tabiting village is the first choice for most travellers. The rooms are large and stylish (corner rooms are the best), and the good restaurant has floor-to-ceiling bay windows that offer great valley views. The name refers to the 'Pure Land' paradise of the Buddha Amithaba.

Gakiling Guest House HOTEL $$
(☑442540; s/d Nu 2280/2760) This locally owned hotel is just behind the Black-Necked Crane Information Centre. The new concrete block of 16 double rooms offers comfortable and warm rest, while the original guesthouse will offer traditional Bhutanese rooms when renovations are finished. There are valley views from the *bukhari*-warmed dining room.

Yue-Loki Guest House GUESTHOUSE $$
(☑17874116; s/d Nu 2160/2640) This new but traditional guesthouse is owned by Dorji Wangmo of the adjacent Wangmo Hand-Woven Carpet Factory. The dining room and all but one of the eight pine-clad rooms are heated by wood-fired *bukharis,* adding to the cosy ambience. Rooms and private bathrooms vary greatly in size and there are some steep stairs to negotiate to get to the upper storey.

Gangtey Goenpa Lodge LUXURY HOTEL $$$
(www.easternsafaris.com; s/d incl breakfast US$600/780; ☎) Although still under construction when we visited, there was no doubting the eventual luxury of this new 12-room hotel. All rooms share excellent views over the valley and the goemba – even

WESTERN BHUTAN PHOBJIKHA VALLEY

HIKING THE PHOBJIKHA VALLEY

There's some great hiking in the valley and surprisingly for Bhutan, it's mostly flat going! The Black-Necked Crane Information Centre suggests the following routes (you should be able to get information on these and other trails there).

A good short walk is the **Gangte Nature Trail** (1½ hours), which leads downhill from the *mani* stone wall just north of the Gangte Goemba to the Khewang Lhakhang. The trail descends to Semchubara village and continues straight at the chorten into the edge of the forest, before descending to a square chorten and the lhakhang. From here you can cross over the metal bridge to the primary school.

You could add on a half-day hike into the valley behind Khewang Lhakhang along the **Tenkhor Yuetshe Sum Trail**, linking up the villages of Gophu, Doksina and Pangsa with Jangchu Goemba in a loop back to Khewa.

Another option is the one-hour **Kilkhorthang Trail**, from the large modern lhakhang at Kingathang across the valley to the Damchoe Lhakhang, south of Tabiting. Alternatively, drive further south from Kingathang to the lovely side valley of Lawog and explore on foot from there.

The tougher half-day **Shasi La Nature Trail** leads up the valley behind Beyta school, though the trail is easier to follow from the track behind the Amankora Gangtey resort. The path leads through rhododendron forests to the village of Ramgokha, a collection of chortens at Mani Thongju and then the Shasi La pass, before descending through old-growth forest to Kalekha on the main Wangdue Phodrang road. Arrange to get picked up here and continue on to Wangdi. This is the traditional route taken by the Gangte *trulku* (reincarnated lama) and local farmers when they leave the valley for the winter. A local guide would be sensible for this route.

The Black-Necked Crane Information Centre can also show you the hike from Gangte Goemba to the **Kuenzang Chholing** retreat centre and on to the **Kumbhu Lhakhang**, a protector chapel dedicated to the ancient Bon deity Sipey Gyalmo.

the baths have postcard views. This company developed a luxury lodge in Myanmar, and just like there, it plans to introduce hot-air ballooning to the Phobjikha valley (flights only after the cranes have left for Tibet).

Amankora Gangtey　　　LUXURY HOTEL **$$$**
(☑ 442235; www.amanresorts.com; s/d full board US$1740/1860; ☎) A side road branches off 1km from just below the goemba to this top-of-the-line lodge. The eight rooms are identical to Thimphu's Amankora and the dramatic picture windows, spa massage and excellent service won't disappoint.

CHHUKHA DZONGKHAG

Unless making an overland crossing to or from India, most Western travellers tend to give Chhukha Dzongkhag a wide berth. For those who insist on taking the land route, the district effectively consists of the winding road that drops from the mountains through the lush tropical foothills of southern Bhutan to Phuentsholing, a boom town on the international border; Jaigaon, its twin settlement, is on the other side. It's a dramatic road trip and it gives you a sense of geographical continuity that flying into Paro doesn't. En route, you'll pass gigantic 'Lost World' ferns that spill onto the road and dozens of silver-threaded waterfalls, cascading off high cliffs into the mist.

Most of this road is a winding and treacherous 1.5-lane highway, regularly blocked for road-widening works. You may want to point out to your driver the superbly cheesy Indian signboards that bear cautionary lines such as 'Speed is the knife that kills life', 'Speed thrills but kills' and 'Impatient on Road, patient of Hospital'!

Thimphu to Phuentsholing

172KM / 5 HOURS

The downhill journey from Thimphu to Phuentsholing follows the first highway in Bhutan, built in 1962 by Dantak, the Indian border-roads organisation. It's still the most important road in the country, and is constantly being widened and improved – you'll meet road crews toiling away on several stretches. Before the highway, this journey could take up to 10 days.

The first stage of the trip is from Thimphu to Chhuzom (31km, 40 minutes). See p91 for a description of this section.

Chhuzom to Chapcha

23KM / 20 MINUTES

A wide two-lane expressway connects Thimphu to Watsa, about 10km from Chapcha. It follows the Wang Chhu valley southward; you can see the road to Haa climbing on the opposite side of the valley. Passing beneath **Dobji Dzong**, which sits atop a promontory high above the river, the road crosses the settlement of Hebji Damchu (2020m). The Chapcha bypass, under construction at the time of writing, should hopefully be finished by the time you read this. But for now the road starts climbing away from the river from tiny Hotel Damchu, making several switchbacks out of the valley.

Finally, the road crests a ridge and passes the **Chapcha Bjha** (Chapcha Rocks) as you squeeze between a vertical rock face to the left and an equally vertical sheer drop to the right. Cross the Chapcha La to reach the Dantak road construction camp at Chapcha (2450m).

Chapcha to Chhukha

34KM / 1 HOUR

Driving out of Chapcha, you can see the dramatic **Thadra Ney Lhakhang**, built into a rock face on a cliff far above to the right. The road switchbacks steeply down through forests to the Tachhong Zam (Most Excellent High Bridge) and the immigration check-post at Tanalung. Another 10km down a forested slope is Bunakha (2270m), where the **Tourist Hotel Bunagu** (☑08-460522; set meal Nu 300) caters to travellers who have booked in advance, and has pleasant balcony seating.

From Bunakha, the road passes a lovely waterfall to the goemba of **Chhukha Rabdey**. A few kilometres further on, in the lower part of Tsimasham (formerly Chimakothi; 2210m), is the new **Chhukha Dzong**, consecrated in 2012 by the Je Khenpo, as the new home for *dzongkhag's* administration and *rabdey* (district monk body). The new dzong shares with old dzongs an imposing presence; however, the external walls are perforated with large windows rather than narrow slits for defensive firing. Its tsechu is celebrated on the seventh to 10th days of the ninth Buddhist month, in March or April.

The road now switchbacks down to the **Chhukha hydroelectric project**. The air gets thicker and warmer, and several side roads lead down to the massive dam site at the valley floor. Beyond the basic Deki Hotel & Bar is the **Thegchen Zam** (Strong High Bridge), which takes the road west of the Wang Chhu. This is the midpoint between Thimphu and Phuentsholing, both around 95km away.

Chhukha to Gedu

38KM / 1 HOUR

The road climbs to a lookout over the Chhukha project, beyond which is the first of several roads leading to the 1020MW

Tala hydroelectric project. This road leads 8.5km to the intake structure where water is diverted into a 22km-long tunnel. From the lookout, you can see the transformers and the transmission station, and beside the distribution station is the yellow-roofed Zangto Pelri Lhakhang and the old Chhukha Dzong. The two projects meet the entire power demand of Western Bhutan, with enough surplus to export to India. The Dam View Restaurant at Wangkha has a Tourist & VIP Room, with great views into the valley as well as self-serve spicy food such as chilli chicken and rice (Nu 150).

The rest of the climb is over the ridge that separates the Wang Chhu valley from the Torsa Chhu drainage. Look out for the spectacular high waterfall visible to the east across the valley. Up ahead is a short bridge over what's left of Toktokachhu Falls (Takti Chhu), much diminished after a flood brought down a collection of huge boulders.

Atop the next ridge, at 2020m, is a Dantak canteen, selling Indian fare such as *masala dosa*, and sweet milky tea. It also has public toilets (the ones to the right are for 'officers only'). Beyond a second road to the Tala project is a road-crew camp at Makaibari (Cornfield). Then comes Asinabari (Field of Hailstones) and the small settlement of **Chasilakha** (*la kha* means 'grazing field'). About 9km before Gedu is the *shedra* of Tsatse Lhakhang.

Another climb leads to Gedu, a biggish highway town with several small restaurants. The best bet for a meal in Gedu is the **Lhamu Restaurant & Bar** (☑05-272332) at the south end of town, with great Nepali-style food and well-brewed tea. The nearby Laptshakha Lhakhang has some new murals.

Beyond Gedu, a side road leads downhill to Mirching and the Tala power station, and rejoins the Phuentsholing road just north of Rinchending. It's open to traffic, though usually only used if landslides or roadworks block the main highway.

Gedu to Rinchending

41KM / 1¼ HOURS

A short distance from Gedu is **Jumja** village at 2050m. Around a sharp bend is the huge Jumja slide that often wipes away the road during the monsoon, holding up traffic for days on end. Passing the Kuenga Chholing Lhakhang in the village of Kamji, the road turns a corner and begins to drop like a stone all the way down to the plains.

At **Sorchen**, a road construction camp houses workers who continually repair damage from landslides. A diversion ('bye pass') was built in 2001 to provide a way around roadblocks, and a new road from Jumja to Phuentsholing via Pasakha is being readied to provide a short cut around this volatile section.

From here, it's 12km past an industrial area and an army camp to the checkpoint at Rinchending. You will pick up an entry or exit stamp here, depending on which way you're headed. Just above the checkpoint is the **Peling Resort** (☏77100865; www.peling resort.com; Rinchending; s/d Nu 2300/2875, ste Nu 4025; ❈☎), an alternative to staying down in dusty Phuentsholing.

Rinchending to Phuentsholing

5KM / 15 MINUTES

If you are heading into Bhutan, Rinchending is the last place to invest in perishable rations such as fruit. As you proceed, the prices rise almost as quickly as the altitude does.

Below Rinchending is the small **Kharbandi Goemba**, built in 1967 by the late Royal Grandmother Ashi Phuentso Choedron, who had a winter residence here. The modern temple houses large statues of Sakyamuni, the Zhabdrung and Guru Rinpoche. In the lush grounds there are examples of eight different styles of Tibetan chortens.

Below Kharbandi, the road switchbacks down to Phuentsholing, offering spectacular views over the Torsa Chhu valley as it spills onto the plains.

Phuentsholing

☏05

The small, sweltering border town of Phuentsholing sits opposite the much larger Indian bazaar town of Jaigaon, separated by a flimsy fence and the much-photographed Bhutan Gate. It's a congested, noisy settlement bustling with hordes of traders, security personnel and migrant riff-raff. Coming from India, however, you will notice an instantaneous improvement in municipal cleanliness and organisation. Unless it's absolutely necessary to halt for the night, you'll find little reason to linger in Phuentsholing apart from clearing immigration. The air here is thick with vehicular pollution, and the infrastructure quite utilitarian. Besides, it can get uncomfortably hot and clammy in summer.

◉ Sights

★ **Zangto Pelri Lhakhang** BUDDHIST, TEMPLE
(☉dawn-dusk) The modern Zangto Pelri Lhakhang is a replica of Guru Rinpoche's celestial abode, though we're guessing the original isn't made of concrete! There's not much to see here, but the surrounding garden is pleasant and the pilgrims spinning prayer wheels offer some photo ops.

Crocodile Breeding Centre ZOO
(SAARC national/adult Nu 20/50; ☉9am-5pm) Got an hour to kill? Perhaps go and snooze with the sleepy marsh muggers and gharials at the Crocodile Breeding Centre, a 10-minute walk north of the bus station. The crocs are fed every other day at noon.

⊨ Sleeping & Eating

The following hotels are all Tourism Council of Bhutan (TCB) approved, and have rooms with private bathrooms. Apart from approved hotels, Phuentsholing also has numerous small hotels with a limited number of air-con rooms, which fill up quickly with Indian businesspeople and travellers. The main hotels all have good restaurants, tossing up palatable Indian, Bhutanese, continental and Chinese fare.

Centennial Hotel 2008 HOTEL $
(☏251663; centennial_hotel@yahoo.com; Phuensum Lam, Lower Market; s/d/ste Nu 1430/1650/2200; ❈☎) The Centennial, in the lower section of town, fits somewhere between a local hotel and a tourist hotel and is used by several agents. Rooms are simple and clean, and the multicuisine restaurant and bar is cool and welcoming. The lift is switched on when needed.

Hotel Sinchula HOTEL $
(☏252589; www.hotelsinchula.com; Phuensum Lam; s/d from Nu 1026/1146, with air-con Nu 2100/2700; ❈) Preferred mainly by local and Indian travellers, this oldish establishment located next to a grand peepul tree has clean, tiled rooms with hot-water bathrooms. Its best feature is the rooftop restaurant and bar where you can grab a cold beer and try a chicken and veg sizzler (Nu 250) accompanied by either rice or fries. Lots of stairs though!

Hotel Peljorling HOTEL $
(☏252833; Zhung Lam; s/d from Nu 450/510, deluxe d Nu 900) The Peljorling has clean but basic rooms lacking air-con, which can be

Phuentsholing

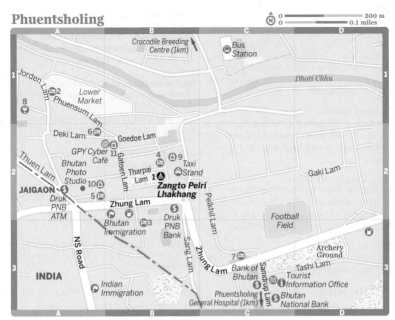

a put-off during summer. However, it scores with its excellent restaurant that tosses up delectable sizzlers and Indian and Bhutanese food. The front restaurant specialises in vegetarian Indian, while the separate rear kitchen serves meaty Bhutanese dishes.

Hotel Namgay HOTEL $

(☑252374; hotel_namgay@yahoo.com; Tharpai Lam; s/d from Nu 1210/1430, ste Nu 2145; ☀) Overlooking the Zangto Pelri Lhakhang, the Namgay is pleasant, with air-con, tropical plants in the lobby and money-exchange services. The reception has helpful staff, which is especially welcome after a tiring road trip.

★ Hotel Druk HOTEL $$

(☑252426; www.drukhotels.com; Zhung Lam; s/d from Nu 3240/3840, ste Nu 8400; ☀ ☎) The Druk is the best hotel in town, boasting comfortable, tastefully furnished rooms spread out around a manicured lawn with garden seating. It's in a secluded spot set well back from the busy road, behind the customs and immigration office. There's a bar and the multicuisine restaurant is the town's finest, serving delicious Indian food.

Lhaki Hotel HOTEL $$

(☑257111; lhakihotel@druknet.bt; Pelkhil Lam; s/d from Nu 2300/2875, ste from Nu 3680; ☎)

Phuentsholing

A modern hotel with clean and spacious rooms built around a bright and airy lobby. The entrance is off a lane in the upper quarters of town, but the back rooms overlook the noisy main road. Be sure to request a nonsmoking room. Other draws include a restaurant with good Indian and quasi-Chinese dishes, and a massage parlour. Booking is advised as many travel agents lodge their groups here.

🔒 Shopping

Phuentsholing has the cheapest consumer goods in Bhutan and many Bhutanese and Indians come here especially on shopping trips. It's also one of the cheapest places to have a *gho* or *kira* (traditional dress for men and women) made.

Bhimraj Stores   FABRIC
Located in the bazaar, here you can buy a range of cloth from Nu200 to Nu400 per metre; you'll need about 4m for a *gho* or *kira*.

Druk Carpet Industries   CARPETS
(📋 252004; ⊙ 9am-8pm Wed-Mon) The factory is north of the town, but this showroom is the place if you are looking to buy. A 46cm by 122cm carpet costs around US$450.

DSB Books   BOOKS
(📋 251898; Gechu Shopping Mall; ⊙ 9am-9pm) Sells novels, newspapers and books on Bhutan.

🍷 Drinking

For a bottle of cold beer (Nu 80), park yourself on the terrace of Hotel Peljorling, with traffic crawling below, or stargaze on the roof terrace of the Hotel Sinchula. The garden bar at the Hotel Green Valley (Jorden Lam) is a good place to get some peace and quiet.

ℹ Information

All the banks will swap Bhutanese ngultrums for Indian rupees, and vice versa. Indian rupees can be used freely in Bhutan, but in bills not exceeding Rs100.

Bank of Bhutan (Samdrup Lam; ⊙ 9am-1pm Mon-Fri, to 11am Sat) Changes foreign currency, including travellers cheques. Has an ATM.

Bhutan National Bank (Samdrup Lam; ⊙ 9am-4pm Mon-Fri, to 11am Sat) Deals in foreign currency.

Bhutan Photo Studio (Gatoen Lam) One of several studios for instant passport photos (Nu 100).

Druk PNB Bank (Zhung Lam; ⊙ 9am-3pm Mon-Fri, to 11am Sat) Changes money and offers limited ATM services.

GPY Cyber Café (per hour Nu 40; ⊙ 9am-9pm) Printing, photocopying and long-distance calls also possible. Behind the Gechu Shopping Mall.

Phuentsholing General Hospital (📋 254825) A 50-bed hospital equipped with a modern lab, operating theatres and a casualty department.

Post office (Samdrup Lam; ⊙ 9am-5pm Mon-Fri, to 1pm Sat) Next to the Bank of Bhutan on a hill above town.

ℹ Getting There & Away

Transport companies such as Dhug, Metho, Pelyab and Sernya run morning Coaster minibuses from the bus station to Thimphu (Nu 210, seven hours) and Paro (Nu 200, six hours), with a few weekly services to Haa (Nu 245, nine hours), Wangdue Phodrang and Punakha (both Nu 400, 10 hours). There are early-morning minibuses to Siliguri (Nu 80, four hours) but these aren't really set up for foreigners, and you would have to detour via immigration en route. Bhutan Post has one 3pm bus to Kolkata (India; Nu 550, 18 hours), but it might cost you an additional slipped disc or two.

Central Bhutan

Off the Beaten Track

➡ Shingkhar (p132)

➡ Chhume (p117)

➡ Zhemgang (p133)

➡ Royal Manas National Park (p135)

➡ Luege Rowe (p127)

Best Views

➡ Trongsa viewpoint (p114)

➡ Tower of Trongsa Royal Heritage Museum (p116)

➡ Jakar Dzong (p120)

➡ Pelseling Goemba (p126)

➡ Kunzangdrak Goemba (p131)

Why Go?

Central Bhutan's forested mountains and fertile valleys comprise the country's cultural heartland. The region boasts several of Bhutan's oldest and most significant temples and monasteries, dozens of great day hikes and several spectacular festivals.

Across the 3420m-high Pele La and the Black Mountains is the magnificent and historically important Trongsa Dzong, commanding the junction of three major roads. From Trongsa, a short, steep drive over the Yotong La (3425m) leads to the four valleys of Bumthang, a magical region of saints and treasure-seekers, great demon-subduing struggles and fabulous miracles, rich with relics, hermitages and sacred sites from the visits of Guru Rinpoche and Pema Lingpa.

Central Bhutan sees fewer tourists than western Bhutan, though Bumthang's new airport looks set to change this. To really get off the beaten track head south to Zhemgang to visit remote village lhakhangs and the almost unexplored Royal Manas National Park.

When to Go

➡ Central Bhutan, particularly the fertile valleys of Bumthang, is a year-round destination: pleasant in summer, and ideal in spring (especially for the rhododendron displays on the mountain passes) and autumn.

➡ Winters can be cold, especially in Bumthang, but days are normally sunny and there are few tourists – just bring some warm clothes and don't be surprised if the passes are closed by snow for a day or two.

➡ Ideally you should time your visit to include at least one of the colourful and fascinating festivals, such as at Ura, Trongsa Dzong, Jampey Lhakhang or Kurjey Lhakhang.

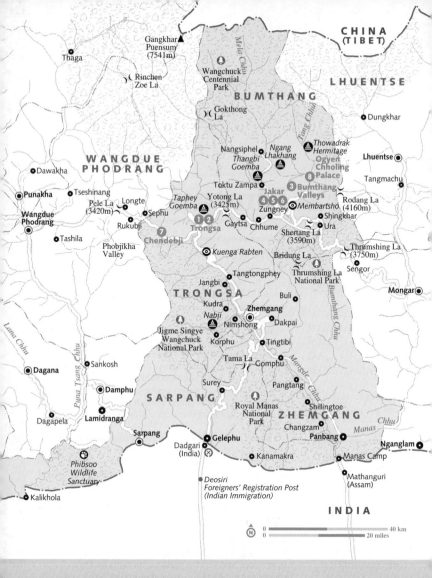

Central Bhutan Highlights

① Explore sprawling **Trongsa Dzong** (p114), a dramatic example of traditional Bhutanese architecture

② Discover the heritage of Trongsa at the **Tower of Trongsa Royal Heritage Museum** (p116)

③ Take one of many hikes in the **Bumthang valleys** (p126)

④ Wander around the **Kurjey Lhakhang** (p127) complex, a legacy of Guru Rinpoche

⑤ Visit one of Bhutan's oldest and most significant temples at **Jampey Lhakhang** (p124)

⑥ Circumambulate **Tamshing Goemba** (p129) wearing a cloak of chainmail made by Pema Lingpa

⑦ Pause for a picnic at **Chendebji Chorten** (p113), patterned after Swayambhunath in Kathmandu

⑧ Detour up the Tang valley to the superb museum of the 100-year-old **Ogyen Chholing Palace** (p131)

History

Central Bhutan is believed to be the first part of Bhutan to have been inhabited, with evidence of prehistoric settlements in the Ura valley of Bumthang and the southern region of Khyeng (around Zhemgang). These and many other valleys were separate principalities ruled by independent kings. One of the most important of these kings was the 8th-century Indian Sindhu Raja of Bumthang, who was eventually converted to Buddhism by Guru Rinpoche. Bumthang continued to be a separate kingdom, ruled from Jakar, until the time of Zhabdrung Ngawang Namgyal in the 17th century.

During the rule of the first *desi* (secular ruler), Tenzin Drugyey, all of eastern Bhutan came under the control of the Drukpa government in Punakha. Chhogyel Mingyur Tenpa unified central and eastern Bhutan into eight provinces known as Shachho Khorlo Tsegay. He was then promoted to Trongsa *penlop* (governor). Because of Trongsa Dzong's strategic position, the *penlop* exerted great influence over the entire country. It was from Trongsa that Jigme Namgyal, father of the first king, rose to power.

Bumthang retained its political importance during the rule of the first and second kings, both of whom had their principal residence at Wangdichholing Palace in Jakar. Several impressive royal residences and country estates remain in the region, including at Kuenga Rabten, Eundu Chholing and Ogyen Chholing.

TRONGSA DZONGKHAG

Wangdue Phodrang to Trongsa

129KM / 5 HOURS

The route between the windswept town of Wangdi (Wangdue Phodrang's colloquial name), in western Bhutan, and Trongsa crosses the Black Mountains over the Pele La (3420m) before entering the broad, heavily cultivated Mangde Chhu valley.

Pele La to Chendebji

27KM / 1 HOUR

From Pele La the road drops through hillsides carpeted with a strange dwarf bamboo called *cham*. This bamboo never gets large enough to harvest for any useful purpose, but when it is small it is a favourite food of yaks and horses. The area near Pele La is one place you might see grazing yaks from the road.

The road drops into the evergreen forests of the Longte valley, passing below the high village of Longte. Nine kilometres from the pass, the cosy Tushita Cafe (☑17608153; Kemepokto village; set breakfast/lunch Nu 250/390) offers fine valley views and a good lunch stop or early breakfast for birders.

Lower down into the valley the vegetation changes to multihued broadleaved species and bamboo. The road passes opposite Rukubji village, with its large school and goemba at the end of a huge alluvial fan believed to be the body of a giant snake. The houses in this village are clustered closely together, an unusual layout for Bhutan. Surrounding the village are extensive fields of mustard, potatoes, barley and wheat.

About 16km from the pass keep an eye out on the left for the roadside rock inscription and mural that was left here in 2002 for the filming of the Bhutanese movie *Travellers and Magicians*. After the Buddhist blessing come the words 'Scene 112, take 101'!

After 1km the road enters a side valley and drops to Sephu (2610m), also known as Chazam, next to the bridge that spans the Nikka Chhu. This is the end point of the epic 24-day Snowman trek through the remote Lunana district. You could stop briefly to examine the woven bamboo mats and baskets for sale here, though most of the products are functional items. The larger baskets, called *zhim,* are tied to horses' pack saddles to transport goods. The lodge-style Norbu Yangphel Restaurant (☑02-441844; set lunch Nu 380), just above the village, offers a good lunch stop and a chance to sample some local *juru jaju* (river moss soup).

The road follows the Nikka Chhu to two chortens that mark the river's confluence with the Nyala Chhu. It is then a gentle, winding descent through rhododendrons, blue pines, spruces, oaks and dwarf bamboo to the village of Chendebji, recognisable by the yellow roof of its lhakhang, on the far bank. This was a night halt for mule caravans travelling from Trongsa during the reign of the second king.

Two kilometres beyond Chendebji village is Chendebji Chorten, at a lovely spot by a river confluence. The large white chorten is patterned after Swayambhunath in Kathmandu and was built in the 19th century by Lama Shida, from Tibet, to cover the remains of an evil spirit that was killed here. The proper name of this structure is Chorten Charo Kasho; it is the westernmost monument in a 'chorten path' that was the route of early Buddhist missionaries. The nearby Bhutanese-style chorten was constructed in 1982.

Just 500m past the chorten is Chendebji Resort (☑ 03-440004; r Nu 2160-2880, set meal breakfast/lunch/dinner Nu 200/300/350), a popular lunch spot and gift shop run by the owner of the Dochu La Resort, who is a renowned artist. The riverside rooms have private bathrooms, some with tubs, and beds with soft mattresses.

Chendebji to Trongsa

41KM / 1¼ HOURS

From Chendebji Chorten the road passes a few farms, crosses a side stream and climbs again to a ridge, passing above the village of Tangsibi. The valley widens and the road turns a corner into the broad Mangde Chhu valley. The shrubs along this part of the road are edgeworthia, which is used to make paper. The brown monkeys you will probably see are rhesus macaques.

At Tashiling village you'll see Tashichholing Lhakhang, home to the Gayrab Arts and Crafts Training Institute. Inside is an impressive 9m-tall statue of Chaktong Chentong, a thousand-armed version of Chenresig (Avalokiteshvara, the Bodhisattva of Compassion). The particularly fine murals were painted by the 40 monks who study here as part of a six-year course in traditional monastic arts.

Further along the road you can see the pretty nearby village of Tsangkha, whose large *shedra* (Buddhist college) specialises in astrology.

After the road weaves in and out of side valleys you finally get a view of Trongsa and the imposing whitewashed dzong that seems to hang in the air at the head of the valley. A viewpoint next to a small chorten in the centre of the road offers a good place for a photo stop and cup of tea from the Viewpoint Restaurant (breakfast/lunch Nu 200/300; ☺ 7am-7pm) underneath the viewing platform. The dzong looks almost close enough to touch but it is still a 14km drive away. From here you can walk to the dzong on the Mangdue Foot Trail, a two-hour

track that drops steeply down to a traditional *baa zam* (cantilevered bridge) over the Mangde Chhu before ascending equally steeply to the western gate of the dzong. Your driver will need to drive ahead to the dzong so that the western gate will be unlocked for your arrival.

Above the viewpoint and road, accessed by a short but slippery driveway, the sprawling and somewhat overblown Raven Crown Resort (☑ 77190799; www.ravencrownresort.com; s/d Nu 4320/5700, ste Nu 5700/7140) offers a top-end alternative to staying in Trongsa town. The 33 spacious rooms are spread across multiple blocks and a spa and swimming pool are planned.

To reach Trongsa, you make a huge detour into the upper reaches of the Mangde Chhu valley, cross the raging river at the Bjee Zam checkpost, and then climb again above the north bank of the river, past a waterfall and the Yangkhil Resort, before pulling into town.

Trongsa

☑ 03 / ELEV 2180M

Trongsa is smack in the middle of the country, set at the strategic junction of roads to Punakha, Bumthang and Zhemgang but separated from both east and west by high mountain ranges. The dzong and surrounding town is perched above a gorge, with fine views of the Black Mountains to the southwest. It's a sleepy and pleasant town, lined with traditional whitewashed shops decorated with pot plants. The town received a large influx of Tibetan immigrants in the late 1950s and early 1960s, and Bhutanese of Tibetan descent run most shops here.

◉ Sights

The main road from the west traverses above the dzong and passes the small weekend vegetable market and tiny Thruepang Palace (closed to visitors), where the third king, Jigme Dorji Wangchuck, was born in 1928. A traffic circle by the centre of town marks the junction of the road south to Gelephu. A short walk along this road offers excellent views of the dzong.

★ Trongsa Dzong   BUDDHIST, DZONG
(☑ 521220; ☺ 8am-5pm, until 4pm in winter) This commanding dzong, high above the roaring Mangde Chhu, is perhaps the most spectac-

ularly sited dzong in Bhutan, with a sheer drop to the south that often just disappears into cloud and mist.

Trongsa Dzong has a rich history dating back to the 16th century. The first construction on the site was carried out by Ngagi Wangchuck (1517–54), the great-grandfather of Zhabdrung Ngawang Namgyal. He came to Trongsa in 1541 and built a *tshamkhang* (small meditation room) after discovering self-manifested hoof prints belonging to the horse of the protector deity Pelden Lhamo. Trongsa ('New Village' in the local dialect) gets its name from the retreats, temples and hermit residences that soon grew up around the chapel.

The rambling assemblage of buildings that comprises the dzong trails down the ridge and is connected by a succession of alley-like corridors, wide stone stairs and beautiful paved courtyards. The southernmost part of the dzong, Chorten Lhakhang, is the location of the first hermitage, built in 1543. The dzong was built in its present form in 1644 by Chhogyel Mingyur Tenpa, the official who was sent by the Zhabdrung to bring eastern Bhutan under central control. It was then enlarged at the end of the 17th century by the *desi*, Tenzin Rabgye. Its official name is Chhoekhor Raptentse Dzong, and it is also known by its short name of Choetse Dzong. The dzong was severely damaged in the 1897 earthquake, and repairs were carried out by the *penlop* of Trongsa, Jigme Namgyal, father of Bhutan's first king.

Trongsa Dzong is closely connected to the royal family. The first two hereditary kings ruled from this dzong, and tradition still dictates that the crown prince serve as Trongsa *penlop* before acceding to the throne.

The dzong's strategic location gave it great power over this part of the country. The only trail between eastern and western Bhutan still leads straight through Trongsa and used to run directly through the dzong itself. This gave the Trongsa *penlop* enviable control over east–west trade and the considerable tax revenue to be derived from it. Today most visitors enter through the main eastern gate, but energetic types can make the steep cardio hike on the Mangdue Foot Trail from the viewpoint and enter the dzong via the western gate, in traditional fashion.

The Trongsa *rabdey* (district monk body) migrates between winter (Trongsa) and summer (Bumthang) residences, just as the

Trongsa

main *dratshang* (central monk body) does between Thimphu and Punakha.

There are 23 separate lhakhangs in the dzong, though what you get to see depends on which keys are available. Most of the existing fine decoration was designed during the rule of the first king, Ugyen Wangchuck.

Rooms to visit include the atmospheric northern **assembly hall** and the southern

Mithrub Lhakhang, which houses the funerary chorten of the founder, Ngagi Wangchuck. Feel for the footprints worn into the wooden floor by one overly enthusiastic prostrator.

The five-day Trongsa tsechu is held in the northern courtyard in December or January and culminates in the unveiling of a large *tongdrol* (a giant *thangka* – a painted or embroidered religious picture). To the side of the dzong is the archery ground and pavilion where the current king (then crown prince) was crowned *penlop* in 2004.

★ **Tower of Trongsa**
Royal Heritage Museum   MUSEUM
(admission Nu 200; ⊙9am-5pm Mon-Sat Apr-May, until 4pm Nov-Mar) This watchtower (Ta Dzong) on the hill above the dzong has been converted into an excellent museum by the same Austrian-financed team that renovated the wonderful Patan Museum in Nepal. The five floors of displays focus on Buddhist art and royal memorabilia, including such varied treasures as the 500-year-old jacket of Ngagi Wangchuk and the football boots used by the teenaged fourth king. The most sacred religious item is a copy of the *Padma Kathang*, a biography of Guru Rinpoche written by his consort Yeshe Tshogyel.

There are two lhakhangs inside the Ta Dzong; the Gesar Lhakhang is dedicated to the 19th-century *penlop* of Trongsa, Jigme Namgyal. Two British soldiers are said to have been kept in the dungeon here for several months during the Duar War. There are sweeping views from the roof, and a cafe on the ground floor provides refreshments (and lunch by prior arrangement).

You can drive here or walk up a staircase from town via two charming, semicircular tower-chapels.

🛏 Sleeping & Eating

Tashi Ninjay Guest House   HOTEL **$**
(☑521531; tashininjay@gmail.com; s/d Nu 1955/2185; 🐾) The views of the dzong are superb from this inn so make sure you get one of the upper-floor rooms with a balcony. Rooms are comfortable, the staff are super friendly and it's the only tourist-grade hotel in the town itself.

Norling Hotel   LOCAL **$**
(☑521171; s/d Nu 1430/1760) This concrete local inn in the bazaar is a good place for lunch and it serves cold Red Panda beer.

The nine upstairs wooden-floored rooms are decent and come with private bathrooms, catering to a mix of locals and visiting NGO staff.

Yangkhil Resort   HOTEL **$$**
(☑521417; www.yangkhil.bt; s/d Nu 3117/3399, deluxe Nu 4054/4428; 🐾) This resort, 1.5km west of town, is a good choice, with 21 rooms constructed in five blocks on a terraced hill facing the dzong. All rooms are spacious and cosy with heating, a balcony and extremely comfortable beds (but no TV). The pleasant grounds, vistas and excellent restaurant make it a great place to relax, so arrange your itinerary to ensure an early arrival or late departure. Request an upper-floor room with a view.

Puenzhi Guest House   HOTEL **$$**
(☑521197; puenzhi@druknet.bt; s/d Nu 2200/2750, deluxe Nu 2750/3300; 🐾) A 4km drive high above the town leads to this place, run by the former governor of Trongsa. The deluxe rooms are the best – airy and spacious with eagle-eye views down to the Ta Dzong, Trongsa Dzong and the Black Mountains. The older rooms are smaller but still cosy and have the same great balcony views. The restaurant balcony is the perfect place for a sunset beer, while more active types can follow the footpath below the hotel directly down to the Ta Dzong.

Oyster House   BHUTANESE **$**
(☑521413; mains Nu 130) This popular restaurant boasts cosy sofa seating and a sunny terrace overlooking the main strip, along with a changing weekly menu of Bhutanese dishes. Pride of place goes to the full-size snooker table, which accounts for Oyster's popularity with Trongsa's teens.

🛍 Shopping

Phuntsho Wangmo Bhutanese Handicraft & General Shop   HANDICRAFTS
(⊙8am-7pm) Phuntsho stocks a small selection of hand-woven textiles, masks and jewellery alongside its less exotic bakery goods.

ℹ Information

Bank of Bhutan (⊙9am-3pm Mon-Fri, 9am-11am Sat) You need a photocopy of the cheque to change travellers cheques here.

Bhutan National Bank (⊙9am-3pm Mon-Fri, 9am-11am Sat)

Post Office (⊙8.30am-5pm Mon-Fri, 8.30am-1pm Sat)

Around Trongsa

Kuenga Rabten

The winter palace of the second king, Jigme Wangchuck, is 23km (one hour) south of Trongsa. It's an interesting drive, passing below Takse Goemba (after 17km), several huge waterfalls, and the fertile rice terraces of the lower Mangde Chhu valley. It's a good half-day or three-quarter-day trip from Trongsa and could even make for a fine bike trip if you can arrange to be picked up at Kuenga Rabten. Traffic is light and it's all downhill from Trongsa!

The palace is under the care of the National Commission for Cultural Affairs (NCCA), so you don't need a special permit to enter. The 1st storey of the U-shaped building was used to store food; the second was the residence of royal attendants and the army; and the third housed the royal quarters and the king's private chapel. Part of this floor has been converted into a library, and books from the National Library are stored here. Sandwiched between the king's and queen's quarters is the Sangye Lhakhang, with statues of Sakyamuni Buddha, the Zhabdrung and Guru Rinpoche.

A 15-minute hike or drive uphill from the building is the **Karma Drubdey Nunnery**, which is currently being expanded by its hard-working *anim* (Buddhist nuns).

A further 25km down the valley is **Eundu Chholing**, the winter palace of the first king, Ugyen Wangchuck. From Kuenga Rabten the road drops down in huge loops, past Refey village to the river and road camp at Yourmu, and then 2km later branches up a dirt road to the palace. The building belongs to a local Dasho (nobleman) but is looked after by the *dzongpen* (lord of the dzong), and tourists can normally visit. The 2nd-floor *goenkhang* (chapel devoted to protective deities; men only) has a highly venerated chorten of Pema Lingpa, as well as a fabulous collection of arms and a lovely *drangyen* (lute). The entry chapel has some of the finest murals you'll see, depicting the mythical kingdoms of Zangto Pelri and Sukhavati.

Taphey Goemba

If you have a spare day in Trongsa, are delayed for some reason or really want to get off the beaten track, consider exploring the hillside north of Trongsa. From Trongsa take the farm road north to Yuling village and lhakhang to start an adventurous day hike up to the *drubdey* (meditation retreat) of Taphey Goemba. A further hour's hike uphill takes you to the ridgeline for fine Himalayan views north all the way to Gangkhar Puensum.

BUMTHANG DZONGKHAG

The Bumthang region encompasses four major valleys: Chokhor, Tang, Ura and Chhume. Because the dzongs and the most important temples are in the large Chokhor valley, it is commonly referred to as the Bumthang valley. A helpful map to refer to is the Bumthang Cultural & Duer Hot Springs map on p181.

There are two versions of the origin of the name Bumthang. The valley is supposed to be shaped like a *bumpa*, the vessel of holy water that is usually found on the altar of a lhakhang. *Thang* means 'field' or 'flat place'. The less respectful translation relates to the particularly beautiful women who live here – *bum* means 'girl'.

Trongsa to Jakar

68KM / 2½ HOURS

The run between Trongsa and Jakar, the main town in Bumthang, is one of the easier and more interesting drives in Bhutan because it passes numerous villages and goembas as it winds through the Chhume valley. With stops you could easily fill an entire day on this lovely drive.

Trongsa to Yotong La

28KM / 1 HOUR

The road zigzags up the ridge above Trongsa, climbing steeply past the Puenzhi Guest House and the cremation ground at Dorji Goemba, to reach the head of the valley. Finally the road traverses the top of the valley to a Tibetan chorten and an array of prayer flags atop the **Yotong La** (3425m). The old trade route to eastern Bhutan parallels the modern road as it crosses the pass.

Yotong La to Zungney

24KM / 1 HOUR

The descent from the pass is through firs, then blue pines and bamboo. The road enters the upper part of the Chhume valley, marked by the small roadside Chuchi Lhakhang at Gaytsa (Gyatsa). On a hill a few hundred metres to the north of Gaytsa is the Nyingma school **Buli Lhakhang**, built by Tukse Chhoying, the son of Dorji Lingpa (1346–1405) and recently renovated with assistance from the American Himalayan Foundation (see www.ahf-bhutan.com for details). On the ground floor is the Jowo Lhakhang, with a lovely seated Jampa (Maitreya; future Buddha) and some impressive 12-sided pillars *(kachens)*. On the upper floor is the Sangye (Sangay) Lhakhang, named after images of the past, present and future Buddhas. The mural by the window depicts Dorji Lingpa. As you climb the stairwell to this upper storey look for a slate carving of the local protective deity, Yoebar Drakpo. The three-day Buli tsechu in February kicks off with an evening *mewang* (fire ceremony connected to fertility rites) that dates back to pre-Buddhist times. A few black-necked cranes winter in the fields to the northeast of the village.

The red roofs of **Tharpaling Goemba** are visible above the trees on a cliff to the northeast. The Tibetan Nyingma (Dzogchen) philosopher and saint Longchen Rabjampa (1308–63) founded Tharpaling as part of eight *lings* (outlying temples) and lived here for many years, fathering two children. It has several temples and houses more than 100 monks who study in the attached *shedra*. It's possible to visit the goemba by driving 10km up a rough road (impassable in rain or snow) through bucolic countryside or by trekking over the hill from Jakar. The downhill makes for a good mountain-bike ride, or you could walk down to the main road via Samtenling Goemba.

Above Tharpaling, at about 3800m, is the white hermitage of **Choedrak**, which consists of two ancient chapels separated by a chorten and a sacred spring. The Thukje Lhakhang to the right has a central 1000-armed statue of Chenresig. The Lorepa Lhakhang, named after the chapel's 12th-century Tibetan founder, contains a stone footprint of Guru Rinpoche and the stone skull of a *khandroma* (*dakini*; female celestial being). Further uphill is the **Zhambhala Lhakhang**, named after the popular God of Wealth. Pilgrims ask for boons here at a set of circular grooves in the rock behind the lhakhang, which contains the surprisingly grand funeral chorten of Nyoshul Khen Rinpoche, an important Tibetan lama who died in 1999. Pema Lingpa revealed several *terma* (sacred texts and artefacts) near these monasteries.

Back on the main road, just past the Tharpaling turn-off, a bridge crosses the Gaytsa Chhu and a signposted gravel road leads off 1km to the **Chumey Nature Resort** (☎ 17114836; www.chumeynatureresort.com; s/d/ste Nu 2250/3000/4200), a relaxing rural retreat surrounded by fields and forests with numerous walking trails, including to Domkhar Dzong (30 minutes). Imported mountain bikes can be hired for fine rides around the valley. The 14 rooms are comfortable, cosy and private, set in cottages beside the main lodge, and a spa and sauna are under construction, along with four sun-facing suites. The resort even has its own lhakhang and can cater for visitors wishing to learn about Buddhism.

The main road continues down the Gaytsa Chhu valley for 2km to Domkhar. A dirt road branches south for 1km to **Domkhar Tashichholing Dzong**, the summer palace of the second king. It was completed in 1937 and is a replica of Kuenga Rabten. It served for years as the residence of the second king's wife, and is now a royal guesthouse and so the interior is closed to visitors (you can visit the courtyard). The monastic school to the south was built in 1968 by the previous reincarnation of the Karmapa, the head of the Karmapa lineage.

Beyond Domkhar village, past Hurjee, is the settlement of **Chhume**, with two large schools alongside more than 500m of straight road, perhaps the longest stretch of its kind in the hills of Bhutan. Speed bumps have been strategically placed to ensure that your driver does not take advantage of this to make up time!

Just before Zungney, at Yamthrak, a paved road branches off 3.5km to **Nimalung Goemba**, an important Nyingma monastery and *shedra* of 100 monks that was founded in 1935 by Dorling Trulku. The ground-floor inner chapel contains a venerated statue of Drolma (Tara) inside an amulet that was brought from Tibet. Walk behind the altar to see the collection of black hats used during the tsechu on the 10th day of the fifth month (around July). In front of the altar is a large metal box which holds a *thondrol* depicting the Guru Tshengye, or eight manifestations of Guru Rinpoche. The upper floor is a *goenkhang*. Outside you might catch the monks playing *khuru*, a game that is part darts, part archery. If you want to stretch your legs, a 15-minute trail leads downhill from a line of giant stupas below the main chapel to Prakhar Goemba.

Back on the main road, a short 500m walk from the Yamthrak junction leads to the **Chorten Nyingpo Lhakhang**, a timeless 16th-century chapel whose main relic is a statue of the Zhabdrung's father, Tenpa Nyima (1567–1619). In the grounds look for the white throne from which Tenpa is said to have preached for three years. Further along the main road, just before Zungney, you pass the pool of the 1.5MW Chhume mini-hydro plant, which supplies electricity to Trongsa and Bumthang.

Five minutes further, stop at the two craft shops at Zungney village to watch weavers and dyers in action. The speciality here is *yathra*, distinctive strips of woven woollen fabric in numerous colours and patterns. You can buy single strips of cloth or finished woollen jackets and blankets. Just west of the **Thokmed Yeshe Handicraft & Yathra Production Centre** (☎03-641124; ⏰6am-8pm) is the tiny Zungney Lhakhang, said by locals to have been built by Tibetan king Songtsen Gampo as one of his demoness-pinning temples. As you leave Zungney look out for the unusual two-storey prayer wheel on the right side.

Zungney to Jakar

16KM / 30 MINUTES

East of Zungney, **Prakhar Goemba** is visible on a promontory on the opposite side of the river. It's a delightful 10-minute walk to the three-storey goemba, which was built as a residence by Dawa Gyaltshen, a son of the famous Pema Lingpa. On the ground floor is a statue of Sakyamuni Buddha crafted by artists from Nepal. On the middle floor are statues of Guru Tshengye, the eight manifestations of Guru Rinpoche. The top floor contains nine small chortens and murals that are as old as the goemba. The Prakhar tsechu is held in the middle of the ninth month (October or November) at the same time as the Jampey Lhakhang Drup. Prakhar means 'White Monkey'.

The road follows the valley down past the apple orchards of Nangar and into blue-pine forests. A new bypass branches off the main road here directly to Ura. It's a short climb to the Kiki La, a crest at 2860m marked by a chorten and many prayer flags. Once over the side ridge, the road descends into the Chokhor valley.

Jakar

📍03 / ELEV 2580M

Near the foot of the Chokhor valley, Jakar (Chamkhar) is the major trading centre of the region. This will probably be your base for several days as you visit the surrounding valleys.

Jakar itself is a bustling two-street town and well worth a wander, though most of the shopfronts are new, rebuilt after three fires destroyed much of the town in 2010. As with other towns in Bhutan, Jakar plans to eventually shift location to the new town of Dekyiling, just north of the Sey Lhakhang. The new town roads are complete, but no date has been given as yet for the big move.

Bumthang's Bathpalathang airport on the east bank of the Chamkhar Chhu opened for regular flights in 2011 and looks set to open up the valley to increasing numbers of tourists.

There is a strong up-valley wind from the south every afternoon, which makes Jakar nippy in the evenings.

YATHRA

Hand-spun, hand-woven wool strips with patterns specific to the Bumthang region are called *yathras*. They mostly have geometric designs, sometimes with a border. Three strips may be joined to produce a blanket-like rain cover called a *charkep*.

In earlier days, *yathras* were often used as shawls or raincoats to protect against the winter cold of Bumthang. They were once made from wool from Tibet; nowadays some of the wool is imported from New Zealand and some wool is used from nearby Australian-supported sheep-breeding projects.

Since Bhutan does not have the carpet-weaving tradition of Tibet, *yathra* pieces have often served the same function as Tibetan rugs. Today *yathras* are fashioned into *toegos*, the short jackets that women often wear over the *kira* (women's traditional dress) in cold weather.

Jakar

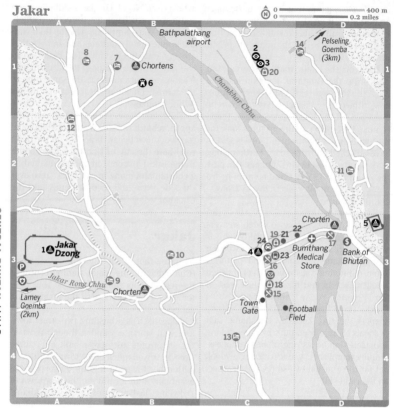

◉ Sights

A traffic circle and the 14th-century **Jakar Lhakhang** mark the centre of the town.

The main street leads east from the town centre to a bridge over the Chamkhar Chhu. Just before you cross the bridge to leave the town, a small **chorten** marks the spot where a Tibetan general's head was buried after the defeat of a 17th-century Tibetan invasion force.

★ Jakar Dzong   BUDDHIST, DZONG

According to legend, when the lamas assembled in about 1549 to select a site for a monastery, a big white bird rose suddenly in the air and settled on a spur of a hill. This was interpreted as an important omen, and the hill was chosen as the site for a monastery and for Jakar Dzong, which roughly translates as 'castle of the white bird'. The Zhabdrung's great-grandfather, Ngagi Wangchuck, founded the monastery.

Jakar Dzong is in a picturesque location overlooking the Chokhor valley. The current structure was built in 1667 and has a circumference of more than 1500m. Its official name is Yuelay Namgyal Dzong, in honour of the victory over the troops of Tibetan ruler Phuntsho Namgyal. The *utse* (central tower) is unusually situated on the outside wall, so there is no way to circumambulate it. A walled passage leads from the dzong down the hill to a nearby spring – a feature that ensured water could be obtained in the event of a long siege.

The approach to the dzong is made on foot along a stone-paved path. The entrance leads into a narrow courtyard surrounded by administrative offices. The *utse* is on the east side of the courtyard, and beyond that is the monks' quarters and the district court. At the west end of the dzong is a slightly larger courtyard surrounded by administrative offices. Behind here, outside the main dzong, is a half-round *ta dzong* (watchtower).

Jakar

⊙ Top Sights
1 Jakar Dzong A3

⊙ Sights
2 Bumthang Brewery C1
3 Cheese Factory C1
4 Jakar Lhakhang......................................C3
5 Lhodrak Kharchu Goemba D3
6 Wangdichholing Palace.......................B1

⊜ Sleeping
7 Amankora B1
8 Hotel Ugyen Ling...................................A1
9 Jakar Village Lodge...............................B3
10 Kaila Guest House B3
11 Mepham Guest House D2
12 Mountain Lodge...................................A2
13 River Lodge...C4
14 Swiss Guest House..............................D1

⊗ Eating
15 Himalayan Pizza...................................C3
16 Kinley Hotel...C3
17 Sunny Restaurant.................................D3

⊕ Shopping
18 Bumthang Handicraft Shop C3
19 Dragon Roots C3
20 Yoser Lhamo Shop C1

⊕ Transport
21 Dragon Ride..C3
22 Druk Air D3
23 Metho Transport...................................C3
24 Taxi C3

Even if the chapels are closed, it's a worthwhile climb for the views of the Chokhor valley from the front courtyard.

Wangdichholing Palace   PALACE
The extensive palace of Wangdichholing was built in 1857 on the site of a battle camp of the *penlop* of Trongsa, Jigme Namgyal. It was the first palace in Bhutan that was not designed primarily as a fortress. Namgyal's son, Ugyen Wangchuck, the first king of Bhutan, was born here and chose it as his principal residence. The entire court moved from Wangdichholing to Kuenga Rabten each winter in a procession that took three days (see the boxed text, p182). Wangdichholing was also for a time the home of the third king, before he moved the royal court to Punakha in 1952.

The grand but rather neglected building is currently used as a *lobdra* (monastic school) but the **Bhutan Foundation** (www.bhutanfound.org) has plans to renovate the building

and convert it into a museum. There are five giant prayer wheels inside square chortens just to the north. The sleek modern building next door is the Amankora resort, which some locals complain is located too close for comfort to its royal neighbour.

Lhodrak Kharchu
Goemba   BUDDHIST, MONASTERY
On the hill to the east of Jakar this large Nyingma monastery was founded in the 1970s by Namkhai Nyingpo Rinpoche and has more than 380 monks in residence. The new Tshokhang (Assembly Hall) has massive statues of Guru Rinpoche, Chenresig and Sakyamuni Buddha. If you're here between 4.30pm and 6pm (April to November), check out the mass debating in the courtyard of the *shedra,* behind the main monastery, where monks reinforce their theological arguments with a stamp of the foot and a victorious slap. Don't disturb the debates with your photography.

⚔ Festivals & Events

Bumthang has some important festivals, of which the most important is the **Jampey Lhakhang Drup**, in the ninth month (October or November). The three-day **Jakar tsechu**, a week earlier, features mask dancing in the dzong, while Tamshing, Ngang and Ura monasteries all have large festivals at other times of the year.

🛏 Sleeping

Most of Bumthang's guesthouses follow a similar design, with pine-clad rooms and separate dining rooms, and the majority are family run. More recently, large travel agencies and hoteliers have built impressive large hotels that provide unequalled luxury but lack the cosy guesthouse atmosphere. Most guesthouses and hotels have *bukhari*s (wood stoves) to heat the rooms. If you're cold, ask the room attendants to light the stove – they start it with a dollop of kerosene and a *whump*! The *bukhari*s heat the room quickly, but don't burn for very long.

🛏 Jakar

The following hotels are either in Jakar town or on the outskirts.

Kaila Guest House   HOTEL **$**
(Map p120; ☑631219; kailaguesthouse94@gmail.com; r Nu 2388; ☏) This is the closest hotel to Jakar bazaar and is a favourite of NGO

workers, who get a 20% discount on the cosy, recently renovated rooms. The owner was the cook at the Swiss Guest House for many years, so the food is very good and the friendly welcome is genuine in this unpretentious establishment. The bar is a great place to plug into what's happening in Bumthang, especially as it has Red Panda beer on draught.

Mepham Guest House
GUESTHOUSE $

(Map p120; ☑631738; mephamgh@druknet.bt; r standard/deluxe Nu 2262/2400; ☎) This hidden guesthouse nestles just below the Lhodrak Kharchu Goemba, making it perfect for Buddhist practitioners headed for dawn prayers. The rooms are simple but there's a sunny restaurant terrace and the corner rooms have views across the valley to the dzong.

Swiss Guest House
HOTEL $$

(Map p120; ☑631145; www.swissguesthouse.bt; s/d Nu 2376/2398) It doesn't get more bucolic than this wooden farmhouse surrounded by apple orchards on a hill overlooking the valley. In 1983 this was the first guesthouse in Bumthang, but there have been plenty of upgrades since then. Rooms in the new wing are spacious and warm, with good beds and clean bathrooms. The cheerful bar is also one of the few places in Bhutan where you can get Red Panda beer on draught, guaranteed fresh, since it's brewed just down the road!

Jakar Village Lodge
HOTEL $$

(Map p120; ☑631242; www.bhutanlodge.com; s/d Nu 2645/2875, deluxe Nu 3220/3450; ☎) Boasting some of the best food in Bumthang, this hotel situated down a narrow village lane below the dzong is run by an ex-*dzongdag* (district administrator) who will regale you with stories as you sample his assortment of teas and freshly ground coffee. The 14 rooms are spotless and comfortable (deluxe rooms are worth the extra money), while the sunny terrace enjoys great views over the valley and up to the dzong.

Mountain Lodge
HOTEL $$

(Map p120; ☑631255; mtlodge90@gmail.com; s/d Nu 2185/2415; ☎) This cosy lodge has wood-panelled rooms in a large two-storey building overlooking Wangdichholing Palace. Friendly staff, tasty food and good rooms and bathrooms make this a very pleasant place to stay, especially now that the new deluxe block has opened, offering rooms with valley views.

Yu-Gharling Resort
HOTEL $$

(Map p125; ☑631948; www.yugharling.com; r standard/deluxe Nu 4025/4945, ste from Nu 5520; ☎) This four-star giant overlooking the valley is as enormous as it is luxurious. Rooms are massive and the views are spectacular, particularly from the seven cottages (with balconies). Though there are no TVs in the rooms, hotel facilities include a spacious bar with foosball and snooker tables, and a spa with massage, Jacuzzi and a hot-stone bath.

Hotel Ugyen Ling
HOTEL $$

(Map p120; ☑631369; www.bhutanhotels.com.bt; s/d Nu 2415/2875; ☎) Owned by one of Bhutan's biggest travel agencies, this compound is close to Wangdichholing Palace and offers above-average accommodation. Standard rooms are almost suites with their separate sitting area heated with a *bukhari* and private balcony. The small bathrooms, however, don't carry the same level of luxury. There is a decent multicuisine restaurant and a relaxing bar.

River Lodge
HOTEL $$

(Map p120; ☑631287; www.drukriverlodge.com; s/d Nu 2268/2388, deluxe from Nu 2700/3000; ☎) This popular place has a variety of rooms overlooking the valley south of town. The lodge has helpful management, a small spa that offers massage and hot-stone baths, and a bright dining room that has great valley views, good food and a warming *bukhari*. Try the homemade organic wild strawberry or plum jam. The owner also runs the rural Mesithang River Lodge in the Tang valley.

Amankora
LUXURY HOTEL $$$

(Map p120; ☑02-331333; www.amanresorts.com; s/d full board US$1744/1860; ☎) The last word in luxury in Bumthang, the sleek dzong-like Amankora sits beside Wangdichholing Palace in apple and pear orchards. Rooms are spacious with king-size beds, soaring ceilings and a central, sumptuous bathtub. Rates include all meals.

🏠 Chokhor Valley

The following hotels are outside Jakar bazaar in the surrounding Chokhor valley but still within easy reach of the town and with quiet rural locations. Several more hotels are currently under construction in the valley.

Gongkhar Guest House
HOTEL $$

(Map p125; ☑631288; tsheringgong@yahoo.com; s/d Nu 2106/2394, deluxe Nu 3600/4200; ☎)

This excellent hotel, 1.5km southeast of Jakar, has spacious, cosy and comfortable rooms with *bukhari*s and super-clean bathrooms. There's a good view of the dzong, garden seating among amazing roses and excellent service, and the food is among the best and most varied in the valley. The eight new deluxe rooms are exceptionally comfortable.

Rinchenling Lodge   HOTEL $$

(Map p125; ☑ 631147; rinchenlinglodge@gmail.com; s/d Nu 2388/2748, deluxe Nu 3600/4200, ste Nu 5400/7080; ☏) This hotel is run by amiable Dasho Jampel Ngedup and family. It has spacious rooms with quality mattresses and an excellent restaurant. Standard rooms line up among the apple trees (avoid the back rooms), and the deluxe rooms in the new block at the back come with modern bathrooms and nice balconies. The hot-stone bath is worth experiencing for its ingenious communication system.

Wangdicholing Resort   HOTEL $$

(Map p125; ☑ 631452; wangdicholingresort@druknet.bt; s/d Nu 1520/2640; ☏) This well-run resort is on a bluff overlooking the valley to the south of town. The highlight is the relaxing balcony terrace festooned with climbing flowers. Rooms are a bit old-fashioned but comfortable; the spacious corner suites are best.

Hotel Pelling   HOTEL $$

(Map p125; ☑ 631222; www.hotelpeling.com.bt; s/d Nu 2645/2875, ste Nu 4320; ☏) This lavish new hotel has huge rooms with balconies and good views, though maintenance is already an issue (most of our electrical outlets seemed to be broken). Wi-fi is patchy outside of the reception. Rooms are heated, but there are no TVs. A hot-stone bath is available.

Leki Guest House   HOTEL $$

(Map p125; ☑ 631231; lekilodge@druknet.bt; s/d Nu 2160/3000) The Leki is one of the oldest hotels in the valley, with 15 rooms in one traditional-style building. The dining room is decorated with homemade weavings for sale (the owner is an accomplished weaver) and textile buffs will enjoy the traditional dyeing demonstration (US$200 per group).

Yozerling Lodge   HOTEL $$

(Map p125; ☑ 631846; yozerling@yahoo.com; s/d Nu 2040/2160, deluxe Nu 3000/3240; ☏) This friendly, family-run place 2.5km from town certainly isn't grand and could do with a lick of paint, but the pine-clad rooms are comfortable and the new deluxe block promises

fresh rooms with valley views. The comfy sofas in the large dining hall make for cosy pre- and post-dinner drinks.

🍴 Eating

The hotels in Bumthang do a great job feeding their guests hearty local and continental food, and there's even some healthy competition among hotels in the culinary stakes. Because of the altitude, buckwheat is the crop of choice in Bumthang and buckwheat noodles *(puta)* and pancakes *(khule)* are a local speciality. The Chamkhar Chhu is also famous for its trout, and despite Buddhist prohibitions on the taking of life, fish do mysteriously appear on hotel dinner plates.

Himalayan Pizza   PIZZA $

(☑ 631437; pizza per slice Nu 45; ☺ 9am-10pm) If you need a break from hotel buffets, this local place at the south end of town produces passable cheese and tomato pizza, as well as beef or cheese *momos* (dumplings) served with a zesty carrot, tomato and chilli sauce. The owner speaks Swiss-German but little English.

Sunny Restaurant   BHUTANESE $

(☑ 17254212; mains Nu 45-90; ☺ 9am-9pm Mon-Sat) There are plenty of small bars and local restaurants along Jakar's main street, though the brightest and cleanest is Sunny Restaurant, with Bhutanese and Chinese dishes served up by a former chef from the Amankora.

Kinley Hotel   BHUTANESE $

(☑ 17681354; mains Nu 60-90) A good place to get an authentic local lunch, with pleasant window seating overlooking the main bazaar.

🛍 Shopping

As in most towns in Bhutan, the shops in Jakar contain a delicious hodgepodge of goods, from shoes, pens, nails and soap to toy cars, dried fish, prayer flags and mobile-phone vouchers. One item in good supply in Jakar is *chugo* (dried cheese). Unless you want to break your teeth, let a piece soften for a long time in your mouth before you bite into it.

Yoser Lhamo Shop   FOOD

(☑ 631193; ☺ 6am-7pm) Yoser Lhamo is the main outlet for the Swiss Farm enterprises. The shop sells Red Panda beer, apple juice, peach brandy and apple or honey wine, as well as soft Gouda or hard Emmental cheese at Nu 410 per kg. This cheese is made for eating off the block, unlike the soft Bhutanese *datse,* which is used only in sauces.

BUMTHANG CHEESE & CHEERS

Bumthang's famous **Swiss Farm** is a mature development project that was established by Fritz Maurer, one of the first Swiss to work in Bhutan. The project introduced cheese-making, brewing, farming machinery and fuel-efficient wood stoves to the valley, as well as its first tourist guesthouse.

One legacy from the project is Bhutan's best beer, **Red Panda**, which is brewed in a state-of-the-art microbrewery. It's possible to tour the **Bumthang Brewery** (☑631197; admission US$3; ☺8am-noon & 1.30-5pm Wed & Sat, 1.30-5pm Mon & Fri, 4-5pm Tue & Thu), where you will learn about the brewing of the Swiss-style unfiltered weiss beer from head brewer Mr Tikaram, before sampling the end product.

Swiss expertise also set up Bhutan's only commercial **cheese factory** (☑17607239; admission US$3; ☺1-3pm daily), which is also open to visitors. If you just want to invest in some cheese and beer for a top-notch Bumthang picnic, head straight to the next-door Yoser Lhamo Shop (p123), which is the main stockist for both enterprises.

Dragon Roots HANDICRAFTS
(☑17120032) The most prominent souvenir shop in town has a decent range of books, masks and the like.

Bumthang Handicraft Shop HANDICRAFTS
(☺9am-6pm) This shop in the bazaar is strong on textiles from eastern Bhutan.

ℹ Information

Bank of Bhutan (☺9am-1pm & 2-4pm Mon-Fri, 9am-noon Sat)

Bhutan National Bank (☺9am-4pm Mon-Fri, to 11am Sat)

Bumthang Medical Store (☺8am-7pm) For medical supplies.

Police At the base of Jakar Dzong.

Post Office (☺9am-5pm Mon-Fri, to 1pm Sat) Just south of the central junction.

ℹ Getting There & Away

Bumthang's new **Bathpalathang airport** currently operates two or three flights a week to Paro. Tickets currently cost around US$175 one-way. **Druk Air** (☑631739) has an office in town.

Metho Transport (☑631439) has Coasters to Thimphu (Nu 323, 11 hours) at 7am. **Taxis** congregate next to Jakar Lhakhang.

The **Dragon Ride** (☑17120032) counter at Dragon Roots souvenir shop rents mountain bikes for Nu 1800 per day, which is a great way to get around the valley's main sights.

Chokhor Valley

To most people the Chokhor valley *is* Bumthang and the Chokhor valley is often called the Bumthang valley or just simply Bumthang. It's possible to visit Jampey and Kurjey lhakhangs in the morning, cross the river and have a packed lunch at Do Zam, and then visit Tamshing Lhakhang in the afternoon. If you want to see a good selection of valley sights and fit in a hike, you really need three or four days here.

Western Side of the Valley

The road that leads up the western side of the valley connects a string of interesting temples which are connected in one way or another with the visit of Guru Rinpoche to Bumthang in 746. A mountain bike would offer a great way to link up the monasteries and continue over to the east bank, or you can walk from Jampey Lhakhang over Do Zam bridge.

SEY LHAKHANG

Beyond the hospital north of Jakar is the **Sey Lhakhang** (*sey* means 'golden'). Properly known as Lhodrak Seykhar Dratshang, this is a monastic school established in 1963. The central figure in the lhakhang is Marpa Lotsawa, a great teacher and translator of the Kagyu lineage.

JAMPEY LHAKHANG

This fabulous **temple** is up a short side road about 1.5km past Sey Lhakhang. It is believed to have been built in 659 by the Tibetan king Songtsen Gampo, on the same day as Kyichu Lhakhang in Paro, in order to subdue a Tibetan demoness.

The temple was visited by Guru Rinpoche during his visit to Bumthang and was renovated by the Sindhu Raja after the Guru restored his life force. It's the one place in the valley that feels truly ancient.

Inside the main Jampey (Jampa) Lhakhang are three stone steps representing three ages. The first signifies the past, the age of the historical Buddha, Sakyamuni. This step has descended into the ground and is covered with a wooden plank. The next age is the present, and its step is level with the floor. The top step represents a new age. It is believed that when the step representing the present age sinks to ground level, the gods will become like humans and the world as it is now will end.

The central figure in the ancient inner sanctum is **Jampa**, the Buddha of the future, with his feet on an elephant. This is the oldest part of the oldest chapel in Bhutan. The entry to the chapel is protected by an iron chainmail that was made by Pema Lingpa. Look up into the alcove above the entry to see a statue of Guru Rinpoche. He sat in this alcove and meditated, leaving behind a footprint. It is said that under the lhakhang there is a lake with several *terma* (sacred texts and artefacts) hidden by Guru Rinpoche.

Chokhor Valley

The inner *kora* (circumambulation) path around the chapel is lined with ancient murals depicting 1000 Buddhas. There are more lovely murals in the atrium. On the right side of the wooden wall divider is an image of Kim-lha, the goddess of the home.

On the northern side of the courtyard is the **Kalachakra Temple** (Dukhor Lhakhang), added by Ugyen Wangchuck when he was *penlop*. The animal-headed deities on the walls are the demons that confront the dead during the 49 days of *bardo* (the state between death and rebirth). Chimi Dorji, the administrator of Jakar Dzong, added the Guru Lhakhang on the south side of the *dochey* (courtyard), which features statues of Guru Rinpoche, Tsepame and Chenresig. Generations of prostrators have worn the wooden boards smooth on either side of the courtyard entryway.

Behind the main temple are two large stone **chortens**; one is in memory of the second king's younger brother, the other in memory of Lama Pentsen Khenpo, spiritual adviser to the first and second Bhutanese kings. The four corners of the complex are anchored by four more chortens, coloured yellow, red, white and blue.

The pile of carved *mani* stones (stones carved with the Buddhist mantra *om mani peme hum*) in the parking lot in front of the goemba is called a *thos* and represents the Guardians of the Four Directions.

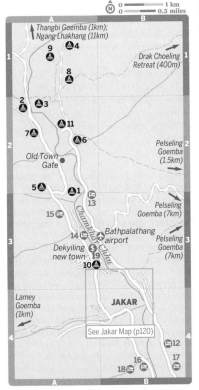

Chokhor Valley

Sights
1 Chakhar Lhakhang A2
2 Deothang Goemba A2
3 Do Zam A2
4 Dorji Bi Lhakhang A1
5 Jampey Lhakhang A2
6 Konchogsum Lhakhang A2
7 Kurjey Lhakhang A2
8 Pema Sambhava Lhakhang A1
9 Rock Painting A1
10 Sey Lhakhang A3
11 Tamshing Goemba A2

Sleeping
12 Gongkhar Guest House B4
13 Hotel Pelling A3
14 Leki Guest House A3
15 Rinchenling Lodge A3
16 Wangdicholing Resort B4
17 Yozerling Lodge B4
18 Yu-Gharling Resort B4

Information
19 Bhutan National Bank A3

WALKING THE BUMTHANG VALLEYS

There are plenty of opportunities for day hikes in the Bumthang region, most of which offer a wonderful combination of remote sacred sights, wide valley views and sublime picnic spots.

The best short walk is between Kurjey Lhakhang and Tamshing Goemba via Do Zam and the nearby rock painting of Dorji Drolo (see p129). You can extend the walk by 15 minutes by walking to Kurjey from Jampey Lhakhang.

Following are the main day hikes:

Pelseling Goemba The half-day hike from the Swiss Guest House in Jakar to the large 'Lotus Grove' Monastery is all uphill (2½ hours), gaining 800m, but is nice and varied, through a mix of forest, meadows and villages, and you are rewarded with great views. A switchbacking 11km dirt road now winds up to the monastery, so you can get picked up there. Alternatively, descend a different route to Tamshing Goemba for a total of about four hours' walking.

Kunzangdrak Goemba (p131) For a remoter hike, drive to Pelseling and then hike over the ridge and around a side valley to this retreat in the Tang valley. Get your vehicle to pick you up there before visiting other sights in the valley.

Tharpaling Goemba (p117) A favourite one-way walk is from Lamey Goemba over the ridge to Tharpaling in the Chhume valley, to meet your vehicle there. The trail branches off a logging road 1km past the goemba, which was built in the 1800s as a residence for King Ugyen Wangchuck and now houses a government office. The first two hours are a hard uphill slog through rhododendron and bamboo, before you finally crest a pass and descend across the bare hillsides of the Chhume valley to the Zhambhala Lhakhang, Choedrak Hermitage and, finally, Tharpaling. The hike offers less in the way of views but has the feel of a pilgrimage, taking in several sacred sites. Check for ticks along this route.

Thangbi Goemba to Ngang Lhakhang A pleasant, largely flat, two- to three-hour hike that avoids the bumpy drive to Ngang Lhakhang by taking the south bank trail of the Chamkhar Chhu, passing the ruins of Draphe Dzong en route.

Drak Choeling Retreat A 90-minute uphill hike from Pema Sambhava Lhakhang takes you up through forest to the white cliffs of this silent retreat centre (don't disturb the hermits), with huge views over the Bumthang valley from a prayer-flag lookout.

Luege Rowe (p127) A charming half-day hike to a remote, little-visited lhakhang that feels untouched by time. Continue the route to Thangbi Goemba or make the more ambitious day hike across the ridge to Shugdrak.

Each October one of the most spectacular festivals in Bhutan, the **Jampey Lhakhang Drup**, is staged here. The festival ground and VIP viewing platform is to the left (south) of the chapel. On one evening, after the lama dances, the monastery hosts a *mewang*, when pilgrims jump through a burning archway. Another late-night fertility rite is the naked *tercham* (treasure dance), normally performed at midnight.

CHAKHAR LHAKHANG

Beside the main road, a short distance beyond Jampey Lhakhang, is Chakhar Lhakhang (Iron Castle Temple). Although it is easy to mistake it for a house, this is an interesting temple and worth a short visit. It is the site of the palace of the Indian king Sendha Gyab, better known as the Sindhu Raja, who first invited Guru Rinpoche to Bumthang. The original palace was made of iron, hence the name Chakhar; it was said to have been nine storeys high, holding within it all the treasures of the world.

The current building was built in the 14th century by the saint Dorji Lingpa. The main statue is of Guru Rinpoche, and there are dozens of masks and black hats that are used during the Jampey Lhakhang Drup festival. Guru Rinpoche took Sindhu Raja's daughter Tashi Khewdoen as his consort – you can see her statue to the left of the altar (flanked by baby elephant tusks), as well as a photo of her stone footprint, one of the lhakhang's most prized relics.

KURJEY LHAKHANG

This large, active and important **temple complex** is named after the body *(kur)* print *(jey)* of Guru Rinpoche, which is preserved in a cave inside the oldest of the three buildings that make up the temple complex. It's at the end of the paved road, 2.5km from Chakhar Lhakhang.

The first of the three temples, the **Guru Lhakhang**, is the oldest and was built in 1652 by Mingyur Tenpa when he was *penlop* of Trongsa. Tucked just below the eaves is a figure of a snow lion with a *jachung* (also called *garuda*) above it, which represents the famous struggle between Guru Rinpoche (appearing as the *garuda*) and the local demon, Shelging Kharpo (as the snow lion).

At the entrance to the lower-floor **Sangay Lhakhang** is a small crawl-through rock passage; Bhutanese believe that in crawling through a narrow tunnel like this you will leave your sins behind. Behind the statues of the three Buddhas is a secret passageway that is said to have once led to Tharpaling.

The upper-floor **sanctuary** is the holiest in the complex. There are a thousand small statues of Guru Rinpoche neatly lined up along the left wall, plus statues of Guru Rinpoche, Pema Lingpa and Drolma (Tara). The main statue in this sanctuary is again of Guru Rinpoche, flanked by his eight manifestations and eight chortens. Hidden behind this image is the **meditation cave**, where he left his body imprint. The far wall has images of Guru Rinpoche, his manifestations, his 25 disciples and various other figures connected with the Guru. The big cypress tree behind the lhakhang is said to have sprouted from the Guru's walking stick.

Ugyen Wangchuck, the first king of Bhutan, built the second temple, the **Sampa Lhundrup Lhakhang**, in 1900, when he was still *penlop* of Trongsa. On the entrance porch are paintings of the Guardians of the Four Directions and of various local deities who were converted to Buddhism by Guru Rinpoche. The white ghostlike figure on the white horse above the doorway to the right is Shelging Kharpo; also here are local protectors Yakdu Nagpo (on a black yak) and Kyebu Lungten (on a red horse). Inside the temple is a towering statue of Guru Rinpoche, this one 10m high, flanked again by his eight manifestations. A smaller image of the Guru sits facing the entrance.

The third building in the complex was built by Ashi Kesang Wangchuck, queen to the third king, in 1984 under the guidance of Dilgo Khyentse Rinpoche. She also had the courtyard in front of the three temples paved with stones and built a wall with 108 chortens around the whole complex. On the porch in front of the temple is a large wheel of life. At the bottom you can see a man being judged, with black and white stones representing his good and bad deeds. There's a mystic spiral mandala on the opposite wall. Interior murals illustrate various monastic rules and regulations, including the strict dress codes.

The elaborately decorated **Zangto Pelri Lhakhang**, a short distance south of the Kurjey Lhakhang compound, features a kitschy 3D depiction of the paradise of Guru Rinpoche and a wall mural of Ashi Wangchuck enjoying life in the western paradise known as Dewachen. The ground floor has a particularly lovely portable chorten shrine known as a *tashi gomang*.

A five-minute walk up the hillside near the entrance is the **Kurjey Drupchhu**, a sacred spring where monks come to wash their socks.

The popular **Kurjey tsechu** is held in June and includes a masked dance that dramatises Guru Rinpoche's defeat of Shelging Kharpo. A large *thangka,* called Guru Tshengye Thondrol, depicting the eight manifestations of Guru Rinpoche, is unfurled in the early morning before the dances, which are performed by the monks from Trongsa.

DEOTHANG GOEMBA

This little-visited but charming private **Deothang (Dawathang) Goemba**, known as the Field of the Moon, is just north of Kurjey Lhakhang and dates from 1949. The surprisingly grand main hall has a large image of Guru Rinpoche, with 12 other interesting metal statues to the side. A small, grey image of Thangtong Gyalpo stands above the cabinet to the left.

LUEGE ROWE

This lovely and little-visited lhakhang at the far northern end of the valley offers a fine half-day hike. From Kurjey Lhakhang drive along the Duer Chhu past Taktu Zampa to the village of Menchugang. Hike for 40 minutes to Jusbi village, soon to be connected by road once the bridge at Menchugang is completed. From here the path climbs up the forested hillside, sometimes on wooden planks across marshy bamboo groves. After two hours branch left at a junction and 30 minutes later you'll reach a chorten gateway, from where you can see the lhakhang nestled in a fold in the hills.

The chapel is named 'Sheeps Horns' after the sacred horn prints and hoof prints on the cave roof. Pilgrims walk under the roof's nine mandalas and make a wish. The building is locked when the caretaker is away, but it's still a lovely location.

Back at the junction continue straight for 40 minutes to yak pastures, where a path branches left for the more ambitious hike across the ridge to Shugdrak. After a total of four hours' walking a collection of prayer flags marks a great viewpoint over the Bumthang valley. From here it's less than an hour downhill to Thangbi.

THANGBI GOEMBA

The yellow-roofed Thangbi (Thankabi) Goemba was founded in 1470 by Shamar Rinpoche and, after a dispute, was taken over by Pema Lingpa. The main chapel of the Dusum Sangay (past, present and future Buddhas) is entered under another of Pema Lingpa's famous chainmails. Around 20 gomchen (lay or married monks) live here, celebrating a mani (festival) and fire ceremony in the middle of the eigth lunar month (October).

The goemba is a 3.5km drive north of Kurjey Lhakhang on an unpaved road, branching across the river at Toktu Zampa. Along the main road you'll see what looks like mailboxes; these are actually 'milkboxes', where local herders leave their fresh milk for daily delivery down to Jakar.

Hikes start from here to Ngang Lhakhang and to Luege Rowe. For Ngang Lhakhang walk along the road to a small khonying (traditional stupa-style gateway), visit the nearby rock painting and traditional water mill, and then cross the bridge over the Chamkhar Chhu at Kharsa village.

SHUGDRAK

To get well off the beaten track make the short 10-minute hike up to this sacred Guru Rinpoche cave, 2km past Thangbi. A series of ladders leads pilgrims past a lovely butter-lamp shrine to a rock-face chapel, where a monk can point out the stone footprint, handprint and bootprint of the Guru. Pilgrims have stuffed dozens of ngultrum notes into the cracks of the rock wall.

To get here take the dirt side road to the left, just past Goling and Kharsa villages, then drive for 1km to the parking lot and walk 10 minutes up to the cave.

NGANG LHAKHANG

A bumpy 10km drive up the Chokhor valley from Thangbi Goemba is the small region known as Ngang-yul (Swan Land). The site was visited by Guru Rinpoche, but the present Ngang Lhakhang (Swan Temple) was built in the 15th century by Lama Namkha Samdrup, a contemporary of Pema Lingpa.

Despite the recently renovated exterior, the interior contains some lovely statues and paintings. The primary statue is of Guru Rinpoche, flanked by early Buddhist missionary Shantarakshita and Tibetan king Trisong Detsen. There is a mural of the Zhabdrung on the side wall opposite the altar and an image of Guru Rinpoche on a lotus surrounded by two ducklike swans.

The upper chapel is a goenkhang, with statues of the 'Tsela Nam Sum' trinity of Tsepame, Namse and Drolma, with Chenresig standing to the left. The statue of Guru Rinpoche to the right was fashioned by Pema Lingpa himself. Protector deities lurk in the shadows. Hanging from the rafters are masks used in the three-day **Ngang Bi Rabney**, a festival organised in the middle of the 10th month by the two main clans of the village in honour of the temple's founder.

It's possible to stay overnight at the rural **Balakha Farmhouse** (☎17292062; s/d Nu 1100/1300) homestay right beside the lhakhang. Accommodation is simple but you'll get a comfortable mattress on the floor, a shared organic meal with the family and a clean Western toilet. The friendly owners have looked after the lhakhang for generations.

The new bridge over the Chamkhar Chhu means it's possible to drive up to the lhakhang but it's a much nicer walk (two hours) from Thangbi Goemba along the true left bank of the river. En route you can detour to explore the 17th-century ruins of **Draphe (Drapham, or Damphel) Dzong**, a 30-minute gentle uphill walk from Ngang Lhakhang.

The long day hike over the Phephe La (signed 'Febila') to Ogyen Chholing Palace in the Tang valley also begins here, on what is called the Bumthang Cultural Trail.

NANGSIPHEL

This attractive village high in the valley is starting to lure visitors. Also known as Chhokhortoe, it's a prosperous village that has become wealthy thanks to the centuries-old caravan trade with Tibet and the more recent boom in the *yarsa gomba* (medicinal worm) business.

The annual two-day **Nomad's Festival** is currently held here in the third weekend in February and features a series of traditional sports such as shotput, wrestling, archery, tug of war and even pillow fighting on a pole, along with mask dances. Locals set up stalls selling everything from buckwheat products to fermented cheese.

The village hopes to be a starting point for new treks into the Wangchuck Centennial Park, which is constructing a visitor centre here. The five-hour Orochhoto (Raven's Beak) Trail winds through blue pine and hemlock forest and cliffs above the village, offering fine day-hike potential.

Homestays are available in both Nang-siphel and the surrounding villages of Shabjithang and Dorjung through the community-run **Alpine Organic Homestays** (☑ 17292177, 17670870; s/d Nu 750/850, meals Nu 250). The 20 or so homestays are simple but offer an inside toilet and a hot-stone bath.

Nangsiphel is around 4km north of the turn-off to Ngang Lhakhang, passing the charming Shabjithang Lhakhang after 2km. Figure on an hour's drive from Jakar.

Eastern Side of the Valley

The best way to visit the eastern side of the Chokhor valley is to walk a couple of hundred metres north from Kurjey Lhakhang, then follow a path east to cross a prayer-flag-strewn footbridge. From the bridge you can see a natural formation named **Do Zam**, said to be the remains of a stone bridge that was built by a goddess trying to meet Guru Rinpoche, but destroyed by a demon.

From here you can follow the east-bank trail south for 30 minutes to Tamshing Goemba. A more interesting 45-minute detour is to take a left after the bridge for 10 minutes to a manor house built by relatives of the second king. From here branch left for three minutes to an impressive **rock painting** of Guru Rinpoche in the form of Dorji Drolo, astride a tiger.

Back at the manor house, head uphill to the **Dorji Bi Lhakhang**, with its large white chorten. From here a dirt road descends to Tamshing Lhakhang via the turn-off to Pema Sambhava Lhakhang. You can meet your vehicle at Dorji Bi or Tamshing Lhakhang.

The major influence in the temples on this side of the valley was Pema Lingpa, the great *terton* (discoverer of sacred texts and artefacts) of the 16th century.

TAMSHING GOEMBA

This goemba, formally the Tamshing Lhendup Chholing (Temple of the Good Message), is 5km from Jakar. It was established in 1501 by Pema Lingpa and is the most important Nyingma goemba in the kingdom. Pema Lingpa built the unusual structure himself, with the help of *khandroma*s, who made many of the statues. On the inner walls are what are believed to be original unrestored images that were painted by Pema Lingpa, though recent research has uncovered even older paintings underneath.

The entrance to the lhakhang is via an inner courtyard lined with monks' quarters. To the left is the **Mani Dungkhor Lhakhang**, built in 1914 to hold a huge prayer wheel.

The main lhakhang has an unusual design, with the key chapel screened off in the centre of the assembly hall, almost like a separate building. In the chapel are three thrones for the three incarnations (body, mind and speech) of Pema Lingpa. During important ceremonies the reincarnations sit here, although a photograph is substituted if one of the incarnations is not present.

The primary statue in the inner sanctuary is of Guru Rinpoche flanked by Jampa (Maitreya, the Buddha of the future) and Sakyamuni Buddha. This statue is particularly important because it was sculpted by the *khandroma*s. The statue's eyes are looking slightly upward, following the angels in their flight; another unique aspect of the statue is that the Guru is not wearing shoes. Above the altar are two *maksara*s (mythological crocodiles) and a *garuda*. On the walls are the

---

DON'T MISS

PEMA LINGPA'S CHAINMAIL

At the side of the dimly lit inner *kora* path within Tamshing Goemba is a cloak of chainmail made by Pema Lingpa. It weighs about 25kg, and if you can hoist it on to your shoulders it is an auspicious act to carry it around the *kora* three times.

eight manifestations of Guru Rinpoche, four on each side. A small statue of Pema Lingpa occupies a glass case in front of the chapel.

The upper floor forms a **balcony** around the assembly hall. Pema Lingpa was a short man and it is said that he built the low ceiling of the balcony to his exact height. Around the outside are 100,000 old paintings of Sakyamuni Buddha. In the **upper chapel** is a statue of Tsepame, the Buddha of Long Life, and a large collection of masks that are used for monk dances. Also here, but closed to visitors, is a statue of Pema Lingpa fashioned by the man himself.

There are good views from Tamshing back across the river to Kurjey Lhakhang.

KONCHOGSUM LHAKHANG

Just 400m below Tamshing, in what currently looks like a building site, this historically important temple is being rebuilt after it was almost destroyed by a butter-lamp fire in 2010. The original building probably dates back to a Tibetan design from the 6th or 7th century, though the current core structure dates from the 15th century, when Pema Lingpa restored it. It's worth checking to see if the lhakhang has reopened.

PEMA SAMBHAVA LHAKHANG

Further along the dirt road north of Tamshing, a short steep climb above the valley floor leads to the small Pema Sambhava Lhakhang. The original lhakhang was built in 1490 by Pema Lingpa around the cave where Guru Rinpoche meditated and assumed his manifestation of Padmasambhava. It was expanded by Jigme Namgyal, the father of the first king, and restored in the early 1970s.

There are several rock paintings here, as well as a representation of the local protector Terda Norbu Zangpo who lurks in a corner behind the door beside a leather whip, and the cave itself is painted in rainbow colours. Ask to see the main relic, a conch shell that is said to have flown here from Do Zam. The footpath at the back of the lhakhang leads steeply uphill for 90 minutes to the white cliff of the Drak Choeling retreat centre.

Tang Valley

Tang is the most remote of Bumthang's valleys. As it is higher than Chokhor and the soil is not as fertile, there's not as much agriculture here, although the valley turns bright pink with buckwheat flowers in October. The people of this valley raise sheep and, at higher elevations, yaks.

From Jakar it's 11km to the unpaved road that branches north up the Tang valley. This road climbs past the trail to **Membartsho** (1.3km from the turn-off) and the **Pema Tekchok Choeling Shedra**, a large nunnery where about 160 *anim* (nuns) complete 12 years of study, to reach the turn-off to the jumping-off point for the hike to Kunzangdrak, 7km from the turn-off. The road then climbs high above the river, crossing the bridge at Pangshing and then passing **Gemshong**, a particularly picturesque village and lhakhang perched on a ridge. After a short descent to the river it's 3km to a school at Mesithang and 1km further to the Tang Rimochen Lhakhang. The owner of River Lodge in Jakar runs an eight-roomed rural retreat called the **Mesithang River Lodge** (☎ 03-631287; pemadawa@druknet.bt; s/d Nu 1610/1725) for those wishing to experience authentic rural Bhutan with more comfort than a homestay affords.

The road becomes rougher as it approaches the bridge at **Kizum** (Ki Zam), 22km from the road junction, where a dirt road branches over the river to Ogyen Chholing. The increasingly rough farm road continues a few kilometres further to Gamling and Wobtang.

You can take in all the sites in this section in a long day trip from Jakar, but it's best to overnight at a farmhouse such as the secluded Ogyen Chholing Guest House.

Membartsho

A five-minute walk from a parking spot at a bend in the road leads to a picturesque pool in the Tang Chhu that is known as Membartsho (Burning Lake). The 27-year-old Pema Lingpa found several of Guru Rinpoche's *terma* here. It's a lovely spot, where nature, religion and mythology blur into one.

A wooden bridge crosses the prayer-flag-strewn gorge and offers a good vantage point over the 'lake'. Only the enlightened will spot the temple that lurks in the inky depths. The sanctity of the site is made evident by the numerous small clay offerings called *tsha-tsha* piled up in various rock niches.

Under a rock shrine with a carving of Guru Rinpoche flanked by Sakyamuni and Pema Lingpa is a cave that virtuous people can crawl through, no matter how big they are. Beware: it's quite small, and very dusty.

THE BURNING LAKE

Two of Pema Lingpa's most celebrated discoveries took place at Membartsho.

The first occurred when a dream told him to go to a point where the river forms a large pool that looks like a lake. After a while, standing on a large rock, he saw a temple with many doors, only one of which was open. He plunged naked into the lake and entered a large cave where there was a throne, upon which sat a life-size statue of Lord Buddha and many large boxes. An old woman with one eye handed him one of the chests and he suddenly found himself standing on the rock at the side of the lake holding the treasure.

Pema Lingpa's second treasure find was the most famous. His previous *terma* had instructed him to return to the lake, but when he did, many people gathered to watch the event and the sceptical *penlop* (governor) of the district accused him of trickery. Under great pressure to prove himself, Pema Lingpa took a lighted lamp and proclaimed: 'If I am a genuine revealer of your treasures, then may I return with it now, with my lamp still burning; if I am some devil, then may I perish in the water.' He jumped into the lake, was gone long enough that the sceptics thought they were proven right, and then suddenly he emerged back on the rock with the lamp still burning and holding a statue and a treasure chest. The lake became known as Membartsho (Burning Lake).

Kunzangdrak Goemba

A stiff 45-minute hike up the hillside above Drangchel village leads to one of the most important sites related to Pema Lingpa. He began construction of the goemba in 1488, and many of his most important sacred relics are kept here.

The first chapel, the Wangkhang Lhakhang, has a *kora* path around it, suspended in mid-air, with Chenresig, Guru Nangsi Zilnon (Guru Rinpoche) and his disciple Namkhai Nyingpo inside. Walk around the back of the building to the gravity-defying **Khandroma Lhakhang**, the meditation cave of Yeshe Tshogyel, spectacularly situated against a vertical rock face that seeps holy water. Ask to see the woodblocks and stone anvil bearing the footprint of Pema Lingpa. Finally, cross over the small bridge, past a fire-blackened cleft in the cliff, to the *goenkhang*.

Figure on 2½ hours for the return trip. There are plans to build a road to the goemba.

Ta Rimochen Lhakhang

Ta Rimochen Lhakhang was built by Pema Lingpa in the 14th century to mark a sacred place where Guru Rinpoche meditated. The original name 'Tag (Tak) Rimochen' (meaning an impression of tiger's stripes) is derived from the yellow stripes that appear on the rock cliff behind the building.

There are handprints and footprints of the Guru and his consort Yeshe Tshogyel on the cliff face, as well as several wish-fulfilling stones, sacred symbols and even an invisible doorway. There are more footprints at the top of the steps leading to the temple. Inside the main chapel look for a depiction of local protector Lhamo Remaley.

The two huge rocks below the lhakhang represent male and female *jachung (garuda)*. By the road you can see the roadside bathing tub of the Guru and even the buttock marks of Yeshe Tshogyel, worn into the rock during an epic bout of Tantric lovemaking.

Ogyen Chholing Palace

From Kizum bridge it's a 3km uphill drive to this hilltop 16th-century *naktshang*, originally built by Deb Tsokye Dorji, the onetime *penlop* of Trongsa and a descendant of the *terton* Dorji Lingpa. The present structures, including the *tshuglhakhang* (main temple), *utse* (central tower), *chamkhang* (dance house), *shagkor* (servants' quarters) and *nubgothang* (guesthouse), are more recent, having been rebuilt after their collapse in the 1897 earthquake.

The family that owns Ogyen (Ugyen) Chholing has turned the complex into a museum (admission Nu 150) to preserve its legacy. The fascinating and well-captioned exhibits offer real insights into the lifestyle of a Bhutanese noble family. Highlights include a book of divination, a *dakini* dance costume made of bone and the revelation that petrified yak dung was one of the ingredients for Bhutanese gunpowder. Particularly interesting is the section on the once-thriving trade with Tibet, describing how Bhutanese traders would take tobacco,

English cloth, rice, paper and indigo to trade fairs over the border in Lhodrak, to return laden with bricks of Chinese tea, gold dust, salt and borax (an ingredient in butter tea). Bring a torch. An excellent museum booklet (Nu 350) is for sale.

The rustic **Ogyen Chholing Guest House** (☑03-631221; r Nu 840-1560) in the palace grounds has three comfortable suites with attached toilet and six smaller basic rooms, offering a tranquil, if simple, overnight retreat. Proceeds go to the trust. Your agency can probably also arrange an overnight stay in a nearby farmhouse.

Instead of leaving by road the way you came, consider making the one-hour walk back down to Kizum bridge via the charming **Choejam Lhakhang**, with its *kora* path and room full of festival masks, and the **Narut (Pelphug) Lhakhang**, built around a sacred cave enclosing a Guru Rinpoche footprint and a shrine to the local protector Garap Wangchu.

Thowadrak Hermitage

The remote hermitage of Thowadrak (Thowa Drak) clings to the highest rocks above the north end of the Tang valley. It is said to have been founded by Mandarava, the Indian consort of Guru Rinpoche, and the Guru himself is believed to have meditated here. The goemba was built by Dorji Lingpa. There are numerous small meditation retreats on the hillside above (don't disturb the hermits) and dramatic views over the valley. Texts relate that the upper valley conceals a sealed gateway to one of Bhutan's *bey-yul* (hidden lands). The only sounds here are of rushing water and the rustle of bamboo.

The six-hour return hike is best done as a day trip from the Ogyen Chholing Guest House.

Ura Valley

Southeast of Jakar, Ura is the highest of Bumthang's valleys and is believed by some to have been the home of the earliest inhabitants of Bhutan.

Jakar to Ura

48KM / 1½ HOURS

The road crosses the bridge to the east of Jakar, then travels south along the east bank of the Chamkhar Chhu, winding around a ridge past the turn-off to the Tang valley. As the road climbs, look back at excellent views up the Chokhor and Chhume valleys.

The few houses and lhakhang that make up Tangsibi village are 24km from Jakar. The road climbs to a chorten, then finally crosses the Shertang La (3590m), also known as the Ura La. Just before the pass you'll get a view of Gangkhar Puensum (7541m) to the northwest and the yellow-roofed lhakhang of Shingkhar village below.

It's then a long descent into the Ura valley. The direct descent on foot or mountain bike from the pass makes for a nice hour-long walk into Ura village. A couple of kilometres before the turn-off to the village of Ura, which lies below the road, is the turn-off to Shingkhar.

Shingkhar

POP 250 / ELEV 3400M

The traditional village of Shingkhar, made up of only 35 households, is 9km up a good gravel side road and over the ridge from Ura. The small **Rinchen Jugney Lhakhang**, on a hill just above the village, was founded by the Dzogchen master Longchen Rabjampa (1308–63) and is currently under expansion.

The village's central **Dechen Chholing Goemba** is headed by Shingkhar Lama, whose predecessor featured prominently in the Bhutanese novel *Hero with the Thousand Eyes*, by Karma Ura. The central lhakhang has its floorboards exposed to show the stone teaching throne of Longchen. The protector deities are appropriately fierce, except for Rahulla who looks embarrassed wearing a gorilla mask. The **Shingkhar Rabney** (festival) held here in the ninth month (October) features an unusual yak dance, without the tour groups that often crowd out Ura.

There are several good hiking options in the valley. The easiest option is the two-hour return hike to the cliff-hanging **Shamsul Lhakhang**, which offers fine views down the valley. The trail starts from the dirt road 3km above Shingkhar. A longer hike leads up to the Singmi La, along the former trade route to Lhuentse, and multiday treks continue further through Thrumshing La National Park to Songme in the Lhuentse valley.

Shingkhar Retreat (☑03-323206; masagang@druknet.bt; s/d Nu 2160/2760), just behind the Rinchen Jugney Lhakhang, is a possible base from which to explore the village and surrounding hikes. The rooms are basic but cosy, with mud walls; meals are available.

On the way back to Ura stop at the charming **Somtrang Lhakhang**, with its courtyard megaliths and a meditation retreat in the cliffs above the village. A footpath offers a pleasant walk from here directly down to Ura village. A three-day *kangsoe* festival brings the place to life at the end of the ninth month (November).

Ura

📞 03 / ELEV 3100M

Ura is one of the most interesting villages in Bhutan. There are about 40 closely packed houses along cobblestone streets, and the main **Ura Lhakhang** dominates the town, giving it a medieval atmosphere. In colder weather Ura women wear a sheepskin shawl that serves as both a blanket and a cushion.

Ura gets a rush of visitors during the **Ura Yakchoe**, a notoriously unreliable festival that regularly changes date at the last minute, leaving behind busloads of disappointed tour groups on tight schedules. If you do decide to visit the festival, normally in May, it would be wise to budget a couple of days' leeway in your itinerary. The three days of masked dances starts on the 12th day of the third month with a procession carrying an image of Chana Dorji (Vajrapani) from the nearby Gaden Lhakhang down to the main lhakhang. The eve of the festival sees the frantic brewing of *sinchhang* (a spirit distilled from millet, wheat or rice) and late-night exorcisms. Even if it's not festival time, it's a pleasant 15-minute walk from Gaden Lhakhang down to Ura village.

Hotel Araya Zambala (📞17732699; azher bal05@yahoo.com; s/d Nu 1800/2100), beside the main road above Ura, has six basic rooms with private bathrooms, and can provide simple meals in its roadside inn. Its main business is in herbal medicines and dried mushrooms. It's just above Gaden Lhakhang.

During the Ura festival even camping spots are scarce and some groups commute from Jakar, 90 minutes' drive away. At other times homestays are generally possible in Ura village.

A few hundred metres beyond the hotel (towards Mongar) is the start of the **Ura-Geyzamchu Walking Trail**, a 9km-long, five-hour hike crossing the Wangthang La pass and rejoining the main road at Geyzam Chhu. It's a demanding but rewarding walk through rhododendron, pine forests and alpine meadows along an old trade route.

For information and a local guide visit the **Thrumshing La National Park Visitor Centre** (📞contact Pema Dobgay 17750493; chieftnp@yahoo.com; ⊙9am-5pm Mon-Fri), on the main road, just past the turn-off to Ura village.

The hills around Ura produce some of Bhutan's best matsutake mushrooms (*sangay shamu* in Dzongkha), a fact celebrated with recipes, local stalls and other fungi-related fun in August's **Matsutake Festival**.

SOUTHERN DZONGKHAGS

The two *dzongkhags* of Zhemgang and Sarpang lie on the southern border of central Bhutan. The region is now open to tourism and offers a remote alternative entry or exit route into Bhutan. The region around Zhemgang was once a collection of tiny principalities, collectively known as Khyeng, absorbed into Bhutan in the 17th century.

For tourists the main highlight is Royal Manas National Park, which offers wildlife enthusiasts an amazing experience in an area of extreme biodiversity.

Trongsa to Gelephu

The highway south of Trongsa initially follows the Mangde Chhu river, winding in and out of various convoluted side valleys. The highway passes the Mangdechuu hydroelectric works before reaching the palaces of Kuenga Rabten and Eundu Chholing; see p117 for details of these. From Eundu Chholing to Zhemgang is 61km.

Trongsa to Zhemgang

106KM / 4 HOURS

South of Eundu Chholing the road continues in this direction past the villages of Lungtel and Taksila (with its lhakhang above the road), before descending to the bridge at Tangtongphey, which marks the start or end point of the Nabji trek (p185). Past Koshela and Pangzum takes the road swings round the unstable Riotola cliffs slide area, opening up views of Nabji and Korphu villages in the side valley across the river.

After briefly detouring up a side valley the road reaches the Wangduegang turn-off, where the Zhemgang bypass branches right to offer a direct route to Gelephu. The

CENTRAL BHUTAN TRONGSA TO GELEPHU

access road to the southern end of the Nabji trek also branches off here. The main road zigzags up a side valley, past a mithun cattle breeding centre before finally rolling into Zhemgang.

The sleepy *dzongkhag* centre of **Zhemgang** is a natural place to break the trip. The surprisingly impressive dzong dates back to the 12th century and is home to 70 monks and several statues of the valley protector Dorji Rabten. An annual tsechu here in March culminates in the unfurling of a giant *thondrol*. The picturesque old town, still bearing the original name of Trong, is worth a wander to visit its lhakhang.

The best place to stay (though it's still quite simple) is the **Dangkhar Community Tourism project** (☑17704962; s/d Nu 750/1500, meals Nu 200-350), which boasts three simple cabins and a block of communal outside toilets. Dangkhar is 3km below Zhemgang centre and hard to find – head towards the lower secondary school. The picturesque village lhakhang here features an image of local deity Kiba Luntse, who has his winter residence in the valley. If you have more time, consider the two-hour return hike to Dongbi village and lhakhang.

In Zhemgang town itself, the **Bajay Guesthouse** (☑17680943; s/d Nu 800/1600) is an atmospheric local place for lunch and the attached block has a few rooms. The modern-looking **Sonam Gakeeling Hotel** (☑17389739) is under construction opposite and might be worth a look.

Zhemgang to Gelephu

131KM / 5 HOURS

After leaving Zhemgang the highway quickly swings into a side valley, passing the **Dueduel Namgyel Chorten** to the turn-off at Dakpa, which leads to the remote but historically important lhakhangs of Buli and Dali. Look for golden langurs along this stretch.

The Zhemgang bypass joins the main highway at the bridge across the Mangde Chhu. Just past the bridge near the new town of **Tingtibi** is the turn-off to Gomphu and road and trekking access to the northern part of Royal Manas National Park. Tingtibi offers a potential lunch spot, as well as a shop selling local farm products. A huge hydroelectric project nearby will doubtless boost Tangtibi in coming years. From here it is 22km from Zhemgang, 98km to Gelephu.

The road now starts a long climb, swinging around a Nepali-style chorten below Tama village. Just above the village is the small but atmospheric Lhamo Lhakhang. The older and more significant Tama Lhakhang, founded by Pema Lingpa, is a further 10 minutes' drive up towards the pass, a short walk from the road.

The road crests the **Tama La**, where vehicles make a *kora* around the white chorten. As you descend the hillside on the far side look for wild beehives on the cliffs above Chapcha and the nearby pagoda at Lungsilgang, which offers a viewpoint and picnic potential. The road bottoms out at Samkhar Zam bridge then climbs to **Surey** village, with its mandarin orchards, cardomom fields and lhakhang just above the village. The Gurung Hotel here offers a decent tea spot. Surey's official Dzongkha name is Jigme Choling but most locals use the local Nepali name.

The road climbs past a landslide area with some sphincter-tightening 1000m drops to the right, before reaching a white chorten marking the turn-off to **Shershong tsachhu** (hot spring). The short but steep downhill detour leads to three cosy and clean hot tubs – a surefire way to recuperate from the drive and meet some Bhutanese friends.

The main road hits the floodplain with a bump at the immigration checkpost beside Pasang Zam bridge. A side road here leads to the hilltop Sershong Lhakhang and its important cremation ground. From here it's a short and mercifully flat drive into Gelephu.

Gelephu

☑06 / ELEV 280M

The large border town of Gelephu is the gateway to south-central Bhutan. It's a pleasant enough town but really just a place to overnight before leaving or entering Bhutan.

If you find yourself with time to kill, visit the weekend market, spin the prayer wheels at the large Buddha statue beside the football ground or visit the large distillery operated by the army welfare division. The Nyimalung Tratsang, 1km north of town, is the winter residence for monks from Nyimalung Goemba in the Chhume valley.

🛏 Sleeping

Several local hotels cater to border traffic, including the **Dragon Guest House** (☑17448394; r Nu 1500-2000), **Hotel Chorten** (☑251252) and **Hotel Dechen** (☑251293).

Tshendhen Hotel HOTEL **$**

(📋 251536; bees@druknet.bt; r Nu 1440-2160; ❄🛜) This family-run place is probably the best choice in town, with a charming flower-strewn porch and pleasant balcony seating. The fresh, tiled rooms come with hot-water bathrooms and even a coffeemaker. The hotel is named after Bhutan's national tree, the cypress.

Hotel Kuku HOTEL **$$**

(📋 251435; r Nu 1870-2750; ❄) A lodge-style place that offers spacious deluxe rooms with reliable hot water, air-con, comfy mattresses and a cosy restaurant.

❶ Information

Bank of Bhutan (🕑 9am-3.30pm Mon-Fri, 9am-noon Sat) By the bus station; exchanges cash but no travellers cheques.

Bhutan National Bank (🕑 9am-3pm Mon-Fri, 9am-11am Sat) Exchanges cash only.

❶ Getting There & Away

Planned twice-weekly flights from Paro to Gelephu airport, just west of town, should be available by the time you read this. Sealed roads run north to Trongsa via Zhemgang or northwest to Wangdue Phodrang via Sarpang and Damphu.

The only reliable onward transport to Guwahati (India; five hours, Rs 4000) is to hire a taxi, which your guide will help arrange. The initial section of road from the border to Bongigaon is in poor condition but is currently being upgraded. Whether leaving or entering India, don't forget to get an Indian immigration stamp at the easily missed Foreigners' Registration Post at Deosiri, 10km from the Bhutan border. At the time of writing frequent and unannounced transport strikes in Assam were causing potential havoc with travel schedules.

Royal Manas National Park

After years of being off-limits due to security concerns this remote and enticing national park is now open to visitors. The park is little known, even among agents in Thimphu, and facilities are still limited; only 27 foreigners visited in 2011.

The park's forests are home to a wide variety of animals, including elephants, water buffalos, leopards, between 30 and 50 tigers, clouded leopards, civets, rhinoceros and 350 species of birds. The park abuts the Manas National Park in Indian Assam, forming a transnational conservation area.

Tourism is very much in its infancy here. Agencies can arrange jeep and elephant safaris from the central Manas camp ranger office, as well as boat trips down the Manas between Panbang and Manas camp. November to March are the best months to visit. There are several tsechu festivals in the region in the 10th Bhutanese month (November).

Access is still tricky as there are few roads into the park. Perhaps the best way to experience the park is to make the three- or four-day hike from Gomphu (1460m) to Panbang, overnighting in community-managed campgrounds at Pangtang (240m), Shillingtoe (420m), Changzam bridge and Pangbang river junction (160m). Expect to walk between four and six hours per day. All campgrounds have toilets, water and twin log cabins. Gomphu is itself a three-hour drive from Zhemgang and boasts a lhakhang, a cremation site and the Duenmang Tshachhu (hot spring; a two-hour walk away). A new road shadows the trek route, but a lack of bridges across the Mangde Chhu means there is currently little traffic.

The easiest road access to Pangbang village is actually from Mathanguri in India, just a short boat ride across the Manas River from Manas camp. A little-used 25km road leads from Gelephu to Kanamakra at the southwestern corner of the park and there is also a road entering the park from Nganglam in the east. Depending on your itinerary you may need double-entry Indian and Bhutanese visas, so check with your agent.

Eastern Bhutan

Best Buddhist Architecture

➡ Lhuentse Dzong (p143)

➡ Gom Kora (p150)

➡ Dechen Phodrang (p152)

➡ Trashigang Dzong (p146)

➡ Trashi Yangtse Dzong (p151)

Off the Beaten Track

➡ Hiking around Mongar (p142)

➡ Dungkhar (p143)

➡ Bomdeling Wildlife Sanctuary (p152)

➡ Birdwatching around Sengor (p139)

Why Go?

The wild east of Bhutan sees far fewer tourists than the western regions, which is one reason why we like it. Food and accommodation can be simpler here than in the west but in return hardy visitors will be rewarded with group-free dzongs and temples, beautiful silks and embroidery, and lush, bird-filled forests. Despite its relative remoteness, the rugged east is the most densely populated region. Most of the population live in remote settlements; secreted high above the road or in isolated valleys, some are home to minority ethnic groups comprising less than 1000 people.

The east is opening up to tourism at a pace unmatched anywhere else in Bhutan. New hotels, a new airport at Yongphula and several proposed new trekking routes make this the frontier for adventure travel in Bhutan. If you want to get off the beaten track and are up for some exploring, this is your place.

When to Go

➡ The lower altitudes mean that late spring and summer here are hot, humid and sweaty, with insects aplenty. This is the best time for birdwatching in the lush broadleaf forests.

➡ Monsoon rains between May and August regularly cause havoc on the fragile roads carved into the steep mountains, so expect delays after heavy downpours.

➡ Late February to mid-March is a good time to visit for comfortable temperatures, low-season crowds, interesting festivals and spring blooms.

➡ Snowfalls in winter can also result in temporary road blockages on the high passes.

Eastern Bhutan Highlights

1 Wander the bustling narrow streets of **Trashigang** (p146), one of Bhutan's most attractive and lively towns

2 Fasten your seatbelt for a trip on the dramatic cliff-hugging road over the 3750m **Thrumshing La** (p138)

3 Take the picturesque drive up to **Lhuentse Dzong** (p143)

4 Watch some of Bhutan's finest cloth being woven at the remote weaving village of **Khoma** (p144)

5 Check your sin levels at the serene pilgrimage site of **Gom Kora** (p150)

6 Walk around the tranquil Chorten Kora, and witness traditional crafts in far-flung **Trashi Yangtse** (p151)

7 Explore the remote **Bomdeling Wildlife Sanctuary** (p152), one of the best places to see the black-necked crane

History

In ancient times eastern Bhutan was ruled by a collection of separate petty kingdoms and was an important trade route between India and Tibet. Goods flowed via Bhutan through what is now Singye Dzong in the Lhuentse district to the Tibetan town of Lhodrak.

The most important figure in this region's history was Chhogyel Mingyur Tenpa. When he was *penlop* (governor) of Trongsa, he led his armies to eastern Bhutan to quell revolts in Bumthang, Lhuentse, Trashigang, Mongar and Zhemgang. His efforts were responsible for bringing eastern Bhutan under the rule of the *desi* (secular ruler of Bhutan) and went a long way towards the ultimate unification of the country. Mingyur Tenpa built the dzong at Trongsa and was responsible for the construction of most of the dzongs in eastern, as well as central, Bhutan. In 1668 he was enthroned as the third *desi* and ruled until 1680.

MONGAR DZONGKHAG

The Mongar district is the northern portion of the ancient region of Khyeng. Shongar Dzong, Mongar's original dzong, is in ruins, and the new dzong in Mongar town is not as architecturally spectacular or historically significant as others in the region. Drametse Goemba (p145), in the eastern part of the district, is an important Nyingma monastery, perched high above the valley.

Jakar to Mongar

193KM / 7 HOURS

It takes about seven hours to travel between Jakar and Mongar. The trip crosses two passes and takes in numerous sheer drops on what is one of the most spectacular drives in the country, descending 3200m in a distance of 84km. During winter the Thrumshing La is occasionally closed for a day or two during heavy snowfall.

Ura to Thrumshing La

36KM / 1¼ HOURS

Beyond the office of the Thrumshing La National Park, past the turn-off to the Ura–Jakar bypass, the main road crosses the small Lirgang Chhu on a bridge called Liri Zam to enter the territory of the national park. It climbs past overhanging cliffs and cedar trees, more often than not framed in mist, and crosses a ridge that is labelled Wangthang La on some maps. It then drops into the Geyzam Chhu valley and starts climbing again past a road workers' camp. Because the soil is very sandy, the road is unstable and has left a large scar on the hillside.

Three kilometres before the pass there is a small park that features over 20 species of rhododendron. It's possible to follow the trail inside the **Rhododendron Garden** and hike up through the forest for 40 minutes to the pass. If you have a keen interest in rhododendrons and are here between March and May, it's often possible to get the park ranger to accompany you and point out the different species; mention this to your guide in advance and ask at the national park office in Ura.

If you are lucky enough to travel on a clear day, watch for a view of Gangkhar Puensum (at 7541m it is often cited as the world's highest unclimbed mountain) as you approach the pass. A *mani* wall (Buddhist dry-stone wall with sacred inscriptions) and prayer flags adorn the pass and a fallen sign proclaims: 'You are at highest point'. This is **Thrumshing La** (3750m), 85km from Jakar, and the border of Mongar Dzongkhag; you are now officially in eastern Bhutan.

Thrumshing La to Sengor

22KM / 1 HOUR

Once you've crossed into eastern Bhutan, you'll find this side of the pass much rockier. The road switchbacks down through a fir forest. At about 3000m, 20km from the pass, the route emerges from the trees and enters the pastures of the Sengor valley. The settlement at **Sengor** has a few houses near the road, although the main part of the village, about 20 houses, is in the centre of the valley below. The roadside Dee-Ling Restaurant offers local-style *ema datse* (chillis with cheese), but it's better to continue past the village to the tourist-grade **Kuenzang Hotel** (☑17866423; set meal Nu 450), built by the Tourism Council of Bhutan (TCB) and boasting clean toilets and set lunches.

Sengor to Kuri Zampa

62KM / 1¾ HOURS

The next stretch of road is the wildest in Bhutan. Five kilometres beyond the Sengor valley the road begins a steep descent into the Kuri Chhu valley, clinging to the side of a rock cliff, with numerous streams and waterfalls leaping out onto the road. The

HIKING & BIRDING OFF THE BEATEN TRACK IN
THRUMSHING LA NATIONAL PARK

The wild landscapes between Thrumshing La and Shongar Dzong offer lots of opportunities for some adventurous forest hikes. Hardy birdwatchers in particular will love the three-hour hike from Thrumshing La pass down to Sengor, through beautiful old-growth forest. The two-day walk from Sengor to Yong Khola also takes you through one of the best birdwatching spots in Bhutan (360 species live here) and many birding groups base themselves at the Norbugang campsite around 5km before Yong Khola.

Another good hiking and birding option is to follow the steep day-long hiking trail from Latong La down to Menchugang, via Saling and Shongar. In general, September to November and February to March are the best times to hike in this region.

For more details on these and other adventures and to pick up a local guide (essential) see the Ecotourism department at the Thrumshing La National Park office in Ura (p133).

frequent fog and cloud on this side of the pass makes it difficult to see what's below – for which you should be profoundly grateful, since more often than not, there's nothing.

Ten kilometres past Sengor the road swings past a chorten and telecommunications tower at Latong La. Three kilometres further a turnout offers views down onto the Namling Waterfall, which plunges from beneath the road and is spectacular after monsoonal rainfalls. There are several chortens on this stretch – erected as memorials to the almost 300 Indian and Nepali contract labourers who were killed during the construction of this portion of the road. As you drive along the narrow track that was hacked into the side of a vertical cliff, it's hard not to be concerned that you might well join them soon. Prayer plaques and Shiva tridents offer some limited spiritual protection. There are no settlements here except for a camp at Namling, 20km from Sengor, where a crew works frantically to protect the road from tumbling down the mountainside.

About 17km from Namling, after a long descent that traverses the side of a cliff, the road reaches safer ground and leaves the territory of the Thrumshing La National Park. At Yong Khola it emerges into the upper part of a large side valley of the Kuri Chhu, a lush semitropical land of bamboo, ferns and leeches (and good birdwatching). You pass cornfields and descend past the new Tidangbi Lhakhang to the valley floor on a road that winds around like a pretzel. Rice terraces appear and tropical fruits such as mango and pineapple flourish.

Atop a hill on the opposite side of the river, near Menchugang village at Km 123, is a view of the ruined Shongar Dzong. There's not much to see – just some stone walls almost hidden by trees on the top of a hillock – but this is believed to have been one of the earliest and largest dzongs, perhaps built as early as 1100. Like Trongsa, Shongar was powerful because the dzong was ideally situated to control movements between eastern and western Bhutan. The new dzong was built in Mongar town when the old one was destroyed by fire in 1899. You can hike to the dzong in around 20 minutes on a sweaty trail rich with birdlife.

A couple of kilometres further, Lingmethang (650m), 57km from Sengor, boasts four adjacent roadside hotels, all offering hot drinks, cold beer and early season fruit.

The road swings north at a chorten that marks the junction of the main Kuri Chhu valley. At Kuri Zampa (570m) you finally hit the valley floor with a bump – an amazing descent of 3200m from the pass. Step out of your vehicle and breathe in the thick syrupy air before frantically stripping off three layers of clothing. On the east side of a prayer-flag-strewn bridge is a concrete chorten that is patterned after Bodhnath in Nepal; it is said to contain relics from the original Shongar Dzong. Beside the bridge is a deserted factory that used to extract oil from the wild lemongrass that is so abundant here.

A secondary road leads downstream to the new town of Gyalpozhing and the Kuri Chhu power project, beyond which a new road leads further downstream to Nanglam on the Indian border.

Kuri Zampa to Mongar

25KM / 45 MINUTES

The road to Mongar climbs through chir pine forests up the eastern side of the Kuri Chhu valley. To the north you can see the road to Lhuentse traversing the side of the valley. This road leaves the Mongar road at Gangola, 12km before Mongar, and travels 65km to Lhuentse.

The Mongar road climbs up and up through cornfields towards a cluster of houses on top of the hill. A final switchback leads into Mongar.

Mongar

☑ 04 / ELEV 1600M

Most towns in the west of Bhutan are in valleys. In eastern Bhutan most towns, including Mongar, are on the tops of hills or ridges.

There is little of real interest to see in Mongar, but many people spend a night here before continuing to Trashigang. It takes about 11 hours to drive from Jakar to Trashigang, which often means driving at night, which is a waste in such interesting countryside.

◉ Sights

The pleasant main street is lined with traditionally painted stone Bhutanese buildings decorated with wooden facades with colourful potted plants and prayer wheels on their verandahs. Archers sharpen their aim on the football ground most afternoons.

A large **prayer wheel** near the crumbling clock tower attracts reverential old-timers who come to catch up on local news.

★ Mongar Dzong   BUDDHIST, DZONG

The Mongar Dzong was established in 1930 to replace the original Shongar Dzong, although the original *utse* (central tower) dates from an earlier age. It's unusual because it has two entrances and because the monk and administrative bodies share the same courtyard, though this will change with the construction of a new administrative courtyard and new assembly hall for the 60 resident monks. There are four lhakhangs in the *utse*, including a *goenkhang* (chapel dedicated to protective deities) and a Sangay Lhakhang. The week-long **Mongar tsechu** is held here in November (seventh to the 10th days of the 10th lunar month).

Yakgang Lhakhang   BUDDHIST, TEMPLE

A short drive west of town is this little-visited but interesting lhakhang, founded in the 16th century by the son of Pema Lingpa. As you enter the main hall notice how the original entrance on the far wall was blocked up after the arrival of the road (in the interests of security), leaving a mixture of old and new murals. The handwritten texts in the corner were brought from Tibet.

The caretaker is a *gomchen* (lay monk) whose position is handed down from father to son. Upon request he will often open the lhakhang in the next-door house, where the main relics are displayed. Look for the wood blocks, a lute, and puppets of local protectors Gelong Daksen and Penchen Tsam. The *cham* masks were crafted by Pema Lingpa's son and are used in the annual tsechu on the 10th day of the fifth month, when the most valuable relics are displayed. To get here drive past the Mongar bus station and traditional architecture of the Court of Justice to the Sherub Reldri private secondary school.

🛏 Sleeping

Dolma Hotel   LOCAL $

(☑ 641508; r Nu 715) The best value of several local-style hotels catering primarily to overnighting bus passengers or budget Indian tourists. It's a clean and modern place in a shopping plaza, with corner balconies and private bathrooms.

Wangchuk Hotel   HOTEL $$

(☑ 641522; www.wangchukhotel.com; s/d Nu 3220/3680, deluxe Nu 4600/5175) The impressive and modern Wangchuk is an echoing, tour-group place that dominates the Mongar accommodation scene with 32 spacious rooms, good food and a delightful setting, though it could do with a touch of maintenance. The large carpeted rooms equipped with comfy beds, TV, room safe and fans have views over town or forested hills, and massage is offered. The restaurant terrace is the perfect place to reminisce over the drive from Bumthang with a stiff drink.

Hotel Druk Zom   HOTEL $$

(☑ 641206; hoteldrukzom@yahoo.com; s/d Nu 1800/3000) A bright and welcoming boutique hotel with a range of rooms whose sizes and configurations vary according to what appears to be rather haphazard building plans. All rooms have a ceiling fan, TV and phone. Mattresses, though, are on the firm side and bathrooms vary in size. The multicuisine restaurant is light and bright with views over town.

Druk Zhongar Hotel   HOTEL $$

(☑ 641587; drukzhongar@druknet.com; s/d from Nu 2640/3000, ste Nu 3240) This well-run, friendly hotel has average rooms equipped with TV and fans, and some have a balcony.

Mongar

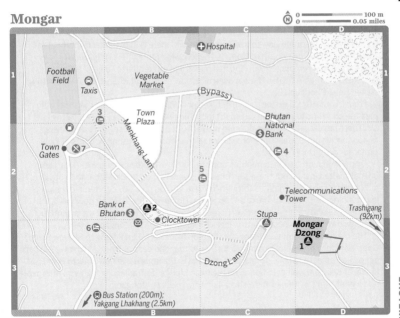

The basement restaurant is also decent, if a little gloomy. Avoid the basement rooms like the plague.

✕ Eating

Almost everyone eats in their hotel, but if you want a light lunch of *momos* (dumplings) or samosas try the local hotels lining the main street.

Phuensom Bakery   BAKERY
(☎641143; ⊗9am-6pm) The Phuensom Bakery is the place to load up on acceptable doughnuts and chocolate éclairs.

✪ Information

Bank of Bhutan (⊗9am-1pm Mon-Fri, 9-11am Sat)
Bhutan National Bank (⊗9am-4pm Mon-Fri, 9-11am Sat)
Hospital (☎641112) Just below the vegetable market.
Post Office (⊗8.30am-5pm Mon-Fri, 8.30am-1pm Sat)

✪ Getting There & Away

The new bus station west of town has buses daily except Sunday to Trashigang (Nu 100, departing at 6am), daily to Lhuentse (Nu 90, 1pm), and daily except Monday to Thimphu (Nu 560, 7am;

overnighting in Bumthang) and Samdrup Jongkhar (Nu 330, 6.30am). Shared taxis to Trashigang are another option at Nu 500 per seat.

LHUENTSE DZONGKHAG

Formerly known as Kurtoe, the isolated district of Lhuentse is the ancestral home of Bhutan's royal family. Although geographically in the east, it was culturally identified with central Bhutan, and the high route over Rodang La was a major trade route until the road to Mongar was completed. Many

HIKES AROUND MONGAR

If you have a half- or full-day spare in your itinerary, there is some fine off-the-beaten-track hiking in the hills south of Mongar. The following route offers ridge walks, valley views and some remote retreats and lhakhangs in a three-quarter-day hike. For an easier 2½-hour walk do it in the opposite direction, starting at Phurji Laptsa and getting picked up at Phongchu La.

From **Yakgang Lhakhang** drive or hike uphill for 45 minutes (take the short cuts past the chortens to avoid the dirt road) to the fine ridgetop monastery at **Phongchu La**. There are expansive views down to the Kuri Chhu and the lushly forested Kheng region to the south, while the monastery itself has some interesting puppets of local protector deity Dorji Gyeltsen.

From Phongchu La it's 25 minutes downhill to tiny **Senlung Goemba**. The main chapel is often locked but there's an unusual personal meditation tent at the entrance.

A steep climb of 40 minutes through forest leads you past two chortens to the ruins surrounding **Jaiphu Lhakhang** on top of the hill. Ten minutes' detour downhill is the charming Jaiphu meditation retreat, home to seven monks. From here trails continue steeply down to the lhakhang and village of Kadam and on to Mongar.

The main route continues along the ridgetop from Jaiphu Lhakhang to Shami (Sainu) Goemba, then continues 20 minutes further to the road pass at **Phurji Laptsa**. You can get picked up here, or hike 40 minutes downhill to the impressive new Zangto Pelri Lhakhang at Kilikhar (Kyilhor) Shedra, on the main Mongar to Trashigang highway. After tea and a chat with the monks, it's a short 4km drive back to Mongar.

Lhuentse women have looms at home and the village of Khoma is especially famous for its *kushutara* (brocade) weaving.

Mongar to Lhuentse

77KM / 3 HOURS

Lhuentse is 63km from the junction at Gangola and a three-hour drive from Mongar. It's a dramatic trip, frequently taking you alongside cliffs high above the river valley, but since you follow the main valley it's a comfortable ride, as long as there have not been any recent landslides.

Mongar to Autsho

38KM / 1¼ HOURS

It is 12km down the hill from Mongar to the junction of the Lhuentse road at Gangola (1110m), where local women sell packets of oranges and peanuts. The Lhuentse road winds around the hill to Chali and Palangphu and then passes the new suspension bridge to Banjor village (the previous bridge further upstream was washed away when a glacial lake burst, sending floodwaters surging down the valley). The road crosses the unstable Dorji Lung slide area (and its protective chortens) to descend to the banks of the Kuri Chhu and the two shops that make up the village of Rewan.

Passing a large, white Tibetan-style brick chorten surrounded by 108 smaller chortens, the road reaches the extensive cornfields and languid riverside location of **Autsho** (920m). Near the river you may be able to spot rhesus monkeys playing on stones, and black cormorants diving for fish. The **Phayul Resort** (☎17624046; r Nu 1000-1250) here has a relaxed vibe and is a good lunch or even overnight stop, with five comfortable rooms.

Autsho to Tangmachu

26KM / 1 HOUR

The road passes towering cliffs, often half hidden in the mist, en route to Fawan. It then switchbacks 100m above the river to the scruffy roadside settlement of Gorgan opposite the large valley of the Noyurgang Chhu, which enters from the west. Near this part of the road, in Umling, are said to be the remains of an ancient underground stone castle built by Bangtsho Gyalpo in about 1500 BC.

After a while the Kuri Chhu valley begins to widen. Beyond a large white chorten, the road crosses to the west bank of the river on a suspension bridge at Thinleypang. On the hillside high above the bridge, above the improbably located settlement of Tangmachu, locals are putting the finishing touches to a colossal 45m-high **statue of Guru Rinpoche** in the form of Guru Nangsi Zilnon. The statue claims to be the tallest Guru statue in the world, beating a similarly Herculean rival in nearby Sikkim, at a cost over US$2 million. See www.drukodiyana.org.bt for details. An unpaved road switchbacks 10km up to the village and high school, 600m above the road, but it is often impassable if it's been raining. Figure on a two-hour detour.

Tangmachu to Lhuentse

13KM / 30 MINUTES

The road traverses the foot of the Tangmachu valley for about 6km, passing a road construction camp and a hydrology station at Sumpa. Rounding a corner there's a view of Lhuentse Dzong, which dominates the head of the valley. A new road bridge leads across the river here, providing access past a huge new chorten and cremation ground to Khoma village.

A short distance on, the valley narrows and the road begins climbing towards the town. Just before the road passes the hospital there is an excellent view of the dzong perched dramatically atop a bluff. The road to Dungkhar branches off by the hospital.

Lhuentse

✍ 04 / ELEV 1440M

There is little to see in Lhuentse and there's no actual village here, but the dzong is one of the most picturesque in Bhutan. Just above the dzong is a new *dratshang* (college) built to house the monastic community, while the hillsides are dotted with new quarters for government officials who have been posted to this remote area where housing is scarce.

It's worth driving up to the Royal Guest House for views of the dzong and the snow peaks at the head of the Kuri Chhu valley. The peak at the head of the valley to the northwest of the guesthouse is Sheri Nyung.

As you leave Lhuentse for Mongar, look out for the ancient ruined bridge down in the valley a couple of kilometres below, just before the bend in the river.

◎ Sights

Lhuentse Dzong   DZONG

Lhuentse Rinchentse Phodrang Dzong, as it is correctly known, sits high on a rocky outcrop overlooking the Kuri Chhu valley, with near-vertical drops on all sides.

Although Pema Lingpa's son Kuenga Wangpo established a small goemba on this site early in the 16th century, the dzong itself was built by the Trongsa *penlop* Mingyur Tenpa in 1654. It has been renovated several times, most recently to repair damage caused by an earthquake in 2009. A three-day *tsechu* fills the dzong to capacity in December/January.

Visitors can visit seven lhakhangs, assuming you can find someone with the keys. The 100 or so resident monks see few tourists and are very friendly, which perhaps explains why visitors here have more freedom to explore than they do in any other dzong in Bhutan.

🍴 Sleeping & Eating

It's best to arrive in Lhuentse with a packed lunch, otherwise you can get *ema datse* and perhaps *momos* at the basic **Shangrila Hotel** (✍545123; mains Nu 80) or the nearby Karma Hotel.

Royal Guest House   GUESTHOUSE $

(✍545102, bookings 17781551; r Nu 300) Lhuentse's only hotel is this 12-roomed government guesthouse, on a hill 100m above the town. It's possible to get a booking here but it's a bureaucratic hassle – you need permission from the *dzongrab* (second in command) and he may want to see permission from the Home Ministry in Thimphu – and you could get bumped at any minute by visiting officials.

❶ Getting There & Away

Buses run three times a week to Thimphu, overnighting in Bumthang.

Around Lhuentse

A recommended excursion from Lhuentse is to the weaving village of Khoma. Several Bhutanese travel companies offer three-day tours of surrounding weaving villages, including Gonpokarpo, Chenling, Shyam, Minje and Nyilamdun (Ngangladung), though all are now linked by farm roads.

Dungkhar

An unpaved but good-quality road runs from Lhuentse for 40km to the small village of Dungkhar, named because the ridge upon which it sits is shaped like a conch (*dungkhar*). Pema Lingpa's son Kuenga Wangpo

WORTH A TRIP

KHOMA

If you are interested in weaving (and even if you're not), it's worth making the 5km drive up to this traditional weaving village. The village produces some of Bhutan's most sought after and expensive *kushutara* weavings and almost all of the 30 or so houses in the village have traditional back-strap looms set up on their porches. The weavings are so elaborate that they resemble embroidery and are generally used as *kiras* (women's traditional dress), though bags and other pieces are produced. The village is comparatively wealthy and most households boast a TV and carbon-fibre archery bows.

The **Zangto Pelri Lhakhang** sits on a spur overlooking the river junction. If you have time to kill, get directions to the **Sangay Lhodrup Lhakhang**, a 20-minute hike on the hillside above Khoma.

Most travel agencies can arrange a homestay in the village. We stayed at the simple but traditional and welcoming **Homestay of Norbu Laden** (☑17700848).

On the drive up to the village look also for the white hermitage of **Drak Kharpo**, visible on the far cliffs across the valley.

settled here, and it is through him that Bhutan's royal family, the Wangchucks, trace their ancestry to the Kurtoe region. Jigme Namgyal, father of the first king, was born here in 1825 and left home when he was 15 to eventually become Trongsa *penlop* and the 51st *desi*.

The road from Lhuentse climbs high above the river to Zhamling before dropping down again to Dungkhar. A return trip here from Lhuentse will eat up at least five hours.

The renovated 16th-century **Dungkhar Naktshang** sits above the village beside the school and houses the government *gewog* (lowest administrative level) offices. A tsechu is held here on the same dates as Lhuentse dzong, on the eighth to 11th days of the 10th lunar month. Just below in the village is the unassuming birthplace of Jigme Namgyal. Much more impressive is the house of the **Choeje Naktshang**, a fine century-old country estate whose family are happy to show visitors their charming rooftop lhakhang.

Guru Rinpoche meditated in a cave at Rinchen Bumpa peak, a hard day's hike high above Dungkhar; locals still make an overnight trek there once a year to circumambulate the peak and visit the small lhakhang. Pema Lingpa visited the Dungkhar area many times and built the Goeshog Pang Lhakhang, a two-hour walk up the valley.

En route to Dungkhar, around 9km from Lhuentse, on the far side of the river is the photogenic country house and large white chorten at **Thimyul**. A suspension bridge offers foot access if you fancy some exploring.

Singye Dzong

Singye Dzong is on the old trade route from Bhutan to Lhodrak in Tibet. Guru Rinpoche meditated here and it's an important pilgrimage place for Bhutanese. The trek takes three days in each direction and there are plans to open it up to tourists.

There's no actual dzong (Singye Dzong is a large rock) but there is a goemba founded by Yeshe Tshogyel, the consort of Guru Rinpoche who concealed many *terma* (sacred texts and artefacts) here.

The route runs from Khoma to Khomagang, Thang Karmo and Singye Dzong (three days), followed by time for exploration of Tshonag (Black Lake) and Tshokhar (White Lake), before returning to Khoma the same way. April to June and the month of October are the best times to go.

TRASHIGANG DZONGKHAG

Trashigang is the heart of eastern Bhutan and was once the centre of important trade with Tibet. There are several goembas and villages that make a visit worthwhile, but a lot of driving is required to reach this remote region.

Mongar to Trashigang

91KM / 3½ HOURS

The Mongar to Trashigang stretch is easier and shorter than the journey from Jakar to Mongar, but you still need about 3½ hours to cover the 91km between the two towns, plus an extra two hours if you detour to Drametse Goemba. The road crosses one low pass, then follows a river valley before making a final climb to Trashigang.

Mongar to Kori La

17KM / 30 MINUTES

Leaving Mongar, the road climbs past fields of corn to the *shedra* (Buddhist college) and new Zangto Pelri Lhakhang at Kilikhar. Soon the road swings into a side valley, passing through a deep forest of rhododendrons and orchids.

About 3km past Kilikhar a paved side road leads down 2km to Wengkhar Lhakhang, founded by the third Zhabdrung near the site of his birthplace. Clothes and relics of the Zhabdrung are displayed here on the 10th day of the third lunar month.

The road passes a new nunnery at Kitar and starts switchbacking at Chompa. A footpath here leads up for 90 minutes or so to the photogenic and little-visited cliffside retreat of Larjung (Larjab Drakar Choeling) Lhakhang. Rather than return the same way, it's possible to continue on foot to the Kori La. The path isn't obvious, so it's a good idea to arrange a guide in advance from the Coffee Café.

About 1km further is the Kori La (2400m), where there is an array of prayer flags, a small *mani* wall, and the Coffee Café (☎17284451; ⊙7am-8pm), where you can get a hot coffee or tea with biscuits. The forest surrounding the pass is a good place for birdwatching; keep an eye out for great Indian hornbills.

Nearby is the start of the Kori La to Golishing Nature Trail, a former trade route which traverses 2.75km (45 minutes) of pleasant downhill forest trail before ending at a side road, 3km from the main road, where your driver can pick you up.

Kori La to Yadi

21KM / 1 HOUR

The road drops from the pass into the upper reaches of the extensive Manas Chhu drainage, switchbacking down through broadleaf forests to the charming private lhakhang near the village of Naktshang.

The road continues its descent past fence-like prayer flags (the Bhutanese equivalent of road safety barriers) to the substantial village of Yadi (1480m). The Choden Hotel General Shop Cum Bar & Lodge (☎04-539113) here is a decent place to break for

a cup of masala tea next to the giant prayer wheel. Passengers pile out of buses from Trashigang to Mongar to breakfast here.

Below Yadi, a dirt road branches off 17km to Shershong (Serzhong) and the two- or three-day pilgrimage trek to Aja Ney. The 'A' of Aja is a sacred letter and 'ja' means 'one hundred'. Guru Rinpoche placed 100 letter As on rocks here, and for devotees it's like a spiritual treasure hunt: the more you see the more merit you gain. Those without sin usually find the most.

Yadi to Thungdari

33KM / 1 HOUR

Beyond Yadi a long stretch of prayer flags lines the road; below are numerous switchbacks, nicknamed the Yadi Loops, that lead down through a forest of sparse chir pine with an understorey of fragrant lemongrass, dropping 350m in 10km. There is a good viewpoint where you can see the road weaving down the hill; pictures taken from here often appear in books and brochures to illustrate just how circuitous Bhutan's roads are.

The community-run Monkey's Shoulder Cafe (☎16920136; set meal Nu 400) at Zalaphangma has pleasant indoor and outdoor seating and serves set meals by arrangement. The unpaved road that heads west from here leads 11km to the village and two lhakhangs of Chaskhar.

After more switchbacks, the road crosses a bridge painted with the eight Tashi Tagye symbols and continues for 10km to Sherichhu (600m). Climb out of the Sherichhu valley to a chorten and cross a ridge to meet the large Drangme Chhu, which flows from the eastern border of Bhutan. The road winds in and out of side valleys for 12km to Thungdari, 71km from Mongar, where a side road leads to Drametse Goemba.

Drametse Goemba

Drametse is the biggest and most important monastery in eastern Bhutan. It's an 18km, hour-long drive on a dirt track off the main road, gaining 1350m, and you'll need a 4WD vehicle if it's been raining.

There are about 90 monks and *gomchen* (lay or married Nyingma monks) at Drametse. The monastery was founded in 1511 by the granddaughter (some say daughter) of Pema Lingpa, Ani Chhoeten Zangmo, in a place she named Drametse, which means 'the peak where there is no enemy'.

The monastery is famous as the home of the Nga Cham drum dance that features in many tsechus and which was proclaimed a masterpiece of oral and intangible heritage by Unesco in 2005.

In the main chapel, to the right of a central Guru Rinpoche, is the gold funeral chorten of Chhoeten Zangmo beside a statue of Pema Lingpa that was fashioned by himself in a dream (and thus is a mirror image). The long box here holds a *thondrol* (painted or embroidered religious picture) depicting Pema Lingpa, which is unveiled at dawn on the 15th day of the 10th lunar month (November) during an annual three-day festival. A *thondrol* is a huge *thangka* that guarantees liberation *(drol)* through the sight of it *(thon)*.

The middle floor has chapels dedicated to the protectors Palden Lhamo (Sri Devi) and the 'horse-necked' Tamdrin (Hayagriva). The upstairs **Goenkhang Chenmo** (Great Protector Chapel) is jam-packed with weapons, a stuffed lynx, a dead flying fox (that looks like it's been blown up with a foot pump), an assault rifle, and the three local protector deities of Pekar, Drametse and Tsong Tsoma. Make an offering to receive a sacred thread, be blessed by the *phurba* (ritual dagger) and then roll the dice to get a reading from an ancient book of divination. The next-door **Tseringma Lhakhang** houses images of the long-life deity, as well as five versions of the Himalayan protector Tseringma, all riding different mythological beasts. Finally, the **Kanjur Lhakhang** houses a box of sacred relics, including the cymbals used in all previous tsechus.

This is potato-growing country, and in autumn there are huge piles of potatoes waiting for trucks to carry them down to eventual sale in India and Bangladesh.

Thungdari to Trashigang

20KM / 45 MINUTES

Back down on the main road you'll catch glimpses of Trashigang Dzong high above the south bank of the Drangme Chhu.

After passing a Public Works Department (PWD) camp at Rolong, the road reaches a 90m-long bridge at **Chazam** (710m). This place was named after the original chain-link bridge here, said to have been built by the Tibetan bridge builder Thangtong Gyalpo in the 15th century (*cha* means 'iron', *zam* means 'bridge'). The large building that formed the abutment of the old bridge has been partially restored and turned into a lhakhang just a short distance upstream of the new bridge. Look for the ruins of watchtowers on the ridge above the old bridge.

On the south side of the bridge is an immigration checkpoint where police inspect your travel permit. The road north from here follows the Kulong Chhu valley and then climbs to Trashi Yangtse.

The road switchbacks up towards Trashigang, passing the turn-off to Samdrup Jongkhar before continuing 3km to Trashigang, well hidden in a wooded valley.

Trashigang

04 / ELEV 1070M

Trashigang (Auspicious Mountain) is one of Bhutan's more interesting towns and a good base for excursions to Trashi Yangtse, Khaling, Radi, Phongme and elsewhere in eastern Bhutan. The picturesque town is at the foot of a steep wooded valley with the tiny Mithidang Chhu channelled through it. Trashigang's focal point is a tiny plaza that becomes crammed with parked cars.

Accommodation here is fairly limited, but there is a variety of restaurants and you're bound to find at least one amusing place to drink among the town's numerous bars. Not many tourists make it to Trashigang, but there used to be many Canadian teachers working here and the people of Trashigang are used to Westerners.

Villagers come to town on holy days, which occur on the first, 10th and 15th of the Bhutanese month, to trade and sample the local *arra* (spirit distilled from rice).

◉ Sights

A large **prayer wheel** sits in the centre of the plaza. The covered pedestal holding the prayer wheel is a favourite sleeping place for villagers waiting for buses and becomes an ad hoc vegetable market most days. Surrounding the plaza are several hotels, restaurants, bars, and a bakery and handicraft shop.

Trashigang Dzong　　　　　　BUDDHIST, DZONG

The dzong is on a thin promontory that overlooks the confluence of the Drangme Chhu and the Gamri Chhu. It was built in 1667 by Mingyur Tenpa, Bhutan's third *desi*. The entire eastern region was governed from this dzong from the late 17th century until the beginning of the 20th century. Several tame *jaru* (*ghoral*; mountain goat) roam the exterior courtyards.

This dzong is unusual in that both the administrative and monastic bodies face onto a single *dochey* (courtyard). By the entry gate look left for the fine *mani* lhakhang and its slate carving of Seng Doma, a local protector that is half-male, half-female.

Inside are a half-dozen lhakhangs, though what you get to see will depend on which monks are around. The 1st-floor *goenkhang* features paintings of a yeti, while another chapel is dedicated to the deity Choegi (Yama) Gyelpo, the wrathful aspect of Chenresig. He is a protector of the faith, the god of death and the king of law, and the one that weighs up the good and evil at the end of a person's life.

Many lama dances are performed in Trashigang to appease Yama, especially during the three-day **tsechu** in November/December, which also includes the unveiling of a large *thangka* and the displaying of a statue of Guru Rinpoche on the last day.

🛏 Sleeping & Eating

A good alternative to staying in Trashigang is to continue 12km southwest of town to the Lingkhar Lodge (p153) at Lengkhar, on the road to Samdrup Jongkhar.

Druk Deothjung Resort HOTEL $
(☑ 521145; s/d Nu 2160/2400, deluxe Nu 2640/3000) This former government guesthouse has charming architecture and fine views down on the dzong, but in return you'll have to put up with simple rooms, patchy hot water and tiny bathrooms. The two top-floor deluxe rooms are marginally better but it's still too basic for some groups. The 'resort' is at Kelling, 1km uphill from the town centre.

Druk Deothjung Hotel LOCAL $
(☑ 521214; drukdeothjung@gmail.com; s/d Nu 2090/2200) This 12-room family-run hotel near the central prayer wheel is the best of the local places in the centre of town. Rooms boast satellite TV and hot-water showers, but also concrete grills in the walls that let in bugs and street noise. Balconies overlook the town plaza, and the very pleasant alfresco dining area serves the best food and coldest beer in town. The attached bakery offers fresh bread and cakes.

**Druk Deothjung
Resort Phomshing** LUXURY HOTEL $$
(☑ 521440; drukdeothjung@gmail.com; s/d Nu 3360/3840, ste Nu 6000/7200) Nothing sums up the changes taking place in eastern Bhu-

Trashigang

◎ **Sights**
1 Prayer Wheel A3

🛏 **Sleeping**
2 Druk Deothjung Hotel A3
3 Hotel KC B2

🍴 **Eating**
4 Pema Bakery & General
    Tsongkhang A3

🛍 **Shopping**
    Druk Deothjung Eastern Rural
    Handicraft .... (see 2)

tan more than this huge luxury investment, a couple of kilometres west of Trashigang. Eventually this behemoth will boast 100 rooms and cottages with a pool, spa and several restaurants with 180-degree views of the valley. Forty smallish rooms have already opened, making it the most comfortable place in town, despite possible construction noise.

Hotel KC HOTEL $$
(☑ 521209; hotelkc4@gmail.com; s/d/ste Nu 2640/3240/4200) This modern, marbley place is comfortable but uninspiring, with a range of rooms, few of which take advantage of the

fine views. Best are the huge suites with kettle and fridge. Standard rooftop rooms are a bit claustrophobic because of the low ceilings. The attached shop has the best selection of imported goodies in town.

Pema Bakery & General Tsongkhang GENERAL STORE $

(☑ 521196) On the road to the dzong, this fascinating general store stocks a decent range of imported goodies from Pringles to Coffee Mate among the pungent odours of dried fish.

🛍 Shopping

Druk Deothjung Eastern Rural Handicraft HANDICRAFTS

(⊘ 9am-7pm) This small shop at the Druk Deothjung Hotel is your last place to load up on crafts like traditional boots, masks and weavings.

ℹ Information

Bank of Bhutan (⊘ 9am-1pm & 2-4pm Mon-Fri, 9am-noon Sat) Changes cash and travellers cheques.

Bhutan National Bank (⊘ 9am-4pm Mon-Fri, 9-11am Sat) Changes cash only.

Kinga Digital and Internet Cafe (per min Nu 2; ⊘ 8am-8pm)

Police Post By the town gate, at the western entrance.

Post Office (⊘ 9am-5pm Mon-Fri, 9am-1pm Sat) Above the town centre, near the high school.

ℹ Getting There & Away

From Trashigang it's 280km to Bumthang (two days), 350km to Trongsa and 550km to Thimphu (three days).

The recently opened airport at Yongphula is about an hour's drive from Trashigang and has weekly flights to Paro. Buy tickets through your agent in Thimphu.

There are daily local buses to Thimphu (Nu 667, two days, 6am), Samdrup Jongkhar (Nu 218, nine hours, 7.30am and 8am) and Mongar (Nu 100, 1pm).

Far Eastern Bhutan

The paved road east from Trashigang travels up the valley of the Gamri Chhu to Rangjung, and then continues as a gravel road and dirt track to Radi and Phongme. Most people headed this way are trekking to Merak and Sakteng. If you're short on time, you won't miss much by skipping this route.

Trashigang to Rangjung

16KM / 45 MINUTES

The road descends from Trashigang, weaving in and out of side valleys to the banks of the Gamri Chhu at 820m. A side road crosses the river here and leads uphill for 19km in great zigzagging gashes to the Chador Lhakhang and *shedra* at **Bartsam**, where the most famous relic is a thumb-sized image of Chana Dorji.

The main Rangjung road stays on the south side of the river, passing through a flat area affected by flooding (the chorten in the middle of the flood plain provides divine protection against floods). Shortly afterwards is the village of **Lungtenzampa**.

After traversing fields for 6km, past the large Vocational Training Institute at Buna, the road crosses the small Kharti Chhu and makes a short climb to **Rangjung** at 1120m. Beyond the secondary school, an elaborate chorten dominates the charming centre of town, which is worth a brief stroll.

Just above the town is the **Rangjung Yoesel Chholing Monastery**, a large Nyingma goemba founded in 1990 by Garub Rinpoche. The main statues are of the Gelog Choksum, the trio of Guru Rinpoche, Indian abbot Shantarakshita and Tibetan king Trisong Detsen. The *torma* (sculptures of barley and butter) depict the five senses, with eyeballs, earlobes, nostrils, a tongue and skin. *Cham* dancing ends a 10-day **drupchen** (festival) in the 12th month (January).

The monastery has a good **guesthouse** (☑ bookings 17110027; s/d Nu 1500/2000) up the hill that is occasionally booked by tourists, particularly Buddhist groups. The 24 rooms have private bathrooms and offer great views over the goemba but must be booked in advance through the Kangri Travel Agency in Thimphu.

Rangjung to Phongme

17KM / 1 HOUR

The dirt road continues east, climbing through large rice terraces and fields of corn for 8km to Radi.

Just 1.5km past Rangjung is **Pema Lhundup Handicrafts** (☑ 16461124), a private house turned weaving centre that sells a beautiful collection of embroidered cloth, shawls and scarfs made from *bura* (raw silk – literally, 'insect fibre') or *sechu* (spun silk) by women from the surrounding villages, including Tzangkhar. *Kiras* vary in price from Nu 10,000 to Nu 55,000, while silk scarves are around Nu 13,000. The knowledgeable owner Peden offers displays on spinning and weaving.

Weaving enthusiasts can also visit **Tzangkhar** from a turn-off by a hairpin loop just before Radi (Km 23). Many of the women here are weavers and you might be able to buy silks direct here.

Beyond Radi (1570m) the road climbs past terraced hillsides for 3km, passing above the large modern **Thekchok Kunzang Choeden Nunnery**, home to 45 nuns. Five kilometres later, past Khardung village, is the collection of shops that is **Phongme** (1840m).

On the hill just before and above the village is the 150-plus-year-old **Phongme Lhakhang**. The central statue is of Chenresig with 1000 arms and 11 heads. A rolled-up *thondrol* (a building-sized *thangka*) hangs from the rafters and *cham* costumes are stored in boxes at the foot of the statues, ready for the annual festival on the 15th of the eighth lunar month (September).

Sakteng Wildlife Sanctuary

From Phongme, ever-advancing roads and foot trails lead southeast to the remote villages of **Merak** and **Sakteng**, which are home to a seminomadic ethnic group called Brokpa (see p186). Rugged Brokpa men often come into Phongme, Khaling and Trashigang to trade. You can recognise them by their sheepskin and red-coloured yak-hair clothing and unusual yak-felt hats called *shamo*, which have hanging spider-like legs that act as rainspouts. The villages and their homestays are currently only reached along trekking routes (see p187) but road construction looks set to change all that in the next couple of years.

Katie Hickman gives a good description of her visit to the region on horseback in her travelogue *Dreams of the Peaceful Dragon*.

Apart from the Brokpas, the sanctuary's most famous resident is the *migoi* (yeti), for whom the park was allegedly established in 2002. The sanctuary office is 1km east of Phongme. The motorable road currently continues to Jyongkhar but will eventually be extended to Sakteng.

TRASHI YANGTSE DZONGKHAG

Previously a *drungkhag* (subdistrict) of Trashigang, Trashi Yangtse became a fully fledged *dzongkhag* (district) in 1993. It borders the Indian state of Arunachal Pradesh, and there is some cross-border trade. The old trade route between east and west Bhutan from Trashi Yangtse, over the mountains to Lhuentse and then over Rodang La (4200m) to Bumthang, is now a trek route. The district lies at the headwaters of the Kulong Chhu, and was earlier known as Kulong.

Trashigang to Trashi Yangtse

53KM / 1¾ HOURS

The drive from Trashigang to Trashi Yangtse takes about 1¾ hours' driving time, but you should budget extra time to visit Gom Kora on the way. There's lots to see en route and it's a great day trip from Trashigang. Even if

---

MIGOI – THE BHUTANESE YETI

The Bhutanese name for a yeti is *migoi* ('strong man') and they are believed to exist throughout northern and northeastern Bhutan, particularly in the Sakteng Wildlife Sanctuary.

The *migoi* is covered in hair that may be anything from reddish-brown to black, but its face is hairless, almost human. It is similar to the yetis of Nepal and Tibet in that the breasts of the female are large and sagging, and both sexes have an extremely unpleasant smell. But Bhutanese *migoi* are special because they have the power to become invisible, which accounts for the fact that so few people have seen them. Another feature that helps them escape detection is that their feet may face backwards, confusing people who try to follow them.

The book *Bhutanese Tales of the Yeti* by Kunzang Choden is a wonderful collection of tales told by village people in Bhutan who have seen, or have met people who have seen, a *migoi*.

you don't have time to drive all the way to Chorten Kora, do make the effort to make the short trip to Gom Kora.

To get from Trashigang to Chazam (9km, 15 minutes), follow the switchbacks down to the bridge at Chazam. Just past Chazam, an unpaved side road leads steeply uphill to Gangthung village and goemba and Yangnyer, where a replica of the Bodhgaya chorten was constructed in 2009. The complex that is visible a short distance up this road is a jail.

From Chazam, the road is level as it winds its way through sparse clumps of chir pine above the west bank of the Drangme Chhu to Gom Kora (13km, 30 minutes). A couple of kilometres before Gom Kora, by the side of the road, is a *ney* (holy spot), where a rock shrine is covered in egg-shaped stones, *tshatshas* (small offerings moulded in clay) and brass images of the Rigsum Goenpo – the Buddhist trinity of Chenresig, Jampelyang (Manjushri) and Chana Dorji. Also here is a natural chorten, wisely painted white since it stands in the middle of the main road!

Gom Kora

Gom Kora is an extraordinarily picturesque temple 13km north of Chazam. The lush green fields, the red robes of the monks and the yellow roof of the temple combine with colourful Buddhist carvings and the rushing river to create an idyllic scene.

The correct name for the site is Gomphu Kora. Gomphu denotes a sacred meditation site of Guru Rinpoche and *kora* means 'circumambulation'. The Guru meditated here and left a body impression on a rock, similar to that in Kurjey Lhakhang in Bumthang.

The central figure in the temple is Guru Rinpoche. To the right is Chenresig, in his 1000-armed aspect. To the far right is an image of the snake demon Gangan Yonga Choephel, who holds a golden mirror in his right hand. The wall murals to the far right are believed to date from the 15th century.

There are numerous sacred objects locked in a glass cabinet that either miraculously appeared here or were brought by the Guru. The largest item is a *garuda* egg, which is a very heavy, perfectly shaped, egglike stone. Other relics include the traditional boot print of the Guru, the footprint of his consort Yeshe Tshogyel (aged eight), the hoof print of Guru Rinpoche's horse and a phallus-shaped rock belonging to Pema Lingpa.

Gom Kora's celebrated old *thondrol,* unique because it is painted, not appliquéd, is either kept in the box here or in Chorten Kora, depending on which source you believe. Gom Kora has a new *thondrol,* which is displayed at the tsechu on the 10th day of the second lunar month (March/April). This festival is different from most other tsechus and pilgrims circumambulate the goemba and sacred rock throughout the night.

Behind the goemba is a fantastical large black rock. It is said that Guru Rinpoche was meditating in a small cave near the bottom of the rock when a demon in the shape of a cobra suddenly appeared. The Guru, alarmed, stood up quickly leaving the impression of his pointed hat at the top of the cave and then transformed himself into a *garuda,* leaving the imprint of his wings nearby. The Guru then made an agreement with the demon to stay away until the end of his meditation. The contract was sealed with thumb prints, which are still visible on the rock. The serpent also left a light-coloured print, with his hood at the top of the rock.

A small sin-testing passageway leads from the cave to an exit to the side of the rock – one participant reported that you must indeed move like a snake to get through the cave. Visitors also test their sin levels and rock-climbing skills by trying to climb up the side of the rock (the 'stairway of the *dakinis*'; female celestial beings) – only the virtuous can make it. On certain auspicious days, holy water, believed to be the Guru's nectar of immortality, flows down from a crevice in the rock and pilgrims line up to spoon it into bottles. You may also see childless women carrying a hefty holy stone around the *kora* path to boost their chances of conceiving.

Gom Kora to Trashi Yangtse

28KM / 1¼ HOURS

Two kilometres from Gom Kora is the sleepy village of Duksum (860m), the roadhead for many large villages higher in the valley. A couple of shops (try the Dondup Tsongkhag) sell colourful patterned cloth and belts woven by the local women using back-strap looms. Duksum's iron chain-link bridge, believed to be the last surviving example of those built by Thangtong Gyalpo, was destroyed in 2004. Some links were used in the reconstructed bridge at Tamchhog Lhakhang and others lie on display at Gom Kora.

The road turns northwest and follows the Kulong Chhu valley towards Trashi Yangtse. The eastern fork of the river flows from Arunachal Pradesh in India and is known as the Dawung Chhu. A dam is under construction along the upper section of the Kulong Chhu.

Climbing high above the Kulong Chhu the road passes the junction of a paved road at Zangpozor. Die-hards can drive 9km up this road to the ruined walls of **Tshenkarla dzong**, which was built in the first half of the 9th century by Prince Tsangma, the eldest son of Tibetan king Trisong Detsen. The prince established himself in eastern Bhutan after he was banished from Tibet. The old name of this town is Rangthang Woong. The ruins sit in a field of wild lemongrass just above the school. A little further is the charming new Zangto Pelri Lhakhang, which offers a fine place for a picnic with views stretching as far as Arunachal Pradesh.

Back on the main road, the habitation gets more sparse as the valley becomes steeper and less suitable for cultivation. Snowy peaks at the head of the valley come in and out of focus. After traversing along a rocky cliff, an impressive building appears on a promontory where a side stream, the Dongdi Chhu, joins the valley. This is the original **Trashi Yangtse Dzong**, built by Pema Lingpa alongside the former trade route; it now houses the town's community of 300 monks. The *dratshang* (monastic college) has a dramatic main assembly hall and an *utse*, which holds the dzong's most precious relic, a statue of Chenresig that flew here from Ralung in Tibet. The dzong is 1.5km up a side road, past a wonderful traditional cantilevered bridge. The old trade route from Bumthang ended here, as does its modern equivalent; today's eight-day Rodang La trek.

Trashi Yangtse

📋 04 / ELEV 1700M

The orderly settlement of Trashi Yangtse rises just above the Chorten Kora, 3km from the old dzong. The new dzong and town occupies a large bowl in one of the furthest corners of the kingdom, 550km from Thimphu.

The road enters from the south passing the large Chorten Kora before it enters a subdued bazaar area with an elaborately decorated Bhutanese-style chorten. From here, one road leads straight to the headquarters and visitor centre of the Bom-

deling Wildlife Sanctuary and another branches right to the new dzong and administrative offices, on a ridge 130m above the town. The dzong was inaugurated in 1997 and has little historical or architectural significance, though the archery ground below the dzong is worth a visit if a tournament is underway.

The town is known for the excellent wooden cups and bowls made here from avocado wood and maple wood using water-driven and treadle lathes. Trashi Yangtse is also a centre of daphne paper-making, using the *tsasho* technique with a bamboo frame to produce a distinctive pattern on the paper.

◎ Sights

Chorten Kora   CHORTEN

Chorten Kora is large, but not nearly as large as the stupa of Bodhnath in Nepal, after which it was patterned. It was constructed in 1740 by Lama Ngawang Loday in memory of his late uncle, Jungshu Phesan, and to subdue local spirits. The lama went to Nepal himself and brought back a model of Bodhnath carved in a radish. He had it copied here so that people could visit this place instead of making the arduous trip to Nepal. The reason that Chorten Kora is not an exact copy of Bodhnath is because the radish shrank during the trip and distorted the carving.

During the first month of the lunar calendar there is a **kora** here, whereby people gain merit by walking around the main chorten and its inner *kora*. It is celebrated on two separate dates (the 15th and 30th days of the lunar month). The first date (Dakpa Kora) is for the people from the Dakpa community in Arunachal Pradesh, India, who make the three-day pilgrimage here to celebrate the sacrifice of an eight-year-old girl from Arunachal Pradesh who was enshrined in the chorten to appease a troublesome demon. The second *kora* (Drukpa Kora) is for the Bhutanese, who come from all over eastern Bhutan, including from the Merak and Sakteng regions, to attend the local fair and gain some good karma by witnessing the unfurling of a giant *tongdrol*. Dozens of stalls and gambling stands give pilgrims a chance to catch up on some shopping and local gossip. A month before the festival the chorten is whitewashed anew, with funds earned from rice grown in the fields immediately surrounding the chorten.

EASTERN BHUTAN TRASHI YANGTSE

In front of the chorten is a natural stone stupa, the *sertho,* which used to stand atop the chorten and is considered sacred. There's also a small goemba here. The hugely popular Bhutanese film *Chorten Kora* was shot here.

National Institute for Zorig Chusum
ART SCHOOL

(☑781141; ☺9am-noon & 1-3.30pm Mon-Fri, 9am-12.30pm Sat) This art and craft institute south of town was opened in 1997 to provide vocational training opportunities for those who are not continuing in the higher education system. Six of the Zorig Chusum (13 traditional arts and crafts) are studied here, including *thangka* painting, embroidery, sculpture, metalwork and woodturning. You can visit the school, watch the students at work and take photographs, though the selection of crafts for sale is rather disappointing. The students are on holiday from December to March and for two weeks in July.

🛏 Sleeping & Eating

Karmaling Hotel
HOTEL $

(☑781113; s/d Nu 1440/1800) This is the main tourist hotel in town, with private Western bathrooms with hot-water geysers but no showers or tubs – just a bucket. The four upstairs rooms are best, arranged around a cosy sitting area warmed by a *bukhari* (wood stove). New deluxe rooms are planned. The elderly owner served the second and third kings of Bhutan as a personal clerk.

Bomdeling Wildlife Sanctuary Guest House
GUESTHOUSE $

(☑781155; s/d Nu 400/500) The sanctuary visitor centre complex just to the northwest of town has several simple rooms with private bathrooms and balconies, but the location is a bit isolated. Upper-floor rooms are the best.

🛍 Shopping

Thinley Dendup General Shop & Handicraft
HANDICRAFTS

(☺7am-7pm) This funky local store by the central-town junction stocks textiles, wooden bowls, oboes, brass butter lamps and other religious paraphernalia.

ⓘ Getting There & Away

Public buses run to Thimphu (Nu 704, two days) on Monday, Friday and Saturday.

Around Trashi Yangtse

Dechen Phodrang

Hidden in a side valley high above Trashi Yangtse town is this delightful and little-known pilgrimage site. The current chapel dates from the 18th century and is built around the *kurjey* (body print) of Guru Rinpoche. Pilgrims lift one of two stones in front of the print to increase their chances of getting a boy or girl. With its towering cypress trees, many sacred stones and carved mantras, the site has a dreamy, timeless feel.

The easiest way to get here is along the bumpy, rutted 12km feeder road to the school at Womenang (also called Do Nakpo), from where it's an easy 45-minute hike via Solamang village. Hiking trails continue via Bumdir and Birting villages to either Dongzom village (3½ hours) or the Rigsum Goenpo Lhakhang via Pelri Goemba (four hours).

Bomdeling Wildlife Sanctuary

Bomdeling is a 40-minute drive north of Trashi Yangtse, across the traditional bridge at the north end of town. It is the winter (November to early March) roosting place of around 100 black-necked cranes, though numbers have been dropping in recent years. The sanctuary is also home to black-capped langurs, red pandas, tigers and snow leopards.

The sanctuary **visitor centre** (☑781155; bws@druknet.bt; ☺9am-5pm Mon-Fri) just north-east of Trashi Yangtse town has some vaguely interesting displays on the geology and natural history of the 1520-sq-km sanctuary, and staff can advise on hiking and homestay options in the sanctuary. Bomdeling currently gets only around 50 tourists a year.

A crane information centre and cafeteria is under development at Dongzom village, 9km from Trashi Yangtse, where rangers can lead you to spot roosting cranes at dawn and dusk. Around 3km before Dongzom is the **Phenday Paper Factory**, where you can watch traditional paper being made from local daphne bushes.

Apart from crane-watching, there are good hikes from Dongzom up to the Buddhist sites of Dechen Phodrang and Rigsum Goenpo, the latter a long day hike or easy overnighter. You can combine all three in a leisurely two- or three-day walk around the valley rim, a hike many agents refer to as the Orchid trek.

SAMDRUP JONGKHAR DZONGKHAG

The only reason to make the tortuous drive into southeastern Bhutan is to leave it, at the border crossing with India at Samdrup Jongkhar. Entering the country at this border crossing offers quick access to the east from India's Assam state, though political tensions and strikes in that state made transport options uncertain at the time of writing.

Trashigang to Samdrup Jongkhar

174KM / 6 HOURS

The winding drive from Trashigang to Samdrup Jongkhar takes at least six hours; more at the time of research due to massive road construction.

Trashigang to Kanglung

22KM / 45 MINUTES

Three kilometres from Trashigang bazaar, the southern road turns off the Mongar road and climbs past the town's main petrol station.

Climbing around a ridge and heading south the road passes the settlement of **Pam**, whose main village and lhakhang are on the hillside above. The narrow unpaved road that heads uphill from here leads to Rangshikhar Goemba and an unusual but rather gaudy two-storey statue of Sakyamuni Buddha as a starving ascetic. Locals say it's possible to hike from here over the ridge to Trashigang in three hours.

The road passes the excellent **Lingkhar Lodge** (☑ 77116767; www.lingkhar.com; s/d/ste Nu 3000/3500/4500; ☎), a charming collection of boutique cottages surrounded by orchards and fruit trees. It's well run, peaceful and thoroughly recommended.

Descend into a side valley, cross a stream and climb through rice terraces to the prosperous farming community of **Rongthung**, 17km from Trashigang. The road then climbs to a ridge and enters **Kanglung** (1870m), where you can see the Zangto Pelri Lhakhang near the entrance to the clock tower and extensive campus of **Sherubtse College**.

The late Father William Mackey, a Jesuit priest, was instrumental in setting up Sherubtse (Peak of Knowledge), Bhutan's only college, in the late 1970s. Most foreigners know of the college through reading Jamie Zeppa's *Beyond the Sky and the Earth*, which chronicles her time teaching here as a Canadian volunteer. The clock tower and green lawns give the town the air of a Himalayan hill station.

Kanglung to Khaling

32KM / 1 HOUR

The road climbs through fields of corn and potatoes, then switchbacks around a line of eight chortens. There are fine views down over the college and as far as Drametse Goemba, way across the valley. Hidden on a ridge above the road in a highly improbable hilltop location is **Yongphula airport** (☑ 17170022), Bhutan's second airstrip, which operates a once- or twice-weekly flight to Paro (US$207), weather permitting.

The road crosses the **Yongphu La** (2190m), offering you a last glimpse of the Himalaya, and swoops past Barshong Lhakhang, along the top of the Barshong valley, and past the impressive **Karma Thegsum Dechenling Goemba**, a huge new Kagyudschool institution of 90 monks headed by the eighth Zuri Rinpoche.

Rounding several corners in the convoluted landscape, the road enters **Khaling**, spread out in a large valley high above the Drangme Chhu. Above the valley is a small lhakhang. In the centre of the valley below Khaling is the **National Institute for the Visually Impaired**. This very well-organised institution tries to assimilate students from all over Bhutan who are blind or otherwise disabled into the local educational system by providing special resources and training. One of its accomplishments is the development of a Dzongkha version of Braille.

Three kilometres beyond Khaling is the **National Handloom Development Project** (☑ 04-581140; ☺ 8am-noon & 1-5pm Mon-Fri, 8am-noon Sat Apr-Dec), operated by the National Women's Association of Bhutan (NWAB). It contracts out weaving and provides cotton yarn on credit to about 200 villagers, who then return the finished product to be sold here or at the Handicraft Emporium in Thimphu.

Particularly interesting are samples of the plants that are used to produce the natural dyes, including rhododendrons (pale yellow), an insect secretion called *lac* (purple) and the stem of the madder creeping plant (pale pink). Photography of the workshops and of the design samples is strictly prohibited.

Prices for a length of woven cloth vary from Nu 1000 up to Nu 20,000, and there are also shawls for sale. Most of the basic cotton is imported from Kolkata (Calcutta).

Khaling to Wamrong

27KM / 45 MINUTES

Beyond Khaling, the road traverses above scattered houses and cornfields before climbing to the head of a rhododendron-filled valley and crossing the **Kharung La** at 2350m. There's a short descent through crumbling hills, then another climb to another pass at 2430m.

Curling around the valley, the route descends past a side road to Thrimshing, then curves round the **Zangto Pelri Lhakhang**. This may well be the last Bhutanese goemba you see, so consider stopping to check out the wonderfully detailed murals and ceiling mandalas. Two kilometres below the lhakhang is the pleasant town of **Wamrong** (2130m), where you can get a good lunch at one of the local-style restaurants. Wamrong is a *drungkhag* (subdistrict) and so has a small dzong.

Wamrong to Pemagatshel Junction

20KM / 45 MINUTES

The road here descends for 6km to Riserboo and its Norwegian-funded hospital. There is a good view down the huge valley as the road traverses in and out of side valleys past the hamlet of **Moshi**, halfway between Trashigang and Samdrup Jongkhar. At a bend in the road at Km 77 you get your first glimpse of the Assam plain below.

Before long you meet the junction to **Pemagatshel**, whose name means 'Blissful Land of the Lotus'. This rural *dzongkhag* is Bhutan's smallest district. There are plans to create a multiday trekking route around the village rim, staying in homestays en route.

On the way to Pemagatshel village is **Yongla Goemba**, one of the holiest shrines in eastern Bhutan. It was founded in the 18th century by Kheydup Jigme Kuenduel, who was advised by the great *terton* (discoverer of *terma*) Rigzin Jigme Lingpa to establish a monastery on a mountain that looked like a *phurba* (ritual dagger) and overlooked the vast plains of India. Later the goemba was used as a base for religious ceremonies by Trongsa *penlop* Jigme Namgyal during the great Duar War with the British in 1865. The goemba is currently being rebuilt after damage sustained in the 2009 earthquake.

Pemagatshel Junction to Deothang

55KM / 1¾ HOURS

Below the junction comes the day's most dangerous section of road, the **Menlong Brak** (*brak,* or *brag,* means cliff in Sharchop), high above the upper Bada valley. The fragile road passes prayer flags, prayer plaques and chortens to reach the Dantak-sponsored Hindu shrine at **Krishnagiri**, where your car (and occupants) will get a *tika* (blessing in the form of a mark on the forehead) from the resident Nepali *babu* (holy man or sadhu). It's an amazing descent, with sheer drops putting the fear of Shiva into you.

From the two-road village of **Narphung** (with its one-way system!), the road passes the Narphung La at 1698m. It crosses a ridge and climbs to 1920m before beginning the final descent to the plains.

The road weaves down, reaching the PWD camp at Morong at 1600m, whose workers are responsible for the Indian-style homilies that line the roads here: 'Speed thrills but kills', 'After whisky driving is risky' and our favourite: 'It is not a rally, enjoy the valley'.

The Choekyi Gyatso Institute for Advanced Buddhist Philosophy marks the outskirts of **Deothang** at 850m. Founded by important rinpoche (and film director) Jamyang Khyentse Norbu, the institute recycles all of its refuse in an attempt to become a zero-waste community. The town's old name was Dewangiri, and it was the site of a major battle between the Bhutanese and the British in 1865. Fittingly, the town is dominated by a large Royal Bhutan Army (RBA) camp and to the south is a chorten with the names of all those who died building Bhutan's roads.

Deothang to Samdrup Jongkhar

18KM / 30 MINUTES

The road eventually hits the valley floor with a thud, as a rock painting of Guru Rinpoche marks the end of the Himalayan foothills. The road curves through the final ripples of the continental collision zone passing the Dickensian Bhutan Chemical Industries to the fairly cursory checkpoint at **Pinchinang**, 4km or so before Samdrup Jongkhar.

Samdrup Jongkhar

📞 07 / ELEV 170M

The highway enters the town from the north, passing the small modern dzong with its goemba and traditional-style courthouse. The main road passes the Bank of Bhutan and crosses a bridge then turns left into the compact bazaar area, where you'll find hotels, shops and restaurants. If you go straight instead of turning left, you will hit the border.

There's little reason to linger in this sweltering border town. The streets are jammed with Tata trucks and every morning and afternoon a tide of Indian workers crosses the border to work in the town. If you have time to kill, you can visit the modern **Rabdey Dratshang** behind the dzong or the **Zangto Pelri Lhakhang** down the road near the football ground.

A Bhutanese-style gate decorated with a dragon and *garuda* bids you farewell as you collect your exit stamp in your passport and cross into the heat and chaos of India.

🛏 Sleeping & Eating

TLT Guesthouse   HOTEL $
(📞 251470; fax 251188; r with/without air-con Nu 2040/1560; ❄) This well-run hotel next to the central market area is a decent option, with rooms with clean private bathrooms and satellite TV, though the mattresses are rock hard, and there's a good multicuisine restaurant.

Hotel Mountain   HOTEL $
(📞 251178; fax 251130; r with/without air-con Nu 2160/1680; ❄) Take the stairs up one floor to this modern hotel with spacious rooms with satellite TV and private bathrooms, and a bright, airy, multicuisine restaurant and bar. It suffers from some road noise.

★ Tashi Gasel Lodge   HOTEL $$
(📞 251553; tashigasel@gmail.com; s/d Nu 2400/3000; ❄) Easily the best option, this new hotel is 3.5km north of town by the Pinchigang checkpost. The nine rooms are surrounded

by breezy balconies and terraces overlooking the town below and there's a good restaurant and bar, making it a fine place to toast the end of your tour.

Hotel Menjong   HOTEL $$
(📞 251094; r/ste Nu 2750/4400; ❄) Recently renovated with spacious rooms, good mattresses and flatscreen TVs, though staff can be hard to find.

ℹ Information

Bank of Bhutan (📞 251149; ⊙9am-1pm & 2-4pm Mon-Fri, 9-11am Sat) Will change ngultrum into Indian rupees with your original exchange receipt, passport copy and an application form, but cannot give Indian rupees for US dollars. For small amounts you are better off changing with your guide.

Immigration Office (⊙6am-8.30pm) Your guide will need to get you stamped in or out at this office next to the police booth at the border gate.

RL Internet Cafe (per min Nu 1; ⊙7.30am-8.30pm) Two computers in a shack opposite the prayer wheel park.

ℹ Getting There & Away

The easiest way to get to Guwahati is to arrange an Indian taxi with your hotel; figure on around Nu 2500 for the 100km (three-hour) drive. Check to see if your Bhutanese agent will pay for this. Buses from the Indian town of Darranga, a 10-minute walk or rickshaw ride over the border, depart for Guwahati at 6.30am and 2pm.

You'll need to stop at the Indian Foreigners' Registration Post by the bridge 5km from the border to get an Indian entry stamp (or exit stamp if headed to Bhutan). Bring a photocopy of your Indian visa and passport information pages.

Bear in mind that strikes in Assam can close the border and cripple transport options in Assam without warning and for days at a time.

Due to security concerns, all Bhutanese vehicles have to travel in a convoy as far as Rangiya (convoys depart around 8am and do not run on Thursday or Sunday), 49km from the border. Indian vehicles face no such restrictions.

Treks

Best Cultural Sights on a Trek

➡ Khaine Lhakhang, Rodang La trek (p183)

➡ Jili Dzong, Druk Path trek (p162)

➡ Lingzhi Dzong, Jhomolhari trek (p171)

➡ Laya village, Laya–Gasa trek (p173)

➡ Nabji village, Nabji trek (p186)

Best Views on a Trek

➡ Jangothang, Jhomolhari trek (p166)

➡ Thanza village, Snowman trek (p177)

➡ Pangalabtsa pass, Dagala Thousand Lakes trek (p163)

➡ Chebisa valley, Laya–Gasa trek (p171)

➡ Soi Yaksa valley, Jhomolhari trek 2 (p170)

Why Go?

Almost two-thirds of Bhutan still lies beyond the reach of any road. Composed of rugged Himalayan summits, high passes, pristine forests, turquoise lakes, rolling yak pastures, traditional villages and a healthy sprinkling of exotic wildlife from hornbills to snow leopards, this is perhaps one of the world's best preserved (and least explored) landscapes.

Bhutan offers a wide range of treks, from tough highaltitude expeditions to the base camps of snowcapped Himalayan giants to relaxing community-based village trails linked by subtropical forest. And with walks ranging from two days to one month, there's a trek for everyone.

Perhaps the best part of all is that you can trust your Bhutanese tour agent, guide and cook to take charge of every conceivable camping chore, leaving you to simply relax, enjoy the trail and soak in the extraordinary scenery. Shangri-La indeed.

Top Tips

➡ You'll enjoy your trek much more if you are in decent physical shape, so spend a month or more beforehand doing some training hikes and breaking in your trekking shoes.

➡ During the day you won't have access to your main bag on a trek, so always carry the following items in your daypack: sun hat, rain shell, spare T-shirt, camera, MP3 player, fleece, water bottle and purification, and trail bars.

➡ For the same reason always have the following emergency items on your person: toilet paper, blister kit, sunscreen, first-aid kit, headache tablets, acetazolamide (Diamox), whistle and torch (flashlight).

➡ You won't find much electricity on longer treks so consider a solar-charging device such as a Solio (www.solio.com). During particularly cold nights keep your batteries in your sleeping bag to stop them from draining.

Trek Routes

The Tourism Council of Bhutan (TCB) sanctions around two dozen official trekking routes across the country. Moreover new routes and variations are popping up all the time. Many routes can be trekked in the reverse direction, logistics permitting.

In recent years road construction has taken a real toll on trekking routes and several former routes such as the Gangte trek and Samtengang winter trek are no longer recommended. You'll have to check with your agent to see how road construction is affecting your proposed route and which new routes are fully functioning.

Route Descriptions

Some treks that follow old trade routes are seldom used today. Since there is usually no one around to ask for directions, you need to stay reasonably close to your guide or horsemen to ensure you are on the correct path.

DAILY STAGES

Route descriptions are divided into daily stages, and give an estimate of the number of days required for each trek. The stages are marked by campsites designated by TCB, and the rules state that you must camp at these places, although alternate campsites are sometimes identified.

Before you start out, ensure you have a detailed itinerary, including rest days, worked out in advance. While discussing the trek with your staff, be careful to ensure that everyone agrees on the places where you will camp. In the past, horsemen have sometimes set off for a campsite beyond the expected stage, leaving trekkers stranded in the wilderness. Besides, some Bhutanese trekking staff have a rather relaxed approach to schedules, and late morning starts are common – often resulting in arrivals to camp after dark.

TIMES & DISTANCES

The route descriptions list approximate daily walking times, based on personal experience and information produced by TCB. The estimates are 'tourist times', factoring in a leisurely pace with plenty of breaks and sightseeing. Bhutanese horsemen and overenthusiastic trekkers can reduce walking times considerably. The distances shown are those published by TCB. They are estimates and have not been determined by any more empirical method of measurement.

REST DAYS

The route descriptions are based on a reasonable number of days needed to complete the trek. You will enjoy the trek more if you add the occasional day for rest, acclimatisation or exploration – even at the cost of an extra US$250.

Our Maps

Our maps are based on the best available maps of each region. To make them legible, only those villages and landmarks mentioned in the text are marked. The maps show elevations for peaks and passes only – other elevations, including camps, are given in the descriptions. Trails and roads follow the general direction indicated on the maps; small switchbacks and sharp twists are not marked.

Altitude Measurements

The elevations given are composites, based on measurements with an altimeter or GPS and checked against maps. There is no definitive list of elevations or names of peaks

---

YAK & JIM

Westerners tend to oversimplify the yak's many manifestations into a single name, yet it is only the full-blooded, long-haired bull of the species *Bos grunniens* that truly bears the name yak. In Bhutan, the name is pronounced 'yuck'. Females of the species are called *jim*, and are prized for their butterfat-rich milk, used to make butter and cheese.

Large, ponderous and clumsy looking, yaks can move very quickly when startled. If you are trekking with yaks, give them a wide berth, and don't put anything fragile in your luggage. If an animal becomes alarmed, it charges up a hill, and your baggage could fall off and get trampled while the yak bucks and snorts, even as its keeper tries to regain control.

Though some yaks are crossbred with local cows, there are many purebred yaks in Bhutan – massive animals with thick furry coats and impressive sharp horns.

Treks

40 km
20 miles

CHINA (TIBET)

INDIA

Manas Chhu

Shenkarla

Phongme

Radi

Rangjung

Rongthong

Trashigang

Bartsam

Khaling

Riserboo

Tskenkarla

Shali

Duksum

Chazam

Kanglung

Sherichhu

Dungzam

Trashi Yangtse

See Rodang La Trek Map (p184)

TRASHI YANGTSE

Singye Dzong

Aja Ney

Drametse

Goemba

Yadi

Chali

Mongar

Namling

Ligmethang

Sengor

Autsho

Sheri Chhu

Kuri Chhu

Dungkhar

LHUENTSE

Tangmachu

Kizum

Mesithang

Bumthang Chhu

Zhemgang

BUMTHANG

See Bumthang Cultural & Duer Hot Springs Map (p181)

Chura Gang (6500m)

Gokthong La

Toktu Zampa

Jakar

Gyetsa

Zungney

Ura

Yotang La (3425m)

Thrumshing La (3750m)

Bridung La

Trongsa

Chendebji Chorten

Kuenga Rabten

TRONGSA

Melunghi Gang (7000m)

Kangri (7239m)

Zonphu Gang (Table Mountain) (7100m)

Thanza

Chozo

Thaga

Sephu

Pele La (3420m)

Zelela

Nobding

Gangte Goemba

Phobjikha Valley

TSIRANG

Sankosh

Dagana

See Snowman Trek Map (p176)

Jelekangphu Gang (7300m)

Kangphu Gang (7212m)

Teri Gang (7300m)

WANGDUE PHODRANG

Tseshinang

Tashila

Geynikha

Tsenda Kang (7100m)

GASA

Tsachhu

Damji

Tashithang

Dawakha

Khuruthang

Punakha

Lobesa

Wangdue Phodrang

Wagye La

Masagang (7165m)

Laya

Gasa

Tsachhu

Dodina

Dechencholing

Dochu La (3140m)

Hongtso

Simtokha Dzong

Chhuzom

Bunakha

See Druk Path & Dagala Thousand Lakes Map (p161)

Gangchhenta (6840m)

Gieu Gang (7200m)

Lingzhi

Jangothang

THIMPHU

Thimphu Valley

THIMPHU

Paro

Isuna

Dolpi

Dzong

Jhomolhari (7314m)

See Laya–Gasa Trek Map (p172)

Thangthangka

PARO

Gunitsawa

Taktshang Goemba

Kyichu Lhakhang

Haa

HAA

Gala

See Jhomolhari Treks Map (p165)

Jichu Drake (6989m)

Phajo

Shing Karap

Manas Chhu

and passes in Bhutan, and various maps and publications differ significantly. In most cases, peak elevations are those defined in the mountain database produced by the Alpine Club in Britain. All other elevations are rounded to the nearest 10m.

Directions & Place Names

Bhutan is a complex maze of valleys and rivers that wind around in unexpected twists and turns. It is, therefore, difficult to define the exact compass direction of a river at a particular spot. So instead of referring to north or south banks, the slightly technical 'river right' or 'river left' have been used. This refers to the right or left side of the river as you face downstream, which is not necessarily the direction you are walking. In the route descriptions, right and left in reference to a river always refers to river right or river left.

Several mountains and places in the descriptions do not match names in other descriptions or maps of the same route. The variance occurs because most maps were made before the Dzongkha Development Commission produced its guidelines for Romanised Dzongkha. We use the Romanised Dzongkha standards for all place names in Bhutan.

Health & Safety

Trekking in Bhutan involves trudging over innumerable ascents and descents, which gets more strenuous with altitude gain. You'll enjoy the trek much more if you do some training before coming. Walk up and down hills or inclines as much as possible, breaking in your boots in the process. Try carrying a backpack to increase the strength training associated with walking or jogging.

One thing to watch out for is sore or inflamed knees caused by the mild trauma repeated thousands of times on a trekking descent. Anti-inflammatory pills are helpful, as are walking poles and knee supports.

Bring a good pair of polarising sunglasses to prevent snow blindness over snowy passes and bring two water bottles to help ensure you stay hydrated.

People aged over 45 often worry about altitude and potential heart problems. Relax. There's no evidence that altitude is likely to bring on previously undiagnosed heart disease. If you can exercise to your maximum at home, you should not have an increased risk while trekking. However, if you have a known heart disease and your exercise is already limited by symptoms at low altitude, consult an experienced doctor before committing yourself to a trek.

Losing Your Way

Since you are escorted by a licensed guide familiar with the lie of the land, it's unlikely that you'll get lost in the hills. However, this has happened to trekkers in the past, so tread with caution. Never stray from your group, and keep an eye out for signs while you trek. Watch for the lug-sole footprints of other trekkers or for arrows carved into the trail or marked on rocks by guides. Hoof prints and dung of pack animals can confirm that you are on track. On a major trekking route, the trail is usually well defined, although there may be a few confusing short cuts. If you find yourself descending when the trail should be going up, if the trail vanishes, or if you find yourself alone ahead of the rest of your party, *stop and wait for the other trekkers and guides to catch up*. If you noticed a trail junction some distance back, retrace your steps to try to find where you went wrong.

TREKS HEALTH & SAFETY

THE SHY PREDATOR

Locally referred to as *chen*, the critically endangered snow leopard is a solitary and elusive creature that lives in rocky mountain folds above the tree line, descending to lower altitudes during winter. While its white fur works as a wonderful camouflage in its icy habitat, the snow leopard is also extremely agile in high terrain, and can effortlessly walk through nearly three feet of snow. Preying on blue sheep and the occasional yak calf, it can sometimes stray into human territory in search of food. However, direct confrontations with humans are rare.

The holy grail of an entire generation of wildlife photographers and filmmakers, the snow leopard remains one of the most pursued creatures in the wild, although there's very little data on hand to portray the animal accurately. If you manage to spot one of these cats on your trek, consider yourself blessed.

Rescue

Trekking entails a certain amount of risk, and there's always a possibility of courting illness or injury. However, *do not panic,* as it only makes things worse. Assess the incident with a clear mind before making a decision, without jumping to conclusions. Suspected broken bones may only be bruises, a fever may subside overnight, and a dazed person may wake up and be all right in a few hours. In most areas, horses or yaks will be available to help ferry a sick or injured trekker.

Sometimes, however, the seriousness of the situation may call for immediate evacuation. In this case, the only option is to request a helicopter, since land evacuation may be near impossible. Fortunately, this is a reasonably simple process, but once you ask for a helicopter, you will be charged upward of US$1500, depending on weather conditions, your exact location and the number of rescue attempts made by the chopper. Rescue helicopters come from Indian Air Force bases in Hasimara or Bagdogra airport, after a request – sent out by the guide to the tour operator – reaches the Indian forces through the Tourism Council of Bhutan (TCB) and the Royal Bhutan Army. It's an efficient chain of communication and a helicopter is usually dispatched within a day.

Bhutan Telecom (www.telecom.net.bt) also provides satellite phones using the Thuraya system, which allows direct dialling from anywhere in the country, even on a trek. Some tour operators rent satellite phones to trekkers, though the charges are steep.

DRUK PATH TREK AT A GLANCE

Duration 6 days

Max Elevation 4235m

Difficulty Medium

Season February to May, September to December

Start Paro Ta Dzong

Finish Motithang

Access Towns Paro, Thimphu

Summary This popular trek follows a wilderness trail past remote lakes and a famous meditation retreat. Trekking days are short but the relatively high altitudes make it moderately strenuous.

Druk Path Trek

The Druk Path is the most popular trek in Bhutan. The main draws are the monasteries, the alpine scenery, its convenient length, and the compelling sense of journey that comes from walking between Paro and Thimphu, Bhutan's most popular destinations.

The trek is possible from late February to May and from September to December, although snow sometimes closes the route in late autumn and early spring. Afternoon showers are common in April and May. Days are normally warm, but nights can be very cold and you should always be prepared for snow. Avoid the monsoon season of July and August. It is possible to shorten the trek to five days. For a five-day trek, simply combine days four and five. If you're a masochist, you can even race through the trek in a single day: an old punishment for Bhutanese soldiers was a forced one-day march along this route.

Day 1: National Museum to Jili Dzong

10KM / 3½–5 HOURS / 1115M ASCENT, 40M DESCENT

The first day is fairly short but it's all uphill, gaining more than 1000m. Most groups start from a trailhead outside Paro's National Museum at 2470m. The route follows a dirt road for 30 minutes before making the first of many short cuts that avoid the looping road. After 40 minutes, pass Kuenga Choeling Lhakhang at 2650m. A further hour's climb takes you to the stone houses and apple orchards of **Damchena** (2880m), 10 minutes before a *mani* (carved stone) wall and campsite in a clearing known as **Damche Gom** (2985m).

It's then a long, but not steep, climb through forests of golden moss to a herders' camp just before **Jili La** (3540m). Cross the pass (marked by a cairn and broken chorten) and drop to an excellent camping place in a meadow surrounded by rhododendron forests just below **Jili Dzong** (see the boxed text, p162).

Day 2: Jili Dzong to Rabana

10KM / 3–4 HOURS / 425M ASCENT, 50M DESCENT

Today's walk is a short and enjoyable ridge walk, full of short ascents and descents, so there's plenty of time for a morning visit to Jili Dzong. You might see or hear monal pheasants during the day.

Druk Path & Dagala Thousand Lakes

From the dzong the route first follows prayer flags and then descends through rhododendrons to a saddle at 3550m, before climbing for 40 minutes to great views of Paro and the Bemang Rong valley. If the weather is clear, look for Jhomolhari and other snowcapped peaks in the distance.

The trail crosses to the east side of the ridge offering views down to Gimena village (look for its large goemba). Climb again and traverse around the west side of a cone-shaped hill to a saddle (3750m) and two clearings, the latter below some prayer flags. Five minutes further is **Jangchhu Lakha**, a yak pasture at 3760m. From here a lower trail continues 10 minutes to an often-boggy camping spot at **Tshokam** (3770m). A better option is to take the higher trail for 25 minutes to the yak herders' camp of **Rabana** (3890m), surrounded by mauve rhododendron forests.

Day 3: Rabana to Jimilang Tsho

11KM / 4 HOURS / 370M ASCENT, 375M DESCENT

There are two trails to Jimilang Tsho. Most groups take the high trail (described here) because it offers better views, including (in good weather) Jhomolhari and 6989m Jichu Drakye, the peak representing the protective deity of Paro. The lower trail descends from Tshokham into the upper Bemang Rong valley and then climbs via the yak pasture of Langrithang.

From Rabana a horse trail ascends the ridge diagonally to a viewpoint marked by a lone prayer flag at 3960m. Traverse for 30 minutes to a meadow, then descend through rhododendrons, heading just left of a miniature peak topped with prayer flags. An hour from camp you crest the minor **Langye Ja La** (Ox Hump Pass) at 4070m. You can climb 50m to the top of the mini-peak for impressive 360-degree views.

TREKS DRUK PATH TREK

The rocky descent is hard on the feet, passing a small herders' shelter by an over-hanging rock, and then climbing 80m to a pass for fine views of Jhomolhari. Far below in the Do Chhu valley you can see the yellow roof of Chumpu Ney, a pilgrimage spot famous for its statue of Dorje Phagmo. Five minutes later you see isolated Jimilang Tsho far below you. Descend to a saddle for lunch and then climb and angle around the ridge to a chorten at 4180m for a final view of Jhomolhari. A steep 30-minute descent leads to the shore of Jimilang Tsho, with pleasant camping five minutes' walk further at the far end of the lake (3885m).

Jimilang Tsho means 'Sand Ox Lake', and was named for a bull that emerged from the lake and joined the cattle of a family that uses the area as a summer grazing ground. The lake is also known for its giant trout, which were introduced in the 1970s.

Day 4: Jimilang Tsho to Simkotra Tsho

11KM / 4 HOURS / 820M ASCENT, 400M DESCENT

The trail climbs from the lower end of the lake through yellow rhododendrons to a ridge at 4010m, traverses the ridge, then descends to a single stone shelter. Following the ridge, you crest at some prayer flags at 4050m overlooking Janye Tsho. Descend to a yak herders' camp near the lake at 3880m before climbing again, veering eventually to the right, to a ridge at 4150m and views of overlooking Simkotra Tsho. Descend to some stone ruins and a camp at 4100m.

JILI DZONG

The 15th-century Jili Dzong has long occupied an important site. It was the residence of Ngawang Chhogyel (1465–1540), the cousin of Lama Drukpa Kunley, and the Zhabdrung is said to have meditated here before heading down to Paro to defeat an invading Tibetan army. The impressive main lhakhang contains a large statue of Sakyamuni Buddha almost 4m high. One can only wonder what kinds of mischief the resident monks must have perpetrated to warrant banishment to such a high and isolated monastery!

Be sure everyone is clear on where to camp on this day. Horse drivers often push to continue over the next ridge to a better camp and grazing land at Labana.

Day 5: Simkotra Tsho to Phajoding

10KM / 3–4 HOURS / 130M ASCENT, 680M DESCENT

It's a long climb past three false summits, before the trail descends to Labana camping place at 4110m, near a stone hut beside an almost-dry lake. There's a final longish climb to a group of cairns atop Labana La at 4235m. The hill above the trail marks a seldom-used sky burial site. The trail descends gently to crest a minor pass at 4210m. There are views of Dochu La and Jhomolhari along this stretch.

From here the trail descends to a final 4090m pass marked by a chorten. Below sprawls the entire Thimphu valley. Weather permitting, there are views of Gangkhar Puensum and other Himalayan peaks. The main trail descends northeast towards Phajoding below but after 10 minutes it's worth taking the side trail for 20 minutes southeast down to Thuji Drak Goemba, a remote meditation centre that clings to the side of a precipitous rock face at 3950m.

Meditation centres and lhakhangs are scattered across the hillside. A descent on a maze of eroded trails through juniper and rhododendrons leads to a campsite beside the main Jampa Lhakhang at 3640m. See p71 for details of Phajoding Goemba. Darkness brings the bright city lights far below you and the feeling that you have arrived back at the edge of the world.

Day 6: Phajoding to Motithang

4–5KM / 2½ HOURS / 1130M DESCENT

This day's trek is all downhill through forest so tie your laces tight and keep your trekking poles handy. A wide trail passes a chorten at 3440m, 40 minutes after which there is a trail junction. The left branch descends via Chhokhortse Goemba to the BTC telecom tower at Sangaygang, offering an interesting alternative end to the trek.

The normal route branches right and descends more steeply towards Motithang. There are numerous short cuts, but they all eventually lead to the same place. Pass another chorten at 3070m and descend steeply to a stream, crossing it at 2820m. Climb to a rough road and follow it down to your waiting vehicle.

Dagala Thousand Lakes Trek

This trek is off the beaten track; you will probably encounter no other trekkers along the way. It's not particularly demanding (despite a few steep climbs), and most trekking days are short. The route is best walked in April and late September through October. However, snow in the high country can often block out the route, compelling you to return.

It's a 29km drive from Thimphu to the junction of an unpaved road, which crawls up 8km to a Basic Health Unit (BHU) at Khoma, high above the Geynitsang Chhu at 2850m. The trailhead lies another 3km ahead at the suspension bridge in Geynizampa.

DAGALA THOUSAND LAKES TREK AT A GLANCE

Duration 5 days

Max Elevation 4520/4720m

Difficulty Medium

Season April, September to October

Start Geynizampa

Finish Chamgang

Access Town Thimphu

Summary A short trek near Thimphu, to a number of lovely high-altitude lakes (far fewer, however, than the name suggests).

Day 1: Geynizampa to Gur

5KM / 4 HOURS / 550M ASCENT, 60M DESCENT

Crossing the suspension bridge, the trail turns south along the east side of the Geynitsang Chhu (river left) to a side stream, the Dolungu Chhu. Cross the stream on a log bridge and start uphill on an eroded trail through an oak forest. Currently used only by yak herders, woodcutters and a handful of trekkers, this trail was once a major trading route between Thimphu and Dagana, headquarters of Dagana Dzongkhag. This accounts for the walls, well-crafted stone staircases and other developments along portions of the route.

A long climb leads to an outstanding lookout point at 3220m. The ascent is now gentler, and the trail climbs to the top of the ridge where it makes a hairpin turn at 3350m. The way to the campsite is an inconspicuous path that leads off the trail here, going southward through the forest to Gur, amid yak pastures at 3290m.

Day 2: Gur to Labatamba

12KM / 5 HOURS / 1040M ASCENT, 110M DESCENT

Climb back from camp to the main trail and continue gently up the ridge on a wide track. A long, stiff climb through blue pines leads to a rocky outcrop where the vegetation changes to spruces, dead firs and larches. The trail traverses into a side valley, crosses a stream at 3870m and begins a long, gentle climb through scattered birches and rhododendrons, weaving in and out of side valleys and crossing several tiny

streams. At Pangalabtsa, a pass marked by cairns at 4250m, there is a spectacular view of the whole Dagala range. This is prime yak country, with numerous herders' camps scattered across the broad Labatamba valley. Descend from the pass to the first herders' hut at 4170m and traverse around the head of a small valley to the main valley floor. Climb beside a stream to Labatamba, a camp at 4300m near Utsho Lake, a beautiful high-altitude *tsho* (lake) with a thriving population of golden trout. The area near the lakes bursts with alpine wildflowers in September. There are numerous other pretty lakes in the vicinity, and you could schedule an extra day here to explore them.

Day 3: Labatamba to Panka

8KM / 6–7 HOURS / 260M ASCENT, 520M DESCENT

There are two possible routes ahead, and pack animals will take the lower one. The trail here is undefined (more of a cross-country traverse), and climbs along the western side of the Dajatsho lake to a saddle at 4520m, with good mountain views. If you want a better view, you could scramble to the top of a 4720m peak to the east. From the pass, the trail descends past several herders' camps before dropping to the Dochha Chhu, rejoining the lower trail at about 4200m. Subsequently, it climbs over three ridges and descends to Panka at 4000m. Water is scarce here during spring, and it may thus be necessary to descend to an alternative camp 20 minutes' walk below.

Day 4: Panka to Talakha

8KM / 6–7 HOURS / 180M ASCENT, 1100M DESCENT

The route leads north to a crest at 4100m, where several trails lead off in different directions. The trail to Talakha climbs steeply up a slate slope to the ruins of a house. From here, it is a long traverse to Tale La at 4180m, which offers a view of the Dagala range and Thimphu, far away to the north. Finally, it's a long descent – first through a mixed forest of spruce, birch, juniper and rhododendron, and then through bamboo – to the goemba at Talakha (3080m). The campsite is near the goemba.

Day 5: Talakha to Chamgang

6KM / 3 HOURS / 440M DESCENT

There is a road passing just below the goemba, and you can choose to end your trek here by requesting a 4WD pick-up. However, it's a rough and bumpy ride to Simtokha Dzong, so it's better to walk three hours down the road, taking a few short cuts to avoid switchbacks, and reach Chamgang at 2640m, where you can meet your vehicle. There is an alternate trail that leads to Simtokha, but it is steep and eroded, with numerous apple orchard fences standing in the way, and is best avoided.

Jhomolhari Trek

The Jhomolhari trek is to Bhutan what the Everest Base Camp route is to Nepal: a trekking pilgrimage. With two different versions (the TCB counts them as two separate treks), it's one of the most trodden routes in the

---

JHOMOLHARI TREK AT A GLANCE

Duration 8 days

Max Elevation 4930m

Difficulty Medium–hard

Season April to June, September to November

Start Sharna Zampa

Finish Dodina

Access Towns Paro, Thimphu

Summary Bhutan's popular showcase trek offers a spectacular view of the 7314m Jhomolhari from a high camp at Jangothang.

---

country, and almost 40% of all trekkers who come to Bhutan end up following one of the Jhomolhari routes. The first two days of the trek follow the Paro Chhu valley to Jangothang, climbing gently, but continually, with a few short, steep climbs over side ridges. It crosses a high pass and visits the remote village of Lingzhi, then crosses another pass before making its way towards Thimphu. The last four days of the trek cover a lot of distance and require many hours of walking. The trek also affords an excellent opportunity to see yaks.

The trek is possible from April to early June and September to November; April and October are most favourable. The daylight hours are normally warm, but nights can be very cold, especially above Jangothang. There is a lot of mud on this trail and it can be miserable in the rain. Snow usually closes the high passes mid-November onward, and they don't reopen until April.

The trek traditionally started from the ruins of Drukgyel Dzong at 2580m, but the road now reaches Sharna Zampa, near the army post of Gunitsawa (2810m), close to the border with Tibet. This trek will be further shortened in the future when roads, currently under construction, extend from Dodina to Barshong.

Day 1: Sharna Zampa to Thangthangka

22KM / 7–8 HOURS / 770M ASCENT, 10M DESCENT

Brace yourself for a long, hard day with lots of ups and downs, made worse by all the rock-hopping required to avoid mud holes.

Begin the day by climbing through conifers and rhododendrons flanking the Paro Chhu. If the water is high, you might have to scramble over a few small hills to get around the river in places. About 15 minutes beyond Sharna Zampa are the remnants of an old bridge with a house and a chorten on the other side. Welcome to Jigme Dorji National Park.

After about two hours of trekking through oaks, rhododendrons and ferns, and crossing several streams, you will reach Shing Karap, a stone house and a clearing at 3110m. Consider stopping here for lunch. Further ahead is the stone-paved trail leading left to Tremo La. This is the old invasion and trade route from Phari Dzong in Tibet, and still looks well beaten since it's used by army caravans to ferry rations to the border post. Beware: many trekkers have

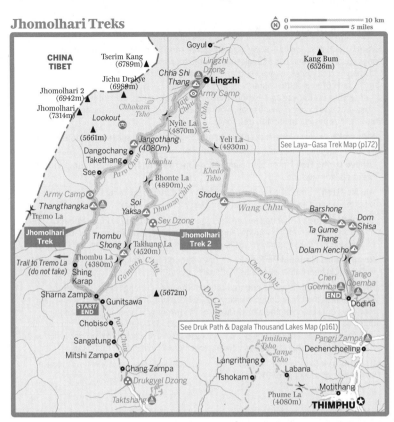

See Laya–Gasa Trek Map (p172)

See Druk Path & Dagala Thousand Lakes Map (p161)

casually ambled down this trail in the past and made a long, exhausting side trip to nowhere.

Immediately after the trail junction is a wooden bridge over a side stream. Climb a short set of switchbacks over a little ridge, then descend and cross the Paro Chhu to river left on a wooden cantilever bridge at 3230m. The route now goes up and down a rocky trail through forests of birch and fir, followed by blue pine, maple and larch, and crossing an old landslide.

About three hours ahead, there's a bridge back to river right at 3560m. The trail climbs to a place where you can see a white chorten on the opposite side of the river. There is a bridge here that leads back across the river. Don't cross it, or it'll take you up the Ronse Ghon Chhu towards **Soi Yaksa**, the campsite on Day 4 of the Jhomolhari trek 2.

Follow the trail on river right and climb over a small ridge as the Paro Chhu makes a

noticeable bend. Fifteen minutes' walk from the bridge is a lovely meadow with Jhomolhari looming majestically at the head of the valley. This is **Thangthangka** (3610m), with a small stone shelter and a Bhutanese-style house in a cedar grove at the edge of the meadow.

Day 2: Thangthangka to Jangothang

19KM / 5–6 HOURS / 480M ASCENT

This is not a long day, but you'll be left breathless due to the significant elevation gain at high altitude.

Wake up early for good views of Jhomolhari, which will disappear behind a ridge as you climb beyond camp. Less than an hour ahead, at 3730m, there's an army camp with rough stone barracks housing personnel from both the Bhutan army and the Indian Military Training Team (IMTRAT).

OFF THE BEATEN TREK

As road construction eats away at existing treks and tourist numbers continue to grow in popular trekking areas at peak seasons, the tourism authorities are trying to introduce new trek routes to avoid bottlenecks and spread tourism development to hitherto unvisited corners of the country.

Ask your Bhutanese agent about the following trek routes, currently in the planning stage but due to come online soon. Figure on some exploring if you tackle these routes, as you'll be among the first to trek them.

Salt trek Five-day winter trek (p174) along a former salt and silk trading route in southeastern Bhutan.

Singye Dzong trek A proposed eight-day return trek (p144) to one of Bhutan's most sacred pilgrimage sites.

Aja Ney trek A proposed six-day trek (p145) from Shershong to this sacred Buddhist pilgrimage site. October to March are the best months.

Shabjithang trek A planned seven-day itinerary from Nangsiphel in the upper Chamkhar valley (Bumthang) through Wangchuck Centennial Park. The route leads to Chamba and Waithang villages, then east to Gomthang for fine views of Gangkhar Puensum.

Royal Manas National Park trek Five days through subtropical and broadleaf forests into the wild heart of Royal Manas National Park (p135).

Bridung La trek This week-long trek through the upper Kheng region starts from Chungphel in the lower Chhume valley, 20km from Ura, and climbs through forest for four days until reaching the plateau lakes of the Bridung La pass and then dropping down to the ancient lhakhang at Buli. April to June and September to November are the best times to trek. The starting point is accessed by farm road from the Pogo junction on the Jakar bypass. Buli is a bumpy 55km (three hours) drive from Zhemgang.

Bumdra trek Overnighter from the Paro valley that links several monasteries to give a short taste of trekking (p89).

The trail crosses a wooden bridge over a fast-flowing stream a short distance beyond the army camp. The hillside on the opposite side of the Paro Chhu is a near-vertical rock face with a few trees clinging to it. Along this stretch the trail can be extremely muddy; there are lots of big stones you can use to rock-hop around mud holes. At 3770m, about one hour from camp, the trail turns sharply right at a whitewashed *mani* wall.

A short climb leads to a small chorten on a ridge. You are now entering yak country and will see these huge beasts lumbering across hillsides and lazing in meadows. There are two trails from here, both contouring up the valley and ending near the river bank, hugging the valley floor as the river bends sharply to the right. Parts of the hillside are covered with larches, which turn a light yellow in autumn. Above the trail is the village of Soe. You cannot see it until you are beyond and above it, but you may meet people herding yaks near the river.

One hour beyond Soe is Takethang, a cluster of stone houses on a plateau at 3940m.

The villagers grow barley and a large succulent plant called *kashaykoni* that is fed to yaks during winter.

The trail follows straight across the plateau, high above the river, crossing a little stream on a bridge made of big stones laid on logs. On the opposite side is a white chorten, an outreach clinic and the few houses of Dangochang. The people of this village raise yaks and a few sheep, and some households grow potatoes, turnips and radishes. This area is snowbound from mid-November until the end of March. From here, it's slow going uphill beside a side stream to the camp at Jangothang (4080m), offering a spectacular view of Jhomolhari.

The guidelines for pack animals require that you now exchange your horses for yaks from Soe or horses from Dangochang. Don't be alarmed when your loads get dumped at the camp and the animals disappear down the valley, leaving you with a mountain of baggage. If all goes well, the replacement pack animals will show up on schedule when you are ready to leave.

Day 3: Acclimatisation Day & Exploration of Jangothang

If you're pressing on to Lingzhi, you should spend a day lazing in Jangothang for acclimatisation. If you are returning to Sharna Zampa via Jhomolhari trek 2, a day in Jangothang is the highlight of the trek; the views don't get any better than here. The horsemen also take the day off, and can be seen lazing around and playing *dego*, a traditional discus game.

There are four major possibilities for day hikes from Jangothang. The first, and best, is a four-hour excursion up the ridge to the north of the camp. There's no trail, but it's a broad open slope and you can just scramble up. The ridge seems endless, but after an hour or so, you get an excellent view of Jichu Drakye. Jhomolhari is hidden behind the ridge here, but becomes visible if you continue to the highest point at 4750m. You are likely to encounter grazing yaks – and, occasionally, blue sheep – on the upper slopes.

An alternative, which can be combined with the walk up the ridge, is to trek up the main valley towards the last house, then continue up the valley towards Jichu Drakye. This is the same country you'll be walking through if, later, you decide to continue trekking over the Nyile La to Lingzhi.

A third hike goes up towards the head of the valley in the direction of Jhomolhari. There is a very rough overgrown trail that cuts across moraines and brush, leading to the foot of the mountain. You can't get very far, but there are good views in the upper part of the valley.

The last option is an expedition to Tshophu, a pair of lakes that sit high on the opposite side of the river to the east, with a good supply of brown trout. To get to the lakes, follow the trail north to the last settlement in the valley. It takes about one hour to get to the top of the ridge and then another 30 minutes following a stream to the lake.

Day 4: Jangothang to Lingzhi

18KM / 6–7 HOURS / 840M ASCENT, 870M DESCENT

If you are having problems with the altitude at Jangothang, consider returning. Otherwise, push ahead past three stone houses inhabited by park rangers. This is the last settlement in the valley and it's extremely isolated. Around a corner, there's a spectacular view of Jichu Drakye.

Descend and cross a log bridge at 4160m to the left bank of the Paro Chhu, then start up a steep traverse heading back downstream. The trail crests at the foot of a side valley and goes eastwards. Jichu Drakye towers above the Paro Chhu valley and soon the top of Jhomolhari appears over the ridge above the camp at Jangothang. The snow peak in the middle is a secondary summit of Jhomolhari.

At 4470m, the trail traverses under the big rocks that were visible from the camp, leads left and enters a large east–west glacial valley with numerous moraines. Apart from a few small gentians, it's just grass, tundra and small juniper bushes that grow here. You may spot blue sheep on the hillside above and see marmots darting into their burrows.

Past a false summit with a cairn at 4680m, the trail approaches the ridge and you can see Jichu Drakye to the northwest. The trail dips and then climbs back up a moraine, offering spectacular views of the sharp ridge jutting out from Jichu Drakye. The final pull is up a scree slope to Nyile La (4870m), about four hours from camp. You can climb higher to the northwest, where you'll see Jhomolhari 2 and Jichu Drakye

CAMPING AT JANGOTHANG

Jangothang is clearly among the most popular campsites in the entire Himalaya. It's packed to its gills with trekkers in October, and the joke among guides is that if you're yearning to catch up with a long-lost mountain-loving pal, simply land up in Jangothang in autumn! You are unlikely to have the camp to yourself even in the lean season.

The campsite derives its name (meaning 'land of ruins') from the remains of a small fortress that sits atop a rock in a side valley leading northwest to Jhomolhari. There's a community hall with a kitchen here for the benefit of trekkers, and several large flat spots for camping. A chain of snow peaks lines the eastern side of the Paro Chhu valley, and it's possible to spot blue sheep on the lower slopes. Despite being located at the foot of Jhomolhari, Jangothang has interestingly never been used as base camp by any expedition scaling the summit.

SUMMIT SAGA

While they may not physically measure up to the iconic 8000m-high peaks in Nepal and Tibet, the mountains of Bhutan are ruggedly beautiful. Jhomolhari was a famous landmark for early Everest expeditions. On the approach march for the 1921 British Everest Expedition, George Leigh Mallory described it as 'astounding and magnificent', but said he felt 'cold and rather horrified' towards the mountain. It was climbed from Tibet in 1937 by F Spencer Chapman and Passang Lama, and again in 1970 by a joint Indo-Bhutanese team.

Michael Ward and Dr Frederic Jackson made an extensive and pioneering survey of Bhutan's mountains from 1964 to 1965. Climbing several peaks of around 5500m, they categorised the Bhutan Himalaya as a defined group of mountains. Climbers were allowed in for a short period from 1983 to 1994. A Bhutanese team scaled Thurigang (4900m), north of Thimphu, in 1983. Jichu Drakye was attempted thrice before being climbed in 1988 by an expedition led by Doug Scott. In 1985, Japanese expeditions climbed Gangri (7239m), Kari Jang, Kang Bum (6526m) and Masang Gang (7165m). Gangkhar Puensum (7541m) still remains the highest unclimbed peak in the world after unsuccessful attempts by Japanese and British teams in the 1980s. Climbing peaks above 6000m was subsequently prohibited in Bhutan, owing to religious beliefs and reservations of villagers residing near them.

on one side, and Tserim Kang (6789m) on the other. Nyile La is frequently very windy, so descend quickly through scree along the hillside, down to a stream on the valley floor at 4450m. There is some vegetation here, mostly grass, juniper and cotoneaster. It's an excellent lunch spot.

The trail now goes north, contouring along the hillside high above the valley. It's a good trail with a few small ups, but mostly down and level. Eventually you can see an army camp near the river below; the white tower of Lingzhi Dzong is visible in the distance. Following a long walk to a lookout at 4360m, the trail now descends into the large Jaje Chhu valley, making many switchbacks through rhododendrons and birches to a yak pasture on the valley floor. Jichu Drakye and Tserim Kang tower over the head of the valley and you can see some remarkable examples of moraines on their lower slopes. The camp is at **Chha Shi Thang** near a large stone community hall (4010m) used by both Bhutanese travellers and trekking groups. **Lingzhi** is up the obvious trail on the opposite side of the Jaje Chhu.

If you take a spare day here, you can make an excursion to **Chhokam Tsho** at 4340m near the base camp of Jichu Drakye. During the hike you may encounter blue sheep and musk deer. If you are continuing to Thimphu, schedule a rest day here. The village and dzong at Lingzhi are worth visiting, and it's useful to rest up for the following strenuous trek day.

Day 5: Lingzhi to Shodu

22KM / 8–9 HOURS / 940M ASCENT, 920M DESCENT

Start early today; you have a long and tiring trek ahead of you. Climb towards a white chorten on a ridge above the camp, then turn south up the deep Mo Chhu valley. The trail stays on the west side of the valley, crossing numerous side streams, most without bridges. About three hours from camp, it crosses the Mo Chhu. There is no bridge and the river has broken into many small channels, presenting a tedious route-finding exercise through hummocks of grass and slippery rocks.

The trail climbs steeply up the side of the main valley and crosses into a large side valley, climbing above a stream. It then makes an impressive climb up the headwall, zigzagging through rocks to a large cairn atop **Yeli La** at 4930m. Avoid walking with the pack animals because the trail here is carved into a rock cliff and is quite narrow. From the pass, on a clear day, you can see Jhomolhari, Gangchhenta and Tserim Kang.

Descending to a hanging valley after passing a small lake at 4830m, the trail tracks the outflow from the lake, and goes down to another huge valley with a larger lake, **Khedo Tsho**, at 4720m. Watch for grazing blue sheep. The trail then crosses the upper reaches of the Jaradinthang Chhu and descends along the valley, following the river southwards, crossing several side streams. After crossing back to the east bank on a log bridge at 4340m, the trail reaches a chorten at 4150m where it turns eastwards into the upper Wang Chhu valley. Descending and crossing to the south bank (river right) on a log bridge, the trail traverses a narrow, sandy slope to a camping spot at Shodu (4080m), just at the tree line.

Day 6: Shodu to Barshong

16KM / 5–6 HOURS / 250M ASCENT, 670M DESCENT

Upon leaving Shodu, you cross to river left and pass an abandoned army camp and a small alternative campsite. The trail traverses under steep yellow cliffs with a few meditation caves carved into them, where the Zhabdrung supposedly spent some time. Down a steep stone staircase, the trail reaches the river, crossing it on a log bridge at 3870m. For the next three hours, the trail crosses the river five more times, slopping through muddy cypress forests on the south slope and hugging the steep canyon walls and crossing large side streams on the north slope, eventually ending up on the north bank (river left) at 3580m.

The route climbs gradually for one hour to Barshong, where there is a dilapidated community hall and the ruins of a small dzong. The designated camp is below the ruins at 3710m, but it is located in a swampy meadow and most groups elect to continue to a better camp by the river, about 1½ hours beyond.

Day 7: Barshong to Dolam Kencho

15KM / 4–6 HOURS / 290M ASCENT, 640M DESCENT

The trail descends gently through a dense forest of rhododendrons, birches and conifers, and then drops steeply on a rocky trail to meet the Wang Chhu. Thirty minutes of walking through a larch forest leads to a clearing known as Ta Gume Thang (Waiting for Horses) at 3370m. Most groups camp here or 15 minutes further on at Dom Shisa (Where the Bear Died) instead of Barshong.

Stay on river left, climbing over ridges and descending to side streams. From here, the route then makes a steep climb to 3340m. After traversing for about 30 minutes through rhododendron forests, a trail leads off to the right. This descends to Dolam Kencho, a pleasant camp in a large

meadow at 3320m. If your group has elected to shorten the trek and continue on to Dodina, stay on the left-hand trail, bypassing Dolam Kencho, and climb to a crest at 3430m.

Day 8: Dolam Kencho to Dodina

8KM / 3–4 HOURS / 500M ASCENT, 930M DESCENT

From the camp, a track climbs back to the main trail, reaching a crest with a cairn at 3430m. The trail descends to a stream at 3060m, then climbs again to a pass at 3120m. Another short descent and climb through bamboo forest leads to a rocky stream bed, which the trail follows down to the remains of a logging road along the Wang Chhu at 2720m. It is then a 15-minute walk south along a rocky route to the road head at Dodina (2640m), opposite the bridge that leads to Cheri Goemba.

Jhomolhari Trek 2

If you fancy sighting Jhomolhari and Jichu Drakye from up close, but nonetheless want to avoid the tiring slog all the way to Lingzhi, this trek is just for you. While it's possible to return from Jangothang to Sharna Zampa by the same route taken on the way up, most trekkers choose to take an alternate route described here, which is less strenuous than the classic Jhomolhari trek and can be completed in less time. Despite its relative ease, however, this route still reaches an elevation that could cause problems.

JHOMOLHARI TREK 2 AT A GLANCE

Duration 6 days

Max Elevation 4890m

Difficulty Medium

Season April to June, September to November

Start/Finish Sharna Zampa

Access Town Paro

Summary The shorter and easier version of the main Jhomolhari trek goes to the Jhomolhari base camp at Jangothang, returning either via the same route or by an alternate trail.

Days 1–3: Sharna Zampa to Jangothang

Follow Days 1 to 3 of the main Jhomolhari trek.

Day 4: Jangothang to Soi Yaksa

16KM / 6–7 HOURS / 810M ASCENT, 1090M DESCENT

From Jangothang, the return trail initially leads north to the last settlement in the valley, before dropping to the Paro Chhu, crossing it on a wooden bridge. After crossing the river, you begin a gradual climb, following a set of sharp switchbacks for about 300m up the side of the hill. Along the way, you can get fabulous views of Jhomolhari, Jhomolhari 2, Jichu Drakye and Tserim Kang if the weather is good. From here, it's a relatively even and smooth hike all the way to a large cirque nestling the lakes of Tshophu (4380m), a pair of splendid high-altitude water bodies inhabited by a flock of ruddy shelducks and known to foster a healthy population of brown trout deep in their placid waters. While it's possible to set up camp in between the two lakes, you could always carry on along the trail, which now climbs high above the eastern side of the first lake, passes the second lake along the way and finally climbs across a scree slope to the crest of a ridge. From here, it descends into a hidden valley, before climbing steeply to Bhonte La (4890m), the highest point on this route.

YUGYEL DZONG

Built by the third *druk desi* (secular ruler), Mingyur Tenpa, who ruled from 1667 to 1680, Yugyel Dzong (also called Lingzhi Dzong) is perched on a hill about 200m above Lingzhi village and is quite close to the Tibetan border. The dzong was destroyed in the 1897 earthquake, but was rebuilt in the 1950s to serve as an administrative headquarters.

The dzong is quite small, with a few offices along the outside wall and a two-storey *utse* (central tower) in the centre. Until some years ago, the basement was used as a jail to house murderers and temple robbers. However, the facilities were quite primitive and the dzong is no longer used for this purpose. The dzong is also home to a few monks.

Descending from Bhonte La, the route now runs past a scree slope, and then winds down a ridge with a lot of criss-crossing yak trails. Finally, it switchbacks down to the Soi Yaksa valley (also known as the Dhumzo Chhu valley), a beautiful setting for a camp at 3800m with rocky cliffs, wild-flower meadows, a few nomadic settlements and a waterfall at the end of the valley. All through this day, keep your eyes trained on the wilderness for a host of regional wildlife, such as blue sheep, golden marmots and the elusive snow leopard.

Day 5: Soi Yaksa to Thombu Shong

11KM / 4–5 HOURS / 720M ASCENT, 340M DESCENT

Starting out from camp, today's walk initially takes you past hillsides lush with a crop of azalea and rhododendron, before gradually climbing above the tree line. You will also cross forests of birch and oak on the way. The trail ascends about 100m over a ridge, before dropping to a meadow with a chorten and a *mani* wall, and a babbling stream. If you have enough time on your hands, you can make a quick detour to the ruins of the Sey Dzong, in a side valley nearby. Otherwise, you can simply continue ahead from the *mani* wall, cross the stream on a wooden bridge, and follow the trail heading up the hillside. Not long after, it drops into a small side valley, before emerging onto a ridge. Here the trail bifurcates, and it can be quite confusing since both the tracks look very similar. Don't go left – this route will eventually take you to Lalung La, a pass that leads on to an extremely roundabout way back to Drukgyel Dzong. Go right instead. The track will first take you through a wooded area, and then climb steeply for about an hour, ascending past a few huts and chortens to Takhung La (4520m). Spectacular views of Jhomolhari, Jichu Drakye and Tserim Kang can be seen from the pass, and on a clear day, the formidable Kanchenjunga (8586m) can be sighted far away on the western horizon.

From Takhung La, the trail holds out for a while, before gradually meandering down to Thombu Shong (4180m). It's a grassy pasture dotted with three yak herders' huts, and has traditionally been used by animal herders as a campsite through various times of the year.

Day 6: Thombu Shong to Sharna Zampa

13KM / 4–5 HOURS / 200M ASCENT, 1650M DESCENT

After breaking camp, follow the trail leading out of the valley through a marshy patch. From here, the well-defined track suddenly begins to gain elevation, and climbs steeply for a good 200m. This hike can prove tiring, especially since you now have an entire week's vigorous trekking behind you, although you will have adjusted well to the altitude by now, if that's any consolation. All along, you will be traversing through a gloriously beautiful garden of wildflowers, also rich with a crop of rhododendron, which is especially breathtaking through late spring and summer. At the end of the climb you will finally cross over **Thombu La** at 4380m, where the trail eventually exits the valley. Stop here for a last good look at Kanchenjunga and Drakye Gang (5200m), among other peaks.

On the other side of Thombu La, the trail begins to amble down steeply through upland forest, and the long descent ahead can prove to be rather brutal on your knees. Leading down from the pass, the total loss in elevation all the way to the end of the trek is a whopping 1800m, all within a span of about three hours. The first part of the descent is gradual, winding down to about 4000m, after which the trail makes a steep descent, zigzagging down the ridge through wildflower bushes, mostly edelweiss, before finally reaching the helipad at **Gunitsawa** (2730m). Cross the river and go upstream to reach your Day 1 starting point at **Sharna Zampa** (2580m).

Laya–Gasa Trek

This trek takes you into remote and isolated high country, introducing you to the unusual culture of the Layap community and allowing you to cross paths with takins (Bhutan's national animal). If you're lucky, you might also spot the exotic blue poppy, Bhutan's national flower.

The trek begins in the Paro valley and follows the same route as the Jhomolhari trek as far as Lingzhi, before heading north into the highlands. Snow can sometimes close the high passes, but they are generally open from April to June and mid-September to mid-November. The best trekking month in the Laya region is April.

LAYA–GASA TREK AT A GLANCE

Duration 12 days

Max Elevation 5005m

Difficulty Medium–hard

Season April to June, September to November

Start Sharna Zampa

Finish Gasa

Access Towns Paro, Punakha

Summary This trek is an extension of the Jhomolhari trek, with a pit stop at the far-flung village of Laya. It offers diverse flora and fauna, and a good opportunity to spot blue sheep.

Days 1–4: Sharna Zampa to Lingzhi

Follow Days 1 to 4 of the Jhomolhari trek.

Day 5: Lingzhi to Chebisa

10KM / 5–6 HOURS / 280M ASCENT, 410M DESCENT

Cross the stream below the Chha Shi Thang camp on a wooden bridge and climb up the opposite side to a chorten below **Lingzhi Dzong**, sitting at 4220m atop a ridge and accessible via a diversion from the trail. Also known as Yugyel Dzong, it was built to control travel over the Lingzhi La, a trade route between Punakha and the Tibetan town of Gyantse.

Walk down from the dzong and rejoin the lower trail leading into Lingzhi village, hidden in a valley formed by the ridge. Wheat and barley fields carpet the upper part of the side valley. The trail crosses the lower part, dotted by a few houses, a school and a post office (with a telephone) at 4080m. The Lingzhi region has a wide variety of herbs, many of medicinal value. The National Institute of Traditional Medicine in Thimphu has a herb-collecting and -drying project here.

About one hour from Lingzhi, the trail turns into a side valley past a cairn and prayer flags on a ridge at 4140m. It then makes a long gradual descent to **Goyul** (3870m), a cluster of unusual stone houses by a stream, with dramatic rock walls towering above. Leaving Goyul, the trail climbs for an hour to a chorten. A short descent leads into the spectacular

Laya–Gasa Trek

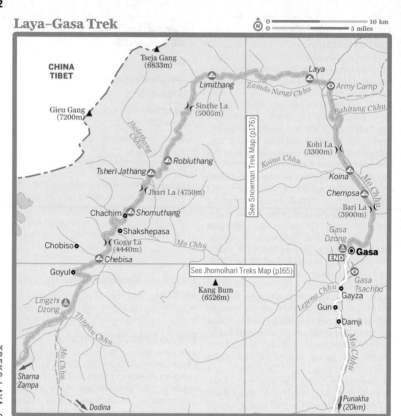

Chebisa valley, with a frozen waterfall at its head. The campsite is on a meadow opposite **Chebisa** (3880m). Upstream of the camp is the village of **Chobiso**.

Day 6: Chebisa to Shomuthang

17KM / 6–7 HOURS / 890M ASCENT, 540M DESCENT

Start out by climbing the ridge behind Chebisa, and then tackling a long, steep ascent up a featureless slope. There are large herds of blue sheep living in the rocks above. Watch for bearded vultures and Himalayan griffons flying overhead. At about 4410m the trail levels out and traverses to **Gogu La** (4440m), before crossing a ridge and descending into a side valley through rhododendrons.

Descend to a stream at 4170m, and then climb over a small ridge through a cedar forest. The trail crests the ridge at 4210m and descends on a muddy path into the main Jholethang Chhu valley, in a deep forest of fir and birch. There's a little climb over the

side of the valley and down to **Shakshe-pasa** (3980m), the site of a helipad, marked by a big 'H'. Below, there's a marsh and a messy stream crossing, with a good lunch spot on the other side.

The trail now goes up the northern side of the valley, levelling out at about 4200m, passing a couple of herders' huts and traversing high above the valley floor on river right to **Chachim**, a yak pasture at 4260m. The camp is in a cluster of brush beside a stream at the base of the valley, at **Shomuthang** (4220m).

Day 7: Shomuthang to Robluthang

18KM / 6–7 HOURS / 700M ASCENT, 760M DESCENT

The trail climbs up the valley, starting on river right, crossing to river left and then crossing back again at 4360m. Edelweiss abounds along the trail; the snow peak visible to the southeast is Kang Bum (6526m).

Climb out of the valley through desolate country to Jhari La (4750m), about two hours from camp. North of the pass, the trail switchbacks down to a little stream at 4490m, then becomes a rough, rocky route through rhododendrons on the stream's left. Follow the stream gently downhill through bushes on river left as it makes its way to the main valley. It's a gradual descent to a meadow by the Jholethang Chhu at 3990m, which you cross on a log bridge about 1km upstream.

There is a camp called Tsheri Jathang by the river. Herds of takin migrate to this valley in summer and remain here for about four months. Takins are easily disturbed by the presence of other animals, including humans. Sometimes it might be necessary to take a one-hour diversion in order to leave the beasts undisturbed. The valley has been declared a special takin sanctuary and yak herders have agreed not to graze their animals in the valley while the takins are here.

The trail climbs steeply on the northern side to a crest at about 4150m. It then traverses into a side valley past a tiny lake. There are good camping places in a rocky meadow named Robluthang at 4160m.

Day 8: Robluthang to Limithang

19KM / 6–7 HOURS / 850M ASCENT, 870M DESCENT

Climb past the remnants of a burned forest and up the hillside through some boggy patches. Switchback to a shelf at 4390m, before turning into another large glacial side valley. Follow a stream for a while, crossing to river right on an icy log bridge at 4470m, then climb onto a moraine and traverse past lots of marmot holes. You may be able to spot blue sheep high on the slopes to the north before the trail crosses back to stream left.

It's a tough climb from here to the pass at Sinche La (5005m), passing a false summit with a cairn. The trail levels out a little before reaching the cairns and prayer flags on the pass, with the snow-covered peak of Gangchhenta filling the northern horizon.

The descent is on a rough, rocky trail that follows a moraine into another glacial valley. Eventually you arrive at the Kango Chhu, a stream below a terminal moraine that forms the end of another valley to the west.

Cross the Kango Chhu to river left on a log bridge at 4470m. A short distance beyond is a yak pasture and camping spot next to a huge rock. However, it's best to continue to Limithang to camp. Follow the valley northwards, staying high as the stream falls away below you. Beyond an uninhabited stone house, the trail descends steeply to the valley floor. It switchbacks down with the terminal moraine looming above, crossing the Kango Chhu on a bridge at 4260m. After a short climb through rhododendrons, the trail levels out on a plateau

LORE OF LAYA

Spread out over a hillside near the Tibetan border, Laya is one of the highest and remotest villages in Bhutan, at 3700m. The terrain forms the country's primary yak-breeding area. Villagers raise turnips and mustard and produce a crop of wheat or barley each year before winter. During summer people move to high pastures and live in black tents woven from yak hair.

The Layaps have their own language, customs and distinct dress. The women keep their hair long and wear conical bamboo hats with a bamboo spike at the top, held on by a beaded band. They dress in black woollen jackets with silver trims and long woollen skirts with a few stripes in orange or brown. They wear lots of silver jewellery on their backs; on many women, this display includes an array of silver teaspoons.

The village women are easily encouraged to stage an evening 'cultural show', which consists of Bhutanese circle dancing accompanied by traditional Bhutanese and Layap songs. The womenfolk often offer to sell their bamboo hats for about Nu 200. Be wary of the ones offering to sell beads, as they are often family heirlooms. Laya women also frequent trekking camps selling jewellery; most of this is made in Nepal.

Zhabdrung Ngawang Namgyal passed through Laya, and in a small meadow below the village is a chorten with the footprints of the Zhabdrung and his horse. The region is believed to be a bey-yul (hidden land) protected by an ancient gate that leads to Laya village. The Layaps perform an annual ceremony in honour of the protective forces that turned all the stones and trees around the gate into soldiers to repel Tibetan invaders.

above the Zamdo Nangi Chhu. It's then a short walk through a cedar forest interspersed with small meadows to **Limithang** (4140m), a lovely campsite in a big meadow by the river. Gangchhenta towers over the campsite in the distance.

Days 9–10: Limithang to Laya

10KM / 4–5 HOURS / 60M ASCENT, 340M DESCENT

After 20 minutes of walking, the trail crosses to river left and enters a deep cedar forest, crossing several muddy side streams. Ahead, there's a herders' hut of stone where the vegetation changes to fir trees draped with lichen.

Cross a large stream that flows in from the north and make a steep rocky descent down the side of the valley to the river at 3800m, then cross to river right on a wooden cantilever bridge. A short distance later, cross back and make a stiff climb.

It's a long walk through the heavily wooded, uninhabited valley. Descend to cross a waterfall flowing across the trail, then traverse several small ups and downs. Near a point where you can see a single house on a ridge to the east, there is an inconspicuous trail junction. The lower trail leads to the lower part of the village. If you take the upper trail, you will cross a ridge and see the stone houses and wheat fields of **Laya** laid out below you with some abandoned houses and a goemba above.

Gangchhenta dominates the skyline to the west of the village, and from some places you can get a glimpse of Masang Gang (7165m). In the village centre is a community school, a hospital, an archery field and the first shop since the Paro valley. You can camp in the fields below the school at 3840m. Many groups include a rest day in Laya.

Day 11: Laya to Koina

19KM / 6–7 HOURS / 260M ASCENT, 1070M DESCENT

Layaps are not noted for their punctuality, so horses may arrive late. Below the village, the trail drops back to the river. The trail exits the village through a *khonying* (arch chorten), then passes another chorten at Taje-kha as it descends on a muddy trail to a stream.

There is an alternative camping place on a plateau at 3590m, next to the large Togtsherkhagi Chhu. Cross the river on a wooden bridge and climb to the stone buildings of the **army camp**. There's a radio station here, and a checkpoint where your names will be registered.

The route now follows the Mo Chhu downstream to Tashithang. About 30 minutes from the army post is an inconspicuous trail junction at 3340m, where the route for the Snowman trek leads uphill on a tiny path. The route to Gasa keeps going downstream on a muddy trail. Soon, it turns a corner into a side valley before crossing the **Bahitung Chhu** at 3290m, the lunch spot for the day.

From there, the trail trudges along the Mo Chhu to an overhanging rock forming a cave, then crosses to river right at 3240m on a cantilever bridge. The canyon closes in, and the trail makes several climbs over side ridges while making its way downstream. Beyond, another cave formed by a large overhanging rock is a long steep climb, cresting on a ridge at 3390m. It's a 150m descent to a clear side stream, and the trail then wanders up and down near the river, before climbing once again to **Kohi La** at 3300m.

The muddy trail stays high for about 30 minutes until it reaches a stone staircase, where it turns into a side valley, before dropping to the Koina Chhu. Welcome to **Koina**

THE SALT TREK

This brand-new trek was scoped out in 2013 and is so new, even we haven't had a chance to try it yet. The five-day route from Cheya (south of Trashigang) to Samdrup Jungkhar via Pemagatshel follows a former salt- and silk-trading route through subtropical and temperate broadleaf and pine forest, overnighting in Denchung, Demrizam, Mongling, Radhingphu and Nelang. Figure on four to five hours' walking a day.

The starting point is at a campsite by Cheya Tsho, down a farm road that branches off the main highway at Khentongmani. The trail follows the Khaling Chhu for the first couple of days before climbing to Mongling on the Tshelingkhor–Pemagatsel highway for views of Deothang and Pemagatshel regions and a visit to nearby Yongla Gomeba. Days four and five are all downhill. Because of the low elevations this is a great winter-season trek and walkable between October and March. Come in November to time your trek with the three-day Pemagatshel tsechu.

(3050m), a muddy bog in the forest filled with ankle-deep sludge. This is the worst camp on the whole trek. A considerably drier camp has been identified about two hours ahead at Chempsa (3700m). Feel free to use it instead.

Day 12: Koina to Gasa

14KM / 6–7 HOURS / 900M ASCENT, 1710M DESCENT

Today's walk sees you tackling one last obstacle on this trek – the Bari La.

Cross the bridge at Koina and start up the hill. Parts of the trail are so muddy that logs have been placed to form little bridges. The muddy trail keeps going through a deep forest of fir for almost three hours, until you reach a small rock cairn and a few prayer flags atop Bari La (3900m). Then it's a reasonably level walk to another chorten.

The route then begins to descend, sometimes steeply, through a bamboo forest to a stream. At 3080m it rounds a corner where you can finally see Gasa Dzong (p99) on the opposite side of a large wooded side valley. The trail descends past an old chorten, then crosses a ridge into a big side valley. It drops and crosses a large stream at 2780m, then traverses along the side of the valley to four chortens on the ridge at 2810m.

The chortens mark the southern boundary of Gasa town (2770m). The trail traverses above the football and archery ground, past several small teashops, then intersects Gasa's main street. Trek downhill to the bazaar, where there is a handful of shops and a police checkpoint. The police post checks permits, providing a perfect excuse to stop for a soft drink or beer at one of the shops.

You can camp in a field near the town or possibly 1½ hours downhill near the tsachhu (hot spring). If it's raining, the remainder of this trek is perfect country in which to closely study how leeches become attached to humans. Gasa is where you meet the roadhead, and your operator can arrange to have you picked up from here and driven down to Punakha via Damji and Tashithang.

Snowman Trek

The combination of distance, altitude, remoteness and weather makes this trek a tough journey, and when trekking fees were raised, it suffered a sharp decline in the number of trekkers attempting it. Even though there are reduced rates for long treks, many baulk at the cost of a 24-day trek.

SNOWMAN TREK AT A GLANCE

Duration 24 days

Max Elevation 5320m

Difficulty Hard

Season September to October

Start Sharna Zampa

Finish Sephu

Access Town Paro

Summary The Snowman trek travels to the remote Lunana district and is said to be one of the most difficult treks in the world. Fewer than half the people who attempt this trek eventually finish it, either because of problems with altitude or heavy snowfall on the high passes.

If you plan to trek this route, check your emergency evacuation insurance. If you get into Lunana and snow blocks the passes, the only way out is by helicopter, an expensive way to finish an already expensive trek. Another obstacle that often hampers this trek is bridges in remote regions that get washed away by deluges.

The Snowman trek is frequently closed because of snow, and is impossible to undertake during winter. The season for this trek is generally considered to be from late September to mid-October. Don't plan a summer trek; this is a miserable place to be during the monsoon.

This classic trek follows the Jhomolhari and Laya–Gasa treks to Laya. Many walking days can be saved by starting in Gasa (via Punakha) and trekking north over the Bari La.

Days 1–4: Sharna Zampa to Lingzhi

Follow Days 1 to 4 of the Jhomolhari trek.

Days 5–9: Lingzhi to Laya

Follow Days 5 to 9 of the Laya–Gasa trek.

Day 10: Rest & Acclimatisation Day in Laya

If you have trekked from Sharna Zampa, you should spend a day recuperating in Laya and preparing for the rigours ahead. If

Snowman Trek

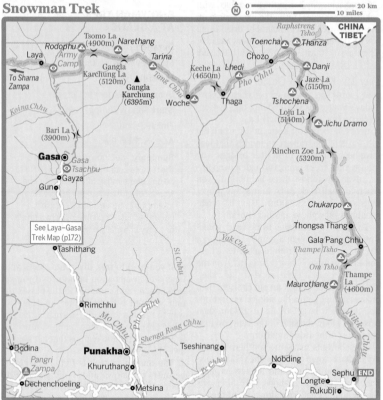

you've trekked from Gasa, you should also walk up to Laya to acclimatise. The army camp below Laya has a radio; you will need to send a runner here with a message in an emergency.

Day 11: Laya to Rodophu

19KM / 6–8 HOURS / 1030M ASCENT, 70M DESCENT

The trek leads down to the Lunana trail junction, then climbs for 40 minutes to a hilltop with good views over the Mo Chhu and the Rhodo Chhu. It continues up the Rhodo Chhu valley, first through mixed conifers, then through rhododendron, above the tree line. Atop a large rock slide there is a view of the glacial valley and a massive glacier on Tsenda Kang (7100m). The **Rodophu** camp is just beyond a wooden bridge across the Rhodo Chhu at 4160m.

If you're acclimatising here for a day, consider a short 2km hike up the valley to a knoll with excellent views of the valley

and mountains, continuing to the base of the glacier. Another option is to follow a small trail starting about 500m upstream from camp and up the hill to the north, ending in a small yak pasture with a hut at 4500m.

Day 12: Rodophu to Narethang

17KM / 5–6 HOURS / 720M ASCENT

The path crosses the wooden bridge and follows the river for 20 minutes through rhododendron shrubs before turning right up the hill. Climb to a high open valley at 4600m and then through meadows to **Tsomo La** (4900m), which offers good views towards the Tibet border and Jhomolhari. Next up is a flat, barren plateau at around 5000m with yak trails criss-crossing everywhere – your guide will know the way. The camp is at **Narethang** (4900m), below the 6395m peak of Gangla Karchung.

Day 13: Narethang to Tarina

18KM / 7–8 HOURS / 270M ASCENT, 1200M DESCENT

It's a one-hour climb to the 5120m **Gangla Karchung La**, with Kang Bum (6526m) to the west and Tsenda Kang, Teri Gang (7300m) and Jejekangphu Gang (7100m) due north. The path descends along a large moraine to the edge of a near-vertical wall with breathtaking views. A massive glacier descends from Teri Gang to two deep turquoise lakes at its foot, 1km below you. The glacial lake to the left burst through its dam in the early 1960s, causing widespread damage downstream, and partially destroying Punakha Dzong.

The path now becomes very steep as it descends into the valley. When wet, this stretch can be rather nasty, with lots of roots and slippery mud. At the base of the U-shaped valley, the trail turns right, following the Tang Chhu downstream. There are several good campsites along the river, both before and after the trail crosses the river at **Tarina**.

Day 14: Tarina to Woche

17KM / 6–7 HOURS / 275M ASCENT, 330M DESCENT

The walk leads through conifers down the Tang Chhu on river left, passing some impressive waterfalls. The trail climbs gently out of the valley past several huge landslides, and eventually climbs steeply to the northeast into the high side valley of **Woche**. The first village in the Lunana region, Woche is a small settlement of five houses at 3940m.

Looking up the valley you can see the following day's route to Lhedi. There have been reports of theft here; keep all your gear safely inside your tent.

Day 15: Woche to Lhedi

17KM / 6–7 HOURS / 980M ASCENT, 950M DESCENT

The trail climbs the Woche valley, crossing a stream and going over a moraine before descending to a wooden bridge across the Woche Chhu. It then climbs on a wide trail past a clear lake to **Keche La** (4650m), with excellent views of the surrounding mountains, including Jejekangphu Gang's triple peak, the source of the Woche Chhu.

The route now descends into the Pho Chhu valley and reaches **Thaga** village (4050m). Dropping towards the Pho Chhu, the path then turns northeast towards Lhedi. Passing a few scattered settlements and crossing be-

low a waterfall on a wooden bridge, the trail descends to the banks of the Pho Chhu, continuing along the river bed to **Lhedi** at 3700m.

Lhedi is a district headquarters with a school, Basic Health Unit (BHU) and wireless station, but there is no shop here (or anywhere else in the Lunana district). Everything is carried in by yak trains across 5000m passes. Strong winds blow up the valley in the late afternoon, making it bitterly cold in autumn and winter.

Day 16: Lhedi to Thanza

17KM / 4–5 HOURS / 400M ASCENT

The trail follows the north bank of the Pho Chhu past several small farms. Floods have destroyed parts of the trail so an alternative path winds its way among boulders in the river bed. Around lunchtime the trail passes **Chozo** village at 4090m, with a dzong.

If you are pressed for time, you can take a direct trail to Tshochena from here, but most trekkers continue to Thanza (4100m), a couple of hours up the valley. The first part of the trail leads through yak pastures on river flats, giving way to a large expanse of fine glacial sand. Eventually, the trail leaves the river bed and climbs a bluff overlooking the villages of **Thanza**, straight ahead, and **Toencha**, on the other bank of the river. The 7100m Zongophu Gang (Table Mountain) forms an immense, 3000m-high wall of snow and ice behind Thanza. Most groups camp in Toencha (4150m), but there are places to camp in Thanza as well.

Day 17: Rest Day in Thanza

Schedule a rest day here. This is as far as yak drivers from Laya go, and it takes time to round up yaks for the rest of the trek. Capitalise on the day by exploring the villages and glacial lakes up the valley. The closest lake, **Raphstreng Tsho**, is 100m deep and caused a flood in 1994 when a moraine holding back its waters burst. A large crew of Indian workers dug a channel through the moraine to prevent a recurrence, but there are other lakes in the area posing a similar risk.

Day 18: Thanza to Danji

8KM / 3–4 HOURS / 80M ASCENT

If you're feeling fit, you can hike to Tshochena in one day, but it's a long, hard walk at high altitude and is best split in two parts.

Climbing to a large boulder on the hill south of the village, the trail turns east up

OWL TREK

Keen to sample some 'nightlife' out in the mountains? Well, you could always consider walking the Owl trek, a new route in the Bumthang region that owes its name to the frequent hooting of owls which can be heard at campsites through the night. A three-day itinerary, the Owl trek starts at Menchugang village (5km north of Toktu Zampa) and ends at either Jakar Dzong or Tharpaling Goemba. October to December and March to May are the best times for trekking, though spring can be muddy. See the map on p181 for this route.

Day 1 From Menchugang the trail climbs for 1½ hours to an old water-driven flour mill at Chutigang, before climbing a further 2½ hours to Rabtense, and then a three-hour climb through ancient forests of birch, fir and spruce to Shona campsite. Some itineraries visit Duer village en route.

Day 2 The climb continues to Rang La (Drangela) pass and then up to 3870m Kitephu ridge for magnificent views towards Gangkhar Phuensum and the main Himalaya range. There's plenty of time in the afternoon to savour the views or hike up to the top of the ridge.

Day 3 Takes you for 1½ hours to impressive Tharpaling Goemba and nearby Choedrak hermitage (where Guru Rinpoche is said to have meditated). From here you have the choice of meeting your vehicle, descending on foot via Samtenling Lhakhang to Domkhar in the Chhume valley, or climbing back over the ridge behind Tharpaling to descend through forest to Jakar.

a side valley. After a couple of hours of easy walking, the trail enters **Danji**, a yak meadow with some herders' huts. It's an excellent camp, with blue sheep often grazing above and occasionally walking into camp.

A few hundred metres up the valley, a small trail climbs the ridge to the left, leading to a higher valley. The top of the ridge offers excellent views of surrounding mountains.

Day 19: Danji to Tshochena

12KM / 5–6 HOURS / 490M ASCENT, 240M DESCENT

From the junction near camp, the trail up the valley leads to Gangkhar Puensum base camp and Bumthang. The path to the end of the trek crosses the creek and leads up a rocky side valley – a long climb across several false summits to **Jaze La** at 5150m, with views of mountains in all directions. From the pass, the path descends between snow-covered peaks past a string of small lakes. The camp is near the shore of **Tshochena** at 4970m. This is the first of two nights' camping above 4900m.

Day 20: Tshochena to Jichu Dramo

14KM / 4–5 HOURS / 230M ASCENT, 140M DESCENT

The trail follows the shore of the blue-green lake before climbing to a ridge at 5100m, with a 360-degree panorama of snowy peaks. Far below, the Pho Chhu descends towards Punakha. The road and microwave tower at Dochu La are visible in the distance.

The path makes several ups and downs over small rounded hills, but the altitude can slow you down. Past a glacial lake before **Loju La** at 5140m, many trails wander around high-altitude yak pastures, and it's easy to wander astray. The correct path is across a small saddle at 5100m into a wide glacial valley, and then down to the camp at **Jichu Dramo** (5050m), a small pasture on the east of the valley.

Day 21: Jichu Dramo to Chukarpo

18KM / 5–6 HOURS / 320M ASCENT, 730M DESCENT

The trail climbs through a moraine to the picturesque Rinchen Zoe La (5320m), dividing the Pho Chhu and Mangde Chhu drainages. Rinchen Zoe peak (5650m) towers above, and Gangkhar Puensum is visible in the east, while the Thampe Chhu valley stretches below to the south.

Descending into a broad, marshy valley with a string of lakes, the trail follows the left (east) side of the valley. Eventually, it descends steeply down the face of a moraine to a yak pasture in the upper reaches of the Thampe Chhu. Cross to the west bank (river right) here, as there is no bridge further down. The vegetation begins to thicken, and consists of rhododendron and juniper. The camp is a couple of hours away at **Chukarpo** (4600m); a better site sits an hour ahead at **Thongsa Thang** (4400m).

Day 22: Chukarpo to Thampe Tsho

18KM / 5–6 HOURS / 400M ASCENT, 640M DESCENT

Descend along the right bank of the river until you reach a yak pasture at Gala Pang Chhu (4010m). From here, the path begins to climb steeply through junipers and silver firs towards Thampe Tsho. The path generally follows a stream to the beautiful, clear, turquoise lake, set in a bowl and surrounded by steep mountain walls. The camp is at the far end of the lake at 4300m.

Day 23: Thampe Tsho to Maurothang

14KM / 5 HOURS / 280M ASCENT, 1020M DESCENT

The trail climbs steeply to Thampe La at 4600m. You may see blue sheep high on the slopes above the trail.

The path descends to Om Tsho, a sacred site where Pema Lingpa found a number of *terma* (sacred texts and artefacts). The path skirts the northwestern shore of the lake before crossing its outlet, marked by prayer flags, and then drops steeply past a waterfall to a smaller lake, about 100m lower.

From the second lake to the headwaters of the Nikka Chhu is a descent so steep that even yaks are reluctant to come down this stretch. The path eventually levels out, following the left bank of the Nikka Chhu. After about 2km, it reaches a large open glade near the confluence of a major tributary coming from the east. A wooden bridge crosses the Nikka Chhu to river right, where a broad path leads through mixed forest to Maurothang (3610m), a large clearing by the river beside a few herders' huts.

Day 24: Maurothang to Sephu

18KM / 5–6 HOURS / 990M DESCENT

If horses are not available at Maurothang, your guide will probably send someone ahead to arrange for them further down. Yaks cannot walk all the way to the road because of the low altitude and the many cows in the area.

A well-used trail continues down the west side of the Nikka Chhu for about 30 minutes before crossing to the east bank into a mixed deciduous and bamboo forest. It descends gradually through forests and pastures, emerging onto a large grassy area overlooking the road and Sephu village. There are many confusing trails here; look for a large track about 25m above the river and you'll soon pass a large suspension bridge over the Nikka Chhu, which you shouldn't cross. Soon the trail turns into a narrow tractor road leading to the main road at Sephu, next to the Nikka Chhu bridge at 2600m, marked by shops and a small restaurant.

Bumthang Cultural Trek

This trek has changed over the last few years due to the construction of roads in the region. Many people now do the trek in a single day, staying at simple accommodation in Ngang Lhakhang and Ogyen Chholing at the start and end of the walk. The walk is short but packs in a tiring 750m climb to the Phephe La.

If you want to make it a two-day camping trek it is possible to start from Thangbi Goemba, walk up the true left bank of the Chamkhar Chhu and camp at Sambitang,

---

TREKKING WITHOUT A TENT IN THE BUMTHANG VALLEY

There are so many great hiking trails in the Bumthang valley that it's possible to link together a string of day hikes to make a multiday walk that avoids the inconvenience, discomfort and expense of a full camping trek. For details of the following Bumthang day hikes, see p126.

From Menchugang you could start with a full day hike to Luege Rowe (or even Shugdrak), before hiking up the south bank of the Chamkhar Chhu to Ngang Lhakhang. Overnight at Ngang Lhakhang or a homestay in nearby Tsangling or Tashiling, before making the long day hike over the Phephe La to Ogyen Chholing (ie the Bumthang Cultural trek).

For day three make the rewarding return day hike to Thowadrak Hermitage. Then on day four return to Jakar by car or drive to Kunzungdrak Goemba and hike over the ridge to Pelseling Goemba and then down to the Swiss Guest House or Tamshing Goemba.

For a full week's walking with some camping, add on the three-day Owl trek in the reverse direction, starting at Tharpaling Goemba and picking up this itinerary at Menchugang.

BUMTHANG CULTURAL TREK AT A GLANCE

Duration 1–2 days

Max Elevation 3360m

Difficulty Medium

Season March to May, September to November

Start Ngang Lhakhang

Finish Ogyen Chholing

Access Town Jakar

Summary Delightful forests and interesting lhakhangs and villages at the start and end points make this a good option if you fancy a challenging day walk with flush toilets at either end!

about a 30-minute walk from Ngang Lhakhang. There is a second camping spot at Tahung at the far end of the trail but most groups continue to nearby Ogyen Chholing, now that it is connected by road.

Day 1: Ngang Lhakhang to Ogyen Chholing

18KM / 7 HOURS / 750M ASCENT, 670M DESCENT

The day's walk starts out with a short climb to a meadow at the base of **Draphe Dzong**, which is worth the short detour to explore the ruins of this formerly strategic fort. From here the trail drops to the **Sambitang** campsite. The trail continues across meadows, with a lot of dwarf bamboo, before climbing up to a cold, sunless forest of birch, sycamore and lots of tall bamboo. Spanish moss drapes the ancient trees, giving an eerie feel to the steep climb.

The climb continues through a rhododendron forest in a dry gully to a rock cairn and a little stone shrine. Tattered prayer flags stretch across the path atop **Phephe La** (3360m), on a forested ridge with big birch and fir trees.

The trail leads down to a stream at 3200m, then into a side valley covered in dwarf bamboo, passing a small *mani* wall and a *khonying* chorten. Breaking out into broad yak pastures, it continues down through ploughed fields into a broad valley, where the most prominent of several trails leads downhill to a large stream and a wooden bridge at 2790m near the village of **Tahung**.

From here a rough farm road leads down to **Tang** village and the main Tang valley. Your vehicle can pick you up here and take you to Ogyen Chholing or you can continue on foot to **Gamling**, a large, wealthy village noted for its *yathra* weaving, about 45 minutes downstream, where a footpath climbs up to a ridge, reaching four chortens and several large houses at 2760m. **Ogyen Chholing** is atop the hill to the right. Rooms in the guesthouse (p132) are simple but cosy.

Duer Hot Springs Trek

This is a less-walked route, owing to its high difficulty rating. It's possible to extend this trek to the base camp of Gangkhar Puensum itself, although the trail is remote and little trekked. It's also possible to vary either the upward or return route, and travel via the Mangde Chhu valley to meet a gravel road leading west from Trongsa.

This trek can also form an alternative ending to the Snowman trek, branching off the main trial at Thanza and making the remote five-day trek to Duer Hot Springs via the Tsorhim lakes, the 5230m Gophu La, Geshe Woma, the Saka La pass and Warathang.

Snow covers the route during winter, so the trek is usually open from March to April and from September to early November. Its starting point, Duer village, is 30 minutes (5km) of rough driving from Toktu Zampa. The trek includes a day at a *tsachhu* (hot spring).

DUER HOT SPRINGS TREK AT A GLANCE

Duration 8 days

Max Elevation 4700m

Difficulty Medium–hard

Season March to April, September to November

Start/Finish Duer

Access Town Jakar

Summary This trek takes you on the old expedition route to Gangkhar Puensum, the world's highest unclimbed peak, and offers a full day at the hot springs.

Day 1: Duer to Gorsum

18KM / 6 HOURS / 380M ASCENT

Starting at Duer, the route goes north, following the valley of the **Yoleng Chhu** (also known as Gorzam Chhu), which is famous for its trout population. En route, you will cross the Lurawa Goemba. The campsite for the day is at **Gorsum** at 3120m; for those who want to push ahead, there's an alternate site about two hours ahead.

Day 2: Gorsum to Lungsum

12KM / 5 HOURS / 40M ASCENT

The route travels through a forest of cypress, juniper, spruce, hemlock and maple. The trail is muddy and climbs gradually to the camp at **Lungsum** (3160m). On the way, you might cross paths with Bhutanese wild dogs. Keep your cameras ready.

Day 3: Lungsum to Tsochenchen

15KM / 6–7 HOURS / 620M ASCENT

Today's trek remains more or less the same as yesterday's, passing through similar terrain and flora. Along the way you'll come across a bifurcation; from here, the trail to the right leads to Gangkhar Puensum via Thole La. The left trail leads to the springs. Towards the end of today's hike, the vegetation begins to thin out, before camp is reached at **Tsochenchen**, above the tree line at 3780m.

Day 4: Tsochenchen to Duer Hot Springs

18KM / 8–9 HOURS / 1340M ASCENT, 1530M DESCENT

The day starts with a long climb to a small lake and on to **Juli La** (4700m), a rocky saddle with a few prayer flags and a good view of the surrounding mountains. After

Bumthang Cultural & Duer Hot Springs

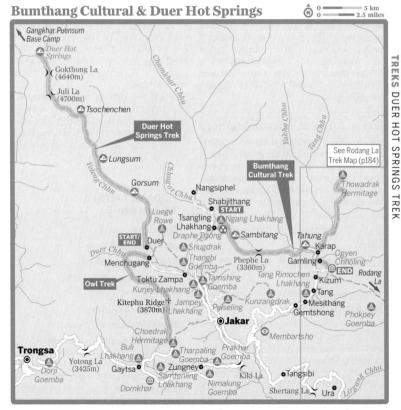

THE ROYAL HERITAGE TRAIL

Every autumn during the rule of the second king (1926–52) the entire royal court would pack up their belongings onto 300 porters and 100 pack horses and set off on a twice-annual migration between the summer palace at Bumthang and a warmer winter residence at Kuenga Rabten. Today only the occasional herder uses this former royal processional way but trekkers can re-enact the route as part of an interesting three-day cultural trek. The little-trekked route links together two passes, three former palaces, several meditation retreats and some lovely scenery into a low-elevation cultural trek.

From Wangdicholing Palace in Jakar groups hike over the Kiki La ridge to Tharpaling Goemba (p117), before descending via Samtenling Goemba to a camp near Domkhar Dzong (alternatively, get a more comfortable night's sleep at the nearby Chumey Nature Resort; p118). Day two climbs past the royal lunch spot of Dungmai (3680m; four hours) to a campsite at Jamsapang (4020m; two hours). The final day starts with a short climb to a chorten at the Tungli La for fine views of the distant Black Mountains. From here it's all downhill via Jopchisa to a lunch spot at Saphay Pang (2860m; four hours) and then a final four-hour downhill hike to the impressive palace at Kuenga Rabten. An alternative route climbs over the Ngada La before descending to either Saphay Pang or Eundu Chholing. Expect some road construction on the final hour or two of the walk.

crossing the pass, the trail goes all the way down to a lake at 4220m, before climbing again to **Gokthong La** (4640m). Finally, it switchbacks steeply down through jungle to a camp near the **Duer hot springs** at 3590m. It may be possible to see musk deer, Himalayan bears and blue sheep through the day's trek.

Day 5: A Day at Duer Hot Springs

Take a rest day to relax in the *tsachhu*. There are several wooden tubs set into the ground inside a rough wooden shelter for you to soak in. A new campsite, simple community-run guesthouse and drinking water supply was constructed here recently.

Days 6–8: Duer Hot Springs to Duer

Return via the same route from the hot springs to Duer.

Rodang La Trek

Ever since a highway was rolled out to connect its end points, this once important trade route has remained largely untrodden by locals. However, its high difficulty level can come as a draw for the more adventurous types. You can add a day onto this trek by starting in Ngang Lhakhang and adding on the Bumthang Cultural trek.

Rodang La is subject to closure because of snow, and is best trodden in October, early November or late spring. The trek crosses the road near Lhuentse, which breaks up the continuity of the trekking experience but offers a chance to visit the remote dzong.

Roads are nibbling away at the trail in four different directions, so check with your agent to see how developments have affected the trek. There are even plans to build a road over the Rodang La, which will effectively kill this walking route.

RODANG LA TREK AT A GLANCE

Duration 6–8 days

Max Elevation 4160m

Difficulty Medium–hard

Season October to November

Start Ogyen Chholing

Finish Trashi Yangtse

Access Town Jakar

Summary This trek across eastern Bhutan is tough and involves a tremendously long, steep descent. The logistics are complicated and horses are often difficult to obtain for the final four days of the trek.

Day 1: Ogyen Chholing to Phokpey

17KM / 5–6 HOURS / 920M ASCENT

The long climb to Rodang La takes two days. Above **Ogyen Chholing**, the trail is rutted with cattle hoof prints, and can be slippery when wet. The trail levels out around 2900m, meeting a stream. At about 3000m the cow trails turn into a small footpath through muddy fields and dwarf bamboo.

At 3400m the trail crosses a meadow. High on the opposite hill is the Phokpey Goemba. Climb through the meadow and traverse through forest to another steep, high meadow, finally turning a corner into a side valley, and heading to **Phokpey**, a camp at 3680m.

Day 2: Phokpey to Pemi

20KM / 6–7 HOURS / 480M ASCENT, 1160M DESCENT

The trail goes through a small notch onto a ridge at 3700m. After a long crossing at 3770m is the final climb to the pass, up stone slabs and a steep stone staircase. **Rodang La** (4160m) is about two hours from camp.

Across the pass, it's a steep descent of nearly 2500m to the valley floor, down an unbelievably long and steep stone staircase. This is a tough route for horses, and it is said that even the king had to walk downhill here. Part of the route is along a vertical face, and the trail is on wooden galleries fastened into the side of the cliff. Past a few meadows, the trail winds through a region where sightings of ghosts and *migoi* (yetis) have been reported.

Leaving the rhododendrons and conifers, the trail descends to a big meadow called **Pemi** at about 3000m. Up ahead are the ruins of a royal granary and a campsite at 2950m. Water is 30 minutes down the side of a hill, so go easy on the washing or, better, continue to **Ungaar** campsite where water supplies are more abundant.

Day 3: Pemi to Khaine Lhakhang

21KM / 7–8 HOURS / 350M ASCENT, 1340M DESCENT

Much of today's trail criss-crosses a new farm road, so check to see if alternative trails are available. The current trail tumbles into the Noyurang Chhu valley, leading through dwarf bamboo and a damp, mossy, rock-filled gully. Around 2600m, the vegetation changes to ferns and tropical species, and the trail goes down towards a meadow

KHAINE LHAKHANG

Some people believe that the remote Khaine Lhakhang is one of the 108 temples built by King Songtsen Gampo in AD 659. Three small statues from here are said to have flown of their own accord to Konchogsum Lhakhang in Bumthang, believed to have been built at the same time. The primary statue is a 2.5m Sakyamuni Buddha figure. A statue of the Karmapa is on his right and Zhabdrung Rinpoche is above him on the left. There are also smaller statues of Milarepa and Guru Rinpoche. The main protective deity is a ferocious god named Taxan, who is depicted riding a horse.

A two-day festival is celebrated here in mid-November.

called **Sang Sangbe** (2300m), apparently haunted by a ghost. The trail drops to a bridge over a stream at 1700m. It's then a short walk across rice fields to a suspension bridge over the Noyurgang Chhu at 1660m.

Cross to river left and start climbing through ferns and tropical jungle to the village of **Bulay** (1800m). Next is **Kulaypang** (1930m) – with a few simple houses and cornfields – where there's a false trail going down towards the next ridge; the correct trail goes up.

The trail passes below **Gomda** village (2040m). Passing a chorten, it crosses a stream at 2000m, then climbs to a *mani* wall at 2020m. Then it's a level walk to Gongdra. Beyond Chanteme, you cross a stream and climb to **Khaine Lhakhang**. Follow the cement irrigation canal and climb onto the ridge where the temple sits at 2010m. There are two tall cedars by the monastery and fields of soya beans surrounding it. Pephu Goemba is high above and the town below is Songme.

Day 4: Khaine Lhakhang to Tangmachu

18KM / 6–7 HOURS / 520M ASCENT, 810M DESCENT

The trail goes down to a stream and up to a BHU and community school in **Gorsam** (an alternative campsite). It then climbs to 2130m, levelling out for 15 minutes, before climbing gently through trees. You can see a glimpse of the road at the bottom of the Kuri Chhu valley.

Rodang La Trek

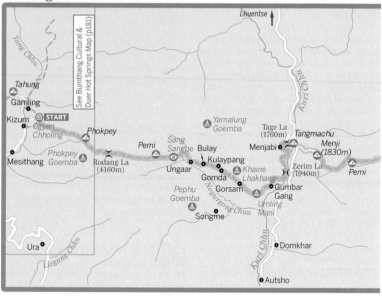

The Tibetan-style **Umling Mani** at 2180m is at the corner between the Noyurgang Chhu and the Kuri Chhu valleys. It was built by a lama from Tibet and marks the boundary between the two *gewogs* (administrative blocks). Here the route turns north up the Kuri Chhu.

Traversing through four large side valleys, you then descend to a stream and climb to the next ridge. The trail emerges from the first valley at **Gumbar Gang** (2120m). After going up to a chorten on **Zerim La** (1940m), it winds down to the head of a valley at 1840m, with a chorten and a prayer wheel, then starts climbing back through chir pines to 1890m, traversing grassy slopes to another ridge and several herders' huts.

Descend to a *mani* wall, pass **Menjabi** village, cross the stream at 1540m, then start a long climb on a grassy slope with chir pines to some chortens and a *mani* wall on **Tage La** (1760m). Southeast of the pass is the Tangmachu High School and the towering 45m statue of Guru Rinpoche, which is worth a visit. If you have time, you could request a vehicle to meet you here and drive you 21km north to Lhuentse to visit the dzong, and then drop you back at **Tangmachu** or Menji for the night. The vehicle can then drive on to Trashi Yangtse to pick you up four days later.

Day 5: Tangmachu to Menji

16KM / 4–5 HOURS / 690M ASCENT, 620M DESCENT

A feeder road now connects the main road with Menji, so check with your agent to see if you are hiking or driving this section and how this impacts the following days. From the bridge (1140m) below Tangmachu, the hiking trail goes gradually up through rice terraces and cornfields to Chusa. It then becomes a steep haul up a treeless slope, although the path is beautifully scented with wild mint, lemongrass and artemisia. Camp is at 1830m, above **Menji**, beside the Darchu Pang Lhakhang.

Day 6: Menji to Pemi

10KM / 3–4 HOURS / 620M ASCENT

Continue uphill through the thick, humid forest packed with a dense foliage of ferns and creepers and a constant whistle of cicadas. The trail is narrow, steep and rutted. Climb steadily for two hours to a ridge-top meadow, then plunge back into the forest to reach some herders' huts at **Pemi** (2450m) on a narrow ridge-top clearing with a view to a forested gorge. Menji villagers use this area as a summer pasture. Much of the trail for the next two days has fallen into disuse and is narrow and slippery.

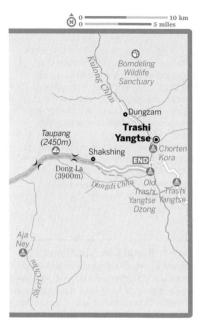

Day 8: Taupang to Trashi Yangtse

24KM / 8–9 HOURS / 720M DESCENT

The path through the forest beside the river is damp and muddy with huge ferns, red-berried palms and occasional leeches. The forest is alive with birds and monkeys. Two hours of sloshing through mud or stone-hopping brings you to **Shakshing**, a cluster of houses surrounded by corn, millet, banana and grazing cows. The logging road from Trashi Yangtse now reaches Shakshing and will probably extend further to Taupang.

If you decide to continue walking, the trail stays on the ridge to the north of the valley, passing above Tongshing village. It then descends past swampy areas, crossing to the southern bank of the Dongdi Chhu on a large bridge. The small, old **Trashi Yangtse** dzong suddenly appears on a hilltop above the river. The trail crosses back to the north bank of the river below the dzong on an old cantilever bridge. Finally, it crosses the Kulong Chhu at 1730m. Your vehicle will either be waiting here, or at the old dzong.

Day 7: Pemi to Taupang

21KM / 7–8 HOURS / 1450M ASCENT, 1450M DESCENT

The trail stays largely in damp, cold forest, with occasional pastures. The area is a botanist's delight, with shrubs of every kind, pungent with a sweet fermented smell, thick with humus. The trail then traverses nine passes, nicknamed the **Nine Sisters**, the highest of which is **Dong La** (3900m), with good mountain views and some prayer flags on a pile of rocks.

Cross the remaining ridges, each adorned with prayer flags, and descend steeply through thick evergreen forests on a trail strewn with rocks, logs and slippery leaves to a ridge-top meadow called Lisipang. The last part of the trek is easy at first, turning right and down through a pasture at Yesupang (an alternative campsite), but then becomes rocky and muddy near the Dongdi Chhu. There's no bridge, and once you rock-hop across, it's even muddier and rockier on the other side, and parts of the trail are layered with logs placed in a bridge-like manner to provide smoother walking. The camp is at **Taupang** (2450m), a clearing with a wooden cowherds' shelter.

Nabji Trek

If you are looking for a low-altitude winter trek, or if village life, bird-spotting and family interactions are more important than mountain views, the Nabji trek could well be your cup of tea.

The trail is an early stab at community-based tourism in Bhutan, in which local villagers are employed on a rotating basis to offer services and amenities such as porterage, village tours, cultural shows and food at

---

NABJI TREK AT A GLANCE

Duration 6 days

Max Elevation 1635m

Difficulty Easy

Season October to March

Start Riotala

Finish Tongtongphey

Access Town Trongsa

Summary A low-altitude trek passing through the land of the isolated Monpa people.

MEET THE BROKPAS

The 6000 or so Brokpas of Merak and Sakteng trace their origins from Tshona in southern Tibet but have lived in Bhutan for centuries now. They are culturally distinct from neighbouring ethnic groups and are recognisable by their unique dress; most notable is their *shamo*, a beret-like black hat made from the chest hair of a yak, with spiderlike tentacles descending from its edges to deflect rainwater. Women wear a red- and white-striped silk dress called a *shingkha*, while men wear a red wool jacket known as a *tshokhan chuba*. Most practise transhumance, moving with their yaks between the highlands in summer and lower pastures in winter.

The Brokpas still engage in the barter system, and travel down to Phongme, Radi and Trashigang in winter to trade their stocks of *chora* (fermented cheese), butter and dried meat in exchange for salt, tea and grains. Most families own livestock, barring a few who stay back in their village dwellings through the cold season. With the introduction of tourism the entrepreneurial Brokpas have started to open homestays and offer equipment rental.

semi-developed campsites along the route. Campsite fees go into a community fund to support education, conservation and tourism development.

The trailheads of this winter trek are on the road between Trongsa and Zhemgang, and the trek itself offers a chance to spot some exotic local creatures such as the golden langur, the rufous-necked hornbill and the serpent eagle, among others.

As with so many treks in Bhutan, roadbuilding is nibbling away at the beginning and end of the trek. Roads are planned to reach as far as Nabji itself. This trek can easily be done in the opposite direction. See Map p112 for this route.

PEOPLE OF DARKNESS

Numbering around 3000 individuals, the Monpas inhabit a cluster of ancient villages dotting the mountain slope overlooking the Mangde Chhu near Jangbi. The word Monpa loosely translates to 'people of darkness', and refers to their isolated existence in Bhutan. Believed to be the earliest settlers in Bhutan, the tribe's ethnic roots can be traced back to Arunachal Pradesh in India, where their population currently exceeds 45,000.

The Monpas practise a mix of Buddhism and animistic shamanism. While they were originally hunters and gatherers, the Monpas have, over time, developed artisanal skills such as cane weaving, bamboo crafting and basket making.

Day 1: Riotala to Nimshong

6.5KM / 3–4 HOURS / 625M ASCENT, 365M DESCENT

From the Wangduegang turn-off just north of Zhemgang, a farm road descends to the Mangde Chhu, offering access to the Nabji valley. Depending on how far the road has reached you might start walking in Matling (800m), or even Nimshong (1170m), which would do away with this first-day's walking.

Nimshong is a village of about 60 households at 1320m. You will be welcomed into the village with much song and dance, before being served dinner cooked by villagers.

Day 2: Nimshong to Korphu

14KM / 5–6 HOURS / 200M ASCENT

After a village tour of Nimshong, hike through a lush broadleaf forest teeming with regional fauna, such as golden langurs and rufous-necked hornbills, to make a final ascent to Korphu, a village of about 600 people perched at 1500m. Visit the village temple, housing the sacred relics of Pema Lingpa. The community-run campsite offers fine views over the valley.

Day 3: Korphu to Nabji

13KM / 2–3 HOURS / 200M DESCENT

It's a short and pleasant walk down to the river and then up to the expansive paddy fields of Nabji (1300m), giving you plenty of time to explore the village. Visit the temple here and the historically important stone pillar commemorating an 8th-century peace treaty negotiated by Guru Rinpoche and signed between King Sindhu of Bumthang and King Nauchhe (Big Nose) from Assam.

In the village, you'll also see the rocky remains of a blacksmith, believed to be connected to Pema Lingpa. The camp is located amid rice fields near the village.

Day 4: Nabji to Kudra

13–14KM / 6–7 HOURS / 335M ASCENT

Today's trek leaves Nabji at a spot marked by a holy tree, before passing through a dense forest of clippers, orchids and bamboo. The forest is supposedly a habitat for tigers and leopards, although sightings are rare. The campsite at Kudra (1635m) is smack in the middle of the forest, with three Monpa households nearby.

Day 5: Kudra to Jangbi

13–14KM / 6–7 HOURS / 265M DESCENT

Today's trail is littered with fabulous evidence of Guru Rinpoche's visit to the region – footprint, dagger, hat, you name it. Lunch is at Phrumzur village (1400m), which has a temple from where you can take in good views of the valley. From Phrumzur, it's an easy hike to Jangbi village (1370m), where you'll pitch tent in a scenic spot overlooking the Mangde Chhu valley.

Day 6: Jangbi to Tongtongphey

8.5–9.5KM / 3–4 HOURS / 640M ASCENT, 950M DESCENT

After breaking camp, descend steeply to the bridge crossing the Mangde Chhu, before one last push to Tongtongphey (1060m), where you will be met by your vehicle and driven back to Trongsa.

Merak–Sakteng Trek

Closed to foreigners from 1995 to 2010, this trek in the far-eastern corner of the country promises an unparalleled cultural and natural experience, for the moment at least.

The trek passes through the Sakteng Wildlife Sanctuary, an unspoilt and delicate ecosystem that's home to the endangered snow leopard and red panda, the Himalayan black bear, the Himalayan red fox and perhaps even the legendary *migoi* (yeti). The region is also home to the isolated Brokpa people, one of the Himalaya's most interesting ethnic groups.

As with so many trekking routes in Bhutan, roads are inching towards both Merak and Sakteng villages and will probably reach them within the lifetime of this book. Alter-

---

MERAK–SAKTENG TREK AT A GLANCE

Duration 5 days

Max Elevation 3480m

Difficulty Medium

Season Mid-March to May, September to November

Start Jaling

Finish Phongme

Access Town Trashigang

Summary A star attraction offering a sneak peek into one of the most secluded regions in Bhutan.

---

native paths will doubtless be found to avoid the bulk of the roads. Homestays are already available in both villages. April and May are the best months to visit for lovely spring blooms.

It's possible to start the trek from alternative locations at Jaling, Khardung and Phongme, depending on how far you want to drive on farm roads. The 4WD road currently reaches Damnongchu, so it is possible to skip day one of this itinerary if you want a shorter trek. See Map p137 for this route.

Day 1: Jaling to Damnongchu

7 HOURS

Starting out of Trashigang, drive to Rangjung and take the feeder road 3km past the village. The trailhead is at Jaling (or Chaling), a further hour's drive past the residence of Garab Rinpoche. You'll need an early start to make it over the 3675m Mindrula pass to the campsite at Damnongchu (3070m), criss-crossing feeder roads as you ascend. For a shorter day, stop at the Shatimi campsite.

Day 2: Damnongchu to Merak

5 HOURS

The trail leading out of Damnongchu involves a series of gentle ups and downs along a stream. About 45 minutes before Merak you pass the village and lhakhang at Gengu, which is said to house the mummified body of Buchang Gyalwa Zangpo, the son of Thangtong Gyelpo.

The final stretch is an easy and gradual ascent through yak meadows into the village

TREKS MERAK–SAKTENG TREK

of **Merak** (3480m), home to 140 families. Camp will be made just before the village, in a spot offering fantastic views of the mountains and the village. Alternatively, you can choose to stay at the village guesthouse or in a local homestay. The Samtenling Lhakhang boasts the saddle and phallus of local mountain deity Jomo Kuenkhar's horse.

Day 3: Merak to Miksa Teng
7–8 HOURS

Today's trek scales the 4140m Nagchung La pass for fine Himalayan views, after which the route descends steadily to a river. After following the river for an hour, it's another steep one-hour climb and then descent to **Miksa Teng** (2850m). A *teng* is a ledge or terrace. The campsite is surrounded by rhododendrons, which are in riotous bloom in April.

Day 4: Miksa Teng to Sakteng
4 HOURS

From Miksa Teng, you climb 300m to a small pass, then descend through beautiful woods to **Sakteng** (2985m). If you're lucky, you might see a red panda amid the greens along the way. There's a campsite on the outskirts of the village, but you can also sleep at the village guesthouse if you want. Some groups include a rest day in Sakteng, which is a good idea.

Day 5: Sakteng to Jyongkhar
6–7 HOURS

After a small pass, today's walk is mostly downhill, along a plain path, to the village of **Jyongkhar** (1850m), which is the current trailhead.

Understand Bhutan

Bhutan Today

Bhutan remains a unique and special country, but for better or worse, the country has opened its doors and hearts to the outside world and joined the global community. There is now at least one mobile phone for every two Bhutanese and there are more than 63,000 registered vehicles (though there are still no traffic lights). The challenge ahead for the government is to bring the benefits of globalisation and capitalism to Bhutan without undermining the very things that Bhutanese cherish about their unique culture.

Best in Print

The Raven Crown (Michael Aris) Definitive history of Bhutan's monarchy, lavishly illustrated with rare photographs.

The Hero with a Thousand Eyes (Karma Ura) Historical novel based on the life of Shingkhar Lam, a retainer who served in the court of the second, third and fourth kings of Bhutan.

The Circle of Karma (Kunzang Choden) Story of a young woman's journey across Bhutan to find her destiny, revealing the rich detail of everyday life and ritual.

Bhutan: The Land of Serenity (Matthieu Ricard) Superb coffee-table book that sensitively and strikingly reveals Bhutan at its most picturesque.

Married to Bhutan (Linda Leaming) Engaging account of finding love and much more in Bhutan.

Best on Film

Travellers & Magicians (Khyentse Norbu) Whimsical tale tackling the conflict of new and old, set along twisting mountain roads and in mysterious dark forests.

The Other Final (Johan Kramer) Nicely crafted record of what happens when the world's bottom football (soccer) team, Montserrat, meets second from bottom, Bhutan.

Democracy & Parliament

In 2005 Bhutan's much-loved king announced that he would abdicate in favour of the crown prince and he set about drawing up the country's first ever constitution to prepare for democratic elections in 2008. This peaceful ceding of power in favour of a parliamentary democracy stood in stark contrast to that other Himalayan former monarchy, Nepal.

In March 2008 the world's eyes were focused on this small mountain kingdom as its populace went to the polls. With royal encouragement the sparse population spread over a rugged country managed a remarkable 80% turnout. And the result was extraordinary and unpredicted – a landslide victory to one of the two contesting parties. The Druk Phuensum Tshogpa (DPT) party grabbed 45 of the 47 seats in the parliament's lower house, the National Assembly. The People's Democratic Party (PDP) won the other two seats. In 2013 it was time for the second election and, in a climate of economic uncertainty, the PDP was swept into power winning 32 seats to the DPT's 15.

Bhutan's parliament consists of the king (Druk Gyalpo), the National Council (upper house) and the aforementioned National Assembly. The National Council consists of 25 members, 20 of whom each represent one of the *dzongkhags* (political districts) and there are five additional members nominated by the king. Interestingly, candidates for the National Council must not be members of a political party.

For the first and second elections, the National Assembly had 47 seats across the 20 *dzongkhags*. The constitution allows for adjustments to be made to the National Assembly as the population increases (to a maximum of 55 seats), and as the distribution of voters across *dzongkhags* changes.

Modernisation & Gross National Happiness

Despite the rapid uptake of technology, democracy and global trends, Bhutan is very aware of the dangers of modernisation and the government continues to assume a protective role in Bhutanese society. Bhutan was the world's first country to ban not only smoking in public places but also the very sale of tobacco. Also banned are Western-style advertising billboards and plastic bags.

Issues of sustainable development, education and health care, and environmental and cultural preservation are therefore at the forefront of policy making; as are the tenets of Buddhism, which form the base of Bhutan's legal code. Every development project is scrutinised for its impact on the local population, religious faith and the environment. Bhutan's strict adherence to high-value, low-impact tourism is a perfect example of this. Bhutan is one of the few places on earth where compassion is favoured over capitalism and wellbeing is measured alongside productivity. This unique approach is summed up in the much-celebrated concept of Gross National Happiness.

Challenges

Bhutan is a tiny nation with abundant natural riches and a small, sustainable population surrounded by much larger countries with massive populations and economies. This situation has presented opportunities (the export of hydroelectricity to India provides around 50% of government revenue), but also threats in recent decades.

A rapidly growing economy has resulted in increased consumerism, leading to soaring imports, primarily from India. The flow of Indian rupees (to which the Bhutanese ngultrum is pegged) out of the country resulted in a cash crisis in 2012. The government responded by placing a ban on many imports, including cars, and restrictions on bank withdrawals. Although the complex situation is said to be exacerbated by the large Indian workforce sending their pay 'home', many Bhutanese say they have simply caught the global bug of overspending and overborrowing. For example, easing finance restrictions has led to land speculation, particularly in the capital. The irony of this happening in the country that introduced Gross National Happiness is not lost on the Bhutanese and is openly discussed.

POPULATION: **736,417**

LIFE EXPECTANCY: **69 YEARS**

GDP: **US$1055 PER CAPITA**

INFLATION: **8.45%**

if Bhutan were 100 people

50 would be Bhote
35 would be Nepali
15 would be tribal

belief systems
(% of population)

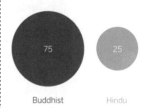

Buddhist   Hindu

population per sq km

BHUTAN   USA   INDIA

⚊ ≈ 20 people

History

Bhutan's early history is steeped in Buddhist folklore and mythology; it features tremendous deeds and beings with supernatural powers. It's said that a saint who had the ability to appear in eight different forms, one of them being Guru Rinpoche, visited Bhutan on a flying tiger and left the imprint of his body and his hat on rocks. School texts describe demons that threatened villages and destroyed temples until captured through magic and converted to Buddhism. Tales abound of ghosts who destroyed temples, and angels who rebuilt them.

The Centre for Bhutan Studies (www.bhutan studies.org.bt) is dedicated to promoting research and scholarship on Bhutan; it publishes many detailed historical research articles, among other subjects.

Lost in the Mists of Time

Researchers have attached dates to many events and protagonists in Bhutan's vibrant history, though these often do not seem to fit together into a credible and accurate chronology. When reading Bhutanese history, it's easier to let your imagination flow. Try visualising the spirit of the happenings rather than rationalising events as historical truth. This will, in part, help prepare you for a visit to Bhutan, where spirits, ghosts, *migoi* (yetis), medicine men, and lamas reincarnated in three different bodies are accepted as a part of daily life.

Bhutan's medieval and modern history is better documented than its ancient history, but is no less exotic. This is a time of warlords, feuds, giant fortresses and castles, with intrigue, treachery, fierce battles and extraordinary pageantry all playing feature roles. The country's recent history begins with a hereditary monarchy that was founded in the 20th century and continued the country's policy of isolationism. It was not until the leadership of the third king that Bhutan emerged from its medieval heritage of serfdom and seclusion.

Until the 1960s the country had no national currency, no telephones, no schools, no hospitals, no postal service and no tourists. Development efforts have now produced all these – plus airports, roads and a national system of health care. Despite the speed of modernisation, Bhutan has been famously cautious in opening its doors to tourism, TV and the internet in an effort to preserve its national identity and the environment. More recently the exceedingly popular fourth king ensured

TIMELINE	1500–2000 BC	6th century AD	7th century
	Present-day Bhutan is inhabited by nomadic herders who seasonally migrated between low-lying valleys and alpine pastures.	The animist Bon religion is established across the Himalayan region including several valleys of what is now Bhutan.	Buddhism becomes established in Bhutan with the first Buddhist temples built in AD 659, including Kyichu Lhakhang near Paro, and Jampey Lhakhang in Bumthang.

his special place in history and the beginning of a new era for Bhutan by forsaking absolute power, introducing democracy and abdicating in favour of his son.

Early History & the Arrival of Buddhism

Archaeological evidence suggests the low-lying valleys of present-day Bhutan were inhabited as early as 1500 to 2000 BC by nomadic herders who moved their grazing animals to high pastures in summer. Many Bhutanese still live this way today. The valleys of Bhutan provided relatively easy access across the Himalaya, and it is believed that the Manas Chhu valley, in particular, was used as a migration and trade route from India to Tibet.

Some of the early inhabitants of Bhutan were followers of Bon, the animistic tradition that was the main religion throughout the Himalayan region before the advent of Buddhism. It is believed that the Bon religion was introduced in Bhutan in the 6th century AD.

Buddhism was possibly first introduced to parts of Bhutan as early as the 2nd century AD, although most historians agree that the first Buddhist temples were built in the 7th century under the instruction of the Tibetan king Songtsen Gampo.

Many of the important events in the emerging country's early history involved saints and religious leaders and were therefore chronicled only in scriptures. Unfortunately, most of these original documents were destroyed in fires in the printing works of Sonagatsel in 1828 and in Punakha Dzong in 1832. Much of what was left in the old capital of Punakha was lost in an earthquake in 1897 and more records were lost when Paro Dzong burned in 1907. Therefore, much of the early history of Bhutan relies either on reports from British explorers, on legend and folklore, or the few manuscripts that escaped these disasters.

Guru Rinpoche

Guru Rinpoche (Precious Master) is one of the most important of Bhutan's historical and religious figures and his visit to Bumthang in AD 746 is recognised as the true introduction of Buddhism to Bhutan. He is a notable historical figure of the 8th century and his statue appears in almost all Bhutanese temples built after this first visit.

He is also regarded as the second Buddha possessing miraculous powers, including the ability to subdue demons and evil spirits, and his birth was predicted by Sakyamuni, the historical Buddha. His birthplace was Uddiyana in the Swat valley of what is now Pakistan. Uddiyana is known in Dzongkha (the national language of Bhutan) as Ugyen, and some texts refer to him as Ugyen Rinpoche. He is also known as Padmasambhava. *Padma* is Sanskrit for 'lotus flower' and is the origin of the Tibetan and Bhutanese name Pema; *sambhava* means 'born from'.

Artistic styles and traditional practices are greatly similar between Buddhists and Bonpo, followers of Bon. Noteworthy differences: Bonpo circumambulate their temples anticlockwise and vote in their lamas, whereas Buddhist lamas are reincarnated.

HISTORY EARLY HISTORY & THE ARRIVAL OF BUDDHISM

746

Guru Rinpoche (Padmasambhava) is invited by the king of Bumthang to visit his land and subdue evil spirits. He is credited with converting the king and others to Buddhism.

841

The Tibetan king Langdharma bans Buddhism in Tibet and banishes his brother prince Tsangma to eastern Bhutan.

DAN BANNISTER / GETTY IMAGES ©

➠ Buddhist monks in Bumthang (p117)

ORIGIN OF THE NAME BHUTAN

Few agree on the origin of the name Bhutan. It may have evolved from the Sanskrit Bhotant, meaning 'the end of Tibet', or from Bhu-uttan, meaning 'high land'. Early British explorers called it Bootan or Bhotan, and they believed the name derived from Bhotsthan, meaning 'Land of the Bhotias' (Bhotia is Sanskrit for people from Tibet).

Although now known as Bhutan to the outside world, the country has been known as Druk Yul, 'Land of the Thunder Dragon', to its inhabitants since the 13th century. The people call themselves the Drukpa.

He travelled in various manifestations throughout Tibet, Nepal and Bhutan, meditating in numerous caves, which are now regarded as important 'power places'. He preserved his teachings and wisdom by concealing them in the form of *terma* (hidden treasures) to be found by enlightened treasure discoverers called *tertons*. His consort and biographer, Yeshe Tshogyel, urges us not to regard Guru Rinpoche as a normal human being, because by doing so we will fail to perceive even a fraction of his enlightened qualities.

Bhutanese and Tibetans differ over a few aspects of his life; we refer here to the Bhutanese tradition.

Guru Rinpoche is credited with the founding of the Nyingma lineage – also known as the old 'Red Hat' sect – of Mahayana Buddhism, which became for a time the dominant religion of Bhutan. Its followers are known as Nyingmapa.

The Story of Kurjey Lhakhang

In 746 Guru Rinpoche made his first visit to Bhutan. At this time, the Indian Sendha Gyab had established himself as the king of Bumthang, with the title Sindhu Raja. He was feuding with Naochhe (Big Nose), a rival Indian king in the south of Bhutan, when Naochhe killed the Sindhu Raja's son and 16 of his attendants. The raja was so distraught that he desecrated the abode of the chief Bumthang deity, Shelging Kharpo, who then angrily took revenge by turning the skies black and stealing the king's life force, bringing him near to death.

One of the king's secretaries thus invited Guru Rinpoche to Bumthang to use his supernatural powers to save the Sindhu Raja. The Guru came to Bumthang and meditated, leaving a *jey* (imprint) of his *kur* (body) in the rock, now surrounded by Kurjey Lhakhang.

Guru Rinpoche was to be married to the king's daughter, Tashi Khuedon. He sent her to fetch water in a golden ewer. While she was away the Guru transformed into all eight of his manifestations and, together, they started to dance in the field by the temple. Every local deity appeared to watch this spectacle, except the stony-faced Shelging Kharpo who stayed hidden away in his rocky hideout.

9th century	10th century	12th century	1180
Many Tibetan Buddhists take up refuge in Bhutan as the Bonpo gain power and Buddhists are persecuted.	Further turmoil and the decline of Buddhism in Tibet sees various schools of Tibetan Buddhism established in Bhutan.	Gyalwa Lhanangpa, founder of the Lhapa Kagyu lineage, establishes Tango Goemba in the Thimphu valley and a system of forts based on Tibetan dzongs.	The founding of Druk Monastery in Ralung (Tibet) by Lama Tsangpa Gyarey Yeshe Dorji signals the beginning of Drukpa Kagyu lineage.

Guru Rinpoche was not to be set back by this rejection, and when the princess returned he changed her into five separate princesses, each clutching a golden ewer. The sunlight flashing off these ewers finally attracted Shelging Kharpo, but before he ventured out to see what was going on, he first transformed himself into a white snow lion. On seeing the creature appear the Guru changed into a *garuda,* flew up and grabbed the lion and told Shelging Kharpo in no uncertain terms to behave himself. He therefore recovered Sendha Gyab's life force, and for good measure converted both the rival kings to Buddhism, restoring the country to peace.

Shelging Kharpo agreed to become a protective deity of Buddhism; to seal the agreement the Guru planted his staff in the ground at the temple – its cypress-tree descendants continue to grow and tower over the Kurjey Lhakhang.

Further Visits by Guru Rinpoche

The Guru returned to Bhutan via Singye Dzong in Lhuentse and visited the districts of Bumthang and Mongar as well as Lhuentse. He was returning from Tibet where, at the invitation of the Tibetan king Trisong Detsen, he had introduced Nyingma Buddhism and overcome the demons that were obstructing the construction of Samye Monastery.

At Gom Kora, in eastern Bhutan, he left a body print and an impression of his head with a hat. He flew in the form of Dorji Drakpo (one of his eight manifestations) to Taktshang in Paro on a flaming tigress, giving the famous monastery Taktshang Goemba the name 'Tiger's Nest'.

Sampa Lhundrup Lhakhang, part of the Kurjey Lhakhang complex in Bumthang's Chokhor valley, houses an impressive 10m statue of Guru Rinpoche flanked by his eight manifestations.

PAINTINGS & STATUES OF GURU RINPOCHE

Most representations of Guru Rinpoche are in his manifestation as Padmasambhava, wearing royal robes and holding the insignia of spiritual realisation.

Often, a statue of Padmasambhava will be flanked by two statues of female devotees. These are the Indian princess Mandarava, the lady of wisdom, and the Tibetan *khandroma* (female celestial being) Yeshe Tshogyel, who is regarded as an incarnation of Saraswati, the goddess of knowledge. She was gifted with such a perfect memory that she was able to remember the Guru's every word and became his sole biographer. She is depicted as a white, heavenly being with traditional ornaments and flying scarves; Mandarava is usually depicted as an Indian hill princess.

Guru Rinpoche's celestial abode or paradise is a copper-coloured mountain named Zangto Pelri. The Guardians of the Four Directions guard the four gates, and in the centre is a three-roofed pagoda, with Guru Rinpoche enthroned on the ground level, flanked by his two consorts.

12th century	1184–1251	1433	1450–1521
Many Drukpa lamas leave Tibet for Bhutan because of persecution at the hands of the rival Gelugpa. Most settle in western Bhutan and establish Drukpa monastic orders.	Lifespan of Lama Phajo Drukgom Shigpo, who establishes Drukpa Kagyu as the dominant school of Buddhism in Bhutan, giving the region its distinctive form of Buddhism.	Thangtong Gyalpo, the Iron Bridge Lama, visits Bhutan from Tibet in search of iron ore and builds eight bridges.	The much-heralded life of Pema Lingpa, the most important *terton* (discoverer of sacred texts) in Bhutan.

HISTORY GURU RINPOCHE

BUDDHISM

It is believed that Guru Rinpoche also made a third visit to present-day Bhutan during the reign of Muthri Tsenpo (764–817), the son of Trisong Detsen and the 39th king of Tibet.

The Eight Manifestations of Guru Rinpoche

The Guru is depicted in eight forms (Guru Tshengay). These are not really different incarnations, but representations of his eight main initiations, in which he assumed a new personality that was symbolised by a new name and appearance. Because initiation is equivalent to entering a new life, it is a form of rebirth. Therefore the eight forms follow the chronology of Guru Rinpoche's life.

He emerged as an eight-year-old from a blue lotus on Lake Danakosha in Uddiyana, and was adopted by King Indrabodhi. Then he was called Tshokye Dorji (Diamond Thunderbolt Born from a Lake). He later renounced his kingdom and went to receive teachings and ordination from the master Prabhahasti in the cave of Maratrika (near the village of Harishe in eastern Nepal), becoming Sakya Senge (Lion of the Sakya Clan). In this form he is identified with Sakyamuni, the historical Buddha.

After studying the teachings of the Vajrayana and mastering the sciences of all Indian *pandits,* he obtained full realisation and was able to see all the gods and deities. Then he was called Loden Chogsey (Possessor of Supreme Knowledge). He took as his consort Mandarava, the daughter of the king of Zahor (in the Mandi district of Himachal Pradesh, India). This enraged the king, who condemned them both to be burned, but through his powers the Guru turned the pyre into a lake and converted the kingdom to Buddhism. Then he was called Padmasambhava.

He returned to Uddiyana to convert it to Buddhism, but was recognised as the prince who had renounced his kingdom and was condemned to be burned along with his consort. Again he was not consumed by the fire and appeared sitting upon a lotus in a lake. This lake is Rewalsar – also called Tsho Pema (Lotus Lake) – in Himachal Pradesh, and is an important pilgrimage spot. His father, King Indrabodhi, offered him the kingdom and he became Pema Gyalpo (Lotus King), remaining for 13 years and establishing Buddhism.

When he was preaching in the eight cremation grounds to the *khandromas* (female celestial beings), he caught the life force of the evil deities and he turned them into protectors of Buddhism. Then he was called Nyima Yeozer (Sunbeam of Enlightenment). Later, 500 heretic masters tried to destroy the doctrine of Buddha, but he vanquished them through the power of his words and brought down a thunderbolt destroying the non-Buddhists in a flash of hail and lightning. He was then called Sengye Dradrok (Roaring Lion).

The three main lineages spreading Buddhist teachings in Bhutan were the Nyingmapa, the Kagyupa and the Sakyapa. A fourth school, the Gelugpa, emerged in Tibet in the 15th century. This lineage was viewed by the Bhutanese from the 17th century onwards as hostile to Bhutan.

1455–1529	1616	1621	1627
Lifespan of Lama Drukpa Kunley, the Divine Madman, who travelled throughout Bhutan preaching an unconventional approach to Buddhism and life.	The first Zhabdrung, Ngawang Namgyal, arrives in Bhutan from Ralung, Tibet, marking the ascendancy of the Druk Kagyu lineage.	First monk body established at Cheri Goemba, which was built by Zhabdrung Ngawang Namgyal a year earlier.	Portuguese Jesuits, Fathers Cacella and Cabral, are the first European visitors to Bhutan.

When he came to Bhutan the second time and visited Singye Dzong in Kurtoe and Taktshang in Paro, he was in the form of Dorji Drakpo (Fierce Thunderbolt). He subdued all the evil spirits hindering Buddhism and blessed them as guardians of the doctrine. In this form, Guru Rinpoche rides a tigress.

Medieval Period

The grandson of Trisong Detsen, Langdharma, ruled Tibet from AD 836 to 842. As a follower of Bon, he banned Buddhism, destroyed religious institutions and banished his brother, Prince Tsangma, to Bhutan. It is believed that many monks fled from Tibet and took refuge in Bhutan during this period. Despite the assassination of Langdharma and the re-introduction of Buddhism, Tibet remained in political turmoil and many Tibetans migrated to western Bhutan.

Between the 9th and 17th centuries numerous ruling clans and noble families emerged in different valleys throughout Bhutan. The various local chieftains spent their energy quarrelling among themselves and with Tibet, and no important nationally recognised political figure emerged during this period.

The Divine Madman by Keith Dowman is a wonderful translation of the poems and works of the extraordinary Lama Drukpa Kunley.

Establishing the Bhutanese Form of Buddhism

Back in Tibet, Lama Tsangpa Gyarey Yeshe Dorji (1161–1211) founded a monastery in the town of Ralung, just east of Gyantse, in 1180. He named the monastery Druk (Dragon), after the thunder dragons that he heard in the sky as he searched for an appropriate site upon which to build a monastery. The lineage followed here was named after the monastery and became known as Drukpa Kagyu.

In the 11th and 12th centuries there was a further large influx of Tibetans into Bhutan. Many Drukpa lamas left Tibet because of persecution at the hands of the followers of rival Buddhist lineages. Most of these lamas settled in western Bhutan and established branches of Drukpa monastic orders. Western Bhutan became loosely united through the weight of their teachings. Charismatic lamas emerged as de facto leaders of large portions of the west, while the isolated valleys of eastern and central Bhutan remained separate feudal states.

One of the most important of these lamas was Gyalwa Lhanangpa, who founded the Lhapa Kagyu lineage. He established the Tango Goemba on a hill above the northern end of the Thimphu valley and built a system of forts in Bhutan similar to the dzongs found in Tibet.

Lama Phajo Drukgom Shigpo (1184–1251), a disciple of Lama Tsangpa Gyarey, came to Bhutan from Ralung and defeated Lama Lhanangpa. He and his companions developed the small Dho-Ngen Dzong on the west bank of the Wang Chhu and took control of the Tango Goemba. Lama

1629	1637		1639
A coalition of five Bhutanese lamas representing opposing lineages attacks Simtokha Dzong, the first dzong in the country, and challenges the Zhabdrung.	Punakha Dzong is constructed as the second dzong in country. The town remains capital of Bhutan until the mid-1950s.		Tibet finally recognises Zhabdrung Ngawang Namgyal as the supreme authority in Bhutan.

DIANA MAYFIELD / GETTY IMAGES ©

➜ Punakha Dzong (p96)

Phajo is credited with forging the Bhutanese form of Buddhism by converting many people to the Drukpa Kagyu lineage. Other lamas resented his presence and success, and they tried to kill him through the casting of magic spells. Phajo, though, turned the spells back on these lamas, destroying several of their monasteries.

Between the 13th and 16th centuries, the Drukpa Kagyu lineage flourished and Bhutan adopted a separate religious identity. Several important Druk Kagyu teachers from Ralung were invited to preach and set up monasteries in western Bhutan. Among the visitors to Bhutan during this period was Lama Ngawang Chhogyel (1465–1540). He made several trips and was often accompanied by his sons, who constructed several monasteries. They are credited with building the temple of Druk Choeding in Paro and Pangri Zampa and Hongtsho goemba near Thimphu.

Perhaps the most famous Druk Kagyu teacher was the colourful and unconventional Drukpa Kunley (1455–1529). He is remembered today with immense affection and faith by the Bhutanese and is closely associated with the beautiful temple of Chimi Lhakhang between Lobesa and Punakha.

Hidden Treasures & Pema Lingpa

Between the 11th and 16th centuries numerous *terma* hidden by Guru Rinpoche in caves, rocks and lakes were discovered, as he had prophesied, by tantric lamas called *tertons*.

Pema Lingpa (1450–1521) was one of the five great *tertons* of Nyingma Buddhism, and the most important *terton* in Bhutan. The texts and artefacts he found, the dances he composed and the art he produced have significantly shaped Bhutan's cultural heritage. He is also considered to be a reincarnation of Guru Rinpoche.

He was born in the hamlet of Drangchel in Bumthang's Tang valley, near Kunzangdrak Goemba. As a boy he learned the craft of blacksmithing from his grandfather; indeed, two of the chainmails he forged are still on display at Tamshing and Thangbi Goembas.

At age 25 he discovered his first *terma* after he dreamed a monk handed him a scroll in *dakini* script that gave instructions on how to find a treasure chest deep in a pool in the Tang valley. Pema eventually managed to translate the scroll but this was a huge project, because in *dakini* script each word stands for 1000 human words. Later, assisted by the *khandromas (dakinis)*, he used the text as a basis for teachings. His residence at the time was in Kunzangling, which is on a cliff above the Tang valley and is now the site of the Kunzangdrak Goemba.

In his visions, Pema Lingpa often visited Zangto Pelri, Guru Rinpoche's celestial paradise, where he observed the dances (*pa-cham*) of the *khandromas* and *yidam* (tutelary deities). He taught three of these dances to his disciples, and several are still performed as part of Bhutan's tsechus.

1668	1705	1730	1768
Mingyur Tenpa is enthroned as the third *desi* (secular ruler). He rules for 12 years, during which time he extends the boundaries of Bhutan westwards to Kalimpong, now part of India.	The much-delayed announcement of the demise of the Zhabdrung Ngawang Namgyal.	Druk Desi Mipham Wangpo assists Gya Chila, the ruler of Cooch Behar, to defeat invaders and to settle a family feud; Bhutan is then allowed to station a force in that southern kingdom.	The *desi* tries to suppress the influence of the religious establishment in Bhutan. To do so he establishes alliances with the Panchen Lama in Tibet and with King Prithvi Narayan Shah of Nepal.

During Pema Lingpa's life he found a total of 34 statues, scrolls and sacred relics in Bhutan and as far away as Samye in Tibet. Many of the statues and relics he discovered are preserved in lhakhangs throughout Bhutan, including Bumthang's Tamshing and Kunzangdrak Goembas, which he founded.

After his death he was reincarnated in three forms, consisting of *ku* (body), *sung* (speech) and *thug* (mind) and these lineages continue to this day.

Through his six sons, one daughter and numerous reincarnations, Pema Lingpa's legacy still influences much of Bhutan. One of his grandsons, Gyalse Pema Thinley, who was also a reincarnation of Pema Lingpa, founded Gangte Goemba in the Phobjikha valley, and the Gangte Trulku lineage continues there, with Kuenzang Pema Namgyal, born in 1955, as the ninth 'mind' reincarnation. The royal family of Bhutan, the Wangchuck dynasty, is also descended from this line.

The Rise of the Zhabdrung

By the 16th century the political arena was still fragmented between many local chiefs, each controlling their own territory and engaging in petty feuds with the others. There were numerous monasteries competing for superiority and the lamas of western Bhutan were working to extend their influence to the east of the country.

Everything changed in 1616 when Ngawang Namgyal (1594–1651) came to Bhutan from Ralung, the original home of the Drukpa Kagyu in Tibet. He was a descendent of Tsangpa Gyarey, the founder of Ralung Monastery. At age 12 he was recognised as the reincarnation of Pema Karpo, the prince-abbot of Ralung. This recognition was challenged by the ruler of another principality in Tibet, and Ngawang Namgyal found his position at Ralung very difficult. When he was 23, the protective deity Yeshe Goenpo (Mahakala) appeared to him in the form of a raven and directed him south to Bhutan. He travelled through Laya and Gasa and spent time at Pangri Zampa (Thimphu), which was established by his great-great-grandfather, Ngawang Chhogyel.

As Ngawang Namgyal travelled throughout western Bhutan teaching, his political strength increased. Soon he established himself as the religious ruler of Bhutan with the title Zhabdrung Rinpoche (Precious Jewel at Whose Feet One Prostrates), and so becoming the first in the line of Zhabdrungs. He built the first of the current system of dzongs at Simtokha, just south of present-day Thimphu. While the primary function of earlier Bhutanese dzongs was to serve as invincible fortresses, the Simtokha Dzong also housed a monastic body and administrative facilities, as well as fulfilling its defensive function. This combination of civil, religious and defensive functions became the model for all of Bhutan's subsequent dzongs.

The arrival in 1616 of the Zhabdrung Ngawang Namgyal marks the transformation of Bhutan and the ascendancy of the Druk Kagyu lineage.

During his reign, Zhabdrung Ngawang Namgyal ordered the construction of many monasteries and dzongs throughout Bhutan. Of these, the dzongs at Simtokha, Paro, Punakha and Trongsa are still standing.

1772	1774	1776 & 1777	1783
Bhutan invades Cooch Behar and kidnaps its king. The British East India Company agrees to assist Cooch Behar in return for payment.	George Bogle leads a trade mission to Bhutan and Tibet, and plants potatoes in Bhutanese soil.	Dr Alexander Hamilton travels to Punakha and Thimphu to negotiate land disputes between Britain and Bhutan.	Captain Samuel Turner leads a grand British Raj expedition to Bhutan and Tibet.

FATHERS CACELLA & CABRAL MEET THE ZHABDRUNG

The first Western visitors to Bhutan were two Portuguese Jesuit priests. In early 1627 Fathers Cacella and Cabral travelled from Calcutta to Bhutan en route to Shigatse in Tibet. They stayed for a few months in Cheri Goemba, north of Thimphu, with the Zhabdrung.

There is no complete account of their journey, but one of their letters provides an insight into Ngawang Namgyal's character: 'He received us with a demonstration of great benevolence, signifying this in the joy which he showed on seeing us and on knowing where we had come from, where we were from, that is from what country or nation, and he asked the other questions normal at a first meeting.'

The Zhabdrung's rule was opposed by the leaders of rival Buddhist lineages within Bhutan. They formed a coalition of five lamas under the leadership of Lama Palden and attacked Simtokha Dzong in 1629. This attack was repelled, but the coalition then aligned itself with a group of Tibetans and continued its opposition. The Zhabdrung's militia thwarted the Tibetans in battle on several occasions, and the influence of the rival lineages diminished. Finally, after forging an alliance with the brother of King Singye Namgyal of Ladakh, the Zhabdrung's forces defeated the Tibetans and their coalition ally. In 1639 an agreement was reached with the Tsang Desi in Tibet recognising Zhabdrung Ngawang Namgyal as the supreme authority throughout Bhutan.

A Political and Religious History of Bhutan by CT Dorji chronicles the major personalities in the religious and political spheres of Bhutan's history.

The Zhabdrung further enhanced his power by establishing relations with neighbouring kings, including Rama Shah, the king of Nepal, and Raja Padmanarayan of Cooch Behar (India). It was at this time that the king of Ladakh granted the Zhabdrung a number of sites in western Tibet for the purpose of meditation and worship. These included Diraphuk, Nyanri and Zuthulphuk on the slopes of the holy Mt Kailash.

The Bhutanese administration of these monasteries continued until the Chinese takeover of Tibet in 1959. Other Tibetan monasteries that came under Bhutanese administration were Rimpung, Doba, Khochag and De Dzong, all near Gartok. A Bhutanese lama was sent as representative to Nepal, and Bhutanese monasteries were established at Bodhnath (Chorten Jaro Khasho) and Swayambhunath in Kathmandu. Bhutan administered Swayambhunath until after the Nepal-Tibet war of 1854–56, when it was retaken by Nepal on the suspicion that Bhutan had helped the Tibetans.

The Zhabdrung established the first *sangha* (community of monks) at Cheri Goemba near Thimphu. When Punakha Dzong was completed in 1635, the *sangha* was moved there and became the *dratshang* (central monk body), headed by a supreme abbot called the Je Khenpo.

1826	1828	1832	1862
Bhutan and Britain start bickering over the sovereignty of the *duars* (southern Bhutanese hills).	Many original historical documents are destroyed in fires in the printing works of Sonagatsel.	Further losses of historical documents occur in the devastating fire in the library of Punakha Dzong.	Birth of Ugyen Wangchuck, the son of 'the Black Regent' Jigme Namgyal, the battle-hardened Trongsa *penlop*.

Invasions from Tibet

In the meantime, strife continued in Tibet, between the Nyingmapa (known as 'Red Hat') group of Buddhists and the Gelugpa ('Yellow Hat'); the latter are headed by the Dalai Lama. The Mongol chief Gushri Khan, a patron of the Dalai Lama, led his army in an attack on Tibet's Tsang province, where he overthrew the Rinpong dynasty and established the supremacy of the Gelug lineage in the region.

In 1644 the Mongols and Tibetans, who were used to the extremely high plains of Tibet, launched an assault from Lhobrak into Bumthang, but found themselves overpowered by the forests and heat of Bhutan. Zhabdrung Ngawang Namgyal personally led the successful resistance and several Tibetan officers and a large number of horses were captured. Drukgyel Dzong was built at the head of Paro valley in 1647 to commemorate the victory and to prevent any further Tibetan infiltration.

One of the strongest of Tibet's Dalai Lamas was the 'Great Fifth'. During his administration, he became jealous of the growing influence of the rival Drukpa on his southern border and mounted further invasions into Bhutan in 1648 and 1649. Each attempt was launched via Phari in Tibet, from where the Great Fifth's forces crossed the 5000m-high Tremo La into Paro valley. They were repelled, and again the Bhutanese captured large amounts of armour, weapons and other spoils. Some of this booty may still be seen in the National Museum in Paro.

Ngawang Namgyal's success in repelling the Tibetan attacks further consolidated his position as ruler. The large militia that he raised for the purpose also gave him effective control of the country. Mingyur Tenpa, who was appointed by the Zhabdrung as *penlop* (governor) of Trongsa, undertook a campaign to unite all the valleys of the central and eastern parts of the country under the Zhabdrung's rule, which he accomplished by about 1655. At this time the great dzongs of Jakar, Lhuentse, Trashi Yangtse, Shongar (now Mongar), Trashigang and Zhemgang were constructed.

A Bhutanese Identity Emerges

The Zhabdrung realised that Bhutan needed to differentiate itself from Tibet in order to preserve its religion and cultural identity. He devised many of Bhutan's customs, traditions and ceremonies in a deliberate effort to develop a unique cultural identity for the country.

As a revered Buddhist scholar, he had both the astuteness and authority to codify the Kagyu religious teachings into a system that was distinctively Bhutanese. He also defined the national dress and instituted the tsechu celebrations.

Much of the armour and many weapons that were taken during the 1644 battle with the Mongols and Tibetans are on display in Punakha Dzong.

1864	1865	1865	1870
The ill-fated Ashley Eden expedition gets a humiliating reception in Punakha and sours relations between Bhutan and Britain.	Bhutan and Britain go to war over the *duars*; it is finally resolved with the Treaty of Sinchula, which sees Bhutan's territory greatly reduced.	After the *duar* war, the saying goes that Bhutan's border is where a rock rolled down the hill finally stops.	The Penlop of Trongsa, Jigme Namgyal, is enthroned as the 51st *desi*, consolidating his growing power and influence.

The Zhabdrung created a code of laws that defined the relationship between the lay people and the monastic community. A system of taxes was developed; these were paid in kind in the form of wheat, buckwheat, rice, yak meat, butter, paper, timber and clothing. The people were subject to a system of compulsory labour for the construction of trails, dzongs, temples and bridges. These practices lasted almost unchanged until the third king eliminated them in 1956.

In the 1640s the Zhabdrung created the system of Choesi, the separation of the administration of the country into two offices. The religious and spiritual aspects of the country were handled by the Zhabdrung. The political, administrative and foreign-affairs aspects of the government were to be handled by the *desi* (secular ruler), who was elected to the post. The office of the Zhabdrung theoretically had the greater power. Under the system at that time, the Zhabdrung was the spiritual ruler and the Je Khenpo was the Chief Abbot and official head of the monastic establishment. The Je Khenpo had a status equal to the *desi* and sometimes held that office.

The first *desi* was Tenzin Drugyey (1591–1656), one of the monks who came with Ngawang Namgyal from Ralung Monastery. He established a system of administration throughout the country, formalising the position of *penlop* as that of provincial governor. There were initially three districts: Trongsa in the centre, Paro in the west and Dagana in the south. The *penlops* became the representatives of the central government, which was then in Punakha. There were three officers called *dzongpens* (lords of the dzong) who looked after the affairs of the sub-districts of Punakha, Thimphu and Wangdue Phodrang.

Zhabdrung Ngawang Namgyal went into retreat in Punakha Dzong in 1651. He didn't emerge again, and although it is likely that he passed away very early in the period of retreat, his death remained concealed until 1705. It is believed that the four successive *desis* who ruled during this period felt that the continued presence of the Zhabdrung was necessary to keep the country unified and Tibet at bay. Nonetheless, Tibet mounted seven attacks on Bhutan between 1656 and 1730.

Several records of the early European exploration and missions to Bhutan have been reprinted by Indian publishers and are readily available in bookshops in Thimphu, Delhi and Kathmandu.

Civil Wars

When the Je Khenpo finally announced the death of the Zhabdrung in 1705, he said that three rays of light emanated from the Zhabdrung's body, representing the *ku sung thug* of Ngawang Namgyal. This indicated that the Zhabdrung would be reincarnated in these three forms, though only the reincarnation of the Zhabdrung's mind was considered to be the head of state. Because the position of *zhabdrung* was a continuing one, it was necessary for the mind incarnation to be reborn after the death of the previous incarnation.

1878
At just 16 years of age Ugyen Wangchuck, the son of Jigme Namgyal, is briefly taken hostage in Paro's Ta Dzong while accompanying his father's campaign to recapture Paro Dzong.

1885
After decades of civil unrest and the Battle of Changlimithang, Ugyen Wangchuck emerges as the most powerful figure in the country.

STEVE GEER / GETTY IMAGES ©

➜ Paro Dzong (p77)

This structure resulted in long periods when the *zhabdrung* was too young to rule and the *desi* often became the de facto ruler. Because the *desi* was an elected position, there was considerable rivalry among various factions for the office. These factions also took advantage of uncertainty over which of the three incarnations of the Zhabdrung was the 'true' incarnation. None of the successive incarnations had the personal charisma or political astuteness of Ngawang Namgyal.

The next 200 years were a time of civil war, internal conflicts and political infighting. While there were only six mind incarnations of the Zhabdrung during this period, there were 55 *desis*. The longest-serving *desi* was the 13th incumbent, Sherab Wangchuk, who ruled for 20 years; and the most important was the fourth, Gyalse Tenzin Rabgye, who ruled from 1680 to 1694. Few of the rulers finished their term; 22 *desis* were assassinated or deposed by rivals.

The political situation became so unstable that some of the rival factions appealed to the Tibetans for assistance. In 1729 and 1730 Tibet took advantage of Bhutan's instability and invaded the country three times. The lamas in Tibet initiated a truce that eventually ended the hostilities. The rival Bhutanese factions submitted their case to the Chinese emperor in Beijing for mediation. But the issue was only finally resolved when several of the Bhutanese protagonists died, leaving the currently recognised mind incarnation of the Zhabdrung as the ruler. At the same time, formal diplomatic relations were established between Bhutan and Tibet, which the late historian Michael Aris said 'helped to guarantee the fact of Bhutanese independence'.

Involvement of the British

In his book, *Lands of the Thunderbolt,* the Earl of Ronaldshay wrote: '...it was not until 1772 that the East India Company became conscious of the existence, across its northern frontier, of a meddlesome neighbour.' The first contact the British had with Bhutan was when the claimants to the throne of neighbouring Cooch Behar (in present-day West Bengal) appealed to the East India Company to help drive the Bhutanese out of their kingdom.

Because the East India Company was a strictly commercial enterprise, its officers agreed to help when the deposed ruler of Cooch Behar offered to pay half of the revenues of the state in return for assistance. In December 1772 the British governor of Bengal, Warren Hastings, sent Indian troops and guns to Cooch Behar and, despite suffering heavy losses, routed the Bhutanese and restored the king to the throne. However, Cooch Behar paid a very high price for this assistance. Not only did its rulers pay Rs50,000, but in 1773 they also signed a treaty ceding substantial powers and future revenue to the East India Company.

Bhutan and the British by Peter Collister is a comprehensive account of the interaction between Britain and Bhutan from 1771 to 1987.

1897	1904	1906	1907
On 12 June the great Assam earthquake destroys the dzongs and many original documents in Punakha and Lingzhi, and severely damages many other buildings.	Ugyen Wangchuck assists Francis Younghusband in his invasion of Tibet and assists with the negotiations for a treaty between Britain and Tibet.	Sir Ugyen Wangchuck is invited to Calcutta to attend the reception for the Prince of Wales.	Ugyen Wangchuck is unanimously elected as the hereditary ruler of Bhutan, the Druk Gyalpo (Dragon King), in Punakha.

The British pushed the Bhutanese back into the hills and followed them into Bhutan. The British won another major battle in January 1773 at the garrison of Chichacotta (now Khithokha) in the hills east of what is now Phuentsholing. A second battle was fought near Kalimpong in April 1773. The Bhutanese troops were led by the 16th *desi* but, after the second defeat, he was deposed by a coup d'état.

First Treaty with the British

The new *desi* wanted to make an agreement with the British and appealed to the Panchen Lama in Tibet for assistance. The Panchen Lama then wrote what the British described as 'a very friendly and intelligent letter' that was carried to Calcutta (now called Kolkata) by an Indian pilgrim. The British, although more eager to establish relations with Tibet than to solve the issue of Bhutan, agreed to comply with the Tibetan request. The result was a peace treaty between Bhutan and the British signed in Calcutta on 25 April 1774. In this treaty the *desi* agreed to respect the territory of the East India Company and to allow the company to cut timber in the forests of Bhutan. The British returned all the territory they had captured.

The British in India attached their own names, derived from Sanskrit, to the titles used by the Bhutanese. They called the Zhabdrung the '*dharma raja*', and the desi '*deb raja*'.

Exploration by Western Travellers

Some of the most interesting stories of Bhutan, and much of Bhutan's recorded history, came from the descriptions provided by early European explorers. These records provide an insight into what they observed and also reveal the extraordinary attitudes of some of the envoys Britain sent to negotiate with Bhutan.

George Bogle

The first British expedition arrived in Bhutan in 1774, just after the first British treaties with Bhutan and Tibet were signed. The Court of Directors of the East India Company sent a mission to Tibet via Bhutan to find out about goods, 'especially such as are of great value and easy transportation'. The expedition team, led by George Bogle, planted potatoes wherever they went, providing a new food crop for Bhutan and a lasting legacy of this mission. They spent five months in Thimphu and then travelled on to Tibet. The written account of this mission provides the first Western view into the isolated kingdom of Bhutan. Bogle found the Bhutanese 'good-humoured, downright, and so far as I can judge, thoroughly trustworthy'. He did, however, note that the practice of celibacy by many monks led to 'many irregularities' and the cold resulted in 'an excessive use of spirituous liquors'.

Although the *duars* were excellent for growing tea, they were also a malarial jungle, and the British had a very difficult time keeping their troops healthy.

1907	1910	1926	1927
Numerous collections of historical documents and treasures are lost when Paro valley's Rinpung Dzong is engulfed in a devastating fire.	The Treaty of Punakha is signed, guaranteeing Bhutan's sovereignty and giving Britain a hand in its external relations.	His Majesty Ugyen Wangchuck dies and is succeeded by his son Jigme Wangchuck, the second Druk Gyalpo.	British officer Lt Col FM Bailey attends the official coronation of the second king of Bhutan, Jigme Wangchuck.

Alexander Hamilton & Samuel Turner

In the next few years two small expeditions travelled to Bhutan. Dr Alexander Hamilton led a group to Punakha and Thimphu in 1776, and another in 1777, to discuss Bhutanese claims to Ambari Falakati (a town northwest of Cooch Behar) and to consolidate transit rights through Bhutan to Tibet that had been negotiated by Bogle's mission.

The next major venture into Bhutan was in 1783, when Samuel Turner led a grand expedition with all the accoutrements of the British Raj. They travelled through the *duars* (southern Bhutanese hills) in palanquins (sedan chairs) and followed Bogle's route to Thimphu. They also visited Punakha and Wangdue Phodrang before crossing to Tibet. Among the members of the 1783 expedition was Samuel Davis, who was a draftsman and surveyor. His journal and outstanding paintings provide one of the earliest views of Bhutan. Much of Davis' material is presented in *Views of Mediaeval Bhutan* by Michael Aris.

The Humiliation of Ashley Eden

Minor British expeditions to Bhutan were made in 1810, 1812, 1815 and 1837, for the most part in order to settle border disputes and conflict over the *duars*. The Ashley Eden expedition attempted to settle these issues.

The British had managed to extend their influence into Sikkim, making it a British protectorate, and subsequently decided to send a mission to Bhutan to establish a resident British representative and encourage better communication. Among the members of Eden's expedition was Captain HH Godwin-Austin of the Indian topographical Survey. Godwin-Austin had explored (present-day) Pakistan's Baltoro Glacier in 1861 and on some maps K2, the second-highest peak in the world, is named after him.

Despite reports of political chaos in Bhutan, Ashley Eden, the secretary of the government of Bengal, set out from Darjeeling in November 1864 to meet the *desi* (or '*deb raja*'). Ignoring numerous messages from the Bhutanese that the British mission was not welcome, Eden pushed on past Kalimpong, through Daling, Haa and Paro, reaching Punakha on 15 March.

It's not clear whether it was more by accident or by design, but Eden's party was jeered, pelted with rocks, made to wait long hours in the sun and subjected to other humiliations. Both Bhutanese and British pride suffered badly. As Eden describes it in *Political Missions to Bootan:* 'The Penlow [*penlop*] took up a large piece of wet dough and began rubbing my face with it; he pulled my hair, and slapped me on the back, and generally conducted himself with great insolence.'

Eden exacerbated the situation by sending the Lhengyal Shungtshog (Council of Ministers) a copy of a draft treaty with terms that he had been instructed to negotiate. His actions implied that this was the

Political Missions to Bootan by Ashley Eden is a pompous Victorian account of the history of Bhutan. After reading a few pages, you'll have some idea as to why Eden was treated so badly when he arrived in Punakha.

1928	1931	1949	1952
The future third king, Jigme Dorji Wangchuck, is born at Thruepang Palace in Trongsa on 2 May.	Lt Col JLR Weir travels to Bumthang to present King Jigme Wangchuck with the insignia of Knight Commander of the Indian Empire.	Bhutan signs a treaty with newly independent India in Darjeeling and gains a small concession of land bordering the region known as the *duars*.	King Jigme Wangchuck dies and is succeeded to the throne by his 24-year-old son Jigmi Dorje Wangchuck.

final version of the treaty that the Bhutanese were to sign without any discussion. The Bhutanese took immediate exception to Eden's high-handedness and soon presented him with an alternative treaty that returned all the *duars* to Bhutan. One clause in the treaty stated: 'We have written about that the settlement is permanent; but who knows, perhaps this settlement is made with one word in the mouth and two in the heart. If, therefore, this settlement is false, the Dharma Raja's demons will, after deciding who is true or false, take his life, and take out his liver and scatter it to the winds like ashes.'

Reading this, it's little wonder that Eden feared for the safety of his party. He signed the treaty, but under his signature added the English words 'under compulsion', which, naturally, the Bhutanese could not read.

Eden's party crossed the Cheli La from Haa into the Paro valley in February and had an extremely difficult time in the deep snow. Some years later, John Claude White suggested that Eden might have been given incorrect directions, perhaps on purpose. It is astounding that, even having admitted failure, Eden still viewed his as a 'friendly mission'. His report certainly was a major factor in British annexation of the *duars*. He advocated a punitive policy to teach the Bhutanese that they would not be allowed to 'treat our power with contempt'. He later went on to build the toy train in Darjeeling.

Lands of the Thunderbolt, Sikhim, Chumbi & Bhutan by the Earl of Ronald-shay is a very readable, very British account of regional history and an expedition to Bhutan in the early 20th century.

John Claude White

There were no formal expeditions to Bhutan for more than 40 years after Eden's, but the Survey of India sent several agents disguised as lamas and pilgrims to explore Bhutan and Tibet in 1883 and 1886.

By 1905 the Bhutanese and British were friends due to the assistance that the *penlop* of Trongsa, Ugyen Wangchuck, had provided the 1904 Younghusband expedition to Lhasa. John Claude White, a British political officer, came to present the insignia of Knight Commander of the Indian Empire to the *penlop*. White had been a member of the 1904 expedition and was an old friend of Ugyen Wangchuck.

White and his large party travelled from Gangtok, in Sikkim, into Haa and Paro, en route to the investiture ceremony in Punakha. Later, White and his party were guests of Ugyen Wangchuck at his new palace of Wangdichholing in Bumthang. The expedition later returned with the first photographs of dzongs and the court of Bhutan.

In 1906 White made a reconnaissance through eastern Bhutan to southern Tibet. He made a third trip in 1907 when he was invited as the British representative to the coronation of Ugyen Wangchuck as the first king of Bhutan. A summary of White's account appeared in the April 1914 issue of the *National Geographic,* and made Bhutan known to the world for the first time.

1953	1956	1958	1959
The 130-member National Assembly (Tshogdu), the country's first legislature, is established by the king to promote democratic governance.	The age-old system of serfdom is abolished by King Jigme Dorji Wangchuck, who also decrees that all derogatory terms associated with serfs be abolished.	The Indian prime minister, Jawaharlal Nehru, and his daughter, Indira Gandhi, visit Bhutan to symbolise improving communications with India.	Bhutan loses administrative control of several monasteries on the slopes of Mt Kailash and near Gatok after the Chinese annexation of Tibet.

Other British Political Officers

Between 1909 and 1947 the British government dealt with Bhutan in the same way as it did with other Indian princely states, but it never specifically defined its relationship with Bhutan. Starting with CA Bell in 1909, several British political officers visited Bhutan and presented the king with decorations. In 1921 the Earl of Ronaldshay, who was described as a 'closet Buddhist', travelled to Bhutan as a guest of the first king. He travelled from Gangtok to Paro, where he was met with great fanfare. The party visited Taktshang Goemba and witnessed the Paro tsechu, but never met the king, who was in Punakha, ill with influenza.

The Duar Wars & the Rise of Ugyen Wangchuck

The area of plains between the Brahmaputra River up to and including the lowest of the hills of Bhutan was known as the *duars* (literally, 'doors or gates'). The western part of this area, known as the Bengal Duars, had been annexed by the third *desi,* Mingyur Tenpa, in the late 17th century and the Bhutanese considered it their territory. The eastern part, the Assam Duars, had long been administered in a complex rental agreement between Bhutan and Assam.

After the Burmese war (1825–26), the British took over the peculiar land rental arrangement for the Assam Duars, along with what were described as 'very unsatisfactory relations of the Assamese with the Bhutanese'. Disagreements over payments and administration between Britain and Bhutan escalated into military skirmishes. Other than the area's strategic importance, the British were attracted to the *duars* because they were excellent tea-growing country.

The British annexed the two easternmost *duars* in 1840 and the rest of the Assam Duars in September 1841, agreeing to pay Bhutan an annual compensation of Rs10,000. Lord Auckland wrote to the *deb* and *dharma rajas* that the British were '...compelled by an imperative sense of duty to occupy the whole of the duars without any reference to your Highnesses' wishes, as I feel assured that it is the only course which is likely to hold out a prospect of restoring peace and prosperity to that tract of country.'

Perhaps more revealing is a letter from Colonel Jenkins, the agent of the governor-general, outlining the need for taking over the Assam Duars. He wrote: 'Had we possession of the Dooars, the Bhootan Government would necessarily in a short time become entirely dependent upon us, as holding in our hands the source of all their subsistence.'

In 1931 Lt Col JLR Weir travelled to Bumthang to denominate the king Knight Commander of the Indian Empire – the basis for the book and TV documentary *Joanna Lumley in the Kingdom of the Thunder Dragon.*

Sikhim and Bhutan, Twenty-one Years on the North-east Frontier by J Claude White describes the 1905 expedition to present the first king, Ugyen Wangchuck, with the insignia of Knight Commander of the Indian Empire.

1961	1964	1968	1971
Bhutan warily emerges from self-imposed isolation and begins a process of controlled development, undertaking modernisation.	Prime Minister Jigme Palden Dorji, a leading proponent of change, is assassinated on 5 April in Phuentsholing.	King Jigme Dorji Wangchuck continues to reform the government by surrendering his veto power on the decisions of the National Assembly.	Bhutan finally joins the UN as a full member after spending three years holding observer status.

The Trongsa Penlop Gains Control

During this period the Trongsa *penlop*, Jigme Namgyal (1825–82), established effective control of the country through a series of shrewd alliances. This was the first time peace had prevailed since the time of the first Zhabdrung. Jigme Namgyal was working to strengthen his power and that of the central government when he had an inconvenient visit from the British government representative Ashley Eden.

Although the British considered Eden's mission a failure, and reprimanded him for his conduct, they continued the dispute with Bhutan over payment for the Bengal Duars. The Bhutanese, in turn, were furious the British had renounced the treaty Eden had signed. In November 1864 the British summarily annexed the Bengal Duars, gaining effective control of the entire south of Bhutan. Jigme Namgyal mounted a carefully planned counterattack. His troops, protected by shields of rhinoceros hide, captured two British guns and drove the British forces out of Bhutan in January 1865.

The British regrouped and recaptured various towns, including Samtse (then called Chamurchi). A fierce battle at Dewangiri on 2 April essentially ended the war, with the British destroying all the buildings and slaughtering their captives. Negotiations continued through the summer. Eventually the Bhutanese returned the captured guns and accepted a treaty. The treaty of Sinchula was signed, under duress, by the Bhutanese on 11 November 1865. In it the Bhutanese ceded the *duars* to Britain forever and agreed to allow free trade between the two countries.

Through this treaty, Bhutan lost a major tract of valuable farmland and a large portion of its wealth. Its borders became the foot of the hills bordering the plain of India. It is often said that Bhutan's border is where a rock rolled down the hill finally stops. Among the important landmarks the Bhutanese lost were the town of Ambari Falakati, northwest of Cooch Behar, the town of Dewangiri (now called Deothang) in the east and the territory on the east bank of the Teesta River, including what is now the town of Kalimpong.

Back in Bhutan's heartland there were continuing civil wars, but Jigme Namgyal retained his power and in 1870 was enthroned as the 51st *desi*. The next 10 years were again a time of intrigue, treachery, power broking and continual strife. The *penlop* of Paro and the *dzongpens* of Punakha and Wangdue Phodrang conspired to challenge the position of Desi Jigme Namgyal and his successor, who was his halfbrother. After he retired as *desi*, Jigme Namgyal remained in firm control of the country and in 1879 appointed his 17-year-old son, Ugyen Wangchuck, as Paro *penlop*.

Michael Aris' book *The Raven Crown* gives a detailed description of Bhutan in the early 20th century; it is lavishly illustrated with rare photographs and provides a perspective based on Bhutanese accounts.

1972	1974	1974	1980s
King Jigme Dorji Wangchuck is succeeded to the throne by his son, 16-year-old Jigme Singye Wangchuck.	The official coronation of King Jigme Singye Wangchuck, the fourth Druk Gyalpo.	The first 'tourist group' explores the country's sights, paving the way for international visitors.	Government policies aimed at preserving national identity begin to polarise the Nepali-speaking southerners.

After Jigme Namgyal died, his son consolidated his own position following a feud over the post of *penlop* of Trongsa. At the age of 20, Ugyen Wangchuck marched on Bumthang and Trongsa and in 1882 was appointed *penlop* of Trongsa, while still retaining the post of *penlop* of Paro. Because his father had enhanced the powers of the office of the Trongsa *penlop,* this gave him much more influence than the *desi.* When a battle broke out between the *dzongpens* of Punakha and Thimphu, Ugyen Wangchuck tried to mediate the dispute.

He sent in his troops after unsuccessful negotiations and his forces defeated the troops loyal to both *dzongpens* and seized control of Simtokha Dzong. The monk body and the *penlop* of Paro tried to settle the conflict and in 1885 arranged a meeting at the Changlimithang parade ground in Thimphu. During the meeting a fight broke out, the representative of the Thimphu *dzongpen* was killed and the *dzongpen* fled to Tibet. Following the battle, Ugyen Wangchuck emerged as the most powerful person in the country, assumed full authority, installed his own nominee as *desi,* and reduced the post to a ceremonial one.

The First Dragon King

In order to re-establish Bhutan's sovereignty and help consolidate his position, Ugyen Wangchuck developed closer relations with the British. He accompanied Francis Younghusband during his invasion of Tibet in 1904 and assisted with the negotiations that resulted in a treaty between Tibet and Britain. The British rewarded the *penlop* by granting him the title of Knight Commander of the Indian Empire. In 1906 the then Sir Ugyen Wangchuck was invited to Calcutta to attend the reception for the Prince of Wales and returned to Bhutan with a better appreciation of the world that lay beyond the country's borders.

In 1907 the *desi* died and Ugyen Wangchuck was elected as the hereditary ruler of Bhutan by a unanimous vote of Bhutan's chiefs and principal lamas. He was crowned on 17 December 1907 and installed as

THE 1897 EARTHQUAKE

One of the most devastating natural disasters in Bhutan was the great Assam earthquake that occurred at 5.06pm on 12 June 1897. The epicentre was about 80km south of Bhutan in Assam and had an estimated magnitude of 8.7 on the Richter scale, which seismologists categorise as 'catastrophic'. The earthquake destroyed the dzongs in Punakha and Lingzhi and severely damaged the dzongs of Wangdue Phodrang, Trongsa, Jakar and the *utse* (central tower) of Trashi Chhoe Dzong. Paro Dzong escaped largely unharmed.

1983	1988	1991	1992
Bhutan's national airline, Druk Air, commences international flights between Paro and Kolkata.	The government conducts a nationwide census aimed at identifying illegal immigrants, defined as those who could not prove family residence before 1958.	The start of an eventual mass movement of Nepali-speakers from Bhutan to refugee camps just over the border in Nepal.	Up to 80,000 Nepali speakers who claimed they were from Bhutan are housed in seven camps in the Jhapa district of southeastern Nepal.

head of state with the title Druk Gyalpo (Dragon King). This coronation signalled the end of the *desi* system and the beginning of a hereditary monarchy – among the youngest in existence today. King Ugyen Wangchuck continued to maintain excellent relations with the British, partly in an effort to gain some security from the increasing Chinese influence in Tibet.

Karma Ura's book *The Hero with a Thousand Eyes* gives a wonderful insight into the protocol and workings of the Bhutanese court in the days of the second king, Jigme Wangchuck, and is available in Thimphu.

The Treaty of Punakha

British-Bhutanese relations were enhanced in the treaty of Punakha, which was signed in 1910. This treaty stated that the British government would 'exercise no interference in the internal administration of Bhutan'. It was agreed, though, that Bhutan would 'be guided by the advice of the British Government in regard to its external relations'. The compensation for the *duars* was doubled to Rs100,000 per year and Bhutan agreed to refer disputes with Cooch Behar and Sikkim to the British for settlement.

Bhutan still refused to allow the appointment of a British resident, and continued to maintain a policy of isolation aimed at preserving its own sovereignty in an era of colonisation. In 1911 King Ugyen Wangchuck attended the great *durbar* (royal court) held by King George V at Delhi and was given the additional decoration of Knight Commander of the Order of the Star of India.

The Second King

Ugyen Wangchuck died in 1926 and was succeeded by his 24-year-old son, Jigme Wangchuck. He ruled during the time of the Great Depression and WWII, but these catastrophic world events did not affect Bhutan because of its barter economy and isolation.

Of Rainbows and Clouds: The Life of Yab Ugyen Dorji as Told to His Daughter by Yab Ugyen Dorji and Ashi Dorje Wangmo Wangchuck is a fascinating and intimate account of life in changing Bhutan.

Jigme Wangchuck refined the administrative and taxation systems and brought the entire country under his direct control. He made Wangdichholing Palace in Bumthang his summer palace, and moved the entire court to Kuenga Rabten, south of Trongsa, in the winter.

After India gained independence from Britain on 15 August 1947, the new Indian government recognised Bhutan as an independent country. In 1949 Bhutan signed a treaty with independent India that was very similar to its earlier treaty with the British. The treaty reinforced Bhutan's position as a sovereign state. India agreed not to interfere in the internal affairs of Bhutan, while Bhutan agreed to be guided by the government of India in its external relations. The treaty also returned to Bhutan about 82 sq km of the *duars* in the southeast of the country, including Dewangiri, that had been annexed by the British.

1993	1998	1998	1999
The exodus of Nepali speakers stops and the UN High Commissioner for Refugees establishes a screening centre at Kakarbhitta on the Nepal–India border.	King Jigme Singye Wangchuck transfers full executive authority to an elected Council of Ministers.	Taktshang Goemba, the most famous monastery in Bhutan, is all but destroyed in a fire.	TV and the internet are officially introduced to Bhutan in a managed continuation of the modernisation process.

The Third King & the Modernisation of Bhutan

King Jigme Wangchuck died in 1952. He was succeeded by his son, Jigme Dorji Wangchuck, who had been educated in India and England and spoke fluent Tibetan, English and Hindi. To improve relations with India he invited the Indian prime minister, Jawaharlal Nehru, and his daughter, Indira Gandhi, to visit Bhutan in 1958.

When the Chinese took control of Tibet in 1959, it became obvious that a policy of isolationism was not appropriate in the modern world. The king knew that in order to preserve Bhutan's independence, the country had to become a member of the larger world community. In 1961 Bhutan emerged from centuries of self-imposed isolation and embarked on a process of planned development.

Bhutan joined the Colombo Plan in 1962. This gave it access to technical assistance and training from member countries in Southeast Asia. The first 'five-year plan' for development was implemented in 1961 and

King Jigme Dorji Wangchuck, the third king, became known as the father of modern Bhutan owing to his reforms to society and economics.

THE BEGINNING OF TOURISM

Until the beginning of King Jigme Dorji Wangchuck's modernisation efforts in 1960, most of the non-Indian foreigners who entered Bhutan were British explorers. A few foreigners were permitted into the country during the 1960s, but only the royal family had the authority to issue invitations, so almost all visitors were royal guests.

Early trekkers included Desmond Doig, a friend of the royal family who trekked in 1961 on assignment for *National Geographic*. In 1963 Professor Augusto Gansser travelled throughout the country studying geology, and in 1964 a group of British physicians, Michael Ward, Frederic Jackson and R Turner, mounted an expedition to the remote Lunana region.

The coronation of the fourth king in 1974 was the first time that a large number of foreign visitors had entered the kingdom. After the coronation, small groups of tourists were allowed into the country and given permission to visit the dzongs and goembas in Thimphu and Paro. From these beginnings, the pattern for Bhutan's tourism industry evolved.

The first group of paying tourists arrived in 1974, organised and led by Lars Eric Lindblad, founder of Lindblad Travel in Connecticut, USA, a pioneer of modern-day group tours. Lindblad encouraged the government to limit tourism and to charge high fees.

Paro airport was opened in 1983 and the newly formed national airline, Druk Air, started operating flights from Kolkata. The airport runway was extended in 1990 and Druk Air began operating jet aircraft, with direct international connections. Until 1991 tourists were handled by the Bhutan Tourism Corporation, a government agency. Tourism was privatised that year and soon numerous agencies were established, most run by ex-employees of the now-disbanded government agency.

2001	2001	2003	2003
Drafting of the first Constitution of the Kingdom of Bhutan begins.	A verification process of refugees in the Nepal camps is initiated under a bilateral process between Nepal and Bhutan.	The Royal Bhutan Army, led by the fourth king, removes Bodo militant camps from Bhutanese territory.	Disagreements over appeals from the first round of verification escalate and officials are attacked in one refugee camp.

SOUTHERN BHUTANESE & CONFLICTS ACROSS THE BORDER

Along the southern border of Bhutan, immigrants from Nepal, seeking to break free from the rigid caste system of their home country, began settling in the late 19th and early 20th centuries. They are called Lhotshampa (literally, 'the people of the southern border') and are mainly Hindu and form approximately 25% of Bhutan's population.

Major problems between the Drukpa and the Lhotshampa emerged in the late 1980s. At that time, the government began to focus on preserving what it saw as Bhutan's threatened national identity. Mindful of Bhutan's porous border and attractiveness because of its fertile land, low population and free health and education facilities, the government conducted a nationwide census to identify illegal immigrants.

Thousands of ethnic Nepalis lacked proper documentation and a sense of fear and insecurity led to an exodus of Nepali-speakers from Bhutan. How much of the migration was voluntary remains a matter of debate, but tens of thousands of Nepali-speakers left Bhutan for camps in neighbouring Nepal between 1988 and 1993. In 2013 there were about 38,000 people left in the United Nations High Commissioner for Refugees (UNHCR) protected camps, despite around 100,000 refugees being resettled in the West.

In 2004, on another porous border, Bhutanese troops flushed out Assamese separatist militants from Bhutanese territory, destroying their jungle refuges. While the struggle for independence, or at least some form of autonomy, from Delhi in this region of India continues, the security of the bordering Bhutanese lands remains compromised and travel in Assam complicated (see p273).

The northeastern region of India has suffered years of separatist violence carried out by militants, some of whom have established bases in the jungles of southern Bhutan from which they mount assaults. The actions of these groups have claimed the lives of more than 20,000 people in the Indian state of Assam.

The Bodos are Mechey tribal people that have two militant groups, the Bodo Liberation Tiger Force and the Bodo Security Force, both of which are fighting for a Bodo homeland. The United Liberation Front of Assam, more commonly known as ULFA, is a separatist group formed in 1979 with the goal of an independent Assamese nation. It has staged numerous attacks on trains, buses and vehicles carrying both Bhutanese and Indian citizens.

In December 2003, after the government felt it had exhausted all peaceful means, the Royal Bhutan Army, led from the front by the king, flushed out the militants from Bhutanese territory. The continued presence of these militants across the border has made travel in the southeastern part of the country risky for both Bhutanese and tourists and is the reason for restrictions on visiting such places as Royal Manas National Park and Pemagatshel.

India agreed to help finance and construct the large Chhukha hydroelectric project in western Bhutan. Not all Bhutanese approved of the pace of change. There were clashes between rival power groups, and the prime minister, Jigme Palden Dorji, who was a leading proponent of change, was assassinated on 5 April 1964.

2005 & 2006	2007	2007	2008
The fourth king abdicates and the draft Constitution for the Kingdom of Bhutan is released.	First-ever election to vote for the 20 members each representing a *dzongkhag* (district) of the 25-member National Council (upper house).	The major political parties, Druk Phuensum Tshogpa (DPT) and Peoples Democratic Party (PDP), are formed for the inaugural democratic election.	Bhutanese vote again, this time for the 47-member National Assembly (lower house). The DPT wins 45 seats.

Bhutan joined the Universal Postal Union in 1969 and became a member of the UN in 1971. In the same year, Bhutan and India established formal diplomatic relations and exchanged ambassadors.

The king's domestic accomplishments were also impressive. In 1953 he established the Tshogdu (National Assembly) and drew up a 12-volume code of law. He abolished serfdom, reorganised land holdings, created the Royal Bhutan Army (RBA) and police force, and established the High Court. However, as he led Bhutan into the modern world, he emphasised the need to preserve Bhutanese culture and tradition.

The Fourth King & the Introduction of Democracy

King Jigme Dorji Wangchuck died in 1972 at age 44. He was succeeded by his 16-year-old son, Jigme Singye Wangchuck. Like his father, he was educated in India and England, but he also received a Bhutanese education at the Ugyen Wangchuck Academy in Paro. He pledged to continue his father's program of modernisation and announced a plan for the country to achieve economic self-reliance. This plan took advantage of Bhutan's special circumstances – a small population, abundant land and rich natural resources. Among the development goals set by the king was the ideal of economic self-reliance and what he nicknamed 'Gross National Happiness' (GNH). GNH is not a simple appraisal of the smiles on the faces of the populace; rather it encompasses explicit criteria to measure development projects and progress in terms of society's greater good. A more sustainable happiness for the individual is believed to derive from such an approach.

The coronation of King Jigme Singye Wangchuck as the fourth Druk Gyalpo on 2 June 1974 was a major turning point in the opening of Bhutan, and was the first time that the international press was allowed to enter the country. A total of 287 invited guests travelled to Thimphu for the event, and several new hotels were built to accommodate them. These hotels later provided the basis for the development of tourism in Bhutan.

The fourth king emphasised modernisation of education, health services, rural development and communications. He continued the reforms begun by his father in the areas of administration, labour and justice, including the introduction of a secret ballot and the abolishment of compulsory labour. He was the architect of Bhutan's policy of environmental conservation, which gives precedence to ecological considerations over commercial interests. He promoted national identity, traditional values and the concept of 'One Nation, One People'.

The UN refugee agency (www.unhcr.org) provides the latest facts and figures on the refugee camps in Jhapa, Nepal.

2008	2008	2009	2009
Formal coronation of the fifth Druk Gyalpo Jigme Khesar Namgyel Wangchuck on 6 November 2008.	The Constitution of the Kingdom of Bhutan is officially adopted.	Bhutan and India agree on the construction of 10 new hydropower projects in Bhutan to provide 10,000MW of electricity.	A 6.1 magnitude earthquake centred in eastern Bhutan shakes the entire country leaving several dead and many homeless.

In 1988 the royal wedding solemnised the king's marriage to the sisters Ashi Dorji Wangmo, Ashi Tshering Pem, Ashi Tshering Yangdon and Ashi Sangay Choedon. In 1998 he gave up absolute power, sharing authority with the National Assembly and Council of Ministers.

In December 2005 the 50-year-old king announced a plan to abdicate the throne in favour of his eldest son, Crown Prince Jigme Khesar Namgyel Wangchuck, and help move the country from an absolute monarchy to a democratic constitutional monarchy in 2008. He is quoted as saying 'Monarchy is not the best form of government because a king is chosen by birth and not by merit'.

The Fifth King & the First Elected Parliament

King Jigme Singye Wangchuck did not wait until 2008. He formally abdicated in December 2006, bestowing all his authority to his eldest son, who was already travelling to every corner of the country to explain the new constitution, the upcoming election, and their beloved fourth king's dramatic decision.

In December 2007 the first elections for the new parliament were held for the 25-member upper house, called the National Council. This was followed in March 2008 with the first election for the 47-member National Assembly (lower house). This election became a landslide victory for Druk Phuensum Tshogpa (DPT; Bhutan Peace & Prosperity) party, which won 45 of the 47 seats. The Peoples Democratic Party (PDP) won the other two seats. For more on Bhutan's system of government and political parties, see p190.

The most authoritative and complete history of Bhutan in English is Michael Aris' *Bhutan, the Early History of a Himalayan Kingdom.*

The unprecedented sight of the former king crowning the new king with the raven crown was witnessed on 6 November 2008 at the official coronation of 27-year-old Jigme Khesar Namgyel Wangchuck. The momentous occasion took place in the Golden Throne room of Thimphu's Trashi Chhoe Dzong in front of national and international dignitaries. The following day, the fifth king gave his coronation speech to a packed Changlimithang Stadium, in which he pledged: 'As the king of a Buddhist nation, my duty is not only to ensure your happiness today but to create the fertile ground from which you may gain the fruits of spiritual pursuit and attain good Karma.'

2011	2011	2012	2013
The Royal Wedding. King Jigme Khesar Namgyel Wangchuck marries commoner Jetsun Pema at Punakha Dzong on 13 October.	A 6.9 magnitude earthquake with an epicentre in Sikkim causes one death in Bhutan and damages several historic buildings.	Bhutan is rocked by the complete destruction by fire of Wangdue Phodrang Dzong, one of the country's oldest dzongs. Plans for its reconstruction start immediately.	Bhutan goes to the polls for the second time. The tables are turned and the Peoples Democratic Party (PDP) is swept to power in the National Assembly.

The Bhutanese Way of Life

Bhutan was relatively isolated until the early 1950s and this tiny country has witnessed more change in the last 60 years than in the previous 400 years. To date, Bhutan has retained many of its traditional social structures and has actively sought to preserve its cultural identity in the face of modernisation and increasing external influences.

Bhutan decided long ago that we will never be a military power, we will never be an economic force, so to survive we must have a distinct identity. This is the identity you see; our clothes, language, the architecture. You look around and you feel that you are in a different world. This is not an accident.

Dasho Kinley Dorji, Secretary, Ministry of Information and Communication

Until the mid-20th century there were no large urban settlements in Bhutan. By 2005, the population of Thimphu was over 50,000.

The Bhutanese are a warm and open people – quick to smile and laugh. The smiles of the children walking to school in the morning light, the laughter overheard in a family house, the shy greetings from women weaving outside their homes – these will quickly entrance the traveller. As with the other peoples of the Himalaya, the Bhutanese have an infectious sense of humour and quickly overcome barriers to communication. You should not be surprised to be offered a seat and a cup of tea even if you do not speak Dzongkha or one of the other 18 languages of Bhutan. These simple acts are spontaneous and provide the traveller with both fond memories and a brief insight into the generous nature of the Bhutanese.

Everyday Buddhism

Maybe it's your first sight of the monumental Buddha that watches over the Thimphu valley, or the way your driver swerves clockwise around a chorten stuck in the middle of the road, but as a new visitor you quickly realise how Buddhism permeates life in Bhutan. Prayer flags flutter throughout the land, prayer wheels powered by mountain streams clunk gently by the roadside, images of the Buddha and other religious figures are carved into cliffs, reminding the visitor that every aspect of daily life is shaped by Buddhist beliefs and aspirations. This can be daunting, even alien, for many Western visitors, and a basic knowledge of Buddhism will go a long way towards understanding the Bhutanese. The idea of accumulating merit, having a deep respect of the natural and often sacred environment, respect for religious practitioners: all are central elements of the unique fusion of Buddhism and older non-Buddhist beliefs.

Buddhism is practised throughout the country; however, in the south, most Bhutanese people of Nepali and Indian descent are Hindu. Relations between Buddhists and Hindus are very good, with major Hindu festivals marked by national holidays. Minority groups practise various forms of ancient animistic religions, including Bon, which predates Himalayan Buddhism.

Urban Bhutan

Until the 1960s there were no major urban settlements. Since then Thimphu, Paro and Phuentsholing have both grown significantly, leading to pressure on land availability in these areas. Elsewhere there has been an increase in land acquisition and settlement, most notably in Gelephu.

Literacy in Bhutan is 72% for males and 55% for females (2012). For more information on education in the Himalaya, and on supporting young students, see www.loden.org.

As a result of the opportunities created by education and the development of service-industry jobs (such as civil servants, teachers, travel guides, army personnel or police), Bhutan has experienced unprecedented social mobility in recent decades. The rate of rural–urban migration continues to increase, and there has been growing concern over the increasing unemployment rate among educated school leavers, as well as rapidly rising property values and rents in Thimphu.

The Living Standard Survey 2012 revealed that 34% of Bhutanese now live in urban areas, and over half of the country's household income is generated by wages. Averaged across the country, agriculture accounts for only 10% of income. For many living in urban areas average household expenditure can represent all or most of their salary, which is why many Bhutanese women now work to supplement the household income through some form of small business enterprise.

Rural Life

Despite rapid urbanisation, the majority of people, 66% of all households, still live in rural Bhutan, most dependent on the cultivation of crops and livestock breeding.

Life for most rural households starts around dawn and ends with sunset; daily life revolving around the care of crops and livestock. Each morning the family will make offerings, typically of water, before the household shrine and a simple breakfast of rice will be prepared. Men and women share equally in the day-to-day care of the children, and although women are usually in charge of the household, men are equally able, and expected, to assist with the cooking. Meals consist of rice and a selection of simple shared dishes – *ema datse* (chillis with cheese), perhaps a meat dish or some buckwheat noodles. Children are expected to help with the household and farm chores, like cleaning, collecting water or firewood, or herding the livestock.

The main crops grown in central Bhutan are rice, buckwheat, barley and potatoes. Chillies are also grown, then dried on the roofs of houses before being stored.

In the evening, the water from the offering bowls will be poured away and a butter lamp may be lit and left to burn before the household shrine.

Traditionally Bhutanese were very self-sufficient, often making their own clothing, bedding, floor and seat covers, tablecloths, and decorative items for daily and religious use. There remains a degree of self-sufficiency among the rural Bhutanese, though many everyday items are imported from Bangladesh, China, India and Thailand.

BHUTAN BEAT

The music scene in Bhutan is small and the most popular music, *rigsar*, is still evolving. *Rigsar* is typically performed on modern instruments, notably electric piano and synthesiser. *Rigsar* blends elements of traditional Bhutanese and Tibetan tunes, and is influenced by Hindi film music. Popular male and female *rigsar* performers often appear in locally produced films.

While contemporary and traditional Bhutanese music is widely available from little booths throughout Bhutan, groups struggle in a small market where massively popular karaoke has all but plundered every centimetre of available stage space. Check out Mojo Park (p65) in Thimphu for the latest in live music.

Farmer tends his crops, Bumthang (p117)

Learning

Until the introduction of Western-style education by the third king in the 1960s, the only education available in Bhutan was from the monasteries. Prior to this a few students travelled to Darjeeling or Kalimpong to receive a secular education. Western-style education has expanded to cover the whole country.

The school system aims to provide basic literacy skills, and knowledge of Bhutan's history, geography and traditions. Most villages have a primary school, though it is not uncommon for children to board at a junior high school or high school. Free education and textbooks are provided to all students until tertiary level. Morning prayers and the national anthem start the day for all students throughout Bhutan. The government provides adult education classes, especially aimed at improving literacy.

A key aspect of Bhutan's development plan involves training doctors, engineers and other professionals, as well as teaching important trade skills such as plumbing, construction and electrics. The Royal University of Bhutan was established in 2003 to provide tertiary education in Bhutan.

Women in Bhutan

Compared to other areas of South Asia, Bhutanese women enjoy greater equality and freedom with men. The right to inherit often passes property to the woman of the household rather than the man.

Traditionally, women look after the household, preparing food and weaving textiles for family use and for sale. However, they also work in the fields, notably at harvest times when all available labour is required. Usually women brew the homemade alcohol such as *arra*, *bang chhang* or *sinchhang*. Decisions affecting the household are jointly made.

Rural women are often presented as the custodians of traditional values. Urbanisation and increasing rural–urban migration have brought new challenges for women separated from their families and social networks.

Travelling in Bhutan you will notice that Bhutanese women are independently minded and possess a strong entrepreneurial spirit. In Thimphu and the emerging urban centres such as Trongsa, Gelephu and Phuentsholing, women may seek to boost family income by engaging in trade, selling goods from home or renting a small shop.

The introduction of education in the 1960s enabled Bhutanese women to become literate and to seek employment outside of both their homes and their local villages. Teaching, the civil service and other office positions provided important opportunities for young, educated Bhutanese women.

The women of Laya are particularly noted for their distinctive conical bamboo hats and long black wool dresses.

However, there are areas in which Bhutanese women are still not equal with their male counterparts. Levels of literacy remain higher among men than women, though this is being tackled by the government through adult learning classes. Although some women have been appointed to higher positions in the government and NGOs, including the first female district court judge appointed in 2003, there remains a gender imbalance at all levels of government. In the first and second elections for the parliament's National Council, women accounted for four and none, respectively, of the successful 20 candidates. For the 47-member National Assembly elections in July 2013, only three women (all from the victorious Peoples Democratic Party; PDP) were successful.

The major women's organisation in the country is the National Women's Association of Bhutan. It was established in 1981 and headed by Dasho Dawa Dem, one of the few women to have received the honorific title of Dasho. In 2004, Respect, Educate, Nurture & Empower Women (Renew; www.renewbhutan.org), an NGO for women, was established by HM Queen Mother Sangay Choeden Wangchuck. RENEW is highly respected and tackles major issues facing contemporary Bhutanese women.

Yeewong magazine is Bhutan's women's glossy, launched in 2009 and published three times a year. While the poses and the prettiness are globally glamorous, the food and fashions are decidedly Bhutanese.

Marriage

In the past, marriages were arranged. However, since the 1970s the majority of marriages are love matches. The minimum age is 16 for women and 21 for men. In rural areas, it is quite common for the husband to move into his wife's household and if they divorce he will return to live with his own family.

Polyandry, the practice of taking more than one husband, still exists in certain parts of Bhutan and polygamy is restricted. There remains a large number of Bhutanese couples who, although living together as a couple, are not formally married. The divorce rate is increasing and there is legal provision for alimony to be paid to take care of children.

DOMA

Doma is an integral part of Bhutanese culture. A popular gift throughout Bhutanese society, it is made up of three main ingredients: *doma* (areca nut; *Areca catechu*), *pani* (betel leaf; *Piper betel*) and *tsune* (lime; calcium carbonate).

Eating *doma* was an aristocratic practice, with the various ingredients kept in ornate rectangular silver boxes called *chaka*, while lime had a separate circular box with conical lid called *trimi*. JC White, the British political officer who attended Gongsar Ugyen Wangchuck's enthronement in 1907, reports that *doma* was served to those attending the enthronement. Today people may keep their *doma* in bamboo *bangchung* or a cloth pouch called a *kaychung*. While the red sprays of *doma* spit still stain many walls and floors, young people appear to be slowly turning away from the habit as health warnings begin to make inroads.

TRADITIONAL MEDICINE

Historically, Bhutan was referred to as the 'Land of Medicinal Herbs' and exported herbs to Tibet. Bhutanese were trained in medicine, known as So-ba Rig pa. It represents a blending of Ayurveda from India with Chinese medicine, in the reading of pulses. The earliest medical works date from the 7th and 8th centuries and the main medical teachings are believed to have been transmitted from the Medicine Buddha, Sangye Menlha. They are contained in four volumes, called the *Gyuzhi*.

When the Zhabdrung Ngawang Namgyal came to Bhutan, he brought with him a highly esteemed physician, Tenzin Drukey, who spread the teachings on So-ba Rig pa in Bhutan. Although the basic texts are the same, the Bhutanese tradition of So-ba Rig pa developed independently from its Tibetan origins. Since 1967 the Bhutanese tradition has been formally incorporated into the national health system.

The decision about the kind of treatment necessary for a particular condition is made mainly through reading of the pulses. Unlike Western medicine, which only uses reading of pulses to detect anomalies of the circulatory system, using the So-ba Rig pa method it is possible to detect diseases of organs. The eyes, tongue and urine are also examined for signs that will help with the diagnosis.

Several forms of treatment are applied in Bhutanese traditional medicine. Hundreds of medicinal plants, minerals and animal parts from the basic medicines are used by the practitioner. These basic ingredients are processed and mixed in different combinations to make 300 medicines in the form of pills, tablets, syrups, powders and lotions. The practitioner may also offer advice on, or treatment for, diet and lifestyle.

There are also procedures that include *gtar* (bloodletting), *bsregs* (cauterisation by herbal compounds), *gser bcos* (acupuncture with a golden needle), *tshug* (cauterisation with instruments of different materials), *dugs* (applying heat or cold to parts of the body), *byugs pa* (medicated oil massage), *sman chu* (stone heated bath), *tsha-chhu* (bath at a hot spring, such as the springs in Gasa) and *lum* (vapour treatment).

What's in a Name?

The system for personal names in Bhutan differs between the north and south of the country. In the north, with the exception of the royal family, there are no family names. Two names are given to children by monks a few weeks after birth. These are traditional names of Tibetan origin and are chosen because of their auspicious influence or religious meaning. Two names are always given, although a few people have three names.

It is often impossible to tell the sex of a Bhutanese person based on their name. A few names are given only to boys, and others apply only to girls, for example Choekyi, Drolma and Wangmo, but most names may apply to either.

In the south, with an evident Hindu influence, a system resembling family names exists. Brahmans and Newars retain their caste name, such as Sharma or Pradhan, and others retain the name of their ethnic group, such as Rai or Gurung.

Bhutanese do not shout a person's name at night, as it's believed this may attract a ghost.

Health & the Wheel of Life

Bhutan's rapid modernisation has included significant progress in its provision of health facilities and it provides free health care to all its citizens. Over 90% of Bhutanese have access to clean drinking water.

The main hospital is the National Referral Hospital in Thimphu, with two further regional referral hospitals in the south and east. There are also smaller hospitals in each district, and in remote areas health care is provided through Basic Health Units staffed with a health assistant, nurse midwife and a basic health worker.

Spectators at Paro tsechu (p23)

The Wheel of Life, often evident at the entrances to goembas, reminds Bhutanese that death is part of the cycle of samsara separating loved ones and leading to rebirth. Accordingly, death is treated as a major life event. Family and friends are informed and monks, *gomchen* (lay or married monks) or nuns begin to recite from the *Bardo Thodrel* to guide the deceased through the intermediate phase.

Of approximately 5000 formal monks in Bhutan, half are under the patronage of the Je Khenpo, the other half subsidised by private support.

Until the cremation, the deceased is placed in a wooden box and covered in a white cloth and kept separate from the family. At the cremation, the corpse is placed on the pyre facing the officiating lama. The first funeral service is held on the seventh day after death, with other rituals performed on the 14th, 21st and 49th days. The lama reminds the deceased that they are dead and during the ritual seeks to help them move on to their next and (it is hoped) fortunate rebirth, either as a human being or preferably in a Buddha realm.

At the end of the 49 days the ashes of the deceased may be scattered; some are placed in a sacred image and donated to a monastery or temple. The anniversary of the death will be marked for the following three years.

Titles & Forms of Address

Titles are extremely important in Bhutan. All persons of rank should be addressed by the appropriate title followed by their first or full name. Members of the royal family are addressed as 'Dasho' if they are male, and 'Ashi' if female. A minister has the title 'Lyonpo' (pronounced 'lonpo').

The title Dasho is given to those who have been honoured by the king, receiving also the accompanying red scarf. In common practice, many senior government officials are addressed as Dasho even if they have not received the title, but officially this is incorrect.

You would address a senior monk or teacher with the title 'Lopon' (pronounced 'loeboen') or, if he has been given the title, as Lam. A *trulku* (reincarnate lama) is addressed as 'Rinpoche' and a nun as 'Anim'.

A man is addressed as 'Aap' and a boy as 'Busu'; a woman is addressed as 'Am' and a girl as 'Bum'. If you are calling someone whose name you do not know, you may use 'Ama' for women and 'Aapa' for men. In the same situation, girls are 'Bumo' and boys 'Alou'. When Bhutanese talk about a foreigner whose name they don't know, they use the word 'Chilip', or in eastern Bhutan 'Pilingpa'.

White silk scarves called *kata* are exchanged as customary greetings among ranking officials and are offered to high lamas as a sign of respect, but they are not exchanged as frequently as they are in Tibet and Nepal.

Bhutan's first foray into the Olympic Games happened when an archery team of three men and three women participated in the 1984 games. Since then Bhutan has participated in all the Olympics.

Dress: Gho & Kira

Bhutan's traditional dress is one of the most distinctive and visible aspects of the country. It is compulsory for all Bhutanese to wear national dress in schools, government offices and on formal occasions. Men, women and children wear traditional clothing made from Bhutanese textiles in a variety of colourful patterns.

Men wear a *gho*, a long robe similar to the Tibetan *chuba*. The Bhutanese hoist the *gho* to knee length and hold it in place with a woven cloth belt called a *kera*. The *kera* is wound tightly around the waist, and the large pouch formed above it is traditionally used to carry a bowl, money and the makings of *doma*. One man suggested that the best part of the day was when he was able to loosen his uncomfortably tight belt.

According to tradition, men should carry a small knife called a *dozum* at the waist. Traditional footwear is knee-high, embroidered leather boots, but these are now worn only at festivals. Most Bhutanese men wear leather shoes, trainers or trekking boots.

Ghos come in a wide variety of patterns, though often they have plaid or striped designs. Flowered patterns are taboo, and solid reds and yellows are avoided because these are colours worn by monks; otherwise patterns have no special significance. Historically, Bhutanese men wore the same thing under their *gho* that a true Scotsman wears under his

---

DRIGLAM NAMZHA

The Zhabdrung Ngawang Namgyal established a code of etiquette for monastic and government officials. Over the centuries this system of etiquette spread to lay people. Called *driglam namzha*, the code of conduct specifies how to dress when visiting a dzong, the polite way to greet one's boss and officials, the correct way to sit, eat and so forth. Many of the ceremonies performed at the start of an official event *(chipdrel, marchang)*, or an archery match are part of *driglam namzha*.

The government has actively promoted *driglam namzha* since 1989 in an attempt to preserve Bhutanese traditions, notably enforcing the requirement to wear *gho* and *kira* when visiting government offices, dzongs and temples.

Closely linked to *driglam namzha*, *thadamthsi* refers to the Bhutanese belief in respect towards ones' parents, elders and other members of the community. Based on the Buddhist teachings on devotion, *thadamtshi* is an important concept in Bhutanese society. It is often illustrated by the story of the Four Friends (see p237).

Linked to *thadamtshi* and less formal than *driglam namzha* is the concept of *bey cha*. *Bey cha* emphasises the aesthetics of performing everyday tasks gracefully and with care and consideration for others.

FOOTBALL

kilt, but today it's usually a pair of shorts. In winter it's correct to wear thermal underwear, but it's more often a pair of jeans or a tracksuit. Formality in Thimphu dictates that legs may not be covered until winter has arrived, which is defined as the time that the monks move to Punakha.

Formal occasions, including a visit to the dzong, require a scarf called a *kabney* that identifies a person's rank. The *kabney* has to be put on correctly so it hangs in exactly the right way. In dzongs, and on formal occasions, a *dasho* or someone in authority carries a long sword called a *patang*.

Ordinary citizens wear a *kabney* of unbleached white silk and each level of official wears a different coloured scarf: saffron for the king and Je Khenpo; orange for *lyonpos*; blue for National Council and National Assembly members; red for those with the title Dasho and for senior officials whom the king has recognised; green for judges; white with a central red stripe for *dzongdags* (district governors); and white with red stripes on the outside for a *gup* (elected leader of a village).

Women wear a long floor-length dress called a *kira*. This is a rectangular piece of brightly coloured cloth that wraps around the body over a Tibetan-style silk blouse called a *wonju*. The *kira* is fastened at the shoulders with elaborate silver hooks called *koma* and at the waist with a belt that may be of either silver or cloth. Over the top is worn a short, open, jacket-like garment called a *toego*. Women often wear large amounts of jewellery. The whole ensemble is beautiful and Bhutanese women are very elegant in their finery.

The *kira* may be made from cotton or silk (usually synthetic these days) and may have a pattern on one or both sides. For everyday wear, women wear a *kira* made from striped cloth with a double-sided design, and on more formal occasions they wear a *kira* with an embellished pattern woven into it. The most expensive *kiras* are *kushutaras* (brocade dresses), which are made of handspun, handwoven Bhutanese cotton, embroidered with various colours and designs in raw silk or cotton thread. Lhuentse is celebrated for its *kushutara* designs.

When visiting dzongs, women wear a cloth sash called a *rachu* over their shoulders or simply over their left shoulder in the same manner as men wear a *kabney*.

Bhutanese at Play

Bhutan's national sport is *datse* (archery). It is played wherever there is enough space and remains the favourite sport for all ages. There are archery tournaments held throughout the country.

Archery contests act as an affirmation of Bhutanese cultural identity as well as popular entertainment. The tournaments begin with a short ceremony and breakfast. The targets are placed 140m apart. Players often stand close to the targets and call how good or bad the aim of their opponent is – if the contestant hits the target, his team mates will perform a slow dance and sing his praises, while he slips a coloured scarf into his belt. If he misses, the opposition mock his ability.

Bhutanese footballers came to the world's attention in 2002 when Bhutan played against the small island of Montserrat. *The Other Final* documentary narrates the lead-up to the football match between the world's two lowest ranked teams and the crowd's enthusiastic participation.

DZOE – SPIRIT CATCHER

Sometimes you will come across a strange construction of twigs, straw and rainbow-coloured thread woven into a spiderweb shape. You may see one near a building or by a roadside, with flower and food offerings. This is a *dzoe* (also known as a *tendo*), a sort of spirit catcher used to exorcise something evil that has been pestering a household. The malevolent spirits are drawn to the *dzoe*. After prayers the *dzoe* is cast away, often on a trail or road, to send away the evil spirits it has trapped.

BHUTAN'S SILVER SCREEN

The first feature film produced by a Bhutanese film-maker for a non-Bhutanese audience was *The Cup* by Khyentse Norbu, which was nominated as best foreign-language film for the 2000 Academy Awards. *Travellers and Magicians* (2003), also produced by Khyentse Norbu, is the first Dzongkha-language film to be made for an international audience. The film contains two parallel tales and its main theme remains pertinent to contemporary Bhutan. The main story focuses on a young frustrated civil servant, Dhundup, who dreams of leaving Bhutan for the USA. He likes rock and roll and Western clothes. Yet on the road to the capital, he encounters a series of people who suggest that contentment can be found among his own people.

Bhutanese of all ages enjoy these films, and part of the enjoyment for many is identifying friends and relatives, as well as the locations. Bhutanese films such as *Khorwa*, made for a Bhutanese audience, often tackle contemporary social problems such as domestic violence, the issues facing stepchildren, alcoholism and, more recently, unemployment. The production values and acting are of varying quality, yet a stronger sense of Bhutanese film-making is gradually appearing, with annual awards recognising local film-makers. One recent film, *Thank You Sir*, bagged 12 awards at the 12th National Film awards in Thimphu 2013. But it was the feel-good *Jarim Sarim Yeshey Tshogay*, about a girl's quest against the odds to be Miss Bhutan (played by the inaugural Miss Bhutan), that won best film that year.

Women, usually wearing their finest clothes and jewellery, often stand to one side of the archery field and act as cheerleaders. They dance and sing during breaks from the shooting. Their songs and shouts can be quite ribald!

Khuru is a darts game played on a field about 20m long with small targets similar to those used by archers. The darts are usually homemade from a block of wood and a nail, with some chicken feathers for flights. If a chicken can't be found, bits of plastic make a good substitute. Teams compete with a lot of shouting and arm waving, designed to put the thrower off his aim. The game is a favourite of monks and young boys; beware of dangerous flying objects if you are near a *khuru* target or an archery field.

Other sports, notably basketball, football (soccer), cricket, cycling, golf, tae kwon do and tennis, continue to grow in popularity.

Buddhism in Bhutan

Buddhism is inscribed into the very landscape of Bhutan – prayer flags, white-and-red chortens and portraits of Buddhist saints carved into the rock dot the countryside. Whether you are visiting a dzong or chatting to your guide, if you want to understand Bhutan it is essential to have a basic understanding of Buddhism. In essence everything from festival dances and monastery art to government policy serves the same purpose in Bhutan: to encapsulate and promulgate basic Buddhist teachings.

To learn more about Tibetan Buddhism try the book *What Makes You Not a Buddhist* by Dzongsar Jamyang Khyentse, the celebrated Bhutanese *rinpoche* (reincarnated lama) and director.

The Buddha

Buddhism originated in northern central India around the 6th or 5th century BC, from the teachings of Siddhartha Gautama – better known as Sakyamuni Buddha. Little is known for certain about the young Siddhartha. According to legend his parents, King Suddhodana and Queen Maya, lived in a small kingdom, Sakya, which lay on the border between the present-day states of Nepal and India. Shortly after his birth a wandering ascetic prophesied to King Suddhodana that the young prince would either be a world-conquering king or a liberator of living beings from suffering. The king took various precautions to ensure that his son would never have cause to follow a spiritual path. However, the young prince grew restless and during various excursions from his palace Siddhartha Gautama saw a number of examples of suffering that inspired him to escape from his sheltered palace life.

After fleeing the palace (and leaving his wife and child behind), Siddhartha became a wandering ascetic, fasting and meditating. Finally at Bodhgaya in Bihar, India, Siddhartha began meditating beneath a bo (peepul) tree, declaring that he would not stop until he had achieved enlightenment. He had realised there must be a middle path between the extremes of his luxurious palace life and the severe ascetic practices that brought him only exhaustion. As dawn broke on the morning of his third night of meditation Siddhartha became a Buddha (an awakened one).

Schools of Buddhism

Buddhism is perhaps the most accommodating of the world's religions. As Buddhism has spread, it has adapted to local conditions and absorbed local beliefs and aesthetics, creating new schools of thought. Over the centuries two principal schools of Buddhism emerged: Theravada and Mahayana.

Theravada, sometimes referred to as Hinayana, focused on pursuing liberation for the individual. Mahayana took Buddhism in a different direction, emphasising compassion and the liberation of all living beings. The Theravada teachings retreated to southern India before becoming established in Sri Lanka, Thailand, Myanmar (Burma) and Cambodia. The Mahayana teachings were developed in the new Buddhist universities in northern India before being transmitted northwards in a huge arc along the Silk Road to China, Tibet, Bhutan, Japan and Korea. It is the Mahayana teachings on compassion that permeate the religious beliefs and practices of the Bhutanese.

Despite these differences, the basic tenets of Buddhism have remained the same and all schools of Buddhism are united by their faith in the value of the original teachings of Buddha.

Tantrism (Vajrayana)

A new school called Vajrayana (Diamond Vehicle) emerged from the Mahayana in about AD 600. Both the Theravada and Mahayana schools studied the Sutras that recorded the teachings of Sakyamuni; however, the followers of Tantrism believed that he had left a collection of hidden esoteric teachings to a select few of his early disciples. These were known as Tantra *(gyu)*.

Over the centuries tantric Buddhism in Tibet gradually divided into various schools, each with their own philosophical, spiritual and political emphasis. In central and eastern Bhutan, the oldest school of Himalayan Buddhism, Nyingmapa, is most popular. The Nyingmapa school was introduced during the earliest phase of Buddhist propagation and experienced a revival through the discovery of *terma* (hidden texts believed to have been buried by Guru Rinpoche at various sites across Bhutan). In other parts of Bhutan, particularly the west, the Drukpa Kagyupa school is preeminent. The Drukpa school was founded in Ralung in Tibet by Tsanpa Gyare (1161–1211) and spread to Bhutan in the 13th century.

Tantra (Sanskrit meaning 'continuum') most often refers to the literature dealing with tantric teachings. Tantrism relies heavily on oral transmission between teacher and student, as well as the practice of identifying with a tutelary deity through meditation and the recitation of mantras. The two most well-known mantras are *om mani padme hum* of Chenresig (Avalokiteshvara) and *om vajra guru padme siddhi hum* of Guru Rinpoche (Padmasambhava).

In Bhutan ritual objects such as the *dorji* (thunderbolt), *drilbu* (bell), skull cup and hand drum are all derived from tantric teachings, as is much of the imagery on the walls of monasteries and temples. They display the many different aspects of enlightenment – at times gentle, at other times wrathful.

Pilgrims earn merit from the donation of food, money and oil for butter lamps, from sponsoring religious ceremonies or prayer flags or simply attending a festival or religious ritual on a particularly auspicious date.

DOS & DON'TS WHEN VISITING TEMPLES

Himalayan Buddhism has a generally relaxed approach to religious sites, but you should observe a few important rules if you are invited to enter a lhakhang (temple) or goemba (monastery).

➡ It is customary to remove one's shoes and hat upon entering the important rooms of a temple. You will most likely be escorted by a caretaker monk, and you can follow his example in removing your shoes at the appropriate doorway. Leave cameras, umbrellas and hats outside.

➡ Always move in a clockwise direction and do not speak loudly. If there is a ceremony being performed inside, always check that it's OK before entering.

➡ It is customary to leave a small offering of money (Nu 10) on the altar. When you make this offering, the monk accompanying you will pour a small amount of holy water, from a sacred vessel called a *bumpa*, into your hand. You should make the gesture of drinking a sip of this water and then spread the rest on your head.

➡ While male visitors may be permitted to enter the *goenkhang* (protector chapel), always ask before entering and remember that these are off limits to all women. Do not walk behind an altar set before the *goenkhang*.

Buddhist Concepts

Shortly after gaining enlightenment, the Buddha gave his first public teaching in the Deer Park at Sarnath. The Buddha started his teachings by explaining that there was a middle way that steered a course between sensual indulgence and ascetic self-torment. The Middle Way can be followed by taking the Eight Fold Noble Path, underpinned by the Four Noble Truths. The Four Noble Truths set out the laws of cause and effect. Buddhism is thus not based on a revealed prophecy or divine revelation but rather is firmly rooted in human experience. In a modern sense, Buddhist thought stresses nonviolence, compassion, equanimity (evenness of mind) and mindfulness (awareness of the present moment).

Buddha's first sermon at Sarnath's Deer Park is commemorated by the bronze statues of two deer flanking the Wheel of Law that adorns each monastery roof.

Four Noble Truths

The Four Noble Truths underpin Buddhist philosophy and are the basic tenets linking ignorance and enlightenment, suffering and freedom set forth by the Buddha in his first formal discourse in Sarnath.

The first Noble Truth is that life is suffering, the Truth of Suffering. This suffering is the result of an unenlightened life and is maintained by the constant process of rebirth in the different realms of existence. Inherent in the suffering of life is the pain of ageing, sickness and death, the loss of things we are attached to and the failure to achieve the things we desire.

The reason for this dissatisfaction and suffering is contained in the second Noble Truth, which refers to our desire for things to be other than they actually are. This dissatisfaction leads to actions and karmic consequences that merely prolong the cycle of rebirths.

The third Noble Truth was described by the Buddha as True Cessation – the stopping of all delusions, desires and attachment to samsara (the cycle of birth, death and reincarnation). With the cessation of desire and attachment, we are able to break the cycle of rebirth and suffering and reach a state of nirvana, the ultimate goal of Buddhism.

LUSO (FOLK RELIGION)

Vestiges of Bon, the pre-Buddhist belief system prevalent across the Himalaya, can still be found in Bhutan and are closely tied to the rich folk religion known as *luso*. Customs such as hanging prayer flags from a mountain pass have their roots in Bon practice. Every locality, mountain, lake, river or grove of trees in Bhutan has its own sacred geography and the invocation of these local and protective deities is an essential part of daily ritual in Bhutan. In the morning, most Bhutanese burn aromatic herbs (juniper) or incense as an offering to the mountain deities. On certain days, a single flag is raised on every house and particular deities are invoked.

Bhutanese folk beliefs are also concerned with a range of spirits or *nep* (local deities) who act as the custodian of particular valleys, such as Chungdu in Haa, or Radak in Wangdue Phodrang. There are also *tshomen*, mermaid-like goddesses who inhabit the lakes, and *lu* or *naga* – snake-bodied spirits who dwell in lakes, rivers and wells. *Sadak* are lords of the earth and *tsen* are air spirits who can bring illness and death.

Many of the local deities are believed to have originally been Bon deities converted to Buddhism by Guru Rinpoche. Bon traditions and rituals are still practised in parts of Bhutan, especially during the celebration of local festivals. Many Bon traditions have subsequently merged into mainstream Buddhism.

An interesting, if rare, category of female religious figures is the *delog*. *Delog*s are women, occasionally men, who have died and travelled to the other side, where they have watched the judgement of the dead and encountered various Buddhas (eg Chenresig or Guru Rinpoche), before returning to life. The *delog*s stress the importance of leading virtuous lives and refraining from causing harm to living beings.

OTHER RELIGIONS

Not all Bhutanese are Buddhist. Many of the Lhotshampas, the descendants of Nepali migrants, are Hindu – as are the majority of the casual labourers from Assam and Bengal. There are still traces of animistic pre-Buddhist beliefs in the countryside and there's a small number of Christian converts. Bhutan is tolerant of all religions but does not permit proselytisation. The constitution upholds freedom of belief and does not make any religion the official religion of Bhutan. It does, however, recognise the importance of Bhutan's Buddhist heritage to Bhutan's cultural identity.

The Fourth Noble Truth, True Paths, set out by the Buddha refers to the correct means through which an individual is able to overcome attachment and desires in the pursuit of liberation from samsara. These are often described as the Eight-Fold Path: with dedication and practise it may lead to accumulation of merit, then enlightenment and liberation. The eight components of the path to enlightenment: right understanding, right thought, right speech, right action, right livelihood, right effort, right mindfulness and right concentration.

The doctrine of the Four Noble Truths is the foundation on which the whole path to liberation and enlightenment is built. Therefore a deep understanding of these truths, cultivated through reflection and meditation, is an indispensable basis for following the Buddhist path.

Rebirth & the Wheel of Life

In Buddhism, life is seen as a countless cycle of rebirths as living beings 'wander' in samsara. There is not just one world but a myriad of worlds in which beings may be reborn – according to Buddhist doctrine there are six different realms of existence. It is important during one's lifetime to accumulate enough merit to avoid being reborn in one of the three lower realms. Rebirth, or cyclic existence, emerges from fundamental ignorance through a process known as the 12 links of dependent origination. When this fundamental ignorance is reversed, cyclic existence itself can be reversed and nirvana attained, free from suffering and the processes of rebirth. The six realms of existence and the 12 links of dependent origination are what is depicted in the popular Wheel of Life illustration at monastery entrances.

Karma

As beings are reborn in samsara their rebirths in the different realms of existence are determined by their karma, a kind of psychic baggage that follows each being from rebirth to rebirth. In Buddhist doctrine, karma refers to three important components: actions, their effects and their consequences. Buddhist teachings liken karma to a seed (action) that ripens into a fruit (effect).

Mahayana teachings say it is important to dedicate the merit of one's wholesome actions to the benefit of all living beings, ensuring that others also experience the results of one's positive actions. The giving of alms to the needy and to monks, the relinquishing of a son into the monkhood and acts of compassion are all meritorious and have a positive karmic outcome.

The Eight Auspicious Symbols (Tashi Tagye) are associated with gifts made to Sakyamuni and appear as protective motifs across Bhutan. They are the knot of eternity, wheel of law, lotus flower, fair of golden fishes, victory banner, previous umbrella, white conch and vase of treasure.

Buddhism in Modern Bhutan

The modern state of Bhutan reflects an age-old system constructed by the first Zhabdrung. At the pinnacle of the new structure was the Zhabdrung. Below him he created the Je Khenpo (Chief Abbot), who was responsible for all religious matters. His secular counterpart was the *desi,* who was responsible for all political matters. For a background to the origins of Buddhism in Bhutan and the important historical figures that influenced the spread and organisation of Buddhism in Bhutan, see the History chapter (p192).

Organisation of the Religious Community

The *dratshang* (central monk body) refers to the government-supported monks who are under the authority of the Je Khenpo. He is assisted by five *lonpons* (masters), each in charge of religious tradition, liturgy, lexicography or logic. The Je Khenpo moves between Punakha Dzong in winter and Thimphu's Trashi Chhoe Dzong in summer. On these occasions the roads are lined with Bhutanese seeking his blessings along the two-day journey.

Each dzong has a *lam neten,* who is responsible for the monk body in each *dzongkhag.* Each dzong will have a master of grammar, master of liturgy, master of philosophy, an *umdze* (choirmaster) and a *kundun* (disciple master), who carries a rosary of large beads and a whip.

Traditionally, Bhutanese families would, if they were able, send one son to join a monastery. This was viewed as creating merit for the family and household and a blessing for the child. The fourth *desi,* Tenzin Rabgye, introduced a monk tax in the late 16th century. The reason for this tax, which required one child to be sent to become a monk, was to promote the Drukpa Kagyu sect.

Although there is no longer a monk tax, young boys continue to enter the monkhood. Any visitor to Bhutan will see long snaking lines of maroon-robed boy monks walking near the dzongs in Paro and Punakha. Often they come from poor rural families and may or may not have expressed an interest to become a monk. Once in the monastery, their daily lives revolve around learning to read and write.

Typically, the young monks will sit in class with a monk-teacher in the mornings and in the afternoon sit with friends in small groups, reciting their texts. Monastic schools for younger monks are known as *lobdras,* as opposed to more advanced *shedras.* Throughout a monk's education there is an emphasis on memorisation. So each day the monk will memorise a set amount of text and prayers, and will be tested by his teacher. When they are still young the monks do not understand the meaning of the texts. Once they are in the midteens they will be examined individually and they will either proceed to the *shedra* (Buddhist college) or perhaps join the ritual school. The *shedra* develops the young monk's knowledge and understanding of a range of Buddhist texts and teachings, while the ritual college trains the monk in the correct procedures for a wide range of rituals.

While the government currently provides basic needs (accommodation, food and clothing), the monks are permitted to keep money received from lay people for performing rituals. They may be requested to attend the blessing of a new house, the consecration of a new chorten or to conduct prayers for the wellbeing of the household. These events take a great deal of preparation for the sponsor, who will need to ensure that all the necessary ritual items are available. The sponsor will provide food for the monks and often the household will be filled with neighbours attending the ceremony. These events renew and strengthen the bonds between the lay and religious community.

Monks continually take vows, as they progress from novice to fully ordained monk. A few monks join monastic orders after adolescence, but they are not the norm. Monks may renounce or return their vows at any time in order to return to lay life, often to start a family, and have to pay a token fine. These former monks are called *getres* or 'retired' monks and there is no social stigma attached to this choice. Some may even act as lay religious figures, called *gomchens,* and perform prayers and ceremonies for a range of daily activities, especially if there is no monastery nearby.

Bhutan's oldest Buddhist temples are the Kyichu Lhakhang in the Paro valley and Jampey Lhakhang in the Bumthang valley. Both were built by the Tibetan king Songtsen Gampo in the 7th century.

Domestic Rituals

Every house has a *choesum* (altar or shrine room). Each altar usually features statues of Sakyamuni, Guru Rinpoche and the Zhabdrung. In most homes and temples, devotees place seven bowls filled with water on altars. This simple offering is important because it can be given without greed or attachment. If offerings are made to the protective deities, such as Mahakala, then there are only five offering bowls. As all Himalayan Buddhists do, Bhutanese devotees prostrate themselves in front of altars and lamas, first clasping hands above the head, again at throat level and then at the chest. This represents the ultimate desire to attain the body *(ku)*, speech *(sung)* and mind *(thug)* of a Buddha.

Rites are performed for events and crises in life such as birth, marriage, promotion, illness and death. The rituals take place in front of the household shrine, or outside with an altar erected with an image of Buddha (representing the Buddha's body), a religious text (representing the Buddha's speech) and a small stupa or chorten (representing the Buddha's mind). The basic rituals of initiation, purification, consecration and the offering of a *torma* (ritual cake) are included. For example, a water or incense purification ceremony is performed after a birth, while more elaborate rituals involving the offering of the eight auspicious symbols

On special occasions monks prepare *torma* (ritual cake), multicoloured sculptures made from *tsampa* (barley flour) and butter, as symbolic offerings to deities. Each deity is associated with a particular form of *torma*.

PRAYER FLAGS

Prayer flags are ubiquitous in Bhutan, found fluttering on mountain passes, rooftops, and dzong and temple courtyards.

Prayer flags come in five colours – blue, green, red, yellow and white – symbolising the elements of water, wood, fire, earth and iron, respectively. They also stand for the five *dhyani* (meditation Buddhas); the five wisdoms; the five directions; and the five mental attributes or emotions. The prayer for the flag is carved into wooden blocks and then printed on the cloth in repeating patterns.

Goendhar

The smallest prayer flags, *goendhar*s, are those mounted on the rooftops of homes. These white banners have small blue, green, red and yellow ribbons attached to their edges. They invoke the blessings and patronage of Mahakala, the main protective deity of Bhutan. The flags are replaced annually during a ceremony that honours the family's personal local deities.

Lungdhar

The *lungdhar* (wind flag) is erected on hillsides or ridges and can be for good luck, protection from an illness, the achievement of a personal goal, or the acquisition of wisdom. These flags are printed with the Wind Horse (Lungta), which carries a wish-fulfilling jewel on its back.

Manidhar

The *manidhar* is erected on behalf of a deceased person, and features prayers to the Bodhisattva of Compassion, Chenresig. These white prayer flags are generally erected in batches of 108 and are placed at strategic high points from which a river can be seen. In this way, the belief is that the prayers will waft with the wind to the river, and be carried by the river on its long and winding journey.

Lhadhar

The largest flag in the country is the *lhadhar* (god flag). These huge flags can be seen outside dzongs and other important places and represent victory over the forces of evil. There is normally no text on these flags; they are like a giant version of the *goendhar*. The only difference, apart from size, is at the top, where the *lhadhar* is capped by a colourful silk parasol. You must be formally dressed in traditional Bhutanese attire for Bhutanese and in appropriate dress for foreigners to enter any place where a *lhadhar* stands.

Sakyamuni

Jampa

Chenresig

Jampelyang

Chana Dorji

(ie Tashi Tagye) may be offered at a promotion or marriage. Astrology may be used to decide the timing of the rituals. Bhutanese often consult *tsips* (astrologers) before embarking on a journey or a new undertaking. Astrology plays an important role in overcoming misfortune and deciding the most appropriate time to perform rituals to avert misfortune.

Ordinary men and women do not typically engage in meditation or Buddhist philosophical studies, though many will attempt to complete the preliminary practices and will seek the blessings of lamas before embarking on new ventures, for their children and prosperity.

Important Figures of Buddhism in Bhutan

This is a brief guide to the iconography of some of the main figures of Buddhism in Bhutan. This guide is neither exhaustive nor scholarly; rather it seeks to enable you to identify the main figures on altars and in the temple murals encountered during your trip. The Bhutanese names are generally given first with the Sanskrit (where applicable) in parenthesis.

Buddhas

Sakyamuni (Tenpa or Sangye)

Sakyamuni is the historical Buddha (of the present age), whose teachings are the foundation of Bhutanese Buddhism. Typically in Bhutan, as in Tibet, Sakyamuni is represented as seated with his legs crossed on a lotus-flower throne. His tightly curled hair is bluish-black and there is a halo of enlightenment around his head. His right hand touches the ground in the 'witness' *mudra* (hand gesture) and his left rests on his lap, usually with an alms bowl in the left palm. His body is marked with 32 signs of enlightenment, including a top knot, three folds of skin on his neck and elongated ear lobes. He is often seen in the Dusum Sangye; the trinity of past, present and future Buddhas. A bowl of *drilbu* sits in front of all Sakyamuni statues in Bhutan, a recent gift from the fifth king to his people.

Opagme (Amitabha)

The Buddha of Infinite Light is one of the five *dhyani* (meditational or cosmic) Buddhas and resides in the Blissful Pure Land of the West (Sukhavati in Sanskrit or Dewachen in Dzongkha – also the name of several hotels in Bhutan). He is closely associated with Tsepame and Chenresig and represents the transformation of lust into wisdom. He is depicted seated cross-legged on a lotus throne, with his hands resting on his lap in meditative pose and holding an alms bowl. His body is red in colour.

Tsepame (Amitayus)

The Buddha of Longevity, like Opagme, is red and holds his hands in meditation gesture, but he holds a vase containing the nectar of immortality. He is often seen in groups of nine.

Jampa (Maitreya)

The future Buddha is said to be residing as a bodhisattva in Ganden (Tushita), a heavenly realm where bodhisattvas reside awaiting full enlightenment and rebirth, until his time to incarnate on earth as a Buddha. Statues of Jampa, often giant, are the focal point in most older lhakhangs built before the visit of Guru Rinpoche. He is shown seated with his feet on the ground and hands in front of his chest, in the 'turning the wheel' *mudra*.

Sangye Menlha (Medicine Buddha)

A deep-blue Buddha who emanates healing rays of light and teaches the science of *men* (medicine). Buddhism values medicine as a means to alleviate suffering and prolong human life, thereby improving the opportunity to attain enlightenment. The Medicine Buddha sits cross-legged on a lotus throne, with a bowl containing three medicinal fruits. He may be surrounded by a group of eight other medicine Buddhas.

Green Tara

Bodhisattvas

A bodhisattva (hero of enlightenment) seeks enlightenment for the sake of all living beings, out of heartfelt compassion and self-sacrifice, rather than seeking liberation from samsara for her or himself. This altruistic attitude is referred to as *bodhicitta* (mind of enlightenment).

Unlike Buddhas, bodhisattvas are often shown decorated with crowns and princely jewels. Keep a look out in goembas and lhakhangs for the Rigsum Goenpo – a trinity of Chenresig, Jampelyang and Chana Dorji.

Chenresig (Avalokiteshvara)

The white Bodhisattva of Compassion is probably the best-known deity in Bhutanese Buddhism. Chenresig appears in a variety of forms. He is the 'glorious gentle one' – one of the four great bodhisattvas and the special guardian of Bhutanese religion – pictured sitting in a lotus position, with the lower two (of four) arms in a gesture of prayer.

Drolkhar

There is also a powerful 11-headed, 1000-armed version known in Bhutan as Chaktong Chentong or Chuchizey. The head of this version is said to have exploded when confronted with a myriad of problems to solve. One of his heads is that of wrathful Chana Dorji (Vajrapani), and another (the top one) is that of Opagme (Amitabha), who is said to have reassembled Chenresig's body after it exploded. Each of the 1000 arms has an eye in the palm.

Jampelyang (Manjushri)

The 'princely lord of wisdom' – the embodiment of wisdom and knowledge – carries a flaming sword in his right hand to cut through delusion. As the patron of learning and the arts he cradles a scripture in his left arm. He is generally yellow.

Guru Rinpoche

Chana Dorji (Vajrapani)

'Thunderbolt in hand' – this is the god of power and victory. His thunderbolt, representing power, is a fundamental symbol of Tantric faith; it is called a *dorji* in Tibetan and *vajra* in Sanskrit. He is pictured in a wrathful blue form with an angry face and one leg outstretched. You'll often see him flanking the entryway to chapels alongside the red deity Tamdrin.

Milarepa

Drolma (Tara)

There are 21 emanations of Drolma. The two most common representations are as Drolma, a green, female bodhisattva seated on a lotus flower with her right leg extended and said to have been born from a tear of compassion falling from Chenresig's face. The other form, known as Drolkhar (White Tara), is seated in the full lotus posture and with seven eyes, including one in her forehead and two on her palms and the soles of her feet. Drolma is often seen as part of the Tsela Nam Sum longevity trinity, alongside Tsepame (Amitayus) and Namgyelma (Vijaya).

Zhabdrung Ngawang Namgyal

Protective Deities
Nagpo Chenpo (Mahakala)
Mahakala (Great Black One) appears in a variety of forms in Bhutan and is one of the fiercest protective deities, aptly recognised as the guardian deity of Bhutan. He is also known as Yeshe Goenpo, and is a tantric Buddhist form of the Hindu god Shiva. Most Bhutanese monasteries and temples have a shrine dedicated to him and he is invoked to help remove obstacles to a new undertaking, or in times of danger. His worship in Bhutan was popularised by the Zhabdrung Ngawang Namgyal, who adopted the protector as his personal deity. According to legend, Mahakala appeared to the Zhabdrung in his raven form (Gompo Jarodanden) and advised him to go to Bhutan. The raven-headed Mahakala is the inspiration for the Raven Crown worn by the Bhutanese monarchs.

Mahakala is black with reddish hair that rises upwards. He has three eyes, wears a cloak of elephant skin, and is surrounded by fire and smoke. He wears various bone ornaments and a skull garland. He carries a curved knife in his right hand and a skull cup in his left. Depending on the form depicted he may have two, four, six or more arms.

Monks are celibate and must abstain from smoking and drinking alcohol, but they are not required to be vegetarian and may eat in the evening, unlike their counterparts in Southeast Asia.

Palden Lhamo (Mahakali)
The Glorious Goddess is a fierce protective deity and is closely associated with Yeshe Gompo (Mahakala). Palden Lhamo is invoked in times of difficulty and special pujas are performed to avert misfortune, like natural disasters and wars. She has a ferocious appearance and is quite distinctive. Her body is dark blue, while the palms of her hands and the soles of her feet are red. She holds the moon in her hair, the sun in her belly and a corpse in her mouth, and wears a crown of five skulls and earrings made of snakes. She carries a skull cup in her left hand and brandishes a club in her right. She rides on a wild ass and her saddle cloth is a flayed human skin.

Historical Figures
Guru Rinpoche (Padmasambhava)
'The Lotus Born' was an Indian Buddhist adept, saint and tantric magician who, according to local tradition, helped found Buddhism in Bhutan in the 8th century. Popularly known as Guru Rinpoche (Precious Teacher), but also known as Pema Jungne or Padmasambhava (Lotus Born) in Sanskrit, he was born in Oddiyana (Ugyen in Dzongkha) in the modern-day Swat valley. He is viewed as nothing less than the Second Buddha by the Nyingma lineage. Dozens of caves and rock markings across Bhutan claim a sacred connection with the guru.

He is depicted seated in a half-lotus position on a lotus throne. He wears a blue inner robe with a golden robe and an outer red cloak. His hat is known as the 'lotus cap' and is adorned with a crescent moon, the sun and a small flamelike protuberance that signifies the union of lunar and solar forces. The hat is surmounted by a *dorji* (thunderbolt) and also an eagle's feather, which represents the Guru's soaring mind. He has long flowing hair, bug eyes and a curly moustache. In his extended right hand he holds a *dorji* and in his left hand, resting on his lap, is a skull cup filled with nectar. A staff known as a *katvanga* topped with a freshly severed head, a decaying head and a skull rests in the crook of his left arm. A *phurba* (ritual dagger for subduing demons) is tucked into his belt.

Guru Rinpoche commonly appears in eight manifestations known as the Guru Tshengye, of which the most eye-catching is the tiger-borne Dorji Drolo. He is often flanked by his two consorts Yeshe Tshogyel and Mandarava and is joined by his 25 main disciples. He is often depicted in his Copper Mountain paradise known as Zangto Pelri.

PROTECTIVE DEITIES

Even the smallest lhakhang has a *goenkhang* (protector chapel) chock-full of terrifying wrathful deities, often engulfed in flames, dripping blood and holding an array of fearsome weapons. These can be specific local guardian deities, more general *yidam* (tutelary deities) or *dharmapala* (protectors of Buddhism), or symbols of malevolent beings that were subdued and converted by tantric forces. On an entirely other level they can also represent powerful attributes of the mind or ego, man's inner psychological demons if you will, with their many arms and weapons symbolising different powers. Often you'll see a protector deity in *yab-yum* pose of sexual union with a female consort, in a symbolic representation of compassion and wisdom.

Most of Bhutan's valleys have their own local protective deity. Statues of Thimphu's protector, Gyenyen Jagpa Melen, appear in Dechenphu Lhakhang near Dechencheoling and in Neykhang Lhakhang next to the dzong. He is also seen as a national protective deity, with Bhutanese visiting his temple to seek his blessings before a new venture or if leaving the country for any length of time. Among the other regional protective deities are Jichu Drakye in Paro, Chhundu in Haa, Talo Gyalpo Pehar in Punakha, Kaytshugpa in Wangdue Phodrang and, in Bumthang, Keybu Lungtsan and Jowo Ludud Drakpa Gyeltshen. These deities are gods who have not left the world and therefore have not gained enlightenment.

Milarepa

A great Tibetan magician (1040–1123) and poet of the Kagyu lineage, the 'Cotton Clad' magician-poet is believed to have attained the supreme enlightenment of Buddhahood in the course of one life. He travelled throughout the Himalayan borderlands and is said to have meditated at Taktshang in Bhutan, where he composed a song. Most images of Milarepa picture him smiling and holding his hand to his ear as he sings. He is normally depicted in green due to his extended diet of nettle soup.

Some monks may be trained as painters or sculptors, or as tailors and embroiderers for the various items required for the monastery.

Drukpa Kunley

The wandering ascetic, Drukpa Kunley (1455–1529), is one of the main figures of the Druk Kagyu. His ribald songs and poems were unconventional and have earned him the affection of the Bhutanese. In Bhutan he is often depicted with a bow-and-arrow case and accompanied by a small hunting dog. In Chimi Lhakhang, Drukpa Kunley is depicted dressed similarly to the great Indian sages known as the Mahasiddhis, with a bare torso and a loincloth. Elsewhere he is shown wearing normal lay dress with boots.

Pema Lingpa

The blacksmith and *terton* (treasure finder) Pema Lingpa (1450–1521) was born in Tang valley, Bumthang. The best-known statue of Pema Lingpa was made by Pema Lingpa himself and is kept at Kunzangdrak Goemba, Bumthang. Pema Lingpa holds a *bumpa* (vase symbolising long life) in his hands and wears a hat similar to that worn by Guru Rinpoche, with the notable addition of two *dorjis* crossed at the front of it.

Zhabdrung Ngawang Namgyal

The Zhabdrung Ngawang Namgyal (1594–1651) is regarded as the founder of Bhutan, where he arrived from Tibet in 1616. The Zhabdrung has a distinctive white, pointed beard and wears monastic robes, and is seated in the lotus posture. In his left hand he holds a *bumpa* and his right hand is in the 'witness' *mudra*. Over his right shoulder is a meditation belt. The Zhabdrung wears a distinctive ceremonial hat of the Druk Kagyu order.

Traditional Arts

Bhutan's vibrant art, dance, drama, music and even its characteristic architecture has its roots in Buddhism. Almost all representation in art, music and dance is a dramatisation of the Buddha's teachings about the path to liberation and the constant struggle to overcome the delusions that lead to the cycle of rebirth in samsara.

Bhutan's Agency for Promotion of Indigenous Arts has introduced the Bhutan SEAL (www.apic.org. bt/our-projects/ seal-of-origin) to establish a quality and authenticity benchmark for handicraft products.

The Artistic Tradition in Bhutan

The development of Buddhist arts and crafts in Bhutan can be traced to the 15th-century *terton* (discoverer of sacred texts) Pema Lingpa, who was an accomplished painter, metalworker, sculptor and architect. The country's artistic tradition received a further boost when, in 1680, the fourth *desi* (secular ruler), Gyalse Tenzin Rabgye (r 1680–94), opened the School of Bhutanese Arts & Crafts, which has evolved into the National Institute for Zorig Chusum.

Traditional Bhutanese artistry is maintained through the support of all levels of society. The royal family, nobility and clergy continue to provide important patronage. Meanwhile, the common people support the arts because they depend on artisans to provide the wide variety of wooden and metal objects indispensable to typical Bhutanese households and painting, both inside and outside homes.

Traditional art has two important characteristics: it is religious and anonymous. The Bhutanese consider commissioning paintings and statues as pious acts, which gain merit for the *jinda* (patron). The name of the *jinda* is sometimes written on the work so that their pious act may be remembered. However, the artist's name is rarely ever mentioned, although there are some artists whose names do become well known due to the exceptional quality of their work.

There are strict iconographical conventions in Bhutanese art and the Bhutanese artists observe them scrupulously. However, artists do express their own personality in minor details (for example, the shading of clouds or background scenes).

The Thirteen Arts

The Thirteen Arts are the 13 traditional arts and crafts (Zorig Chusum) believed to have been categorised during the reign of the fourth *desi*. Zorig Chusum refers to those physical activities that assist, teach or uplift others.

Shingzo (Carpentry)

Skilled carpenters are involved in a range of activities ranging from building dzongs and temples, houses and palaces, to making tools and other practical instruments used in the everyday life of the Bhutanese people.

Dozo (Masonry)

This covers the building of chortens, dzongs and temples as well as making the heavy millstones and stone pestles.

Traditional Bhutanese woodcarving

Parzo (Carving)

The Bhutanese are highly skilled at wood, stone and slate carving. Examples of their work are evident throughout Bhutan, from the slate carvings depicting the Buddha and other religious figures inserted in stupas, to the wooden printing blocks used for printing sacred texts.

Lhazo (Painting)

Lhazo encompasses drawing and painting in Bhutan. It includes the painting of *thangkas* (religious pictures), murals and frescoes in temples and dzongs, as well as the colourful images on the exterior walls of Bhutanese homes. Drawing and painting are governed by strict geometric rules of proportion and iconography.

Jinzo (Sculpture)

One of the arts in which the Bhutanese excel is the creation of delicate clay sculptures, occasionally set in amazing landscapes. These sculptures, ranging from small- to large-scale statues, are generally created around a hollow frame with the mud or clay built up to form the image.

As well as statues, *jinzo* includes the production of a range of ritual items, notably the moulded *torma* (offerings) and masks worn during tsechu, and the more prosaic activity of preparing mud walls on new buildings.

Lugzo (Casting)

Casting, usually in bronze, refers to the production of musical instruments, statues, tools and kitchen utensils, as well as slip casting for pottery and jewellery.

Garzo (Blacksmithing)

Generally, these craftsmen produce axes, plough blades, chains, knives and swords and other practical items.

> Paintings and sculptures are usually executed by monks or laymen working in specialist workshops. The disciples of a master, as part of their training, will do all the preliminary work, while the fine work is executed by the master himself.

Trozo (Gold- & Silversmithing)

This includes all ornaments made from gold, silver or copper. They are often cut out, beaten, drawn or engraved.

Tshazo (Bamboo Work)

There is a wide variety of these products, as seen in the markets across the country. They include *bangchung* (covered bowls with intricate designs, used to carry food), long *palang* (used to store beer or other liquor), the *tshesip* (box), *belo* (small hat worn for sun protection), *redi* (mat), *luchu* (used for storing grain), *balep* (bamboo thatch) and, of course, the bow and arrow.

Thagzo (Weaving)

Thagzo covers the whole process: from the preparation of the yarn, dyeing and the numerous designs. This is the largest craft industry in terms of the variety and number of craftspeople involved throughout Bhutan.

Tshemzo (Embroidery)

There are two special categories within this craft. The first are those items which are sewn and embroidered (ranging from clothing to intricate and rare embroidered *thangkas*). The second refers to appliqué and patchwork items made from stitching cloth together. This includes the large *thondrols* displayed during tsechu festivals, as well as hats and the elaborate boots worn with the *gho* (traditional dress for men) on official occasions.

Shagzo (Woodturning)

Skilled woodturners produce a range of delicate wooden bowls, turned with expertise from special parts of a tree or roots. The large wooden *dapa* (serving dishes), wooden plates, buckets, ladles and *phop* (small cups), as well as the various small hand drums beaten during religious ceremonies, are among the products of this craft.

Dezo (Papermaking)

The art of making paper from the bark of daphne plant, and more recently bamboo and rice stalks, is under threat from the loss of skilled craftsmen. The word *de* refers to the daphne plant.

Painting

Aside from spectacular architecture, the most visible manifestation of Bhutanese art is painting. There are three forms of traditional painting: *thangkas,* wall paintings and statues. A painting is invariably religious in nature, depicting a deity, a religious story, a meditational object or an array of auspicious symbols (such as the Tashi Tagye – Eight Auspicious Symbols – or Four Friends). Paintings were traditionally done not for sale, but for specific purposes – though this is slowly changing.

Paintings, in particular the portrayal of human figures, are subject to strict rules of iconography. The proportions and features must be precise, and there is no latitude for artistic licence in these works. The initial layout is constructed with a series of geometrical patterns, using straight lines to lay out the proportions of the figure, which are defined in religious documents called *zuri pata*. In other cases the initial sketch is made with a stencil of the basic outline, which is transferred to the canvas by patting the stencil with a bag filled with chalk dust. Traditionally, paints were made from earth, minerals and vegetables, though now chemical colours are also used. The material is first reduced into powder and then mixed with water, glue and chalk. The brushes are handmade from twigs and animal hair.

Bhutan's wonderful wooden bowls are turned from lumpy 'burls' that usually grow around an infection or insect attack on a tree. Only the most intricately patterned burlwood goes into making the magnificent and highly valued *woogzo* bowls, so named for their owl-feather patterns.

If you are interested in creating your own Bhutanese art, look out for *Tibetan Thangka Painting: Methods and Materials* by David P Jackson and Janice A Jackson.

THE FOUR FRIENDS

One of Bhutan's favourite paintings is based on the popular fable of the Four Friends. In Dzongkha the name of the story is *Thuenpa Puen Shi* (Cooperation, Relation, Four) and it illustrates the concept of teamwork. You will see paintings illustrating this story on temples, homes and shops throughout the country.

The story tells how the elephant, monkey, peacock and rabbit combined forces to obtain a continual supply of fruit. The peacock found a seed and planted it, the rabbit watered it, the monkey fertilised it and the elephant guarded it. When the fruit was ripe the tree was so high that they could not reach the top. The four animals made a tower by climbing on one another's back, and plucked the fruit from the high branches.

Thangkas are painted on canvas that is stretched and lashed to a wooden frame. When the painting is completed it is removed from the frame and given a border of colourful brocade, with wooden sticks at the top and bottom used for hanging. Although some *thangkas* are hung permanently, most are rolled up and stored until they are exhibited at special occasions. This applies particularly to the huge appliqué *thondrols* that are displayed briefly in the early morning during a tsechu. The same iconographical rules apply to the images on a massive *thondrol*, which demonstrates the skills of the Bhutanese artisans.

The interior walls of dzongs and lhakhangs are usually covered with paintings. In Bhutan most wall murals are painted on a thin layer of cloth applied to the wall using a special paste. Nowadays old paintings are treasured because of their historic and artistic value; however, until quite recently old wall paintings were often repainted or even painted over during restoration work.

Most statues are finely painted to sharply define the facial features, which are individualised for each figure. Many religious statues in lhakhangs, especially the larger statues, are made from unfired clay. In addition to the face, the entire surface of these large figures is painted, often in a gold colour, giving them a bronze aspect. Examples of these statues can be seen in Punakha dzong. On bronze statues, some of which are quite small, only the face is painted.

Statues only gain their sanctity when sacred texts and juniper incense are secreted inside inside the statue, they are blessed and their eyes are painted open. You'll sometimes see unfinished statues with bandages around their unpainted eyes.

Textiles

Weaving, more than the other Zorig Chusum, is the most distinctive and sophisticated of Bhutanese arts and crafts. The richness of this art form can be seen at the permanent exhibition in the National Textile Museum in Thimphu. Everyday articles such as clothing, wrappers for goods and cushion covers are stitched from cloth woven at home. Until the mid-20th century, certain taxes were paid in cloth and collected at the regional dzong. The authorities distributed the cloth as 'payment' to monastic and civil officials and to monasteries. Until quite recently, it was common to present cloth as a gift to mark special occasions or promotions. Bhutanese women still have trunks filled with fine fabrics that may be sold when money is required.

Unlike *thangka* painting, which has very precise religious rules, weaving provides the weaver with an opportunity to express herself. Designs, colours, sizes and even the finish have always reflected the materials available and the changes in technology and fashion. Bhutan's weavers

Most weaving in Bhutan is done on a simple back-strap loom, similar to looms found throughout Southeast Asia and Tibet. The loom is easily transported and is ideal for setting up in a warm kitchen, on the porch of a house or beside a tent.

The royal Wangchuck dynasty's ancestral home is in the pre-eminent weaving district of Lhuentse, and perhaps this is why royal patronage has been so influential in the development of textile art, with dozens of weavers employed by all the royal households.

TEMPTING TEXTILE TRAVELS

Watching the mesmerising weaving while appreciating the fine skills and sheer hard work is just part of the fun of chasing traditional textiles. With your guide you can start conversing with the weavers, perhaps picking up a few century-old tricks of the trade. Some friendly bartering is sure to follow. Handwoven fabric is the most traditional and useful item you can buy in Bhutan. The quality is almost always good, but the price will vary depending on the intricacy of the design and whether any expensive imported silk was used in the weaving. Handwoven fabric is sold in 'loom lengths' that are 30cm to 45cm wide and 2.5m to 3m long. Bhutanese sew three of these lengths together to make the traditional dress of *gho* and *kira*.

The traditional centres of sophisticated weaving are in eastern Bhutan, especially Dungkhar and Khoma in Lhuentse, Khaling and Radi in Trashigang, and Duksum in Trashi Yangste. Zungney village in Bumthang is the centre for the weaving of wool into strips called *yathra*. For those interested in textiles, visits to these places, in addition to Thimphu's National Textile Museum, will provide an invaluable insight into Bhutan's cultural identity.

specialise in working additional decorative warps and wefts into the 'ground' fabric. The most elaborate weavings are usually for the *kira* (woman's traditional dress) and *gho* and these garments may take up to a year to weave in silk.

Legend states that weaving was introduced to Bhutan by the wife of Songtsen Gampo. Each region has its own weaving traditions and designs, with that of Lhuentse, the ancestral home of the royal family, being the most renowned. The weavers in Lhuentse specialise in decorating *kira* and other textiles with intricate patterns that resemble embroidery. Other parts of eastern Bhutan are famous for their distinctive striped garments woven from raw silk. Bumthang weavers produce another popular fabric – *yathra,* hand-woven strips of woollen cloth, stitched into blankets, jackets, cushion covers and even car seats.

Though *yathra* was traditionally produced on back-strap looms, pedal looms were introduced from Tibet in the mid-20th century, while Indian spinning wheels are faster than the drop spindle. Today, all these technologies can be seen being used by weavers in their homes.

More recently, with assistance from the government, new items such as bags, decorations and even bed and table linen have been developed both for the local and international markets.

MUSIC

For a blend of traditional and modern music, look out for the beautiful recording of chants by Lama Gyurme and Jean-Philippe Rykiel, *The Lama's Chants – Songs of Awakening* (Sony, 1994) and *Rain of Blessings* (Real World Records, 2000).

Literature

The development of *jo yig,* the cursive Bhutanese script, as distinct from a Tibetan script, is credited to a monk by the name of Lotsawa Denma Tsemang. However, the Bhutanese script is based on the Tibetan script introduced by Tonmi Sambhota during the reign of the Tibetan king, Songtsen Gampo. For the most part, the literary culture of Bhutan has been dominated by Buddhism; first as a means of translating Buddhist scriptures from Sanskrit, and second as local scholars began to emerge, as a means of developing Himalayan Buddhist thought.

Wood-block printing has been used for centuries and is still the most common form of printing in the monasteries. Blocks are carved in mirror image, then the printers working in pairs place strips of handmade paper over the inked blocks and a roller passes over the paper. The printed strip is then set aside to dry. The printed books are placed between two boards and wrapped in cloth. There is an excellent exhibition in the National Library, Thimphu, showing the printing process as well as examples of rare texts.

Music

There are four main traditional instruments in Bhutan, beyond the ritual instruments used in religious ceremonies: the ornate *drangyen* or Bhutanese lute; the *pchewang,* with only two strings; *lyem* (bamboo flute); and the *yangchen* (zither) made from hollow wood, with 72 strings which are struck lightly with two thin bamboo sticks.

There are various performers who specialise in folk or religious songs, like Am Thinlay. Jigme Drukpa *(Folk Songs from Bhutan)* performs a wide selection of the two main styles of folk singing: *zhungdra,* which developed in Bhutan in the 17th century, and *boedra,* influenced by Tibetan folk music.

There is a series of four CDs from the Monasteries of Bhutan, with the misleading title *Tibetan Buddhist Rites* (John Levy, Lyrichord). This collection includes a wide range of sacred and folk music, including a hauntingly beautiful recording of a *manip* (an itinerant ascetic) reciting a song recollecting the Zhabdrung Ngawang Namgyal's arrival in Bhutan.

Music of Bhutan Research Centre (www.musicofbhutan.org) promotes traditional music and has recorded many of Bhutan's living repositories of rare and regional music. It sells CDs and books online.

Theatre & Dance

The main forms of dance are the spectacular and theatrical masked dances called *cham,* performed at the tsechus (see p31) and other religious festivals held throughout Bhutan.

The main dances performed at tsechus are described here.

Pacham (Dance of the Heroes)

An energetic dance based on a vision by Pema Linga and is thought to lead believers directly to the presence of Guru Rinpoche. The dancers wear yellow skirts and golden crowns but do not wear masks. They cary a *dri-lbu* (small bell) and a *damaru* (small drum)

Shawa Shachi (Dance of the Stag & Hunter)

Based on the story of Milarepa's conversion of the hunter Gonpo Dorji to Buddhism, the dance is split into two parts. The first part is comic, with the hunter preparing to set out on a hunting expedition and his servants joking very irreverently with him. The second part is more serious. The hunter and his dog are in pursuit of a deer when the deer seeks shelter with the yogi Milarepa, identifiable by his white cotton robe, who sings a song that converts all three to Buddhism. The conversion is symbolised by a rope that both the dog and hunter must jump over.

Dranyeo Cham (Dance with the Drangyen)

This dance celebrates the diffusion of the Drukpa lineage in Bhutan by the Zhabdrung Ngawang Namgyal. The dancers carry swords and wear a circular headdress, felt boots and heavy woollen clothes. One dancer carries a *drangyen,* a stringed instrument similar to a lute.

Folk dances are often performed during breaks in the main tsechu performances. The dancers form a circle or a line and move in an intricate series of steps accompanied by graceful arm movements. One person may lead the singing, with the other dancers picking up the song or answering with a refrain.

Sha Na Cham (Black Hat Dance)

This dance, on one level, commemorates the killing of the anti-Buddhist Tibetan king Langdarma in 842 by the Buddhist monk Pelkyi Dorji. It also represents the transformation of the dancers into powerful tantric yogis, who take possession of the dancing area and drive out all evil spirits as they stamp the ground. The dancers wear brocade dresses, wide-brimmed black hats and black aprons with an image representing protective deities.

Pholay Molay (Dance of the Noblemen & Ladies)

This is less a dance than a crude play about the two princesses left with an old couple by two princes who leave for war. The two princesses and an old woman are corrupted by some *atsaras* (clowns). On their return, the princes are furious and punish the women by cutting off their noses. Eventually, everybody is reconciled and the princes marry the princesses.

Drametsi Nga Cham (Dance of the Drametsi Drummers)

Based on a vision by Kunga Gyeltshen, the son of Pema Lingpa, this dance depicts 100 peaceful and wrathful deities. The dancers wear animal masks and knee-length yellow skirts, and carry a large hand drum in their left hand and a drumstick in their right.

Dungtam (Dance of the Wrathful Deities)

In this dance, the deities are the entourage of one of the eight manifestations of Guru Rinpoche, Dorji Drolo. Dorji Drolo and his entourage are armed with *phurba* (special daggers) that execute and thereby redeem an evil spirit (represented by a small mannequin). This represents Buddhist teachings on the liberation of consciousness from the body. The dancers' costumes are beautiful brocade dresses, boots and terrifying masks.

Raksha Mangcham (Dance of the Rakshas & the Judgement of the Dead)

This is one of the highlights of the tsechu. It represents a spiritual drama as two newly deceased men are brought before the Lord of the Underworld, represented by a large mannequin surrounded by an entourage of *rakshas* (a figure or spirit of the underworld). The first to be judged is a sinner, dressed in black. After hearing from Black Demon and White God, the prosecution and defence, his sins outweigh his good actions and he is dragged to the hell realms. The second figure is dressed in white; again the Lord of the Underworld hears about his good and bad actions, and he is found to be virtuous. After a brief attempt by Black Demon to grab the virtuous man, he is led to the pure lands.

Guru Tshengay (The Eight Manifestations of Guru Rinpoche)

The eight manifestations are different forms of Guru Rinpoche, who is accompanied by his two consorts, Yeshe Tshogyel (on his right) and Mandarava (on his left). This is both a dance and a drama and starts with Dorji Drolo, wearing a terrifying red mask, entering the dance area, followed by a long procession with the eight manifestations.

Chhoeshey (Religious Song)

This commemorates the opening of the eastern gate to the pilgrimage site at Tsari in Tibet by Tsangpa Gyarey, the founder of the Drukpa Kagyu.

In Thimphu, the Royal Academy for the Performing Arts (RAPA) trains young Bhutanese dancers and musicians in religious and folk dances. The quality of the dancing is exceptional and the program they offer is breathtaking in its colour and vitality.

Architecture

Bhutanese architecture is one of the most striking features of the country. Massive dzongs, remote goembas and lhakhangs, as well as the traditional houses all subscribe to a characteristic Bhutanese style. The absence of written plans, however, means there are many variations on the theme, with designs dictated by local topography and available building materials.

Dzongs

Bhutan's dzongs are perhaps the most visibly striking architectural aspect of the kingdom. They are outstanding examples of grand design and construction. These huge white citadels dominate the major towns and serve as the administrative headquarters of all 20 *dzongkhags* (districts) and the focus of secular and religious authority in each.

As well as the large, active district dzongs, there are a few dzongs that have been destroyed or abandoned, or are now used for other purposes, such as Dobji Dzong, south of Chhuzom. And not all dzongs are ancient monuments; for example, a new dzong was inaugurated in Chhukha (near Phuentsholing) in 2012.

Many dzongs had a *ta dzong* (watchtower), which was either part of the building, as in Jakar Dzong, or a separate structure, as in Paro and Trongsa Dzongs. This structure was also used as an ammunition store and dungeon. Many dzongs were accessed by cantilever bridges as an additional protective measure. Most dzongs have inward-sloping walls, an architectural feature known as battered walls, which can fool the eye and make the building look imposing and larger than its actual dimensions.

Bhutan's dzongs were built of stone or pounded mud, and a considerable amount of timber, including massive beams and wooden shingle roofs. This, combined with the large number of butter lamps used in temples, has caused fires in almost all dzongs. All important dzongs have been (or are being) rebuilt using traditional construction methods, though in many places corrugated-iron roofs have replaced wooden shingles.

Bhutanese proclaim proudly that no nails are used to construct dzongs. Furthermore, dzong architects don't prepare any plans or drawings. They rely only on a mental concept of what is to be built, and this was how Thimphu's Trashi Chhoe Dzong was reconstructed in 1966.

> Because dzongs were usually placed on ridges, a tunnel was often constructed to the nearest water supply so that those in the dzong could survive a long siege.

DEFENDING THE DZONG

During the time of Zhabdrung Ngawang Namgyal (1594–1651), the dzongs served their primary function – as fortresses – well, and each was the stronghold of a *penlop* (governor). Many of the feuds and battles for control during the 17th to 20th centuries were waged by *penlops* whose troops attacked neighbouring dzongs. The key to success in these battles was to capture the dzong of the opposing *penlop*, thereby gaining control of that district. Dzongs often feature defensive windows with firing positions and usually have only one massive door, which leads into a small passage that makes two right-angle turns before it enters the main courtyard. This is a design feature to obstruct invaders from storming the dzong.

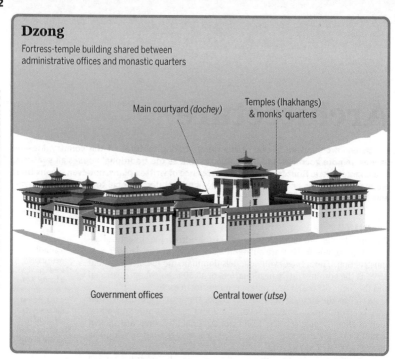

Dzong

Fortress-temple building shared between administrative offices and monastic quarters

Main courtyard *(dochey)*

Temples (lhakhangs) & monks' quarters

Government offices

Central tower *(utse)*

Each dzong has unique details, but most follow the same general design principles. Most dzongs are divided into two wings: one containing temples and monks' quarters and one for government offices. The monastic wing of many dzongs actually serves as a monastery, with the resident monk body called a *rabdey*. In early days, most dzongs had a *rabdey,* but today only the dzongs of Thimphu, Chhukha, Punakha, Paro, Mongar, Trongsa, Jakar, Gasa and Trashigang serve as monasteries. The *dratshang* (central monk body) maintains monastic schools in the dzongs of Punakha, Trongsa and Paro. Punakha Dzong is the seat of the Chief Abbot, His Holiness the Je Khenpo.

The main courtyard of the dzong is the *dochey,* which is paved with large flagstones. Along the outer walls of the dzong are several storeys of rooms and galleries overlooking the paved courtyard; these rooms are the monks' quarters and classrooms. Because the monastic wing of the dzong is physically separate from the secular wing, many dzongs have two *docheys,* the second being surrounded by administrative offices.

The central structure of the dzong is a towerlike building called the *utse.* In most dzongs, the *utse* has a series of lhakhangs, one on each floor. On the ground floor of the *utse* is the primary lhakhang.

Don't-Miss Dzongs
....

Punakha Dzong (Punakha)
....

Paro Dzong (Paro)
....

Trongsa Dzong (Trongsa)
....

Trashi Chhoe Dzong (Thimphu)

Goembas & Lhakhangs

In Dzongkha, a monastery is called a goemba, and the word is pronounced quite differently from the corresponding Tibetan word, *gompa*. A primary reason for selecting the location of a monastery is to have a remote location where the monks can find peace and solitude. This is particularly evident in Bhutan where goembas are built atop rocky crags or on remote hillsides.

All Bhutanese goembas are different, but they all possess certain common features. They are self-contained communities, with a central lhakhang and separate quarters for sleeping. The lhakhang is usually at the centre of a *dochey,* similar to that of the dzongs, which is used as a dance arena during festivals. The term lhakhang can be a bit confusing because it can refer to both the building itself and to the primary chapel inside the building. Some goembas have several lhakhangs within the central building.

On all religious buildings in Bhutan, and on dzongs too, a painted red band called a *khemar* runs just below the roof. One or more circular brass plates or mirrors representing the *nima* (sun) are often placed on the *khemar.*

The following are often depicted at the entrance to goembas:

➡ The Wheel of Life, which is held and turned by Yama, Lord of Death; it is a representation of the cycle of samsara, separating loved ones and leading to rebirth. The inner circle depicts a cockerel (representing desire or attachment) biting a pig (ignorance or delusion) biting a snake (hatred or anger). Surrounding this is a band of figures ascending and descending according to their karma. Outside this are six segments, each depicting the six realms of samsara or rebirth. And outside this are the 12 segments that depict the 12 links of dependant origination representing the processes by which we all live, die and are reborn.

➡ The Six Symbols of Longevity (Tshering Samdrup) are of Chinese origin and include an old man, peach tree, conch-shell-shaped rock, river, cranes (usually a pair) and a deer.

➡ The geometric poem set in a grid of squares (looking somewhat like a quilt) that is dedicated to the Zhabdrung.

One way that lhakhangs in Bhutan differ from those in Tibet is that they feature a pair of elephant tusks alongside the altar to symbolise good. Buddhists revere the elephant because when the Buddha was born, his mother had a vision of a white elephant.

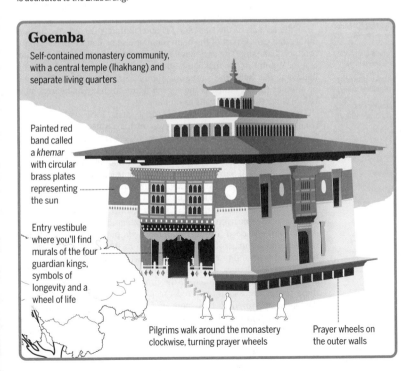

Goemba

Self-contained monastery community, with a central temple (lhakhang) and separate living quarters

Painted red band called a *khemar* with circular brass plates representing the sun

Entry vestibule where you'll find murals of the four guardian kings, symbols of longevity and a wheel of life

Pilgrims walk around the monastery clockwise, turning prayer wheels

Prayer wheels on the outer walls

GUARDIANS OF THE FOUR DIRECTIONS

Paintings or statues of the Guardians (or Kings) of the Four Directions appear on the *gorikha* (verandah) to guard the entrance to most lhakhangs. The guardians have an origin in ancient Mongolian tradition, and each one holds a different object. They are warriors who guard the world against demons and earthly threats.

Chenmizang The red king of the west; holds a chorten and a snake, and is the lord of the *nagas* (serpents).

Yulkhorsung The white king of the east; plays the lute and is the lord of celestial musicians.

Namthose The gold king of the north; holds a mongoose and a banner of victory. He is a god of wealth and prosperity.

Phagchepo The blue king of the south; holds a sword in his right hand.

A typical lhakhang has a cupola and a gilded bell-shaped ornament, called a *serto,* on top of the yellow-painted roof. Most have a paved *kora* path around the circumference of the building. On the outside wall are racks of prayer wheels, which monks and devotees spin as they circumambulate the building.

The entrance to the lhakhang is through the *gorikha* (porch), which is covered with murals, usually depicting the Guardians of the Four Directions or the Wheel of Life. Entry is via a large painted wooden door that is often protected by a heavy cloth or yak-hair curtain. The door opens to a *tshokhang* (assembly hall), also called a *dukhang* or *kunre*. The hall is usually so large that it has rows of pillars to hold up the roof, and the walls are storyboards of Buddhist paintings.

At the far end of the *tshokhang* is an elaborately decorated *choesum* (altar) that can be part of the main room or else be housed in a separate room or lhakhang. The two-tiered *choesum,* with its large gilded statue, is a focal point of the lhakhang, and depending on when and why the lhakhang was built, the statue may be of Sakyamuni, Guru Rinpoche or another figure. Jampa is the central figure in many lhakhangs built before Guru Rinpoche's visits to Bhutan.

On a monastery or chapel altar, you'd see sacred rocks with self-arisen (Rangjung) hand or footprints; a ewer of holy water with a peacock feather in it; a mandala-shaped offering of seeds; a pair of dice used to divine the future; dried seeds; plus elephant tusks and seven bowls of water, referring to the seven first footsteps of Buddha or the first seven ordained monks at Samye in Tibet. On the altar you will also see a delicately carved and usually garishly coloured *torma* (ritual ornamental cake), made from sugar, butter and flour.

The halls often have cymbals, *dungkhar* (conch shell), *jaling* (oboes), and long telescopic trumpets known as *dungchen.* The altar often has the *drilbu* (bell) and *dorji* (thunderbolt), tantric implements that symbolise wisdom and compassion, respectively. Also in the halls are libraries of traditional texts and prayer books, usually wrapped in cloth.

In most lhakhangs, often on the upper floor, is a chapel called a *goenkhang,* which is devoted to the protective deities. The statues in these rooms are usually covered except when rituals are performed. Weapons are stored in this room and may include old muskets, armour, and round shields made from rhinoceros hide. Teams of archers sometimes sleep in a *goenkhang* before a major match, but women are never allowed to enter and the monks are often reluctant to allow entry to visitors.

Temple Highlights

Taktshang Goemba
(Paro)

Kyichu Lhakhang
(Paro)

Chimi Lhakhang
(Punakha)

Kurjey Lhakhang
(Chokhor Valley)

Jampey Lhakhang
(Chokhor Valley)

Houses

If, for the moment, we ignore the concrete blocks that are steadily taking over the major towns, the Bhutanese build distinctive housing depending on the region, particularly the elevation. Thatched bamboo houses predominate in the lower altitudes in the south of the country, whereas at very high altitudes most homes are simple stone structures or even yak-hair tents. In central and eastern Bhutan houses are often made of stone, whereas in the west the walls are usually made of compacted earth, an extremely strong and durable structure.

A typical western Bhutanese house is two storeys high with a large, airy attic used for storage. In rural areas the ground floor is always used as a barn and the upper floor as the living quarters. In most houses, one elaborately decorated room called a *choesum* serves as a chapel.

On the lower floor, an opening for a door, and perhaps some windows, is left in the earth wall that forms the front of the house, which traditionally faces south. The upper floor is supported by wooden beams that fit into holes in the wall. Central columns support the beams, because it is difficult to find a single piece of timber to span the entire width of the house. The earthen walls for the upper floor form only the rear wall and back half of the two side exterior walls. The front portion of the living area is always built of timber, which is sometimes elaborately decorated, with large divided windows facing south. The wooden portion of the house extends out over the front and side earthen walls, giving a top-heavy appearance.

In older houses the windows are sliding wooden panels, not glass. Above all, windows in Bhutan comprise a cut-out of a curved trefoil motif, called a *horzhing*. In Bhutan there are often several explanations for everything, and this motif is said to be either of Persian influence or

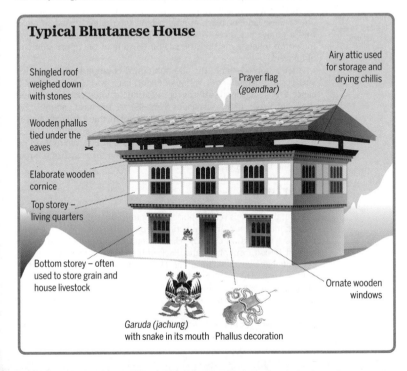

Typical Bhutanese House

Shingled roof weighed down with stones

Wooden phallus tied under the eaves

Elaborate wooden cornice

Top storey – living quarters

Bottom storey – often used to store grain and house livestock

Prayer flag (goendhar)

Airy attic used for storage and drying chillis

Ornate wooden windows

Garuda (jachung) with snake in its mouth   Phallus decoration

POUNDING THE WALLS

The massive compacted earth walls of typical western Bhutanese houses are 80cm to 100cm thick. To build these walls, a wooden frame is constructed then filled with mud. The mud is compacted by being pounded with wooden poles to which a flat ram is attached. When the wall reaches the top of the frame, the frame is shifted upwards and the process begins again.

The pounders are usually teams of women, who sing and dance as they beat the walls. Although Bhutanese women are usually shy and modest with outsiders, they traditionally loosen their inhibitions and exchange ribald comments with men as they perform the pounding, which can take several weeks for a large house. Once the mud wall is finished, it is either left in its natural colour or is whitewashed.

simply a practical design that allows a person to look out of the window while the smoke blows out through the opening above their head.

An elaborate wooden cornice is usually built along the top of the wall directly under the roof of the house. Traditional roofs are pitched and covered with wooden shingles (often weighed down by large stones as safeguards from the wind), but shingles need to be replaced frequently and many people now choose corrugated iron for their roofs. A feature missing in tradition Bhutanese architecture is a gutter – unless a retro-fitted plastic gutter has been installed, expect a soaking when you enter or leave a house during rain.

Many houses are decorated with carved wooden phalluses, often crossed by a sword, which are hung at the four corners of the roof or over the door to ward off evil.

The internal walls, and often parts of the external walls, are built with a timber frame that is filled in with woven bamboo and plastered with mud. This construction is called *shaddam* (weave-mud).

Stairways to the upper floors and attic are often crude ladders made by carving steps into a whole tree trunk. If you find yourself climbing one of these ladders, reach around behind the right edge and you may find a groove cut there to serve as a handrail. Traditional Bhutanese long-drop toilets hang precariously off the side of the upper storey of old houses.

After a house is built, the all-important decoration begins. Wooden surfaces are painted with various designs, each with a special significance. Swastikas, floral patterns representing the lotus, cloud whirls and the Tashi Tagye (Eight Auspicious Symbols) are the most common. Beside the front door are larger paintings, often of mythical animals such as the *garuda,* or large red phalluses. The phallus is not a fertility symbol; it is associated with the Lama Drukpa Kunley and believed to ward off evil. A prayer flag called a *goendhar* is erected on the centre of the roof of all Buddhist homes.

Chortens

A chorten is literally a receptacle for offerings, and in Bhutan all chortens contain religious relics. Chortens are often situated in locations considered inauspicious – river junctions, crossroads, mountain passes and bridges – to ward off evil. The classical chorten shape is based on the ancient Indian form of a stupa. Each of the chorten's five architectural elements has a symbolic meaning. The square or rectangular base symbolises earth. The hemispherical dome symbolises water. The conical or pyramidal spire symbolises fire (the spire has 13 steplike segments that symbolise the 13 steps leading to Buddhahood). On top is a crescent moon and a sun, symbolising air, and a vertical spike symbolising ether or the sacred light of the Buddha. Inside is placed a carved wooden pole called a *sokshing,* which is the life-spirit of the chorten.

Some chortens, such as the National Memorial Chorten in Thimphu, are built in memory of an individual. Others commemorate the visit of a saint or contain sacred books or the bodies of saints or great lamas. Bhutan has three basic styles of chorten, usually characterised as Bhutanese, Tibetan and Nepali.

The Nepali-style chorten is based on the classical stupa. On Nepali chortens the four sides of the tower are painted with a pair of eyes, the all-seeing eyes of Buddha. The prototypes for the Nepali chortens in Bhutan are Swayambhunath and Bodhnath in Kathmandu. The large Chorten Kora in Trashi Yangtse and Chendebji Chorten near Trongsa are two examples of the Nepali style of chorten.

The Tibetan-style chorten has a shape similar to the stupa, but the rounded part flares outward instead of being a dome shape. Thimphu's National Memorial Chorten is an excellent example of this style.

The Bhutanese design comprises a square stone pillar with a *khemar* near the top. The exact origin of this style is not known, but is believed to be a reduced form of the classical stupa, with only the pinnacle and square base. Some Bhutanese chortens have a ball and crescent representing the moon and sun on top.

Several other types of chorten are also found in Bhutan. The *khonying* (two legs) is an archway that forms a gate over a trail. Travellers earn merit by passing through the structure, which is decorated with interior wall paintings and a mandala on the roof. The *mani chukor* is shaped like a Bhutanese chorten but is hollow and contains a large prayer wheel. It is built over or near a stream so that the water turns a wooden turbine below the structure, which then turns the prayer wheel.

When approaching a chorten or *mani* wall, always walk to the left.

ARCHITECTURE CHORTENS

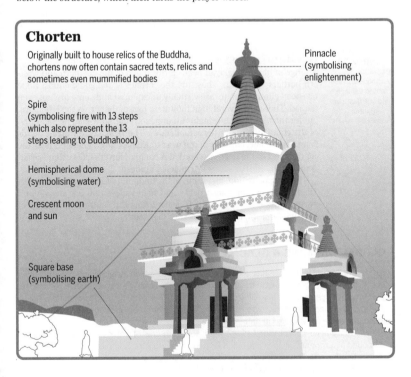

Chorten

Originally built to house relics of the Buddha, chortens now often contain sacred texts, relics and sometimes even mummified bodies

Pinnacle
(symbolising enlightenment)

Spire
(symbolising fire with 13 steps which also represent the 13 steps leading to Buddhahood)

Hemispherical dome
(symbolising water)

Crescent moon
and sun

Square base
(symbolising earth)

Mountains & Valleys

Bhutan is a fascinating corner of the globe. Scientists have long considered the eastern Himalaya to be globally important in terms of biological diversity. Add to this the relatively recent history of isolation, the inaccessibility of much of the country, a low human population coupled with their traditional reverence for all forms of life, and you have the ingredients for an outstanding showcase of nature.

The Lie of the Land

The Himalaya continue to buckle and rise under the influence of plate tectonics and the consequences are regularly felt in Bhutan. In 2009 a 6.1 magnitude quake, centred in Mongar, shook the entire country causing fatalities and destruction. In 2011 the 6.9 magnitude Sikkim earthquake also caused damage and one death in Bhutan.

Bhutan is a landlocked country about 300km long and 150km wide, encompassing 46,500 sq km. It is bounded on the northwest and north by Tibet, and the remainder by India: on the east by the state of Arunachal Pradesh; on the south by Assam and West Bengal; and on the west by Sikkim. Tibet's Chumbi valley, the old trade and expedition route from India to Lhasa, lies between the northern parts of Bhutan and Sikkim.

Virtually the entire country is mountainous, and ranges in elevation from 100m to the 7541m Gangkhar Puensum peak on the Tibetan border. It can be divided into three major geographic regions: the high or Greater Himalaya of the north; the hills and valleys of the Inner Himalaya; and the foothills and plains of the south.

Greater Himalaya

A range of high Himalayan peaks forms much of the northern and western borders of Bhutan. These are the thrones of the gods; almost none has been climbed, many are virtually unexplored and some are not even named. There are several high mountain passes that cross the Himalaya, but for the most part it remains an impenetrable snow-clad barrier (20% of the country is under perpetual snow). The Himalayan range extends from Jhomolhari (7314m) in the west to Kulha Gangri (7554m), near the centre point of the northern border. A chain of lower peaks extends eastwards to the Indian state of Arunachal Pradesh.

The Lunana region, just south of the midpoint of Bhutan's border with Tibet, is an area of glacial peaks and high valleys that are snowbound during winter. A range of high peaks forms the southern boundary of Lunana, isolating it from the rest of the country.

GLOBAL WARMING & GLACIAL TIME BOMBS

It's no small tragedy that the tiny villages of rural Bhutan, which insignificantly contribute to greenhouse gases, are on the front line of global warming's consequences. Across the Himalaya, glacier lakes are filling up with many millions of cubic metres of meltwater, and in recent decades there has been a tenfold increase in glacier-lake outbursts. In Bhutan there are 25 lakes in danger of bursting.

In 1994 a glacier-lake outburst swept 10 million cu metres of water down the Po Chhu. It flooded a number of villages and killed 23 people in Punakha, 80km downstream. Current mitigation efforts include reducing lake levels by digging outflow channels, but the threat of a sudden outburst remains significant.

MOUNTAINS & VALLEYS THE LIE OF THE LAND

DANITA DELIMONT / GETTY IMAGES ©

Mangdue valley (p114)

Inner Himalaya

South of the high peaks is an area of broad, deep valleys and steep forested hills ranging from 1100m to 3500m in elevation. This is the largest region of Bhutan and all the major towns, including Thimphu, are here. This region is a labyrinth of deep ravines formed by fast-flowing rivers. The hillsides are generally too steep for farming, and so most have remained covered in forest.

The greater part of Bhutan's western border is formed by the Himalayan range, including the peaks of Jhomolhari and Jichu Drakye (6989m). Several forested ridges extend eastwards from this range, and these define the large valleys of Thimphu, Paro, Haa and Samtse. Between Punakha and Thimphu lies a well-defined ridge that forms the watershed between Thimphu's Wang Chhu and Punakha's Puna Tsang Chhu. The east–west road crosses this ridge over a 3050m pass, the Dochu La.

A range called the Black Mountains lies to the east of the Puna Tsang Chhu watershed, forming the major barrier between eastern and western Bhutan. Pele La (3500m) is the most important pass across the Black Mountains.

A north–south range of hills separates the Trongsa and Bumthang valley systems. The road crosses this ridge via Yotong La (3425m). Further east, the Donga range of hills follows the border separating the Bumthang and Lhuentse districts, with Thrumshing La (3780m) as the crossing point for the road. Eastern Bhutan, which encompasses most of the Manas Chhu watershed, lies to the east of this range.

Mighty Rivers

Rivers (chhus) play an important role in Bhutan's geography, and their enormous potential for hydroelectric power has helped shape the economy. Most of the rivers have their headwaters in the high mountains of Bhutan, but there are three that flow across borders into the country. The

Millions of years ago the space Bhutan now occupies was an open expanse of water, part of the shallow Tethys Sea. The Tibetan plateau ('Roof of the World') was beachfront property.

Amo Chhu flows from Tibet's Chumbi valley across the southwestern corner of Bhutan, where it becomes the Torsa Chhu, and exits at Phuentsholing. Two tributaries of the Manas, in eastern Bhutan, originate outside the country. The Kuri Chhu has its headwaters in Tibet (where it is known as the Lhobrak Chhu) and crosses into Bhutan at an elevation of only 1200m; the other tributary, the Gamri Chhu, rises in India's Arunachal Pradesh.

All of Bhutan's rivers eventually flow through the *duar*s to become part of the Brahmaputra, which is known in Tibet as the Yarlung Tsampo, with a source near Mt Kailash in the far west. *Duar* is a Sanskrit word meaning 'passes' or 'gates', and is the origin of the English 'door'.

Trees and Shrubs of Nepal and the Himalayas by Adrian and Jimmie Storrs is the best field guide to the forests of Bhutan.

Bhutan's Green Vault

An astonishing array of plants grows in Bhutan: over 5000 species, including more than 600 species of orchid, 300 species of medicinal plants and about 46 species of spectacular rhododendrons. Few countries could boast the variety of habitats from tropical jungle to alpine tundra in such a compact area. Because glaciation had no impact on the lower reaches of the Himalaya, these foothills remain repositories of plants with origins that can be traced back before the ice age. This area is home to some of the most ancient species of vegetation on earth.

Forests are found up to 4500m and serve not only as a source of fuel, timber and herbs, but also as a cultural resource, as they form the basis of many folk songs and ritual offerings. Though the government policy is to maintain at least 60% of the land as forest, the present ratio is higher, with about 65% of the country covered in forests of conifers and mixed broadleaf species.

Warm & Wet Subtropics

Subtropical evergreen forests growing below 800m are unique repositories of biodiversity, but much of the rich vegetation at these lower elevations has been cleared for pasture and terraced farmland. In the next vegetation zone (900m to 1800m) are the subtropical grasslands, including the fragrant lemon grass, and forests of chir pine, oak, walnut and sal. Above groves of bamboo, numerous varieties of orchid and fern grace the branches of forest giants.

Spring is the time to see the magnificent red- or cream-flowering rhododendrons of Bhutan that feature particularly on the mountain passes of Dochu La, Pele La and Yotung La.

Deep & Dark Forests

The subtropical vegetation of the lower altitudes gives way to the diverse, dense and dark forests of oak, birch, maple, magnolia and laurel of the temperate zone (1800m to 3500m). On most hills, the sunny south side takes on many shades of green with a variety of broadleaf species. The damp, shady north side displays a more dour appearance with blue pine and soaring deodars and firs festooned with old man's beard.

POACHING IN SHANGRI LA

While the Bhutanese generally observe their own conservation policies, the open southern and northern borders offer opportunities for poaching of both plant and animal life. Many species are sought for their alleged medicinal or other valuable properties. Killing and poaching are unacceptable in Buddhist tradition, but the high prices that wildlife products such as rhino horn, tiger bone, musk and caterpillar fungus command outside Bhutan present major challenges to conservationists.

The Department of Forests & Park Services operates effective antipoaching programs designed to protect endangered plants and animals, enforce forestry rules, and control trade in wildlife parts and products. A national network of foresters regulates timber harvesting, and road checkpoints are operated throughout the country to monitor the transportation of forest products.

THE BLUE POPPY

The blue poppy, Bhutan's national flower, is a delicate blue- or purple-tinged bloom with a white filament. In Dzongkha it is known by the name *euitgel metog hoem*. It grows to nearly 1m tall, on the rocky mountain terrain found above the treeline (3500m to 4500m). The flowering season occurs during the early monsoon, from late May to July, and the seeds yield oil. Adding to its mystery, fascination and appeal with plant lovers is its strange flowering behaviour. It takes several years to grow, then it eventually flowers for the first and last time, produces seeds, and dies. Poppies can be found atop some high passes from the far eastern parts of the country all the way across to the west.

At one time the blue poppy was considered to be a Himalayan myth, along with the *migoi* (yeti). In 1933 a British botanist, George Sherriff, who was in Bhutan studying Himalayan flora, found the plant in the remote mountain region of Sakteng in eastern Bhutan. Despite this proof, few people have seen one; a mystique surrounds the species in the same way it does the snow leopard.

Alpine Flower Meadows

Between the treeline and the snowline at about 5500m are found low shrubs, dwarf rhododendrons and flowering herbs. Junipers can also be seen in a dwarfed form at altitudes over 4000m.

As the snows begin to melt at the end of winter, the high-altitude grazing lands are carpeted with wildflowers, which remain in bloom until early summer. After the onset of the monsoon, in July, a second and even more vibrant flowering occurs, which extends until late August. Some of the magnificent blooms found at these higher elevations include anemones, forget-me-nots, dwarf irises, primulas, delphiniums and ranunculus.

Wild Rhododendrons of Bhutan by Rebecca Pradhan is a beautiful guide to Bhutan's rhododendrons, with photographs of all 46 species.

Environmental Challenges

Bhutan emerged into the 20th century with much of its forests and ecosystems intact. But now, with an increasing population, improved and expanding roads and limited farming land, a major effort is required to protect the country's natural heritage. Growing awareness of environmental issues has prompted appropriate conservation measures. Among these are nationwide bans on the commercial export of raw timber and the use of plastic bags. Bhutan has consciously decided to forego immediate economic gain from exploitation of its natural resources in order to preserve its environment for long-term sustainable benefits.

Firewood

Wood is used as fuel in rural areas and in most monasteries (in urban areas cooking gas or kerosene is used) and Bhutan's per capita consumption of firewood is one of the highest in the world. It was probably only Bhutan's low population that spared the forests before conservation planning was introduced. Managing firewood harvesting is a major problem in the remote regions, and the government is actively promoting and providing electricity as an alternative source of energy.

Grazing & Farming

Conservation issues centre on human–wildlife conflicts and the deterioration of high-altitude wildlife habitat from grazing pressure. There are government and NGO programs under way to balance the needs of traditional herders and farmers with wildlife protection.

A significant amount of shifting cultivation ('slash and burn', called *tseri* in Dzongkha) is practised in Bhutan, particularly in the east. The practice is officially banned and several methods, including education and fertiliser supply, are being implemented to change this practice.

Between March and May the hillsides are ablaze with the deep red flowers of the etho metho, the country's most famous rhododendron. Ranging from small shrubs to 20m trees, 46 species of rhododendron occur throughout the country.

Wildlife & Sanctuaries

Bhutan boasts a tremendous diversity of plants and animals flourishing in a range of ecosystems from subtropical jungle barely above sea level to snowbound mountains above 7500m. The country's various habitats are believed to contain close to 200 species of mammals and over 600 species of birds.

Mammals

Bhutanese Tales of the Yeti by Kunzang Choden describes Bhutanese beliefs about where and how this mysterious creature may live.

Large mammals abound in the wilds of Bhutan, but unless you are trekking or exploring Royal Manas National Park you will be very lucky to see more than a few examples. The neighbourhood of Royal Manas is home to a large variety of well-known south Asian game species: water buffalo, gaur, serow, wild pig and several species of deer: sambar, muntjac, chital and hog. It is also the best place to see Asian elephants and the very rare greater one-horned rhinoceros.

While trekking on the high trails you may well be lucky enough to spot herds of blue sheep (bharal). Blue sheep are goat-antelopes, taxonomically somewhere between goats and sheep, that turn a bluish grey in winter and are found from 1800m to 4300m. Other mammals that prefer the high life include wolves, yaks and the diminutive, unusual musk deer. The male's musk gland is a highly valued perfume ingredient and this secretive deer is a target for indiscriminate poaching. Fat marmots whistle as you pass their burrows in the high alpine pastures and the curious takins can be seen in northwestern and far northeastern Bhutan. However, the most likely place to spot a takin is in the Motithang Takin Preserve in Thimphu, where six calves were born in 2013 bringing the total herd to 22.

Monkeys

__Best Places to Spot Wildlife__

Bomdeling – capped langurs

Jhomolhari trek – blue sheep

Kori La – hornbills, barbets and more

Phobjikha valley – black-necked cranes

Zhemgang – golden langurs

Several species of monkey are found in Bhutan and some of these are active throughout the day and may be seen not far from villages or a main road – so keep an eye on the roadside trees on those long drives. Most common are the Assamese macaques: reddish-brown, stumpy-tailed monkeys travelling on the ground in troops of 10 to 50 individuals. They are found throughout Bhutan up to 2900m. Rhesus macaques are similar and are the dominant monkey of the Indian plains. In Bhutan the bold rhesus is confined to the southern foothills.

Langurs are elegant, arboreal monkeys with graceful limbs and extraordinarily long tails and a charismatic presence. Three species of langur make a home in Bhutan's forests – up to 3600m in altitude, and usually high up in the forest canopy. The common grey or Hanuman langur is found west of Pele La; the capped langur is found east of the Manas Chhu in eastern Bhutan; while the famous golden langur is only found from the Puna Tsang Chhu in the west to the Manas Chhu in the east. Keep an eye out for troupes of them on the drive from Trongsa to Zhemgang. This beautiful primate's existence was not even known to the scientific community until the 20th century. Not surprisingly, its distinctive feature is its lustrous golden coat.

The grey, golden and capped langurs have a specially adapted stomach for digesting forest leaves and are not an agricultural pest.

MARTIN HARVEY / GETTY IMAGES ©

Red panda

Big Cats

Several species of cat, ranging from the moggy-sized jungle cat to the powerful tiger, prowl the forests, valleys and mountains of Bhutan. The other cats are the Asiatic golden cat, marbled cat, pallas cat, leopard cat, fishing cat, lynx, clouded leopard, common leopard and the enigmatic snow leopard.

The essentially solitary tiger is a symbol of great reverence in Bhutan. They number probably around 100 animals, mostly in and around Royal Manas National park, though tigers roam throughout Bhutan, even to high altitudes (4100m), and as far north as Jigme Dorji National Park. In 2012 a tiger was photographed on a camera trap near Dochu La.

Several tiger-conservation measures have been implemented in Bhutan and, coupled with the strong protected-areas system, has provided a favourable environment for the animal. It is believed the protected regions of Bhutan and India provide sufficient habitat to sustain viable breeding populations.

With its extraordinarily beautiful dappled silver coat, the snow leopard has been hunted relentlessly throughout its range and is in danger of extinction. This elusive cat is almost entirely solitary, largely because a single animal's hunting territory is so vast and its prey is so scarce throughout its high-altitude habitat. However, when its favourite prey, the blue sheep, migrates to lower valleys in winter, the snow leopard follows them. It is then that the sexes meet.

Bears & Red Pandas

There are two species of bear found in Bhutan. The omnivorous Himalayan black bear is a bane to farmers growing corn and fruit near the temperate forests (1200m to 3500m) it frequents, whereas the sloth bear is principally a termite eater and honey pirate found at lower altitudes.

The most authoritative guide to Bhutan's mammals, their identification, behaviour and distribution is *A Field Guide to the Mammals of Bhutan* by Tashi Wangchuk, available in most Thimphu bookshops.

National Parks & Protected Areas

WANGCHUCK CENTENNIAL PARK

Size 4914 sq km
Bhutan's newest and largest national park was inaugurated in 2008. This high-altitude park links Jigme Dorji National Park with Bomdeling Wildlife Sanctuary and protects the headwaters of four major rivers as well as snow-leopard and takin habitat.

JIGME DORJI NATIONAL PARK

Size 4316 sq km
The second-largest protected area in Bhutan with habitats ranging from subtropical (1400m) to alpine (7000m), it protects several endangered species, including takins, snow leopards and tigers. Villagers farm and harvest indigenous plants in the park.

TORSA STRICT NATURE RESERVE

Size 610 sq km
Torsa Reserve is located where the Torsa Chhu enters from Tibet. The reserve was set aside to protect the temperate forests and alpine meadows and is the only protected area with no resident human population.

Thanza

Gasa

Punakha · Trongsa

THIMPHU
Paro · Wangdue Phodrang
Haa

Chhukha · Dagana
Sibsu · Chengmari · Damphu
Samtse · Phuentsholing · Lamidranga
Sarpang · Gelephu
Kalikhola

INDIA (ASSAM)

JIGME SINGYE WANGCHUCK NATIONAL PARK

Size 1730 sq km
Protecting the Black Mountains that separate eastern and western Bhutan, it harbours tigers, Himalayan black bears, red pandas and golden langurs. An amazing 450 species of bird have been catalogued. The Phobjikha valley, wintering place of black-necked cranes, is included in the park.

PHIBSOO WILDLIFE SANCTUARY

Size 269 sq km
On the southern border of Bhutan, it was established to protect the only remaining natural sal forest in Bhutan. Several protected species thrive here, including chital deer, elephants, gaurs, tigers, golden langurs and hornbills.

Protected Areas
Biological Corridors

0 ⬛ 50 km
0 ⬛ 30 miles

THRUMSHING LA NATIONAL PARK

Size 905 sq km
This national park was set aside to protect old-growth temperate forests of
fir and chir pine. It is also home to red pandas and several endangered bird
species including the rufous-necked hornbill and satyr tragopan pheasant.

BOMDELING WILDLIFE SANCTUARY

Size 1521 sq km
The sanctuary protects the habitat of blue sheep, snow
leopards, red pandas, tigers, capped langurs, Himalayan black
bears and musk deer. It also protects a large area of alpine
tundra and is a wintering ground of the black-necked crane.

SAKTENG WILDLIFE SANCTUARY

Size 741 sq km
The sanctuary protects several endemic species,
particularly rhododendrons, within its temperate
forests of blue pine, mixed conifers and rhododendron. It is also renowned as the only reserve in the
world that protects the habitat of the *migoi* (yeti).

CHINA
(TIBET)

Lhuentse

Jakar

Trashi
Yangtse   Sakteng

Trashigang

Zhemgang   Mongar

Wamrong

Pemagatshel

INDIA
(ARUNACHAL
PRADESH)

Panbang   Nganglam   Bhangtar   Daifam

Samdrup
Jongkhar

KHALING WILDLIFE SANCTUARY

Size 335 sq km
In far southeastern Bhutan, the Khaling Wildlife
Sanctuary protects wild elephants, gaurs, leopards,
pygmy hogs, hispid hares and other tropical wildlife.
This sanctuary adjoins a comparable reserve in India.

ROYAL MANAS NATIONAL PARK

Size 1057 sq km
Adjoining India's Manas National Park, it forms a
protected area running from the plains to the peaks. It is
the home of rhino, buffalo, tigers, leopards, bears and
elephants. It is also home to rare species, including the
golden langur, capped langur and hispid hare.

THE TAKIN – BHUTAN'S NATIONAL ANIMAL

The reason for selecting the takin as the national animal is based both on its uniqueness and its strong association with the country's religious history and mythology. When the great saint Lama Drukpa Kunley, the Divine Madman, visited Bhutan in the 15th century, a large congregation of devotees gathered from around the country to witness his magical powers. The people urged the lama to perform a miracle.

However, the saint, in his usual unorthodox and outrageous way, demanded that he first be served a whole cow and a goat for lunch. He devoured these with relish and left only the bones. After letting out a large and satisfied burp, he took the goat's head and stuck it onto the bones of the cow. And then with a snap of his fingers he commanded the strange beast to rise up and graze on the mountainside. To the astonishment of the people the animal arose and ran up to the meadows to graze. This animal came to be known as the *dong gyem tsey* (takin) and to this day these clumsy-looking animals can be seen grazing on the mountainsides of Bhutan.

The takin continues to befuddle taxonomists. The famous biologist George Schaller called it a 'beestung moose'. In summer, takins migrate to subalpine forests and alpine meadows above 3700m to graze on luxuriant grasses, herbs and shrubs. By migrating they escape the leeches, mosquitoes, horseflies and other parasites of the monsoon-swept lower valleys. This is also the time when the alpine vegetation is richest in nutrition and takins gain weight easily: some males become massive, weighing as much as 1 tonne or more. Summer is also the time when takins mate. The gestation period is between seven and eight months, and young – usually a single calf – are born between December and February. Sometimes the Himalayan black bear will follow a pregnant takin and immediately after she has given birth, chase her away and eat the calf.

In late August takins start their slow descent to the lower valleys where the herds begin to break up. They arrive at the winter grazing grounds in temperate broadleaf forests between 2000m and 3000m by late October.

Hunting is banned by law and poaching is limited since there is no high economic value placed on the body parts of the takin. In traditional medicine, however, the horn of the takin, consumed in minute amounts, is supposed to help women during a difficult childbirth.

The major threats that the takin faces are competition with domestic yaks for grazing in the alpine meadows and the loss of habitat in the temperate forests.

Tashi Wangchuk

Bears do occasionally attack humans, probably because their poor eyesight leads them to interpret that a standing person is making a threatening gesture.

The red panda is known in Bhutan as *aamchu donkha* and is most commonly found near Pele La, Thrumshing La and parts of the Gasa district. It is bright-chestnut coloured, about 50cm long, including its bushy, banded tail, and has a white face. The red panda is nocturnal, sleeping in trees during the day and coming to the ground to forage on bamboo and raid birds' nests at night.

Birds of Bhutan by Carol Inskipp, Tim Inskipp and Richard Grimmett is a comprehensive illustrated guide to Bhutan's avian treasures.

Birds

Each year Bhutan's extensive bird list grows longer, a consequence of Bhutan's rich biodiversity and the small amount of systematic birding that has been done in the kingdom. Nonetheless, over 600 species have been recorded and birdwatching tours are extremely popular.

Bhutan is rightly famous for its wintering populations of the vulnerable black-necked crane. Less well known are the winter populations, mainly as solitary individuals, of the endangered white-bellied heron, listed as one of the 50 rarest birds in the world. This graceful bird may – with luck – be seen from the road in the vicinity of Punakha, Wangdue Phodrang and Zhemgang, especially along the Mangde Chhu valley.

Some bird species are even more transient, migrating through Bhutan between Tibet and northern India in autumn and spring. Pallas' fish eagle, which is considered rare, is regularly seen migrating up the Punak Chhu near Wangdue Phodrang in spring. It is often in the company of ospreys, a wide range of ducks, waders such as the pied avocet, and other birds that breed in Tibet.

The raven is the national bird of Bhutan. A raven guided the Zhabdrung to Bhutan in 1616, and it gives its name to the raven-shaped crown worn by the kings of Bhutan.

Winter brings numerous species down to lower altitudes, including accentors, rosefinches, grosbeaks, snow pigeons and pheasants, such as the satyr tragopan, the Himalayan monal and the blood pheasant. Observant early morning walkers can often find these on the mountains and passes around Thimphu. In summer many lowland species move to higher altitudes to breed; these species include the comic-looking hoopoe, various species of minivets, cuckoos (one can commonly hear at least five different species calling), barbets, warblers, sunbirds, fulvettas and yuhinas.

Given the density of forest cover and the steep vertical descents, the road is often the best place from which to spot birds. Recommended stretches include the road down from Dochu La to Wangdue Phodrang (the adventurous can take the old trail, which is even better), from Wangdue Phodrang to Nobding (on the way to Pele La), and before Trongsa. For those who go east, the 2000m descent between Sengor and Lingmethang is spectacular: the rufous-necked hornbill and Ward's trogon have been recorded in this area. But stay on the lookout on all the roads – we spotted a pair of rufus-necked hornbills near Gedu, on the road between Thimphu and Phuetsholing.

Trekking will provide you with a greater chance of seeing high-altitude birds, including the lammergeyer, the Himalayan griffon, the raven, the unique high-altitude wader – the ibisbill – and several colourful pheasants.

> For more on cranes, including a downloadable field guide, visit the International Crane Foundation (www.saving cranes.org).

THE BLACK-NECKED CRANE

The rare and endangered black-necked crane occupies a special place in Bhutanese hearts and folklore. Its arrival every autumn from Tibet inspires songs and dances; it usually heralds the end of the harvesting season and also the time when farming families start migrating to warmer climates.

Many legends and myths exist about the bird, which the Bhutanese call *thrung thrung karmo*. Wetlands of the high mountain valleys of Phobjikha, Bomdeling and Gaytsa serve as the winter habitat for up to 500 birds. Like other cranes, these have an elaborate mating ritual, a dance in which pairs bow, leap into the air and toss vegetation about while uttering loud bugling calls. It can be difficult to distinguish the sexes because the coloration is so similar, but the females are slightly smaller. The crane's preferred delicacies include fallen grain, tubers and insects.

The world's entire population of 5600 to 6000 black-necked cranes breeds in Tibet and Ladakh. As well as in Bhutan, they winter in south-central Tibet and northeastern Yunan province in China.

The **Royal Society for Protection of Nature** (RSPN; www.rspnbhutan.org), which is involved in conservation, education and inspiring the Bhutanese populace, annually monitors the endangered black-necked cranes in the Phobjikha and Bomdeling valleys and has produced videos of the cranes.

THE CATERPILLAR & THE FUNGUS

According to one study, upwards of US$10 billion is spent each year by Asian markets on a fungus with powers matched only by rhino horns, elephant tusks and tiger penises. Most of the purchasers hope it will increase male potency. Some Chinese swimming coaches and practitioners of traditional medicine have so talked up the value of *yartsa goenbub* (winter-worm summer-plant) that it is now one of the, if not *the*, most valuable commodities by weight. Also known as caterpillar fungus or cordyceps, *Ophioordyceps sinensis* is a peculiar fungus that parasitises then kills its moth caterpillar host. It is only found in the high-altitude meadows of the Himalaya and Tibet.

Tibetan yak herders wandering in and out of Bhutan traditionally scooped up the fungus to augment their meagre living, but the increased demand for cordyceps in China has brought dramatic changes with gatherers swarming the meadows of Nepal, Tibet and Bhutan. Not surprisingly; at the time of writing prices were as high as US$100,000 per kilogram!

Bhutan legalised the harvesting of cordyceps in 2004, and since then there has been a massive increase in harvesting effort, raising concerns for its sustainablilty. Although the trade in cordyceps is officially regulated, the high stakes mean unlawful collection and black-market trading is rife.

A tragic knock-on effect linked to this sudden Himalayan wealth bonanza was a swath of poaching of big cats across Asia as increasingly wealthy Tibetans demanded cat skins for new *chuba* (cloaks) and for decorating their homes. This prompted a proclamation by the Dalai Lama for Tibetans to respect nature and discard their cat skins, which was popularly supported with thousands of Tibetans burning their cat skins. Nevertheless, as recent as 2012 the **Environmental Investigation Agency** (www.eia-international.org) found snow leopard skins being offered for sale in China and Tibet, and wild tiger skins being sold alongside Chinese 'farmed' tiger skins. China remains the main destination for products from poached big cats.

National Parks & Protected Areas

There are five national parks, four wildlife sanctuaries and one nature reserve, which together constitute about 43% of the country, or 16,396 sq km. An additional 3307 sq km is designated as a network of biological corridors linking all nine protected areas, putting 52% of the country under some form of protection.

The musk deer is a primitive deer that has no antlers; both sexes have oversized protruding canine teeth, up to 7cm long in males and used in territorial battles.

All but three of the protected areas encompass regions in which there is a resident human population. Preserving the culture and fostering local tradition is part of the mandate of Bhutan's national-park system. The government has developed an integrated conservation and development program to allow people living within a protected area to continue to farm, graze animals, collect plants and cut firewood.

Bhutan established its national-park system to protect important ecosystems, and for the most part they have not been developed as tourist attractions. Apart from one or two exceptions, you won't find the kind of facilities you may normally associate with national parks, such as entrance stations, camping grounds and visitors centres. In many cases you won't even be aware that you are entering or leaving a national park.

Survival Guide

Directory A–Z

Accommodation

Tour operators will book you into hotels approved by the Tourism Council of Bhutan (TCB). Since most visitors effectively pay the same rate across the category, it makes sense to ask for information about the various options when you make your travel arrangements.

Hotels

Accommodation in Bhutan ranges from simple mountain huts to five-star luxury resorts, though most tourists will stay in comfortable midrange tourist hotels equipped with electricity, telephone, TV, private bathroom and hot water. Every hotel has a restaurant that

---

SLEEPING PRICE RANGES

The following price ranges refer to a standard double room at the normal foreign-tourist rates and include the usual 10% tax and either 5% or 10% service charge.

$ less than Nu 2500

$$ Nu 2500 to Nu 5000

$$$ more than Nu 5000

---

serves buffet meals when a group is in residence and offers à la carte dining at other times. Many hotels in Thimphu and Paro have wi-fi, but internet connectivity diminishes as you head away from these centres.

Larger hotels offer standard, deluxe and suite accommodation, although the difference between standard and deluxe in many hotels is minimal. When you book a trip, you may specify which hotel you wish, but your agent may have a list of hotels with whom they have contracts or relationships. Changes and cancellations will be much simpler in these hotels and upgrades more likely. You'll find that smaller agencies often have a hard time getting guaranteed rooms at hotels owned by larger tour companies. During the low season (December to February, June to August), hotels often discount their rooms by as much as 30% so you may be able to negotiate an upgrade during these months.

During tsechu time, tourist hotels add a hefty surcharge, but they still get booked up and you may well find yourself 'bumped' into budget digs, such as the local hotels used by domestic travellers and Indian traders. These can still be comfortable, though the toilet facilities may not be what you're used to.

A confirmed hotel reservation does not always guarantee a booking in hotels as small as those in Bhutan. A large tour group can exert a powerful influence and you may discover that there is an extended negotiation taking place between your guide and the desk clerk when you check in. Don't worry; *something* will be arranged.

Bhutan has a growing number of luxury options, including the Uma, Amankora, Zhiwa Ling and Termalinca resorts. For these you will have to pay a substantial supplement on top of the standard tourist tariff. For these luxury hotels you should get at least a 30% discount off the full rate during the low season.

Winter is cold in Bhutan and central heating is rare. In Thimphu and Paro there are small electric heaters, and in Bumthang many hotel rooms are heated by a wood stove called a *bukhari*, which often has a pile of rocks on the top to retain the heat. Unless you are trekking, you won't need to carry bedding or a sleeping bag, but be aware that hotel pillows tend to be firm and mattresses on the thin side.

If there is an electric water heater (called a geyser) in the room, check that it's turned on when you check in. The better hotels supply bottled drinking water in the rooms, but if you come across an open water flask in your room, don't drink from it.

Indian travellers and resident foreigners often get an automatic 20% or 30% discount on hotel rates, while Bhutanese often get 50%.

Activities

There are plenty of possible day hikes in Bhutan, as well as more serious treks, ranging from three to 24 days. Horse riding is available in Paro and on some treks.

Birdwatching

Bhutan is rightly celebrated for its wintering populations of the vulnerable black-necked crane, but with over 600 recorded bird species and a spectacular range of habitats, this tiny country is a birdwatchers' paradise.

Although these companies specialise in birdwatching tours, Bhutan's plentiful mature forests and lack of hunting makes any travel a bird-spotting opportunity.

Bhutan Birding and Heritage Travels (www.bhutanheritage.com)

Sunbird Tours (www.sunbirdtours.co.uk)

Wings (www.wingsbirds.com)

Fishing

Fishing with lure or fly for brown trout is possible in many rivers, though it is frowned upon by many Bhutanese for religious reasons. A licence (Nu 500 per day) is required (ask your tour agency) and fishing is prohibited within 1km of a monastery, temple, dzong or *shedra* (Buddhist college). A closed season applies from October to December and fishing is banned on many religious days throughout the year.

HOT-STONE BATHS

Most hotels offer a *dotsho* (traditional hot-stone bath), a simple coffin-like wooden box containing water warmed with fire-heated rocks. The red-hot rocks tumble and sizzle into the water behind a grill that protects the bather's skin. More traditional places add natural herbs such as artemisia. You'll need to book a couple of hours in advance for the rocks to heat up; expect to pay around Nu 1500 for the experience, double this in top-end places. Bring a towel and soap in cheaper places.

The most popular lure is the Tasmanian Devil, available in general shops in Thimphu.

Yangphel Adventure Travel (☑02-323293; www.yangphel.com) Operates fly-fishing tours and encourages a 'catch and release' approach.

Golf

The international-standard golf course, Royal Thimphu Golf Club (p58), in Thimphu is open to nonmembers.

Cycling

Mountain biking is popular with Bhutanese and expats alike. Tour companies that specialise in cycling tours, have bikes for hire and can advise on routes include **Yu-Druk Tours & Treks** (Map p54; ☑02-321905; www.yudruk.com) and **Bhutan Wilderness Travel** (www.bhutanbiking.com). Some adventure-travel companies organise trips that allow bikers to bring their own cycles and travel throughout Bhutan accompanied by a support vehicle; otherwise local mountain-bike hire costs an extra US$30 or US$50 per day.

Long journeys are challenging because there's a lot of uphill peddling and vehicles roar approaching from around corners, not expecting cyclists. Local cycling excursions in the Paro, Thimphu and Bumthang valleys offer a safer and less strenuous experience. Suggested places:

Cheli La For a wild ride, get dropped off at the top of this pass and ride 35km nonstop, downhill, either on the main road or on logging roads via Gorina.

Paro valley The paved road to Drukgyel Dzong and the return trip along the unpaved western farm road from Satsam make this a 30km day trip.

Phobjikha Bike trails here are part of the local ecotourism initiative, and there are also new opportunities to follow graded logging roads to Tsele La and overnight to Tikke Zampa.

Punakha Offering several dedicated mountain-bike trails.

Tango and Cheri A fine day trip north of Thimphu, combining biking and hiking.

Thimphu to Paro An interesting ride, though traffic can be heavy as far as Chhuzom (the turn-off to Phuentsholing).

Rafting & Kayaking

Though rafting in Bhutan is still in its infancy, those who have scouted the rivers feel that it has the potential for some of the best rafting on earth. Since 1997 small groups of paddlers have been exploring 14 rivers and over 22 different runs that vary from class II (beginner with moderate rapids) to class V (expert only). However, unless you are a seasoned river rat, and can organise the

TOUR OF THE DRAGON

Bhutan's premier mountain-bike event is the tortuous **Tour of the Dragon** (www.tourofthedragon.com), a race of 268km from Bumthang to Thimphu in just one day. The course gains 3790m and descends 3950m and crosses four mountain passes on Bhutan's winding roads. The tour takes place on the first Saturday in September and international registration costs US$300.

special permission required, there are essentially only two day trips on offer, both in the Punakha valley:

Pho Chhu Combines a hike up the side of the river through forest and farmland to the put-in at Samdinka. The raft trip has a couple of class III rapids and ends in a bang with the 'Wrathful Buddha' rapid next to the Punakha Dzong.

Mo Chhu A very easy scenic float, suitable for all abilities and a good introduction for novices. The run starts about 6km above the Punakha Dzong at the Khamsum Yuelley Namgyal Chorten. As the river meanders through the wide valley, you float past one of the queen's winter residences, the king's weekend retreat and some beautiful farmland before taking out just below the dzong.

Most companies can book you on either of these trips, the fees depend on the group size: five or more US$75 per person; less than five US$375 per raft. The following companies run rafting and kayaking trips.

Needmore Adventures (✆in the USA 888-900 9091; www.needmoreadventure.com) US-based operator.

Druk Rafting Service (www.raftingbhutan.com)

Lotus Adventures (✆02-322191; www.bhutanlotus.com)

Xplore Bhutan (www.xplore-bhutan.com)

Children

Children aged under six are exempt from the minimum daily tariff and six- to 12 year-olds get a 50% discount, so it needn't break the bank if you bring kids along. Kids may become bored with long drives, limited availability to TV and the internet, and little other entertainment available. However, they will be immediately accepted by local kids and their families, and they could make many new friends. Lonely Planet's *Travel with Children* has useful advice.

Bhutan Land of the Thunder Dragon, by Freda Ferne, is a children's book on Bhutan; see www.bhutan-an-introduction.co.uk if you want more info or wish to buy.

Customs Regulations

You will receive a baggage declaration form to complete when you arrive in Bhutan.

For tourists, the main purpose of this form is to ensure that you re-export anything you bring into the country. List any expensive equipment that you are carrying, such as cameras and laptops. Don't lose the form as you must return it when you leave the country.

Duty-free allowances include 1L of liquor. You can bring in only one carton (200) of cigarettes and these attract a 200% duty upon arrival. A packet or two is normally allowed in gratis. There are no restrictions on other personal effects, including trekking gear, brought into the country.

Departure formalities are straightforward, but you'll need to produce the form that you completed on arrival and may need to show all of the items listed on it. A lost form means complications and delays. If you lose the form, let your guide know as soon as possible so that special arrangements can be made to avoid any inconvenience.

The export of antiques and wildlife products is prohibited. If you wish to purchase a souvenir that looks

Climate

Thimphu

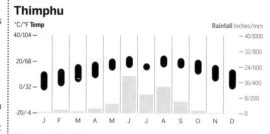

Phuentsholing

old, have your guide clear it as a nonantique item with the **Division of Cultural Properties** (☎02-322694), part of the Department of Culture inside the Ministry of Home and Cultural Affairs. Customs authorities pay special attention to religious statues. It would be prudent to have any such statue cleared, old or not.

Electricity

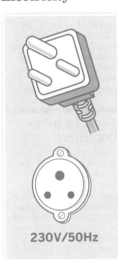

230V/50Hz

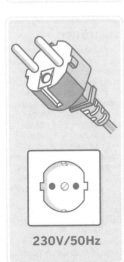

230V/50Hz

Embassies & Consulates

Visas are not available from Bhutanese embassies abroad. All tourist visas must be channelled through a tour company and the TCB in Thimphu, and from there through the Ministry of Foreign Affairs.

Only a handful of foreign countries have an official presence in Bhutan. Bhutan's relations with other countries are handled through its embassies in Delhi and Dhaka.

Bangladeshi Embassy (Map p50;☎02-222362; fax 02-322629; Thori Lam, Thimphu)

Indian Embassy (Map p50; ☎02-322162; www.eoithimphu. org; India House, Zhung Lam; ⊗9.30am-1pm & 2-5.30pm Mon-Fri, closed Indian holidays); Consulate (☎05-252101)

Thai Embassy (Map p50; ☎02-323978; royalthaiconsulate@druknet.bt; Changangkha, Thimphu)

Food

Since most travel in Bhutan is via an all-inclusive package, most of your meals will be in the shape of a hotel or trekking-camp buffet, with a mix of continental, Indian, Chinese and Bhutanese dishes, plus vegetarian options and rice. The food is fine but is specifically created to not offend anyone, so it can be bland. Small groups can often order from the menu, though the buffet meals offer a wider selection. If you find the tourist food bland, request some of what your guide is eating. It will be much tastier, if you can take the heat.

On long day drives or hikes you will not return to your hotel for lunch, and most tour operators arrange either uninspiring packed lunches or a much better hot lunch packed inside a series of metal containers.

The food in hotels is often the best in town, but if you want to sample local restaurants, especially in Thimphu or Paro, your guide can arrange it. Your tour operator should pay for your restaurant meals, with the exception of a few upper-end restaurants in Thimphu. In almost all restaurants it's a good idea to order an hour or more in advance, or expect to wait forever. If you are ordering from a menu, don't be surprised if many of the offerings are not available.

Due to the unique nature of travel in Bhutan, restaurant opening hours have little meaning. Almost all tourists will have breakfast in their hotel and guides will pre-arrange lunch and dinner in restaurants or hotels, which will normally offer a buffet or set meal at whatever time your guide determines. We have listed opening hours where they are fixed, or useful, as in the case of bakeries and private restaurants, but for the most part this guide assumes that restaurants are open for lunch and dinner, with exceptions noted.

Staples & Specialities

The Bhutanese love chillies, so much in fact that some dishes consist entirely of chillies, accompanied by chilli-infused condiments. The mouth-scorching meals will bring tears of joy to the eyes of chilli lovers, and tears of pain to everyone else! Although chillies are ubiquitous, don't expect the aromatically spiced dishes typical of the subcontinent. These can only be found in the Nepali-influenced south of Bhutan or in an Indian restaurant.

Bhutan's national dish is *ema datse*, large green (sometimes red, but always very hot) chillies, prepared as a vegetable, not as a seasoning, in a cheese sauce. Hotel and trekking cooks make some excellent nonspicy dishes, such as *kewa datse* (potatoes with cheese sauce) and *shamu datse* (mushrooms with cheese sauce). More seasonal are the delicious asparagus and unusual *nakey* (fern fronds), the latter typically smothered in the ever-present *datse*. For more menu items see the Food Glossary (p289).

Beef and fish come from India or Thailand, usually flown in frozen and safe. During the summer you are may be limited to chicken, or a vegetarian diet in more remote parts of the country. Yak meat is available, but only in winter.

Foremost among several Tibetan-influenced snacks are *momos,* small steamed dumplings that may be filled with meat or cheese – delicious when dipped in a chilli sauce. Fried cheese *momos* are a speciality of several Thimphu restaurants. Look for the strings of rock-hard,

dried yak cheese, *chugo,* hanging from shop rafters, but be careful of your teeth.

Although there is plenty of white rice, the Bhutanese prefer a locally produced red variety, which has a slightly nutty flavour. At high altitudes wheat and buckwheat are the staples. In Bumthang, *khule* (buckwheat pancakes) and *puta* (buckwheat noodles) replace rice as the foundation of many meals.

Drinks
NONALCOHOLIC DRINKS

Avoid drinking tap water anywhere in Bhutan. Bottled mineral water is widely available.

Indian-style sweet milky tea *(ngad-ja)* is widely available and often referred to as either masala tea or 'ready-made' tea. Less satisfying is the tourist equivalent, a tea bag that you only get some flavour from after endless prodding. Bhutanese frequently drink *sud-ja*, Tibetan-style tea with salt and butter, which is more like soup than tea, and surprisingly tasty and warming on a cold day. Filter coffee and espresso is available in the top-end hotels and a few cafes in Thimphu and Paro, but elsewhere 'coffee' is invariably of the instant variety.

ALCOHOLIC DRINKS

The best beer brewed in Bhutan is the very good Red Panda *weissbier,* a tangy unfiltered wheat beer bottled in

Bumthang. Bhutan Brewery produces Druk Lager and the high-alcohol (8%) Druk 11000. Imported beers were not available at the time of writing, but should imports resume, expect to find cans of Tiger and Singha, and several varieties of Indian beer.

There are several brands of Bhutanese whisky but the most common local brew is *bang chhang,* a warm beerlike drink made from wheat. The favourite hard drinks are *arra,* a spirit distilled from rice, and *sinchhang,* which is made from millet, wheat or rice.

Drinks, including mineral water, are usually charged as extras, and payment is collected at the end of the meal or the following morning when you check out of the hotel.

Gay & Lesbian Travellers

Like most Asians, the Bhutanese believe that what one does in private is strictly a personal matter, and they would prefer not to discuss such issues. Public displays of affection are not appreciated, though, and everyone, regardless of orientation, should exercise discretion. Officially, male homosexuality is illegal.

Insurance

A travel-insurance policy to cover theft, loss and medical problems is always highly recommended. Most policies will cover costs if you are forced to cancel your tour because of flight cancellation, illness, injury or the death of a close relative. This can protect you from major losses due to Bhutan's prepayment conditions and hefty cancellation charges.

Some policies specifically exclude 'dangerous activities', and these can include motorcycling, rafting and even trekking. Read your policy carefully to be sure it covers ambulance rides or an emergency helicopter

LAUNDRY

Most hotels offer a laundry service, for a fee, and larger towns have a laundry or dry-cleaners. During wet weather, smaller hotels may return your laundry damp, or not until the following day. If you are on a tight schedule, ask about the drying facilities before you hand in your laundry.

airlift out of a remote region, or an emergency flight home. Many travel-insurance policies include repatriation and evacuation through the worldwide network of International SOS Assistance. Keep in mind that if you can't afford travel insurance, you certainly won't be able to afford to deal with a medical emergency overseas.

You may prefer a policy that pays doctors or hospitals directly rather than you having to pay on the spot and claim later. If you have to claim later, make sure you keep all documentation. Some insurance companies ask you to call them (they suggest reversing the charges, an impossibility from Bhutan) at a centre in your home country, where an immediate assessment of your problem is made.

Worldwide travel insurance is available at www.lonelyplanet.com/travel_services. You can buy, extend and claim online anytime – even if you're already on the road.

Internet Access

There are internet cafes in most towns, and most tourist hotels offer either an internet-connected public computer or free wi-fi (though this may be limited to the lobby and restaurant and not the rooms).

Language Courses

The **Dzongkha Language Institute** (02-333869; dzongkhalanguageinstitute@yahoo.com) can arrange language classes in Dzongkha from Nu 5000 to Nu 10,000 per month, or private tutors from the Simthoka Language Institute from Nu 500 per hour. Courses last from one to six months.

Legal Matters

Although you will probably notice cannabis growing in any bit of spare dirt, even in the towns, there is not a tradition of use and possession is illegal.

Smoking in public places is prohibited. Bring all the cigarettes you think you'll need but be prepared to be taxed 200% at customs. Don't sell any cigarettes brought into the country as this is illegal.

Maps

There is a dearth of maps of Bhutan and a good map can be hard to source outside the country. Bookshops in Kathmandu are the best bet for finding a map. **International Travel Maps** (www.itmb.com) produces a 1:345,000 *Bhutan & Northern India*, and Nepa Maps produces a 1:380,000 *Bhutan* and *Bhutan Himalaya Trekking Routes*. The laminated Berndtson 1:500,000 *Bhutan* should be available by the time you read this.

In Bhutan, bookshops sell Thimphu and Paro city maps as well as country maps published by the **Survey of Bhutan** (Rm 35, National Land Commission, Motithang). The Survey publishes a large 1:250,000 satellite country map overlaid with roads and major towns and district boundaries, as well as several specialised maps showing historical places and points of interest.

Money

The unit of currency is the ngultrum (Nu), which is pegged to the Indian rupee. The ngultrum is further divided into 100 *chetrum*. There are coins to the value of 25 and 50 chetrum and Nu 1, and notes of Nu 1, 5, 10, 20, 50, 100, 500 and 1000. The Nu 1 coin depicts the eight auspicious symbols called Tashi Tagye, while each note depicts a different dzong.

Indian rupees may be used freely anywhere in Bhutan (don't be surprised if you get change in rupees). Officially 500 and 1000 Indian rupee notes are not accepted due to large amounts of counterfeit notes; however, in practice 500s are usually accepted. Ngultrums cannot be used in India.

It is OK with the Bhutanese if you bring a reasonable amount of Indian currency into Bhutan, though Indian regulations prohibit currency export.

ATMs

At the time of research, only Bank of Bhutan (BoB) and Druk PNB Bank ATMs accepted foreign credit cards. Not all BoB ATMs outside Thimphu and Paro were accepting foreign cards, so get your cash in these centres before heading off east.

Bargaining

Bargaining is not a Bhutanese tradition, and you won't get very far with your haggling skills here, except with trailside vendors on the hike to Taktshang and in the local handicrafts section of the Thimphu Weekend Market.

Cash

If you plan to make a major purchase, for example textiles or art, consider bringing US dollars in cash. Most shops will accept this, and it can save you the hassle of exchanging a large quantity of money in advance and then attempting to change it back if you don't find the exact piece you were looking for.

Credit Cards

Cards are accepted at major handicraft stores and some of the larger hotels in Thimphu, but you will often be charged a surcharge of up to 5% to cover the fees levied by the credit-card companies.

Moneychangers

Tourist trips are fully prepaid, so you could in theory manage in Bhutan without any local money at all, though you'll probably want to change at least US$50 to pay for laundry and drinks, plus whatever you need for souvenirs and tips.

The exchange counters at the airport, larger hotels and the banks in Thimphu and Phuentsholing can change all major currencies, and sometimes Scandinavian currencies. If you are heading to central and eastern Bhutan, you will do better sticking to US dollars. In smaller towns foreign-currency exchange may be an unusual transaction so be prepared for delays. You'll often get a slightly lower rate if changing US$ bills in denominations of US$20 or less.

You may change your unused ngultrums back to foreign currency (though usually only into US dollars) on departure from Thimphu or Paro. Travellers departing via Samdrup Jongkhar didn't have this facility at the time of research. You *may* need to produce your original exchange receipts. Ngultrums are useless outside of Bhutan (except as a curiosity).

Bhutan has two major banks, the **Bank of Bhutan** (www.bob.bt) and the **Bhutan National Bank** (www.bnb.bt), each with branches throughout the country. Both change cash with no commission and charge 1% for travellers cheques. The Bank of Bhutan's main branches are generally open 9am to 1pm

Monday to Friday and 9am to 11am on Saturday, though the branches in Trongsa, Trashigang and Mongar are open on Sunday and closed Tuesday. It also has a branch in Thimphu that stays open later. New banks with forex include the Tashi Group's T-Bank and Druk PNB with limited but expanding branches.

Tipping & Tax

You will usually be accompanied throughout your visit to Bhutan by the same tour guide and probably the same driver. Though it's against the official TCB policy, these people expect a tip at the end of the trip. Many leaders on group tours take up a collection at the conclusion of the trip and hand it over in one packet. With a large group this can be a substantial amount and the practice has created high expectations on the part of Bhutanese guides.

If you've been trekking, it's appropriate to tip the guide, cook and waiter. Horsemen also expect tips, but this can be minimal if they are the owners of the horses or yaks and are making money by hiring out their animals. The stakes go up, however, if they have been especially helpful with camp chores and on the trail.

If arranging tips yourself, hand them over in individual envelopes the evening before you leave, as things get rushed and easily forgotten on the day of departure.

For those paying their own way, most hotels charge 10% Bhutan Sales Tax (BST) and either 5% or 10% service charge, which are included in the rates shown. Most restaurants will charge the same, especially if you want a receipt.

Travellers Cheques

You can cash travellers cheques at any bank, most hotels and the foreign-exchange counter at the airport. There are bank charges of 1% for cheque encashment. You should carry

only well-known brands such as American Express, Visa, Thomas Cook, Citibank or Barclays. There is no replacement facility for lost travellers cheques in Bhutan.

Opening Hours

Reviews mention business hours only if different from these standards.

Government offices 9am to 1pm and 2pm to 5pm in summer, until 4pm in winter, Monday to Friday

Banks 9am to 1pm Monday to Friday, 9am to 11am Saturday

Shops 8am to 8pm or 9pm

Clubs Generally close at midnight on weekdays and at 2am Friday and Saturday

Bars Close at 11pm on weekdays and midnight on Friday and Saturday. Closed Tuesday – the national 'dry' day.'

Photography

Accessories & Printing

Memory cards are available in Thimphu and you will have no problem finding an internet cafe in Thimphu or Paro that can burn digital images to a CD. There are colour-printing facilities in Thimphu and Phuentsholing.

Many of the dzongs and mountain peaks are best photographed at a distance with a telephoto lens. Bear in mind also that there will be little or no opportunity for photography inside buildings, therefore you don't need to organise a flash attachment and tripod for that purpose. Be sure to carry spare batteries, as these are hard to find when in rural Bhutan.

Grab a copy of Lonely Planet's *Travel Photography* for more tips and advice.

Photography enthusiasts should check out the expert-guided itineraries of **Rainbow Photo Tours** (☑in the USA 800-685 9992; www.rainbowphototours.com).

Restrictions

Bhutan is generally liberal about photography by tourists. There are a few places, though, with signs prohibiting photography, such as the telecommunication tower above Thimphu, and it would also be prudent to refrain from taking pictures of military installations.

There are no restrictions on photographing the outside of dzongs and goembas, but photography is *strictly* prohibited inside goembas and lhakhangs. There are several reasons for this. One is that in the past tourists have completely disrupted holy places with their picture taking. Another is the fear that photos of treasured statues will become a catalogue of items for art thieves to steal. And thirdly, some early tourists made photographs of religious statues into postcards that were then sold, which is unacceptable to the Bhutanese religious community.

During festivals you can photograph from the dzong courtyard where the dances take place. Remember, however, that this is a religious observance and that you should behave accordingly. Don't photograph a member of the royal family, even if you happen to be at a festival or gathering where they are present.

There is an extensive set of rules and restrictions, including payment of additional royalties, for commercial movie-making within Bhutan. The TCB publishes a booklet that details all these rules.

Post

The mail service from Bhutan is reliable, and no special procedures are necessary.

Bhutan Post (www.bhutanpost.com.bt) offers both outgoing and incoming Expedited Mail Service (EMS), which is a reliable and fast international mail-delivery facility that is cheaper than courier services. It also has a Local Urgent Mail (LUM) service for delivery within Thimphu.

If you have made a purchase and want to send it home, it's easiest to have the shop make arrangements for you. Keep the receipt and let your guide know what you are doing so they can follow up in case the package does not arrive. Send all parcels by air; sea mail, via Kolkata (Calcutta), takes months.

DHL (Map p50; sangay_wangmo@dhl.com; 19-13 Thori Lam) has an office in Thimphu. A 500g package of documents costs around US$70 to the USA and UK, or US$65 to Australia. There are several smaller courier companies that specialise in service to India.

Postal Rates

Airmail letter Rates Letters up to 20g cost Nu 30 domestic, Nu 50 for Nepal, India and Bangladesh, Nu 55 most foreign countries.

EMS Rates 500g documents cost Nu 645 to India, and Nu 1100/1245/1450 to Australia/USA/UK.

Public Holidays

Public holidays follow both the Gregorian and lunar calendars and are decided by the **Royal Civil Service Commission** (www.rcsc.gov.bt).

Birthday of Fifth King 21, 22 & 23 February

Birthday of Third King 2 May

Coronation of Fourth King 2 June; also marked as 'Social Forest Day'

PRACTICALITIES

➜ **Newspapers** *Kuensel* (www.kuenselonoline.com) is the daily (except Sunday) national newspaper of Bhutan. Private newspapers include: *Bhutan Today* (www.bhutantoday.bt, biweekly); *Bhutan Times* (www.bhutantimes.com, Sunday); *Bhutan Observer* (www.bhutanobserver.bt, Friday); *The Journalist* (Sunday); *The Bhutanese* (www.the bhutanese.bt, biweekly); and *Business Bhutan* (www.businessbhutan.bt, Saturday).

➜ **Magazines** *Faces of Bhutan* is a glossy annual on Buddhism and Bhutanese culture; the monthly news magazine is *Drukpa*; and *Yeewong* is aimed at Bhutanese women.

➜ **Radio** Bhutan Broadcasting Service (www.bbs.com.bt) broadcasts English news at 11am and 2pm on 96FM. Kuzoo FM 105 (www.kuzoo.net) is a private English- and Dzongkha-language station with a mix of music and chat, or try Radio Valley at 99.9FM.

➜ **TV** BBS TV broadcasts evening news in English. Satellite channels such as BBC World and CNN are widespread.

➜ **Weights & Measures** The metric system is used throughout the country. In villages, rice is sometimes measured in a round measure called a *gasekhorlo*. There is a scale called a *sang* that is used for butter and meat.

Coronation of Druk Gyalpo 1 November

Constitution Day/Fourth King's Birthday 11 November

National Day 17 December; the date of the establishment of the monarchy in 1907

The following holidays are set by the traditional lunar calendar and so vary in Gregorian dates:

Losar January/February, New Year

Zhabdrung Kuchoe April/May; death of Zhabdrung

Buddha Paranirvana/Saga Dawa May/June; enlightenment and death of Buddha

Birthday of Guru Rinpoche June/July

First sermon of Buddha July

Dashain October; Hindu celebration

Several major festivals are considered local public holidays, including September's Thimphu *dromchoe* and tsechu. Note that dates for festivals can vary by several weeks each year, especially if they are adjusted to conform to auspicious dates. Before you schedule a trip around a specific festival, check with a tour operator or the **Tourism Council of Bhutan** (TCB; Map p50; ☑02-323251; www. tourism.gov.bt) for the correct dates.

In the Bhutanese lunar system, months have 30 days, with the full moon on the 15th. The eighth, 15th and 30th days of the month are auspicious and you'll notice increased activity and prayers in monasteries across the country.

Safe Travel

Bhutan is a remarkably safe destination, almost completely devoid of the scams, begging and theft that affects its neighbours. There are couple of things to look out for, though.

Altitude

It's unlikely you will have any problems with altitude unless you are trekking. Most of the places tourists visit lie below 3000m and the maximum elevation you can reach by road is around 3800m.

Dogs

Those cute dogs that wag their tails for you during the day turn into barking monsters at night. Bring earplugs. There is little danger of dog bites, but occasional rabies outbreaks occur in rural Bhutan, so be wary of big dogs guarding properties, especially if trekking.

Weather

Inclement weather can obscure the mountain views that you made such an effort to see and can affect Druk Air flights. In the monsoon heavy rain can turn trails into a sea of mud and can wash away bridges, while leeches can be a real irritation in the lower valleys.

Carsickness

If you venture east of Thimphu, you will spend hours driving on rough, winding roads and carsickness is common. Antimotion medication such as Dramamine can help, but bring the antidrowsy versions or you'll spend most of the spectacular drives snoring in the back seat.

Crime

Theft is still minimal in Bhutan, but as elsewhere it is growing along with the population.

Telephone

There are public call offices (PCOs) throughout the country from where you can make long-distance (STD) calls within Bhutan or to India, or international subscriber dialling (ISD) calls overseas. Most hotels can arrange local and international calls for a premium, though few have in-room direct-dial facilities.

Local calls cost around Nu 1 per minute, or Nu 2 per minute long distance. International calls cost Nu 45 per minute, or Nu 5 to India.

Some useful numbers:

☑**140** Domestic directory inquiries

☑**116** International directory inquiries

Mobile Phones

A B-Mobile SIM card is available at any telecom shop in Thimphu for Nu 100 (which includes talk time worth Nu 50); proof of your passport must be shown at the time of purchase. Further top-ups are available in multiples of Nu 100. Apart from **B-Mobile** (www. druknet.bt), there's also **Tashi Cell** (www.tashicell.com), with similar rates but more limited coverage.

Local call charges vary from Nu 0.40 to Nu 0.70 per 15 seconds, depending on the time of day and network called. Text messages are Nu 0.70. ISD charges are Nu 5 per minute for India and from Nu 18 to Nu 45 per minute for the rest of the world.

Time

Bhutan time is GMT/UTC plus six hours; there is only one time zone throughout the country. The time in Bhutan is 30 minutes later than in India, 15 minutes later than Nepal and one hour earlier than Thailand. When it is noon in Bhutan, standard time is 6am in London, 4pm in Sydney, 1am in New York and 10pm the previous day in San Francisco.

Toilets

Most hotels provide Western toilets and toilet paper, though there are some exceptions, particularly in eastern Bhutan. There are very few public toilets, so take full advantage of hotel and restaurant facilities before that long drive. Most public toilets are of the Asian squat variety and toilet paper isn't available, though a container of water should be present.

Tourist Information

The **Tourism Council of Bhutan** (TCB; Map p50; ☎02-323251; www.tourism.gov.bt) has a comprehensive website and it can refer you to tour operators who can assist with arrangements to visit Bhutan. There is no official government tourist office outside Bhutan.

Most of the big travel companies in Bhutan have good general information on Bhutan on their websites.

Travellers with Disabilities

A cultural tour in Bhutan is a challenge for a traveller with physical disabilities, but is possible with some planning. The Bhutanese are eager to help, and one could arrange a strong companion to assist with moving about and getting in and out of vehicles. The roads are rough and pavements, where they exist, often have holes and sometimes steps. Hotels and public buildings rarely have wheelchair access or lifts, and only the newest will have bathrooms designed to accommodate wheelchairs.

Visas

Most countries issue visas from their embassies abroad and stamp it in your passport, but not Bhutan. Visas are issued only when you arrive in the country, either at Paro airport or (if entering by road) at Phuentsholing, Gelephu or Samdrup Jongkhar. You must apply in advance through a tour operator and receive visa approval before you travel to Bhutan.

All applications for tourist visas must be initialised by a Bhutanese tour operator and are approved by the Ministry of Foreign Affairs in Thimphu. The operator submits an online application with a copy of the photo page of your passport to TCB in Thimphu. It, in turn, checks that you have paid for your trip (including the US$40 visa fee) and then issues an approval letter to the tour operator. With this approval in hand, the tour operator then makes a final application to the Ministry of Foreign Affairs, which takes up to three days to process the visa.

It's not necessary to fill in a special visa application form. Just send a scan of your passport photo and your passport information pages to your tour operator/local travel agent. You may also need to provide your permanent address and occupation.

When the visa clearance is issued by the Ministry of Foreign Affairs, it sends a confirmation number to the tour operator and to Druk Air. Druk Air will not issue your tickets to Paro until it receives this number and then rechecks the visa information when you check in for the flight.

The actual visa endorsement is stamped in your passport when you arrive at one of the ports of entry for tourists. You will receive a visa for the exact period you have arranged to be in Bhutan. You will normally have already paid the visa fee of US$40 directly to your tour company. If some unusual event requires that you obtain a visa extension, your tour operator will arrange it.

It's surprisingly efficient considering the time, distance and various levels of bureaucracy involved. When you arrive in Bhutan, the visa officer will invariably be able to produce your approval

INDIAN TRAVELLERS IN BHUTAN

Indian nationals are allowed to travel on their own in Bhutan, with or without the services of a tour operator. If they choose to liaise with an operator, they are currently charged a minimum daily fee of US$135 per person (US$175 for teams of three people or less).

Indians don't require a visa to enter Bhutan, and are given a seven-day entry-cum-stay permit at the border offices upon presentation of a passport or government-issued ID such as a voter's registration card. This permit allows travel only within Phuentsholing, Thimphu and Paro, and can be extended at the **Immigration Office** (☎02-323127) in Thimphu for successive periods of three weeks each. Bring at least two passport photos. One can also request a route permit here to travel beyond the three above-mentioned towns.

Indians without stay permits can wander freely in Phuentsholing during the day, but must return to India before 10pm. There is a **Tourist Information Office** (Map p109; ☎05-251393) in Phuentsholing to assist Indian travellers.

form from the file and the visa will be issued on the spot. It's helpful to have a printout of the scanned visa authority to aid the immigration officials and Druk Air to find your information quickly.

Visas for Neighbouring Countries

INDIA

Nationals of most countries need a visa to visit India. If you are travelling overland to or from Bhutan via the border post in Phuentsholing, Gelephu or Samdrup Jongkhar, you will need an Indian visa.

The government of India strongly prefers that you obtain your Indian visa in the country that issued your passport. It's usually a simple task to get your Indian visa before you leave home, but it's complicated to get one if overseas. It is possible to obtain a seven-day transit visa overseas if you have confirmed flights in and out of India and can produce the appropriate tickets. Otherwise, you must pay a fee to the overseas embassy to send a fax to the Indian embassy in your own country and wait up to a week for a reply. Tourist visas are generally issued for six months, are multiple entry, and are valid from the date of issue of the visa, not the date you enter India. This means that if you first enter India five months after the visa was issued, it will be valid for one month.

NEPAL

Visas for Nepal are available on arrival at Kathmandu airport or at land border crossings, including Kakarbhitta, the road crossing nearest to Bhutan. You will need one passport photo. If you are making a side trip to Bhutan from Kathmandu, be sure to get a double-entry visa the first time you arrive in Nepal. You can also obtain a visa for Nepal in advance from embassies abroad or from the Nepali embassy or consulate in the gateway cities of Bangkok, Delhi, Dhaka or Kolkata.

Travel Permits
RESTRICTED-AREA PERMITS

All of Bhutan outside of the Paro and Thimphu valleys is classified as a restricted area. Tour operators obtain a 'road permit' for the places on your itinerary, and this permit is checked and endorsed by the police at immigration checkpoints located at important road junctions. The tour operator must return the permit to the government after the tour, and it is scrutinised for major deviations from the authorised program.

There are immigration checkpoints in Hongtsho (east of Thimphu), Chhukha (between Thimphu and Phuentsholing), Rinchending (above Phuentsholing), Wangdue Phodrang, Chazam (near Trashigang), Wamrong (between Trashigang and Samdrup Jongkhar) and in Samdrup Jongkhar. All are open from 5am to 9pm daily.

PERMISSION TO ENTER TEMPLES

During times when there aren't festivals, tourists are allowed to visit the courtyards of dzongs and, where feasible, the *tshokhang* (assembly hall) and one designated lhakhang in each dzong, but only when accompanied by a licensed Bhutanese guide. This provision is subject to certain restrictions, including visiting hours, dress standards and other rules that vary by district.

The TCB has a small list of places tourists *cannot* visit, with the assumption that all other places can be visited. You can generally visit any lhakhang that is private or village-run. Dzongs are open to all during tsechus, when you may visit the courtyard, but not the lhakhangs. Your tour company will deal with all the necessary paperwork, so let them know in advance if there are specific goembas or chapels you wish to visit.

If you are a practising Buddhist, you may apply for a permit to visit certain dzongs

and religious institutions usually off limits. The credibility of your application will be enhanced if you include a letter of reference from a recognised Buddhist organisation in your home country.

Volunteering

Bhutan is selective about the type of projects it wants in the country, so the opportunities for volunteer work in Bhutan are limited. The UN has numerous programs in Bhutan, all coordinated through the UN Development Programme (UNDP). Different agencies feed into the program.

Other agencies that operate programs in Bhutan include ACB (Austria), Danida (Denmark), GTZ (Germany), Helvetas (Switzerland), JOCV & JICA (Japan), Save the Children, SNV (Netherlands) and VSA (New Zealand).

Volunteers aren't subject to the normal rules for tourists and the agency employing you will arrange your visa. Volunteers are allowed two visitors a year; the visitors must be close relatives and are not subject to the tourist tariff.

Women Travellers

Women, both foreign and Bhutanese, are not usually subject to harassment and do not need to take any special precautions. Men have a reasonably liberated attitude towards their relations with women. There are several opportunities for misunderstanding if you don't make your intentions clear from the very outset, however. Female travellers should be aware that romantic liaisons between tourists and Bhutanese guides are quite common. You might also be invited to a 'party' at the home of a Bhutanese male and discover too late that you are the only guest.

Women are generally not allowed to enter the *goenkhang* (protector chapel) of a monastery or lhakhang.

Transport

GETTING THERE & AWAY

The majority of travellers to Bhutan arrive by air at Bhutan's only international airport in Paro. Some travellers enter Bhutan by road at Phuentsholing, Gelephu and Samdrup Jongkhar on the southern border with India.

Tours of Bhutan and rail tickets for India can be booked online at www.lonelyplanet.com/bookings.

Entering the Country

Entry procedures are generally simple because your tour guide will meet you on arrival. Be sure to carry your visa authorisation form from the Ministry of Foreign Affairs.

Passport

If your passport has less than six months of validity left, get a new one before setting off, because many countries in this region will not issue visas to persons whose passports are about to expire.

Keep your passport safe. No country other than India has the facility for issuing a replacement passport in Bhutan. If you lose your passport, you must travel 'stateless' to another country to get it replaced. You should carry some additional form of identification and a photocopy of your passport to help in such an event.

Indian and Bangladeshi travellers do not need a passport to visit Bhutan, but will need some form of (photographic) identification, such as a voter's registration card.

Air

Airports & Airlines

Bhutan has one international airport, **Paro** (PBH; ☑08-271423; ☎), and one national airline, **Druk Air** (www.drukair.com.bt), which has an office in **Paro** (☑08-272044; reservationparo@drukair.com.bt; Nemeyzampa, Paro; ⊙9am-1pm & 2-5pm Mon-Fri, 10am-1pm Sat) and **Thimphu** (Map p54; ☑02-323420; drukairthimphu@druknet.bt; Chang Lam Plaza; ⊙9am-1pm & 2-4pm Mon-Fri, 10am-1pm Sat & Sun). A new private airline, **Bhutan Airlines** (www.bhutanairway.com), a division of Tashi Air, is planning to start operating both domestic and international services in late 2013.

The Druk Air schedule changes by season, but normally there are at least three flights per week from New Delhi and a daily flight from Bangkok, either direct or via Dhaka, Kolkata or Bagdogra, depending on the day of travel. Extra flights are put on during the Thimphu tsechu in October and the Paro tsechu in April.

At the time of research only Druk Air was operating international flights to Bhutan. There are only a few

---

CLIMATE CHANGE & TRAVEL

Every form of transport that relies on carbon-based fuel generates CO_2, the main cause of human-induced climate change. Modern travel is dependent on aeroplanes, which might use less fuel per kilometre per person than most cars but travel much greater distances. The altitude at which aircraft emit gases (including CO_2) and particles also contributes to their climate change impact. Many websites offer 'carbon calculators' that allow people to estimate the carbon emissions generated by their journey and, for those who wish to do so, to offset the impact of the greenhouse gases emitted with contributions to portfolios of climate-friendly initiatives throughout the world. Lonely Planet offsets the carbon footprint of all staff and author travel.

aircraft that can operate on a runway that is as short and high as Paro's. All landings and take-offs in Paro are by visual flight rules (VFR), which means that the pilot must be able to see the runway before landing, and see the surrounding hills before take-off. This means that no flights can be operated at night or in poor visibility, so when Paro valley is clouded in, flights are delayed, sometimes for days. When this happens your tour program will have to be changed and everything rebooked. The upside of such a delay is that you can probably add some spontaneity into your schedule in Bhutan and make a few modifications as you go.

➡ Reconfirm your Druk Air flight before departure and also once in Paro, to ensure that the schedule has not changed.

➡ Check in early for Druk Air flights as they occasionally depart before the scheduled time, especially if the weather starts to change for the worse.

➡ Flights are often delayed because of weather and Druk Air recommends that you travel on nonrestricted tickets and allow at least 24 hours' transit time with your connecting flight in order to minimise the complications of delays. It makes sense to budget a couple of days' sightseeing in Kathmandu or Bangkok.

DRUK AIR OFFICES ABROAD

Druk Air Bangladesh
(☎02-891 1066; dhaka@druk air.com.bt; Room 52, Terminal 2, Zia International Airport, Dhaka)

Druk Air India (Kolkata)
(☎033-2290 2429, airport office 033-2511 9976; reservation@ drukairccu.com; 51 Tivoli Crt, 1A Ballygunge Circular Rd, Kolkata)

Druk Air India (New Delhi)
(☎011-4712 7703, airport office 011-4963 3616; sales.delhi@ drukair.com.au; G fl 3, Ansal Bhawan Bldg, 16KH Marg, Connaught Place, New Delhi)

Druk Air Nepal (☎01-423
9988, airport office 01-447 1712; sales@drukair.danfetrav-els.com; Danfe Travel Centre, Woodlands Hotel, Durbar Marg, Kathmandu)

Druk Air Thailand (☎02-
237 92013, airport office 02-134 3040; drukairbkk@drukair.com. bt; Ste 141/4, 5th fl, Skulthai Surawong Tower, Suriyawong, Bangkok)

DRUK AIR SALES AGENTS ABROAD

DNATA (☎02-883 1804; dna-takb@yahoo.com; Ste D1, House 83, 23 Valentine Castle Rd, Gulshan-1, Dhaka, Bangladesh)

Druk Asia (☎6338 9909;
www.drukasia.com; 60 Albert St, 12-03, Singapore)

Global Union Transpor-
tation (☎852-2868 3231; josephlo@aeroglobal.com.hk; Room 505, Nan Fung Tower, 17 Des Voeux Rd, Central, Hong Kong)

Zen International Tours & Travels (☎0353-251
4403; www.zenitt.com; Hotel Central Plaza Market Complex, Mallaguri, PO Pradhan Nagar, Siliguri, India)

Tickets

Because there is little competition with other airlines for flights to Paro, Druk Air fares are relatively expensive. There are no discounts or student fares except for citizens of Bhutan. Moreover, Druk Air rules say that if fares are increased after the ticket is issued, they may collect the difference when you check in. It is possible to purchase Druk Air tickets online using a credit card.

It's also possible to have your agent book your Druk Air ticket and email you the e-ticket. In the event of a cancellation you are likely to get a refund quicker this way and your agent should get direct notifications if there are changes to the flight times. Your agent will also email you a scan of your visa clearance from the Department of Immigration and you will need to show a printout of this when you check-in with Druk Air.

You will need to buy a ticket to and from the place where you will connect to Druk Air. For most travellers this essentially means Delhi, Bangkok, Singapore or Kathmandu, depending on where you are travelling from and which city you'd rather transit through. Delhi,

PARO FLIGHTS

DEPART	ARRIVE	FREQUENCY	COST (US$)
Paro	Kathmandu	daily	220
Paro	Bangkok	daily	390
Paro	Kolkata (Calcutta)	6 weekly	220
Paro	New Delhi	5 weekly	355
Paro	Dhaka	4 weekly	220
Paro	Guhawati	3 weekly	140
Paro	Bagdogra	3 weekly	125
Paro	Singapore	2 weekly	620

IN-FLIGHT ENTERTAINMENT

The Druk Air flight from Kathmandu to Paro provides the most dramatic view of Himalayan scenery of any scheduled flight (snag a window seat on the left if you can). Look for the impressive Bodhnath stupa to the north as the plane takes off. Soon a continuous chain of peaks appears just off the left wing. The captain usually points out Everest (8850m; a black striated pyramid), Makalu (a grey chair-shaped peak) and Kanchenjunga (a huge massif), but if you have trekked in Nepal and are familiar with the mountains you can pick out many more. The elusive Shishapangma (8013m) is sometimes visible inside Tibet. Other recognisable peaks are Gauri Shankar (7185m), with its notched shape, Cho Oyu (8153m), Nuptse (7906m), with its long ridge, Lhotse (8501m) and Chhamlang (7319m).

When you pass Kanchenjunga, look for the dome-shaped peak on the western skyline. That is Jannu (7710m), which some French climbers have described as a 'peak of terror'; the Nepalis have renamed it Khumbakarna. Once past Kanchenjunga, the peaks are more distant. This is the Sikkim Himalaya; the major peaks, from west to east, are Chomoyummo (6829m), Pauhunri (7125m) and Shudu Tsenpa (7032m).

As the plane approaches Paro you may be able to spot the beautiful snow peak of Jhomolhari (7314m) and the grey ridge-shaped peak of Jichu Drakye (6989m). The plane then descends, often through clouds, banking steeply into the wooded valleys of Bhutan. Depending on the approach pattern that day, you may see Taktshang Goemba and Paro Dzong as you descend. Paro airport is often described as the scariest airstrip in the world but it's really not that bad.

Singapore and Bangkok offer the most international connections, but Kathmandu will give you an extra taste of the Himalaya. Other connections via Kolkata or Dhaka are possible, but fewer discounted international airfares are available to these places.

TRANSIT BAGGAGE

Because Druk Air has no interline agreements with other carriers, your ticket to Paro will be separate from your other international tickets. This means you cannot check your baggage all the way through to Paro via a connecting flight. You will need to reclaim your baggage and recheck it at the Druk Air counter. The only exception to this *might* be Thai Airways.

When you depart from Bhutan, Druk Air claims it can check bags through to your final destination if you give them the flight details during check-in but be aware that this information is handwritten on the baggage tags. Call us travel cynics but we don't fully trust the system.

The significance of not being able to check through your luggage is that you may have to go through immigration at your transfer airport to pick up your luggage in order to check in again. Depending on the country this can create visa problems. Bangkok, Singapore and Kathmandu transit is relatively easy, requiring either no visa or free transit visas on the spot, but in Delhi you're likely to need to find a staff member to get your bag from the carousel and recheck it in for you as you can't exit the transit area without an Indian visa.

Border Crossings

Crossing between Bhutan and India (and then to Nepal) is relatively straightforward at the following three points found along Bhutan's southern border.

➡ **Phuentsholing** The primary border crossing from India into Bhutan, on the border with the Indian state of West Bengal.

➡ **Samdrup Jongkhar** Much less used but still possible for exit or entry, in the far east on the border with the Indian state of Assam.

➡ **Gelephu** Again little used but still possible for exit or entry on the border with Assam. May increase in popularity when the the new airport is eventually opened to scheduled flights.

To/From Phuentsholing (India)

The gate between Phuentsholing and Jaigaon (just across the border) opens at 6am and closes at 9pm for vehicles, but people can cross on foot until 10pm. If you are travelling to or from Bhutan via Phuentsholing, all roads lead through Siliguri in West Bengal, the major transport hub in northeast India. Heading into India, you can make road connections from Phuentsholing or Jaigaon to the train station in Siliguri (169km, six hours) or the airport in Bagdogra (which has flights to Paro). From Siliguri it's easy to arrange a share-taxi or bus on to the Indian hill stations of Darjeeling (77km), Gangtok (Sikkim; 114km) or Kalimpong, and also the Nepal border at Kakarbhitta.

The nearest main-line Indian train station to Phuentsholing is in New Jalpaiguri (near Siliguri). From there it's a 12-hour rail journey to Kolkata or a 33-hour trip to Delhi. You can travel by road direct to New Jalpaiguri from Phuentsholing or drive to Siliguri where you can simply flag down a rickshaw.

If you are headed to Bhutan, several Bhutanese transport companies operate a direct bus service at 8am and 2pm daily between Siliguri and Phuentsholing (Rs 90, four hours). In Siliguri, the booking office is on Tenzing Norgay Rd (also known as Hill Cart Rd), opposite the Sher-e-Punjab Hotel. You can sometimes find Bhutanese taxis (yellow-roofed minivans with number plates beginning with 'BT') looking for a return fare. You can technically buy a seat for Rs 350, but you might eventually have to charter the whole taxi for about Rs 1400. Indian bus companies also operate services between Siliguri and Jaigaon on the Indian side of the Bhutanese border.

Bhutanese vehicles may travel freely in India and a Bhutanese tour operator can easily arrange a vehicle to any of these destinations. There are also taxis and shared hire cars available in both Phuentsholing and Siliguri.

Since Phuentsholing offers decent lodging options, few choose to halt at Jaigaon. If you absolutely must stay, try these hotels offering rooms with air-con:

Hotel Anand (☏03566-263783; www.hotelanand jaigon.com; MG Rd; s/d from Rs 1100/1200, d with air-con Rs 2000)

Hotel Kasturi (☏03566-263035; NS Rd; s/d from Rs 500/700) Next to the immigration checkpoint.

FOREIGNERS

Don't forget to get your passport stamped when leaving India. If your transport has already deposited you in Bhutan, you can simply walk back across the border to complete the paperwork.

Your guide will meet you at the gate and help you obtain your Bhutanese visa in Phuentsholing.

INDIAN NATIONALS

To go through immigration at Phuentsholing, Indian nationals are required to submit a passport-size photograph, a copy of their identification document such as passport or voters' identity card, and a filled-in application form at the **Immigration Office** (☏05-253079; Zhung Lam; ⏰6am-1pm & 2-6pm), which sits on the 1st floor of the Regional Revenue and Customs Office, located in front of Hotel Druk. A permit is then handed out by the immigration authorities, which must be stamped in at the checkpoint in Rinchending, en route to Thimphu.

Please note that these rules are changeable upon short notice, especially during politically sensitive periods or due to unforeseen security issues. For more on paperwork for Indian travellers, see p269.

To/From Samdrup Jongkhar & Gelephu (India)

Foreign and Indian tourists are allowed to enter or exit Bhutan at Samdrup Jongkhar and Gelephu. Be aware that *bandhs* (strikes) that affect all road transport and can close borders are relatively common in Assam and can be called at short notice and last for a week. Check on the status of Assamese separatist groups before you decide to travel by land through Assam.

The primary reason you would want to exit into Assam is to avoid the long drive back over the mountains

to Thimphu after visiting central and eastern Bhutan. From Samdrup Jongkhar and Gelephu, drive down to Guwahati in Assam, from where you can fly to Kolkata, Delhi, Bangkok or Bagdogra, or get a train connection to numerous Indian destinations. Due to security concerns, all Bhutanese vehicles have to travel in a convoy so expect delays. Six kilometres from the Samdrup Jongkhar border at Darranga, and 10km from the Gelephu border at Deosiri, is a Foreigners' Registration Post, open 24 hours, where you must get your entry/exit stamp. Carry photocopies of your passport photo pages and Indian visa as these may be asked for.

Another alternative to Guhawati is a long, but flat, drive west through the Indian *duars* (low hills) to Siliguri.

To/From Nepal

Panitanki (aka Raniganj), in northern West Bengal, is opposite the eastern Nepal border town of Kakarbhitta. A long bridge separates the two towns across the Mechi River. Bhutanese tour operators can pick you up or drop you at Panitanki, or you can arrange for them to take you to Bhadrapur or Biratnagar to catch a flight to Kathmandu.

Panitanki is only one hour (35km) from Siliguri (India). Buses run regularly on this route (Rs 25) and taxis are easy to arrange (Rs 500). A cycle-rickshaw across the border to Kakarbhitta costs Rs 30. Buses depart Kakarbhitta at 5pm daily for Kathmandu (NRs 1150 – Nepali rupees, 17-plus hours), a long, rough drive via Narayanghat, Mugling and the Trisuli River valley. See Lonely Planet's *Nepal* for details of what to see and do along this route.

A better option is to take a taxi (NRs 600) from Kakarbhitta to Bhadrapur and take a domestic flight to Kathmandu (US$155). There is a larger airport at Biratnagar, a four-hour drive from the border, from where a flight costs US$130. Yeti Airlines and Buddha Air are the most reliable airlines. **Jhapa Travel Agency** (☎977-23-562020) in Kakarbhitta will be able to book a flight.

GETTING AROUND

Because Bhutan does not have a centimetre of passenger railway track, the only way to see the country is either by foot or by road, though this looks set to change soon with the ongoing development of domestic air services.

There is one main road: the National Hwy, a 3.5m-wide stretch of tarmac that winds its way up and down mountains, across clattering bridges, along the side of cliffs and over high mountain passes. Rivers, mudflows and rockfalls present continual hazards, especially when it rains. The road can easily become blocked due to snow or landslides and can take anywhere from an hour to several days to clear. Take plenty of reading material.

Tour operators use modern buses, minivans and SUVs, depending on the size of the group. These vehicles can take you almost anywhere in the country, but for trips to central and eastern Bhutan during winter (December to February) or the monsoon (June to September) a 4WD vehicle is an advantage, and often a necessity.

If you are travelling on a tourist visa, the cost of all transport is included in the price of your trip and you'll have a vehicle available for both short- as well as long-distance travel.

Air

Bhutan has ambitious plans for domestic air services. Airports have been developed in Yongphula (south of

Trashigang in the far east), Gelephu (in southern Bhutan, near the border with India) and Bathpalathang/Jakar (Bumthang, central Bhutan). At the time of writing, only **Druk Air** (www.drukair.com.bt) flights to Bathpalathang were scheduled, and the other domestic airline, **Bhutan Airlines** (www.bhutanairway.com), had suspended all operations. Check with your tour company to see the current status.

When regular flights are scheduled, the airports in Yongphula and Gelephu in particular could significantly open up travel and improve travel itineraries in that area of Bhutan.

Bicycle

Some travellers bring their mountain bikes to Bhutan, and several companies can help arrange this kind of tour. See p261 for more on cycling.

Bus

Public buses are crowded and rattly, and Bhutan's winding roads make them doubly uncomfortable. The government's Bhutan Post Express and other companies' minibuses have earned the nickname 'vomit comets' as so many passengers suffer from motion sickness when travelling in them. Private operators such as Dhug, Metho and Sernya use more comfortable Toyota Coasters that cost about 50% more than the minibus fare.

Buses run at least once daily from Thimphu to Phuentsholing, Haa, Paro and Punakha. Long-distance buses run between one and three times weekly from Thimphu to Zhemgang, Samtse, Trashi Yangtse, Mongar, Phobjika and Trashigang. Fares are cheap.

A public bus service operates throughout Thimphu

from Chang Lam, including to Dechenchoeling in the north and Simtokha and Babesa to the south. Routes, fares and timetables are available at www.bhutanpost.com.bt.

Car & Motorcycle

Since all transport is provided by tour operators, you normally do not have to concern yourself with driving. If for some reason you are arranging your own transport, you are still far better off using the services of a hired car and driver or a taxi. Driving in Bhutan is a harrowing experience. Roads are narrow and trucks roar around hairpin bends, appearing suddenly and forcing oncoming vehicles to the side. Because most roads are only about 3.5m wide, passing any oncoming vehicle involves one, or both, moving onto the verge.

Motorcycle trips in Bhutan can be arranged through **Himalayan Roadrunners** (www.ridehigh.com) and **Saffron Road Motorcycle Tours** (www.saffronroad.com). The local **Black Dragons Motorcycle Club** (www.bhutandragons.blogspot.com) in Thimphu might be able to offer advice for bikers tackling Bhutan's roads.

Your Own Vehicle

If you drive a vehicle into Bhutan, you can get a 14-day permit at the Phuentsholing border. You will need the help of a tour operator to handle the paperwork. If you are driving a vehicle that is registered overseas, you will need a carnet in order to get through India.

Indian visitors may travel throughout most of Bhutan in their own vehicle, upon getting all relevant documents such as registration papers, insurance policies, emission and fitness certificates and individual driving licences endorsed by the **Road Safety and Transport**

Authority (www.rsta.gov.bt) at the border. Traffic regulations are the same as in India and are strictly enforced.

Driving Licence

NGO staff and volunteers who insist on driving in Bhutan should obtain a driving licence issued by the Road Safety and Transport Authority. Bhutanese licences are also valid throughout India.

An International Driving Permit is not valid in Bhutan. An Indian driving licence is valid in Bhutan, and it's possible for Indian nationals to drive in Bhutan; but unless you are an accomplished rally driver or are from a hill station such as Darjeeling and have experience in motoring in the mountains, it's safer with a professional driver.

Road Rules

Traffic keeps to the left and is much more orderly than in most other south Asian countries. Speeds are low in towns and on rural roads; you will be lucky to average more than 30km/h on the roads in the hills.

As is the case throughout Asia, it is important that the police establish who was at fault in any traffic accident. This means that the police must arrive and make the decision before any of the vehicles can be moved, even if the vehicles are blocking a narrow road. A relatively minor accident can block the road for hours while everyone waits patiently for the police to arrive from the nearest town.

Local Transport

Taxi

There are taxis in Phuentsholing, Paro and Thimphu. Taxis may have meters, but drivers rarely use them. For long-distance trips they operate on a flat rate that is rarely open to negotiation.

You should expect to pay Nu 60 for a local trip within Thimphu, Nu 800 for a full day, and Nu 650 a seat to Nu 2600 (sole use) from Thimphu to Phuentsholing. If you are travelling between Thimphu and Phuentsholing, look for a taxi that is from the place to which you want to go (vehicles with BT-2 number plates are from Phuentsholing and those with BT-1 number plates are from Thimphu or Paro) – you may be able to negotiate a lower price.

Health

The main health concerns in Bhutan are similar to those in other south Asian destinations: there is a relatively high risk of acquiring traveller's diarrhoea, a respiratory infection, or a more exotic infection. The infectious diseases can interrupt your trip and make you feel miserable, but they are rarely fatal. If you go trekking, there are also risks associated with accidents and altitude sickness. Falling off trails, or having a rock fall on you as you trek, is rare but can happen.

The following advice is a general guide only and does not replace the advice of a doctor trained in travel medicine.

BEFORE YOU GO

Pack medications in their original, clearly labelled containers. A signed and dated letter from your physician describing your medical conditions and medications, including generic names, is also a good idea. If carrying syringes or needles, be sure to have a physician's letter documenting their medical necessity. If you have a heart condition, bring a copy of your ECG taken just prior to travelling.

If you take any regular medication, bring double your needs in case of loss or theft. You can't rely on many medications being available from pharmacies in Bhutan.

Insurance

Even if you are fit and healthy, don't travel without health insurance – accidents do happen. Declare any existing medical conditions you have – the insurance company *will* check if your problem is pre-existing and will not cover you if it is undeclared.

You may also require extra cover for adventure activities such as rock climbing. If your health insurance doesn't cover you for medical expenses abroad, consider getting extra insurance; for more information, check **Lonely Planet** (www.lonelyplanet.com). If you're uninsured, emergency evacuation is expensive; bills of over US$100,000 are not uncommon.

Find out in advance if your insurance plan will make payments directly to providers or reimburse you later for overseas health expenditures. (In many countries, doctors expect payment in cash.) You may prefer a policy that pays doctors or hospitals directly rather than you having to pay on the spot and claim later. If you have to claim later, make sure you keep all documentation. Some insurance companies ask you to call them (they suggest reversing the charges, an impossibility from Bhutan) at a centre in your home country, where an immediate assessment of your problem is made.

Vaccinations

Specialised travel-medicine clinics are your best source of information; they stock all available vaccines and will be able to give specific recommendations for you and your trip. Most vaccines don't produce immunity until at least two weeks after they're given, so visit a doctor four to eight weeks before departure. Ask your doctor for an International Certificate of Vaccination, which will list all the vaccinations you've received.

Recommended Vaccinations

The World Health Organization recommends the following vaccinations for travellers to Bhutan (as well as being up to date with measles, mumps and rubella vaccinations):

➡ **Diphtheria and tetanus (for adults)** Single booster recommended if none in the previous 10 years. Side effects include sore arm and fever.

➡ **Hepatitis A** Provides almost 100% protection for up to a year; a booster after 12 months provides at least another 20 years' protection. Mild side effects such as headache and sore arm occur in 5% to 10% of people.

➡ **Hepatitis B** Now considered routine for most travellers, it is given as three shots over six months.

A rapid schedule is also available, as is a combined vaccination with Hepatitis A. Side effects are mild and uncommon, usually headache and sore arm. Lifetime protection occurs in 95% of people.

➡ **Polio** Bhutan's last case of polio was reported in 1986, but it has been reported more recently in nearby Nepal and India. Only one booster is required as an adult for lifetime protection. Inactivated polio vaccine is safe during pregnancy.

➡ **Typhoid** The vaccine offers around 70% protection, lasts for two to three years and comes as a single shot. Tablets are also available; however, the injection is usually recommended as it has fewer side effects. Sore arm and fever may occur.

➡ **Varicella** If you haven't had chickenpox, discuss this vaccination with your doctor.

The following immunisations may be recommended for long-term travellers (more than one month) or those at special risk:

➡ **Japanese B encephalitis** Three injections in all. Booster recommended after two years. Sore arm and headache are the most common side effects. Rarely, an allergic reaction comprising hives and swelling can occur up to 10 days after any of the three doses.

➡ **Meningitis** Single injection. There are two types of vaccination: the quadrivalent vaccine gives two to three years' protection; meningitis group C vaccine gives around 10 years' protection. Recommended for long-term backpackers aged under 25.

➡ **Rabies** Three injections in all. A booster after one year will then provide 10 years' protection. Side effects are rare – occasionally headache and sore arm.

➡ **Tuberculosis** A complex issue. Adult long-term travellers are usually recommended to have a TB skin test before and after travel, rather than vaccination. Only one vaccine given in a lifetime.

Required Vaccinations

The only vaccine required by international regulations is yellow fever. Proof of vaccination will only be required if you have visited a country in the yellow-fever zone within the six days prior to entering Bhutan. If you are travelling to Bhutan from Africa or South America, you should check to see if you require proof of vaccination.

Medical Checklist

Recommended items for a personal medical kit:

➡ antifungal cream, eg Clotrimazole

➡ antibacterial cream, eg Muciprocin

➡ antibiotic for skin infections, eg Amoxicillin/ Clavulanate or Cephalexin

➡ antibiotics for diarrhoea, eg Norfloxacin or Ciprofloxacin for bacterial diarrhoea; Tinidazole for giardiasis or amoebic dysentery

➡ antihistamine, eg Cetirizine for daytime and Promethazine for night

➡ antiseptic, eg Betadine

➡ antispasmodic for stomach cramps, eg Buscopan

➡ contraceptives

➡ decongestant, eg Pseudoephedrine

➡ DEET-based insect repellent

➡ diarrhoea treatment – an oral rehydration solution (eg Gastrolyte), diarrhoea 'stopper' (eg Loperamide) and antinausea medication (eg Prochlorperazine)

➡ first-aid items such as scissors, bandages, gauze, thermometer, sterile needles and syringes, safety pins and tweezers

➡ ibuprofen or other anti-inflammatory

➡ iodine tablets (unless you are pregnant or have a thyroid problem) to purify water

➡ laxative, eg Coloxyl

➡ paracetamol

➡ permethrin to impregnate clothing and mosquito nets

➡ steroid cream for allergic/ itchy rashes, eg 1% to 2% hydrocortisone

➡ sunscreen

➡ throat lozenges

➡ thrush (vaginal yeast infection) treatment, eg Clotrimazole pessaries

➡ Ural or equivalent if you're prone to urine infections

Websites

There is a wealth of travel health advice on the internet. For further information, **Lonely Planet** (www. lonelyplanet.com) is a good place to start. The **World Health Organization** (WHO; www.who.int/ith/) publishes a superb book called *International Travel & Health*, which is revised annually and is available free online.

Another website of general interest is **MD Travel Health** (www.mdtravelhealth. com), which provides complete travel health recommendations for every country and is updated daily. The **Centers for Disease Control and Prevention** (CDC; www.cdc.gov) website also has good general information.

Further Reading

Lonely Planet's *Healthy Travel – Asia & India* is a handy pocket-sized book that is packed with useful information including pretrip planning, emergency first aid, immunisation and disease information, and what to do if you get sick on the road. Other recommended references include *Traveller's Health* by Dr Richard Dawood and *Travelling Well* by Dr Deborah Mills – check out the website www.travelling-well.com.au.

IN BHUTAN

Availability & Cost of Health Care

There are no private health clinics or physicians in Bhutan, but all district headquarters towns have a hospital, and will accept travellers in need of medical attention. The best facility is the **Jigme Dorji Wangchuck National Referral Hospital** (Map p50; 02-322496; Gongphel Lam) in Thimphu. It has general physicians and several specialists, labs and operating rooms. Treatment is free, even for tourists. If you are seriously ill or injured, you should consider evacuation to the excellent medical facilities in Bangkok. It is difficult to find reliable medical care in rural areas. Your closest embassy and insurance company are good contacts.

Self-treatment may be appropriate if your problem is minor (eg traveller's diarrhoea), you are carrying the appropriate medication and you cannot attend a recommended clinic. If you think you may have a serious disease, especially malaria, do not waste time – travel to the nearest quality facility to receive attention. It is always better to be assessed by a doctor than to rely on self-treatment.

In most large towns there are shops that sell medicines. Most of the medical supplies mentioned in this section are available without a prescription.

Infectious Diseases

Coughs, Colds & Chest Infections

Respiratory infections usually start as a virus and are exacerbated by urban pollution, or cold and altitude in the mountains. Commonly, a secondary bacterial infection will intervene – marked by fever, chest pain and coughing up discoloured or blood-tinged sputum. If you have the symptoms of an infection, seek medical advice or commence a general antibiotic.

Dengue Fever

This mosquito-borne disease is becomingly increasingly problematic throughout the tropical world, especially in the cities. As there is no vaccine available it can only be prevented by avoiding mosquito bites. The mosquito that carries dengue bites day and night, so use insect avoidance measures at all times. Symptoms include high fever, severe headache and body ache. Some people develop a rash and experience diarrhoea. There is no specific treatment, just rest and paracetamol – do not take aspirin though, as it increases the likelihood of haemorrhaging. See a doctor to be diagnosed and monitored.

Hepatitis A

A problem throughout the region, this food- and water-borne virus infects the liver, causing jaundice (yellow skin and eyes), nausea and lethargy. There is no specific treatment for hepatitis A – you just need to allow time for the liver to heal. All travellers to Bhutan should be vaccinated against hepatitis A.

TRAVELLER'S DIARRHOEA

Traveller's diarrhoea is by far the most common problem affecting travellers – between 30% and 50% of people will suffer from it within two weeks of starting their trip. In over 80% of cases, traveller's diarrhoea is caused by a bacteria, and therefore responds promptly to treatment with antibiotics, such as Norfloxacin. Keep in mind, though, that a couple of loose stools are little cause for concern.

Loperamide is just a 'stopper' and doesn't get to the cause of the problem. It can be helpful, for example, if you have to go on a long car trip. Don't take Loperamide if you have a fever, or blood in your stools, and seek medical attention quickly if you do not respond to an appropriate antibiotic.

Amoebic dysentery is very rare in travellers but is often misdiagnosed. Symptoms are similar to bacterial diarrhoea, ie fever, bloody diarrhoea and generally feeling unwell. You should always seek reliable medical care if you have blood in your diarrhoea. Treatment involves two drugs: Tinidazole or Metronidazole to kill the parasite in your gut followed by a second drug to kill the cysts.

Giardia lamblia is a parasite that is relatively common in travellers. Symptoms include nausea, bloating, excess gas, fatigue and intermittent diarrhoea. The parasite will eventually go away if left untreated but this can take months. The treatment of choice is Tinidazole.

Hepatitis B

The only sexually transmitted disease that can be prevented by vaccination, hepatitis B is spread by body fluids, including in sexual contact. The long-term consequences can include liver cancer and cirrhosis.

Hepatitis E

Hepatitis E is transmitted through contaminated food and water and has similar symptoms to hepatitis A, but is far less common. It is a severe problem for pregnant women and can result in the death of both mother and baby. There is currently no vaccine, and prevention is by following safe eating and drinking guidelines.

Influenza

Present year-round in the tropics, influenza (flu) symptoms include high fever, muscle aches, runny nose, cough and sore throat. It can be very severe in people over the age of 65 or in those with underlying medical conditions such as heart disease or diabetes; vaccination is recommended for these individuals. There is no specific treatment, just rest and paracetamol.

Japanese B Encephalitis

This viral disease is transmitted by mosquitoes and is rare in travellers. Like most mosquito-borne diseases it is becoming a more common problem in affected countries. Most cases occur in rural areas and vaccination is recommended for travellers spending more than one month outside cities. There is no treatment, and a third of infected people will die, while another third will suffer permanent brain damage.

Malaria

For such a serious and potentially deadly disease, there is an enormous amount of misinformation concerning malaria. You must get expert advice as to whether your trip actually puts you at risk. For most rural areas, the risk of contracting malaria far outweighs the risk of any tablet side effects. Before you travel, seek medical advice on the right medication and dosage for you.

Malaria is caused by a parasite transmitted by the bite of an infected mosquito. The most important symptom of malaria is fever, but general symptoms such as headache, diarrhoea, cough or chills may also occur. Diagnosis can only be made by taking a blood sample.

Two strategies should be combined to prevent malaria; mosquito avoidance and antimalaria medications. Most people who catch malaria are taking inadequate or no antimalarial medication.

Travellers are advised to prevent mosquito bites by taking these steps:

➡ Use a DEET-containing insect repellent on exposed skin. Wash this off at night, as long as you are sleeping under a mosquito net. Natural repellents such as citronella can be effective, but must be applied more frequently than products containing DEET.

➡ Sleep under a mosquito net impregnated with pyrethrin.

➡ Choose accommodation with screens and fans (if not air-conditioned).

➡ Impregnate clothing with pyrethrin in high-risk areas.

➡ Wear long sleeves and trousers in light colours.

➡ Use mosquito coils.

➡ Spray your room with insect repellent before going out for your evening meal.

There are a variety of medications available. The effectiveness of the Chloroquine and Paludrine combination is now limited in many parts of South Asia. Common side effects include nausea (40% of people) and mouth ulcers.

The daily tablet Doxycycline is a broad-spectrum antibiotic that has the added benefit of helping to prevent a variety of tropical diseases, including leptospirosis, tick-borne disease and typhus. The potential side effects include photosensitivity, thrush, indigestion, heartburn, nausea and interference with the contraceptive pill. More serious side effects include ulceration of the oesophagus – you can help prevent this by taking your tablet with a meal, and never lying down within 30 minutes of taking it. It must contiue to be taken for four weeks after leaving the risk area.

Lariam (Mefloquine) is a weekly tablet. Serious side effects are rare but include depression, anxiety, psychosis and fits. Anyone with a history of depression, anxiety, another psychological disorder, or epilepsy should not take Lariam. It is considered safe in the second and third trimesters of pregnancy. Tablets must be taken for four weeks after leaving the risk area.

Malarone is a combination of Atovaquone and Proguanil. Side effects are uncommon and mild, most commonly nausea and headache. It is the best tablet for those on short trips to high-risk areas. It must be taken for one week after leaving the risk area.

Rabies

Rabies is considered to be endemic in Bhutan. This uniformly fatal disease is spread by the bite or lick of an infected animal – most commonly a dog or monkey. You should seek medical advice immediately after any animal bite and commence postexposure treatment. Having a pre-travel vaccination means the postbite treatment is greatly simplified. If an animal bites you, gently wash the wound with soap and water, and apply iodine based antiseptic. If you are not prevaccinated you will need to receive rabies immunoglobulin as soon as possible.

Tuberculosis

While rare in travellers, medical and aid workers, and long-term travellers who have significant contact with the local population should take precautions. Vaccination is usually given only to children under the age of five, but adults at risk are recommended to have pre- and post-travel tuberculosis testing. The main symptoms are fever, cough, weight loss, night sweats and tiredness.

Typhoid

This serious bacterial infection is spread via food and water. It gives a high and slowly progressive fever, headache and may be accompanied by a dry cough and stomach pain. It is diagnosed by blood tests and treated with antibiotics. Vaccination is recommended for all travellers spending more than a week in Bhutan. Be aware that vaccination is not 100% effective so you must still be careful with what you eat and drink.

Environmental Hazards

Food

Eating in restaurants is the biggest risk factor for contracting traveller's diarrhoea. Ways to avoid it include eating only freshly cooked food, and avoiding shellfish and food that has been sitting around in buffets. Peel all fruit, cook vegetables and soak salads in iodine water for at least 20 minutes.

High Altitude

If you are going to altitudes above 3000m you should get information on preventing, recognising and treating Acute Mountain Sickness (AMS). AMS is a notoriously fickle affliction and can also affect trekkers and walkers accustomed to walking at high altitudes. AMS has been fatal at 3000m, although 3500m to 4500m is the usual range.

SYMPTOMS

Mild symptoms of AMS are very common in travellers visiting high altitudes, and usually develop during the first 24 hours at altitude. These will generally disappear through acclimatisation in several hours to several days.

Symptoms tend to be worse at night and include headache, dizziness, lethargy, loss of appetite, nausea, breathlessness and irritability. Difficulty sleeping is another common symptom.

AMS may become more serious without warning and can be fatal. Symptoms are caused by the accumulation of fluid in the lungs and brain, and include breathlessness at rest, a dry irritative cough (which may progress to the production of pink, frothy sputum), severe headache, lack of coordination (typically leading to a 'drunken walk'), confusion, irrational behaviour, vomiting and eventually unconsciousness.

The symptoms of AMS, however mild, are a warning – be sure to take them seriously! Trekkers should keep an eye on each other as those experiencing symptoms, especially severe symptoms, may not be in a position to recognise them.

One thing to note is that while the symptoms of mild AMS often precede those of severe AMS, this is not always the case. Severe AMS can strike with little or no warning.

ACCLIMATISATION

With an increase in altitude, the human body needs time to develop physiological mechanisms to cope with the decreased oxygen. This process of acclimatisation is still not fully understood, but is known to involve modifications in breathing patterns and heart rate, and an increase in the blood's oxygen-carrying capabilities. These compensatory mechanisms usually take about one to three days to develop at a particular altitude. Once you are acclimatised to a given height you are unlikely to get AMS at that height, but you can still get ill when you travel higher. If the ascent is too high and too fast, these compensatory reactions may not kick into gear fast enough.

PREVENTION

To prevent acute mountain sickness:

➡ Ascend slowly. Have frequent rest stops, spending two to three nights at each rise of 1000m.

DRINKING WATER

➡ Never drink tap water.

➡ Bottled water is generally safe – check the seal is intact at purchase.

➡ Avoid ice.

➡ Avoid fresh juices – they may have been watered down.

➡ Boil water – this is the most efficient method of purifying it; let it boil a bit longer at higher altitudes.

➡ Purify water – the best chemical purifier is iodine but this should not be used by pregnant women or those with thyroid problems.

➡ Use water filters – should also filter out viruses; ensure your filter has a chemical barrier such as iodine and a small pore size, eg less than four microns.

➡ Bear in mind the climber's adage 'climb high, sleep low'. It is always wise to sleep at a lower altitude than the greatest height reached during the day. High day climbs followed by a descent back to lower altitudes for the night are good preparation for trekking at high altitude. Also, once above 3000m, care should be taken not to increase the sleeping altitude by more than 400m per day. If the terrain won't allow for less than 400m of elevation gain, be ready to take an extra day off before tackling the climb.

➡ Drink extra fluids. The mountain air is dry and cold, and moisture is lost as you breathe and sweat, which may result in dehydration.

➡ Eat light, high-carbohydrate meals for more energy.

➡ Avoid alcohol as it may increase the risk of dehydration, and don't smoke.

➡ Avoid sedatives.

➡ Take a day off when trekking to rest and acclimatise if feeling overtired. If you or anyone else in your party is having a tough time, make allowances for unscheduled stops.

➡ Don't push yourself when climbing up to passes; rather, take plenty of breaks. Given the complexity and unknown variables involved with AMS and acclimatisation, trekkers should always err on the side of caution and ascend slowly.

TREATMENT

Treat mild symptoms by resting at the same or lower altitude until recovery, usually in a day or two. Take paracetamol or aspirin for headaches. If symptoms persist or become worse, however, *immediate descent* is necessary – even 500m can help.

The most effective treatment for severe AMS is to get down to a lower altitude as quickly as possible. In less severe cases the victim will be able to stagger down with some support; in other cases they may need to be carried down. Whatever the case, do not delay, as any delay could be fatal.

AMS victims may need to be flown out of Bhutan as quickly as possible – make sure you have adequate travel insurance.

The drugs acetazolamide (Diamox) and dexamethasone are recommended by some doctors for the prevention of AMS. However, you should be aware that their use is controversial. They can reduce the symptoms, but they may also mask warning signs; severe and fatal AMS has occurred in people taking these drugs. Drug treatments should never be used to avoid descent or to enable further ascent.

Insect Bites & Stings

Bedbugs and fleas don't carry disease but their bites are very itchy. You can treat the itch with an antihistamine.

Ticks are contracted after walking in rural areas. Ticks are commonly found behind the ears, on the belly and in armpits. If you have had a tick bite and experience symptoms such as a rash at the site of the bite or elsewhere, fever or muscle aches, you should see a doctor. Doxycycline prevents tick-borne diseases.

Leeches are found in humid rainforest areas. They do not transmit any disease but their bites are often intensely itchy for weeks afterwards and can easily become infected. Apply an iodine-based antiseptic to any leech bite to help prevent infection.

Bee and wasp stings mainly cause problems for people who are allergic to them. Anyone with a serious bee or wasp allergy should carry an injection of adrenaline (eg an EpiPen) for emergency treat-

ment. For others, pain is the main problem – apply ice to the sting and take painkillers.

Skin Problems

Fungal rashes are common in humid climates. There are two common fungal rashes that affect travellers. The first occurs in moist areas that get less air such as the groin, armpits and between the toes. It starts as a red patch that slowly spreads and is usually itchy. Treatment involves keeping the skin dry, avoiding chafing and using an antifungal cream such as Clotrimazole or Lamisil. *Tinea versicolor* is also common – this fungus causes small, light-coloured patches, most commonly on the back, chest and shoulders. Consult a doctor.

Cuts and scratches become easily infected in humid climates. Take meticulous care of any cuts and scratches to prevent complications such as abscesses. Immediately wash all wounds in clean water and apply antiseptic. If you develop signs of infection (increasing pain and redness), see a doctor.

Women's Health

In the urban areas of Bhutan, supplies of sanitary products are readily available. Birth-control options may be limited, so bring adequate supplies of your own form of contraception. Heat, humidity and antibiotics can all contribute to thrush. Treatment is with antifungal creams and pessaries such as Clotrimazole. A practical alternative is a single tablet of Fluconazole (Diflucan). Urinary tract infections can be precipitated by dehydration or long road journeys without toilet stops; bring suitable antibiotics.

Pregnant women should receive specialised advice before travelling. The ideal time to travel is in the second trimester (between 16 and 28 weeks), when the risk of pregnancy-related problems are at their lowest and pregnant women generally feel at their best.

During the first trimester there is a risk of miscarriage and in the third trimester complications such as premature labour and high blood pressure are possible. It's also wise to travel with a companion. Always carry a list of quality medical facilities available at your destination and ensure you continue your standard antenatal care at these facilities. Avoid rural travel in areas with poor transport and medical facilities. Most of all, ensure travel insurance covers all pregnancy-related possibilities, including premature labour.

Malaria is a high-risk disease during pregnancy. WHO recommends that pregnant women do *not* travel to areas that have Chloroquine-resistant malaria. None of the more effective antimalarial drugs is completely safe during pregnancy.

Traveller's diarrhoea can quickly lead to dehydration and result in inadequate blood flow to the placenta. Many of the drugs used to treat various diarrhoea bugs are not recommended in pregnancy. Azithromycin is considered safe.

Although not much is known about the possible adverse effects of altitude on a developing foetus, many authorities recommend not travelling above 4000m while pregnant.

Language

The official language of Bhutan is Dzongkha. While Dzongkha uses the same script as Tibetan – and the two languages are closely related – Dzongkha is sufficiently different that Tibetans can't understand it. English is the medium of instruction in schools, so most educated people can speak it fluently. There are English signboards, books and menus throughout the country. Road signs and government documents are all written in both English and Dzongkha. The national newspaper, Kuensel, is published in three languages: English, Dzongkha and Nepali. In the monastic schools Choekey, the classical Tibetan language, is taught.

As a result of the isolation of many parts of the country, a number of other languages survive, and it's common for regional minorities to have their own language. Some are so different that people from different parts of the country can't understand each other. In eastern Bhutan most people speak Sharchop (meaning 'language of the east'), which is totally different from Dzongkha. In the south, most people speak Nepali. Bumthangkha is a language of the Bumthang region. Also spoken are Khengkha from Zhamgang, Kurtoep from Lhuentshe, Mangdep from Trongsa and Dzala from Trashi Yangtse.

PRONUNCIATION

The simplified pronunciation system used in this chapter is based on the official Romanisation system (used for writing Dzongkha in Roman script), so if you read our coloured pronunciation guides as if they were English, you'll be understood.

There are three accent marks: the apostrophe represents a high tone (eg 'ne) or a 'soft' consonant (eg g'), the circumflex accent (eg ê) represents long vowels, and the diaeresis (eg ö) alters the pronunciation of some vowels, namely ä (as the 'a' in 'hat'), ö as the 'ir' in 'dirt' (without the 'r' sound), and ü (like saying 'i' with the lips stretched back).

An h after the consonants c, d, g, l, p and t indicates that they are 'aspirated' (released with a slight puff of air) – listen to the 'p' sounds in 'pip'; the first is aspirated, the second is not.

Practise pronouncing the ng sound (as in 'sing') at the beginning of a word, eg ngawang (a name). The 'dental' consonants, t and th, are pronounced with the tongue tip against the teeth. Note also that c is pronounced as the 'ch' in 'church', and zh as the 's' in 'measure'.

BASICS

Hello.	kuzuzangbo la
Goodbye.	
(by person leaving)	läzhimbe jön
(by person staying)	läzhimbe zhû
Good luck.	trashi dele
Thank you.	kadriche
Yes.	ing/yö
No.	mê
Maybe.	im ong
How are you?	chö gadebe yö?
I'm fine.	nga läzhimbe ra yö
What's your name?	chö meng gaci mo?
My name is ...	ngê meng ... ing
Where are you from?	chö gâti lä mo?
I'm from ...	nga ... lä ing
Where are you going?	chö gâti jou mo?
I'm staying at ...	nga ... döp ing
I know.	nga shê
I don't know.	nga mi shê
Can I take a photo?	pâ tabney chokar la?
Can I take your photo?	chögi pâ ci tapge mä?
That's OK.	di tupbä
It's cold today.	dari jâm-mä
It's raining.	châp cap dowä

Trekking & Country Life

alpine hut	bjobi gâ
alpine pasture	la nogi tsamjo
bridge	zam
cold (weather)	sîtraktra
hills	ri
house	chim
lake	tsho
mountain	gangri
mountain pass	la
mule track	ta lam
plain or meadow	thang
prayer flag	dâshi
river	chhu/tsangchhu
steep downhill	lam khamâ zâdra
steep uphill	khagen gâdra
stone carved with prayers	dogi mani
tired	udû/thangche
trail	lam/kanglam
village	û
warm (weather)	drotokto/tshatokto

Which trail goes to ...?	... josi lam gâti mo?
Is the trail steep?	lam zâdra yö-ga?
Where is my tent?	ngê gû di gâti in-na?
What's the name of this village?	ani ügi meng gaci zeu mo?
Let's go.	jogey-la

bird/chicken	bja
cow	ba
dog	rochi/chi
horse	ta
pig	phap
water buffalo	mahe
yak (male/female)	yâ/jim

barley	nâ
buckwheat	bjô
corn (maize)	gâza/gesasip
husked rice	chum
millet	membja
standing rice	bjâ
wheat	kâ

daughter	bum
elder brother	phôgem
elder sister	azhim
father	apa
friend	totsha/châro
mother	ama
son	bu
younger brother	nucu
younger sister	num/sîm
hers	mogi
his	khogi
mine	ngêgi
yours	chögi

big	bôm
cheap	khetokto
clean	tsangtokto
dirty	khamlôsisi
enough	tupbä/lâmmä
expensive	gong bôm
good	läzhim
happy	gatokto
heavy	jice
not good	läzhim mindu

small	chungku
that	aphidi
this	di

DIRECTIONS & TRANSPORT

What time does the bus leave?	drülkhor chutshö gademci kha jou inna?
I want to get off here.	nga nâ dögobe
How far is the ...?	... gadeci tha ringsa mo?
Is it near?	bolokha in-na?
Is it far?	tha ringsa in-na?
Go straight ahead.	thrangdi song

behind	japkha
here	nâ/nâlu
left	öm
in front of	dongkha
next to	bolokha
opposite	dongko/dongte
right	yäp
there	phâ/phâlu
where	gâti

north	bjang
south	lho
east	shâ
west	nup

EATING & DRINKING

Where is a ...?	... gâti mo?
local bar	changkha
restaurant	zakha
Do you have food now?	chö dato to za-wigang in-na?
I don't eat meat.	nga sha miza
I don't like food with chillies.	nga zhêgo êma dacikha miga
This is too spicy.	di khatshi dû
This is delicious.	di zhim-mä
Please give me a cup of tea.	ngalu ja phöp gang nang
It's enough.	digi lâm-mä

Key Words

food	zhêgo/to
hot (spicy)	khatshi yömi
hot (warm)	tshatom
slices	pa
tasty	zhimtoto

Meat & Vegetables

cabbage	banda kopi
cauliflower	meto kopi
chicken	bja sha
cooked vegetable	tshöse tsotsou
fish	ngasha
meat	ha
potatoes	kewa
radish	laphu
turnips	öndo
vegetable	tshöse

Other Foods

cheese	datse
chilli	êma
corn (maize)	gäza/gesasip
egg	gongdo

Numbers

1	ci
2	nyî
3	sum
4	zhi
5	nga
6	drû
7	dün
8	gä
9	gu
10	cuthâm
11	cûci
12	cunyî
13	cûsu
14	cüzhi
15	cänga
16	cûdru
17	cupdü
18	côpgä
19	cügu
20	nyishu/khächi
30	sumcu/khä pcheda nyî
40	zhipcu/khänyî
50	ngapcu/khä pcheda sum
60	drukcu/khäsum
70	düncu/khä pcheda zhi
80	gepcu/khäzhi
90	gupcu/khä pcheda nga
100	cikja/khänga
1000	ciktong/tongthra ci
10,000	cikthri
100,000	cikbum/bum
1,000,000	saya ci

mushroom	shamu
mustard	päga
noodles	bathu/thukpa
rice (cooked)	to
salad	ezay

Drinks

beer (local)	bang chhang
boiled water	chhu kököu
cold/hot water	chhu khöm/tshatom
tea	ja
water	chhu
whisky (local)	ârra

HEALTH & EMERGENCIES

I'm ill.	nga nau mä
I feel nauseous.	nga cûni zum beu mä
I feel weak.	nga thangchep mä
I keep vomiting.	nga cûp cûsara döp mä
I feel dizzy.	nga guyu khôu mä
I'm having trouble breathing.	nga bung tang mit shubä

doctor	drungtsho
fever	jangshu
pain	nazu

SHOPPING & SERVICES

The word *khang* means building; in many cases it's only necessary to add the word for the type of building.

Where is a ...?	... gâti mo?
bank	ngükhang
bookshop	pekhang
cinema	loknyen
hospital	menkhang
market	thromkhang
monastery	goemba
police station	thrimsung gakpi måkhang
post office	dremkhang
public telephone	manggi jüthrin tangsi
shop	tshongkhang
temple	lhakhang
toilet	chapsa

I want to see ...	nga ... tagobe
I'm looking for ...	nga ... tau ing
What time does it open?	chutshö gademci lu go pchiu mo?
What time does it close?	chutshö gademci lu go dam mo?
Is it still open?	datoya pchidi ong ga?

Politeness

To be polite, you can add -la to the end of almost anything you say in Dzongkha, and even to English words you might use in Bhutan. So when talking to a government minister, a lama or someone older than you, you can say eg 'yes-la' or 'okay-la', and you'll be showing respect.

What is this?	di gaci mo?
I want to change money.	nga tiru sôgobä
How much is it?	dilu gadeci mo?
That's too much.	gong bôm mä
I'll give you no more than ...	ngâgi ... anemci lä trö mitshube
What's your best price?	gong gademcibe bjinni?

TIME & DATES

What is the time?	chutshö gademci mo?
(Five) o'clock.	chutshö (nga)

afternoon	pchiru
day	nyim/za
day after tomorrow	nåtshe
morning	drôba
night	numu
sometime	retshe kap
today	dari
tomorrow	nâba
yesterday	khatsha

Sunday	za dau
Monday	za mîma
Tuesday	za lhap
Wednesday	za phup
Thursday	za pâsa
Friday	za pêm
Saturday	za nyim

GLOSSARY

ABTO – Association of Bhutanese Tour Operators

anim – Buddhist nun

anim goemba – nunnery

atsara – masked clown that badgers the crowd at a *tsechu*

bangchung – round bamboo basket with a tight-fitting cover

BHU – Basic Health Unit

bodhisattva – a being who has the capacity of gaining Buddhahood in this life, but who refuses it in order to be reincarnated in the world to help other beings

Bon – ancient, pre-Buddhist, animistic religion of Tibet; its practitioners are called Bon-po

Brokpa – minority group in eastern Bhutan

bukhari – wood-burning stove

bumpa – vase, usually used to contain holy water in *goembas*

cham – ritual religious dance

chang – north

chhang – beer made from rice, corn or millet, pronounced 'chung'

chhu – river, also water

chilip – foreigner

choesum – chapel

chorten – stone Buddhist monument, often containing relics

Dantak – Indian Border Roads Task Force

datse – traditional archery; also cheese

desi – secular ruler of Bhutan

dharma – Buddhist teachings

dharma raja – British name for the Zhabdrung, the religious ruler, during period 1652–1907

dochey – inner courtyard of a *dzong*

doma – betel nut, also known by its Indian name, *paan*

dorji – a stylised thunderbolt used in rituals; *vajra* in Sanskrit

drak – cave or hermitage

dratshang – central monk body

driglam chhoesum – code of etiquette

driglam namzha – traditional values and etiquette

Druk Gyalpo – the king of Bhutan

Drukpa Kagyu – the official religion of Bhutan, a school of tantric *Mahayana* Buddhism

drungkhag – subdistrict

dukhang – assembly hall in a *goemba;* also called a *tshokhang*

dzong – fort-monastery shared between government office and monks' quarters

dzongdag – district administrator

Dzongkha – national language of Bhutan

dzongkhag – district

dzongpen – old term for lord of the *dzong*

gangri – snow mountain

gho – traditional dress for men

goemba – a *Mahayana* Buddhist monastery

goenkhang – chapel devoted to protective and terrifying deities, usually *Mahakala*

gomchen – lay or married monk

gorikha – porch of a *lhakhang*, literally 'mouth of the door'

Guru Rinpoche – the common name of Padmasambhava, the founder of *Mahayana* Buddhism

gyalpo – ruler or king

himal – Sanskrit word for mountain

IMTRAT – Indian Military Training Team

Je Khenpo – Chief Abbot of Bhutan

kabney – scarf worn over the shoulder on formal occasions

khandroma – a female celestial being; *dakini* in Sanskrit

khenpo – abbot

khonying – archway chorten

kira – traditional dress for women

kora – circumambulation

la – mountain pass

lam – path or road

lama – *Mahayana* Buddhist teacher or priest

lha – god or deity

lhakhang – temple, literally 'god house'

lho – south

Lhotshampa – southern Bhutanese people, mainly Nepali-speaking

Losar – Bhutanese and Tibetan New Year

lu – serpent deities, called *naga* in Sanskrit

Mahakala – Yeshe Goenpo, the guardian god of Bhutan, who manifests himself as a raven

Mahayana – school of Buddhism, literally 'great vehicle'

mandala – cosmic diagram; *kyilkhor* in *Dzongkha*

mani stone – stone carved with the Buddhist mantra *om mani peme hum*

mantra – prayer formula or chant

migoi – the abominable snowman; also known as yeti

naktshang – temple dedicated to warlord or protective deity, literally 'place of vows'

NCCA – National Commission for Cultural Affairs

ney – sacred site

ngultrum – unit of Bhutanese currency

nup – west

Nyingma – lineage of Himalayan Buddhism; its practitioners are Nyingmapa

om mani peme hum – sacred Buddhist mantra, roughly translates as 'hail to the jewel in the lotus'

outreach clinic – health posts in remote villages

PCO – Public Call Office

penlop – regional governor, literally 'lord-teacher'

phajo – priest

prayer flag – long strips of cloth printed with prayers that are 'said' whenever the flag flaps in the wind

prayer wheel – cylindrical wheel inscribed with, and containing, prayers

rabdey – district monk body
RBA – Royal Bhutan Army
rinpoche – reincarnate lama, usually the abbot of a *goemba*
river left – the left bank of a river when facing downstream
river right – the right bank of a river when facing downstream
RSPN – Royal Society for Protection of Nature

SAARC – South Asia Association for Regional Cooperation; this includes the seven countries of Bangladesh, Bhutan, India, Maldives, Nepal, Pakistan and Sri Lanka
Sakyamuni – one name for Gautama Buddha, the Historical Buddha

shar – east
shedra – Buddhist college
shing – wood
sonam – good luck
stupa – hemispherical Buddhist structure from which the *chorten* evolved

terma – texts and artefacts hidden by *Guru Rinpoche*
terton – discoverer of *terma*
thang – plain
thangka – painted or embroidered religious picture
thondrol – huge *thangka* that is unfurled on special occasions, literally 'liberation on sight'
torma – ritual cake made of *tsampa*, butter and sugar
trulku – a reincarnation; the spiritual head of a *goemba*
tsachhu – hot spring

tsampa – roasted-barley flour
tsechu – religious dance festival
tshamkhang – small meditation quarters
tsho – lake
Tshogdu – National Assembly
tshokhang – assembly hall in a *lhakhang*

utse – the central tower that houses the *lhakhang* in a *dzong*

yathra – strips of woven woollen cloth
yeti – see *migoi*

Zangto Pelri – the celestial abode or paradise of *Guru Rinpoche*
Zhabdrung, the – title of the reincarnations of the Zhabdrung Ngawang Namgyal

FOOD GLOSSARY

arra – homemade spirit distilled from barley, wheat or rice

barthu – noodles
bja sha maroo – chicken in garlic and butter sauce

chhang – beer made from rice, corn or millet, pronounced *chung*
chugo – dried yak cheese

dal – lentil soup

ema datse – chilli with cheese sauce

hogey – salad of cucumber, Asian pepper, red chilli, spring onion and tomato

kewa datse – potatoes with cheese sauce
khule – buckwheat pancakes

momo – steamed dumpling filled with meat or cheese

nakey – fiddlehead fern fronds
no sha huentseu – stewed beef with spinach

olo choto – literally 'crow beak', a hooked-shaped broad bean

phak sha laphu – stewed pork with radish
phak sha phin tshoem – pork with rice noodles
puta – buckwheat noodles

shamu datse – mushrooms with cheese sauce
sip – fried, beaten corn
sud-ja – Tibetan-style tea with salt and butter

thukpa – noodles, often served in a soup
tsampa – roasted-barley flour

zao – fried rice

Behind the Scenes

SEND US YOUR FEEDBACK

We love to hear from travellers – your comments keep us on our toes and help make our books better. Our well-travelled team reads every word on what you loved or loathed about this book. Although we cannot reply individually to postal submissions, we always guarantee that your feedback goes straight to the appropriate authors, in time for the next edition. Each person who sends us information is thanked in the next edition – the most useful submissions are rewarded with a selection of digital PDF chapters.

Visit **lonelyplanet.com/contact** to submit your updates and suggestions or to ask for help. Our award-winning website also features inspirational travel stories, news and discussions.

Note: We may edit, reproduce and incorporate your comments in Lonely Planet products such as guidebooks, websites and digital products, so let us know if you don't want your comments reproduced or your name acknowledged. For a copy of our privacy policy visit lonelyplanet.com/privacy.

OUR READERS

Many thanks to the travellers who used the last edition and wrote to us with helpful hints, useful advice and interesting anecdotes:

Derek Bellis, Christa Blessing, Anna Brouwer, Benjamin Bullock, Sarah & Richard Coldwell, Zachary Collier, Vincent Henry, Harvey Hinsz, Joukje Janssen, Kay Klumb, Christine Legler, Lucy Manchester, Marcos Mendonca, Jason Nicholson, David Ochel, Yuvaree Phakdiakson, Steven Sammartino, Deepak Tamang, Sonam Thinlay, Chartchai Tiamsanit, Jeff Tremblay, Ben Tse, Zoltan Valcsicsak, Elien Van Dille, Heinrich Wegenstein, Peter Williams

AUTHOR THANKS

Lindsay Brown

I am very grateful for the guidance of Stan Armington, who pioneered the first two editions of this guide. The following people also provided invaluable assistance in Bhutan: Rinzin Wangchuk, Robin Pradhan and Chador Wangdi, Thuji Dorji Nadik and Kinley Wangdi at the Tourism Council of Bhutan, Wangchuk Wangdi and Sonam Wangdi. Finally, thanks to inspirational coauthor Bradley Mayhew and to Jenny, Pat and Sinead.

Bradley Mayhew

Thanks to Karma Gyeltsen, who did a first-rate job arranging my highly customised tour. Niall Murtagh at the Tourism Council of Bhutan was generous with time and information, and thanks to Pelden Dorji for info on the Salt trek. Cheers as ever to Lindsay and to Suzannah for sending me to such a wonderful country in the first place.

ACKNOWLEDGMENTS

Climate map data adapted from Peel MC, Finlayson BL & McMahon TA (2007) 'Updated World Map of the Köppen-Geiger Climate Classification', *Hydrology and Earth System Sciences*, 11, 163344.

Cover photograph: A Buddhist monk at the doors of Trongsa Dzong, Ami Vitale/Panos.

THIS BOOK

The 1st and 2nd editions of Lonely Planet's *Bhutan* guidebook were researched and written by Stan Armington. The 3rd edition was researched and written by Lindsay Brown and Bradley Mayhew; Stan updated the Trekking chapter and Richard Whitecross wrote the Buddhism in Bhutan and The Culture chapters. The 4th edition was researched and written by Bradley Mayhew, Lindsay Brown and Anirban Mahapatra. Lindsay and Bradley researched and wrote this 5th edition.

This guidebook was commissioned in Lonely Planet's Melbourne office, and produced by the following:

Commissioning Editor
Suzannah Shwer

Coordinating Editors
Carolyn Boicos, Kristin Odijk

Senior Cartographer
David Kemp

Coordinating Layout Designer Frank Deim

Managing Editors Brigitte Ellemor, Martine Power

Senior Editors Catherine Naghten, Karyn Noble

Managing Layout Designer Chris Girdler

Assisting Editors
Charlotte Orr, Gabrielle Stefanos

Cover Research Naomi Parker

Internal Image Research
Jane Hart

Illustrator Michael Ruff

Language Content
Branislava Vladisavljevic

Thanks to Sasha Baskett, Ryan Evans, Larissa Frost, Genesys India, Jouve India, Trent Paton, Adrian Persoglia, Lyahna Spencer, Angela Tinson

Index

Map Pages **000**
Photo Pages **000**

NOTES

NOTES

Map Legend

Sights

- Beach
- Bird Sanctuary
- Buddhist
- Castle/Palace
- Christian
- Confucian
- Hindu
- Islamic
- Jain
- Jewish
- Monument
- Museum/Gallery/Historic Building
- Ruin
- Sento Hot Baths/Onsen
- Shinto
- Sikh
- Taoist
- Winery/Vineyard
- Zoo/Wildlife Sanctuary
- Other Sight

Activities, Courses & Tours

- Bodysurfing
- Diving/Snorkelling
- Canoeing/Kayaking
- Course/Tour
- Skiing
- Snorkelling
- Surfing
- Swimming/Pool
- Walking
- Windsurfing
- Other Activity

Sleeping

- Sleeping
- Camping

Eating

- Eating

Drinking & Nightlife

- Drinking & Nightlife
- Cafe

Entertainment

- Entertainment

Shopping

- Shopping

Information

- Bank
- Embassy/Consulate
- Hospital/Medical
- Internet
- Police
- Post Office
- Telephone
- Toilet
- Tourist Information
- Other Information

Geographic

- Beach
- Hut/Shelter
- Lighthouse
- Lookout
- Mountain/Volcano
- Oasis
- Park
- Pass
- Picnic Area
- Waterfall

Population

- Capital (National)
- Capital (State/Province)
- City/Large Town
- Town/Village

Transport

- Airport
- Border crossing
- Bus
- Cable car/Funicular
- Cycling
- Ferry
- Metro station
- Monorail
- Parking
- Petrol station
- Subway station
- Taxi
- Train station/Railway
- Tram
- Underground station
- Other Transport

Note: Not all symbols displayed above appear on the maps in this book

Routes

- Tollway
- Freeway
- Primary
- Secondary
- Tertiary
- Lane
- Unsealed road
- Road under construction
- Plaza/Mall
- Steps
- Tunnel
- Pedestrian overpass
- Walking Tour
- Walking Tour detour
- Path/Walking Trail

Boundaries

- International
- State/Province
- Disputed
- Regional/Suburb
- Marine Park
- Cliff
- Wall

Hydrography

- River, Creek
- Intermittent River
- Canal
- Water
- Dry/Salt/Intermittent Lake
- Reef

Areas

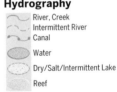

- Airport/Runway
- Beach/Desert
- Cemetery (Christian)
- Cemetery (Other)
- Glacier
- Mudflat
- Park/Forest
- Sight (Building)
- Sportsground
- Swamp/Mangrove

OUR STORY

A beat-up old car, a few dollars in the pocket and a sense of adventure. In 1972 that's all Tony and Maureen Wheeler needed for the trip of a lifetime – across Europe and Asia overland to Australia. It took several months, and at the end – broke but inspired – they sat at their kitchen table writing and stapling together their first travel guide, *Across Asia on the Cheap*. Within a week they'd sold 1500 copies. Lonely Planet was born.

Today, Lonely Planet has offices in Melbourne, London and Oakland, with more than 600 staff and writers. We share Tony's belief that 'a great guidebook should do three things: inform, educate and amuse'.

OUR WRITERS

Lindsay Brown

Coordinating Author, Thimphu, Western Bhutan, Treks Spring in Bhutan is the time for spectacular rhododendron blossoms on the high passes and for sunny days and cool nights. It is also the time for some of Bhutan's more colourful festivals. All the makings for another wonderful adventure in a country that is like no other. A former conservation biologist and Publishing Manager at Lonely Planet, Lindsay has spent the last decade or so writing guidebooks and photographing in Asia and Australia. He has trekked, jeeped, ridden and stumbled across many a Himalayan mountain pass and contributed to Lonely Planet's *South India & Kerala; India; Rajasthan, Delhi & Agra; Nepal* and *Pakistan & the Karakoram Highway* guides, among many others. Lindsay also wrote the Welcome to Bhutan, Bhutan's Top 17, Need to Know, Festivals, Booking Your Trip, Regions at a Glance, Bhutan Today, History, The Bhutanese Way of Life, Traditional Arts, Architecture, Mountains & Valleys and Wildlife & Sanctuaries chapters, and wrote the Survival Guide section.

Bradley Mayhew

Central Bhutan, Eastern Bhutan, Treks A self-professed mountain junkie, Bradley has been trekking in the Himalaya for almost 20 years. For his third time working on this title, he focused on the centre and east of the country, exploring new places in Gelephu, Mongar, Dungkhar, Bomdeling and Zhemgang. Bradley is the coordinating author of Lonely Planet guides to *Tibet, Central Asia* and *Nepal*, and in 2010 was featured in a five-part Arte TV documentary retracing the route of Marco Polo. See what he's up to at www.bradleymayhew.blogspot.com. Bradley also wrote the If You Like..., Month by Month, Itineraries, Planning Your Trek and Buddhism in Bhutan chapters.

Read more about Bradley at:
www.lonelyplanet.com/members/nepalibrad

Published by Lonely Planet Publications Pty Ltd
ABN 36 005 607 983
5th edition – Mar 2014
ISBN 978 1 74220 133 7
© Lonely Planet 2014   Photographs © as indicated 2014
10 9 8 7 6 5 4 3 2 1
Printed in Singapore

Although the authors and Lonely Planet have taken all reasonable care in preparing this book, we make no warranty about the accuracy or completeness of its content and, to the maximum extent permitted, disclaim all liability arising from its use.